Organizational Behaviour in Health Care

Series Editors
Jean-Louis Denis
Ecole Nationale d'Administration
Université de Montréal
Montreal, QC, Canada

Justin Waring
Centre for Health Innovation Leadership and Learning
Nottingham University Business School
Nottingham, UK

Paula Hyde
Birmingham Business School
University of Birmingham
Birmingham, UK

Published in co-operation with the Society for Studies in Organising Healthcare (SHOC), this series has two strands, the first of which consists of specially selected papers taken from the biennial conferences held by SHOC that present a cohesive and focused insight into issues within the field of organisational behaviour in healthcare.

The series also encourages proposals for monographs and edited collections to address the additional and emergent topics in the field of health policy, organization and management. Books within the series aim to advance scholarship on the application of social science theories, methods and concepts to the study of organizing and managing healthcare services and systems.

Providing a new platform for advanced and engaged scholarship, books in the series will advance the academic community by fostering a deep analysis on the challenges for healthcare organizations and management with an explicitly international and comparative focus.

More information about this series at
http://www.palgrave.com/gp/series/14724

Paul Turner

Leadership in Healthcare

Delivering Organisational Transformation and Operational Excellence

palgrave
macmillan

Paul Turner
Leeds Business School
Leeds Beckett University
Leeds, UK

Organizational Behaviour in Health Care
ISBN 978-3-030-04386-5 ISBN 978-3-030-04387-2 (eBook)
https://doi.org/10.1007/978-3-030-04387-2

Library of Congress Control Number: 2018963215

This Palgrave Macmillan imprint is published by the registered company Springer Nature Switzerland AG
The registered company address is: Gewerbestrasse 11, 6330 Cham, Switzerland

To my brother Ian Turner

This book is dedicated to the hard-working healthcare professionals who support our lives by their dedication, knowledge, and skill.

Preface

The delivery of effective health services requires the right leadership in the right place at the right time with the right level of capability, credibility, and knowledge of organisational dynamics. At the highest levels of the organisation, leaders will not only require knowledge of how to develop long-term strategy but also the ability to deliver it. However, the growing awareness that leadership is a non-hierarchical activity—often separate from the formal role of leader—means that interest in the subject now extends to creating a culture in which leadership can thrive at all levels of the organisation. Without effective leadership, there will not be an engaged followership, and this will have an impact on the quality of care and societal or business outcomes. In whatever way it is defined, leadership in the health sector carries significant responsibility. The effect of a health leader's actions impacts countless lives and the right leadership fit is therefore crucial. The nature and shape of best 'fit' is an ongoing challenge facing all organisations in the sector.

Leeds, UK
Paul Turner

Acknowledgements

Liz Barlow, Palgrave Macmillan
Lucy Kidwell, Palgrave Macmillan
Michelle Fitzgerald-Shaw, NHS Leadership Academy
Fiona Rodden, NHS Leadership Academy
Ryan Changcoco and Gabriela Ammatuna, Association for Talent Development, USA
Adam Turner, NHS Health Education England
Xiaoxian Zhu and Feirong Wang, Teesside University
Tomasz Ingram, University of Katowice
Niki Kyriakidou, Leeds Beckett University
Mr Kostas Papagiannopoulos, Mmed Thorax, Md (Cth)

Gail Turner

Contents

List of Figures

List of Tables

1

Leadership in Dynamic and Diverse Health Sector Organisations

No Leaders Without Followers; No Followers Without Leaders

It is a universal truth that there will be no health service without a health workforce (WHO 2014). It is equally true that the delivery of the health service will require the right leadership in the right place at the right time with the right level of capability and credibility for it to be effective. Leadership is an essential health sector practice, which has a significant impact on both clinical and organisational outcomes (Delmatoff and Lazarus 2014; Longenecker and Longenecker 2014; Redknap et al. 2015: 266; Kumar and Khilijee 2016; Sarto and Veronesi 2016). Health sector leaders will have a focus on delivering to the patients, communities, and societies for which they have responsibility and to the workforce in their organisations and to meet the expectations of 'governance' stakeholders, including shareholders in private sector health organisations or government agencies in public sector ones.

To satisfy such a diverse and wide-ranging group will require those who are in leadership roles to match up to stringent requirements in terms of capability and credibility and who are able to deliver excellence and transformation at times of volatility, uncertainty, complexity, and

P. Turner, *Leadership in Healthcare*, Organizational Behaviour in Health Care,
https://doi.org/10.1007/978-3-030-04387-2_1

ambiguity. At the highest level, this means leaders with the knowledge of how to craft a long-term strategy and with the nous, traits, skills, attitudes, and behaviours to deliver it; it means creating a pipeline of those with leadership potential to ensure continuity of strategy and operations; and finally, it means ensuring that leadership, governance, policy, and stewardship are in harmony and aligned to identified organisational goals and objectives. Those in formal 'leader' roles will provide direction to managerial, clinical, medical, technical, and professional groups, diverse healthcare workers, and all relevant stakeholders. However, leadership is not confined to the few people in the most senior roles. Instead it is a concept based on social relationships rather than organisational position. And so, a culture in which devolved leadership practice can take place effectively will also be critical. Leadership is situational and non-hierarchical (Goffee and Jones 2006); it is increasingly collaborative and dependent upon effective networking across agencies or business units. Both observations resonate in health sector organisations with unclear lines of demarcation between activity and with fluid organisational networks or matrices replacing hierarchical structures. Effective formal or positional leadership and a culture of devolved leadership provide the basis for an engaged followership which will contribute to quality of care and positive societal or business outcomes.

Leadership Is a Mysterious Process

It is not only the fact that leadership is important to success but also the fact that leadership style and approach are open to interpretation that creates such a fascination with the subject—framed within the questions of identifying who 'has what it takes' to be a leader and the type of leadership that is required. Leadership has a high profile but is also a 'mysterious process' (Howieson and Thiagarajah 2011). Whilst the person or competences required to be a leader can be readily defined and recognisable, that of the successful application of leadership is less predictable. Chapter 3 covers the debate about these areas and analyses some of the many theories surrounding leaders and leadership. The diversity of opinion occurs because leadership is not an abstract philosophical concept that can be easily categorised. It is a complex process with a series of social relationships between people in organisations as they move towards the achievement of objectives, a 'process that involves the ability to influence and motivate individuals or groups towards common goals' (Ellis and Abbott 2014; Chobanuk and James 2015). In some instances a leader, such as a Chief Executive, will have an overall responsibility for delivering these goals through strategy setting, delegating part of her or his authority, and engaging the workforce. In others, appointed leaders (Heads of Department, Directors) will assume devolved responsibility for leadership in a specific unit or area as part of a formal executive process. But critically, leadership will also take place at many locations by those who don't have the 'leader' title. A fundamental premise is that leadership is the act of engaging others to come together in the quest for a common objective, wherever the objective resides in the organisation's structure and whoever takes responsibility for delivering it through people.

Given the potential benefits, it is no surprise that the profile of leadership has been raised. The question once asked of 'how are we going to develop the leadership skills, imagination and strategies required for implementing desirable policy measures and the overhaul of health care organisations?' (Levey et al. 2002: 68) remains particularly relevant today. Leadership is one of the solutions to the many challenges that the health sector faces, and there are calls throughout the world for more and better leadership (McDonald 2014: 227; Saravo et al. 2017: 2). Identifying appropriate concepts and adapting them to complex health environments is therefore a priority.

Healthcare Leaders 'Mobilise Intelligence'

But this is a challenge. Research has shown that there are more than 200 definitions of leadership 'with descriptions ranging from traits and characteristics to behaviours and processes' (Chobanuk and James 2015). For some health sector organisations, leaders are transformational or charismatic, focusing on innovation and change, 'leading from the front,' and making decisions quickly to respond to external forces or demands. For other health sector organisations, leaders are transactional, reflective, consultative, and inclusive, crafting a way for the organisation to deliver operational outcomes in complex social or political environments. The significant number of studies of leadership in health creates a patchwork of approaches and leadership styles. Amongst these are the generalist (Barr and Dowding 2008; Gopee and Galloway 2009; Gunderman 2009; Dye 2010); there are those which discuss transformational leadership (Levey et al. 2002; Maccoby et al. 2013; Choi et al. 2016), servant leadership (Tropello and Defazio 2014), ethical leadership (Sahne et al. 2015), complexity leadership (Weberg 2012), coaching as leadership style (Hicks 2014), authentic leadership (Read and Laschinger 2015), leadership for improvement (DaCosta 2012) and shared or distributed leadership (Fitzgerald et al. 2013; Rogers 2014). The amount of intelligence on the subject arises from studies in health leadership in the North American, Asian, and European health sectors, from insights on leadership in African healthcare (Amasawa and Crisp 2014), and from global agencies such as the World Health Organization. The scale and scope of these studies demonstrate the positive and also the contextual nature of leadership; they also reflect the willingness on the part of health sector organisations to embrace different ideas about the meaning of leadership and the role of leaders. Because of this, views of leadership have ebbed and flowed over time. As the popularity of transformational leadership wanes, authentic and inclusive leadership rise in its place; as hero leadership falls out of favour, distributed leadership becomes more popular. More recently, there is some agreement on the need to extend the definition of leadership beyond the 'role of charismatic individuals…in setting compelling visions to which all organizational actors are expected to subscribe' (Collinson and Tourish 2015), because such definitions don't take enough account of power dynamics, the importance of organisational and environmental context, and the significance of follower engagement. Opinion, therefore, varies widely about the 'right' way to lead, and the discussion of leadership in the health sector in Chap. 4 will show how many different applications of leadership theory and style have taken place over the past 30 years. In whatever way it is defined, leadership in the health sector carries significant responsibility. The effect of a health leader's actions impacts countless lives (Reed 2009), and as a result, health leadership performance receives a good deal of scrutiny.

External and Internal Forces and Organisational Dynamics and Structure Have an Impact on Leadership Style

A dramatic convergence of forces has had a significant impact on what is needed to meet these expectations. The challenge is made more complex by the dynamic and fast-moving change within the sector, increasingly requiring that health providers view their proposition as a 'continuum of care' from inpatient to physician offices to ancillary services to home health, pharmacy, and nursing homes and, for most, towards providing excellent service at reduced cost (Larkin 2015). External forces, as part of this dynamic mix, include social change and expectation and a broader definition of what is understood by the meaning of health, extending beyond a purely biomedical view (Salomon et al. 2003), to one in which health is regarded as a 'state of complete physical, social and mental well-being, and not merely the absence of disease or infirmity' (WHO 2016). Health relates to everyday life not just the object of living, with a moving of the dial from illness to wellness and well-being. Added to the complexity of this fundamental change, shifting demographics, the impact of ageing on society, and the growing risk of non-communicable diseases require a more holistic health proposition involving leadership across multiple health delivery agencies, affecting health performance outcomes in both the quantity and quality of healthcare. These forces place new pressures on health sector leaders who increasingly have to satisfy multiple stakeholders—from health service users to politicians and business or financial shareholders, from employees to suppliers, and from lawmakers to quality agencies. Often these interactions take place in an uncertain environment, with sometimes contradictory or complex demands requiring, for example, cost reduction and service increase simultaneously, or the simplification of approach in increasingly complex structures or supply chains, or the movement towards a vertically integrated delivery system (Love and Ayadi 2015). Furthermore, there is a demographic urgency to deal with the leadership question because in some geographies, the turnover rate for certain groups in key leadership roles is high and is expected to surge as baby boomers retire (Putre 2013). Attracting, retaining, and developing health sector leaders at all levels is a priority.

A convergence of forces means that as health sector organisations change (e.g. with the application of new technologies), there is a demand across the spectrum of health professionals for skills in innovation, creativity, teamwork, and decision-making 'which consists of a challenge for even the best…. and because of this leadership is considered a relevant skill for the achievement of the collective and organisational goals' (Silva et al. 2017). Leadership in a steady-state environment would be hard pushed to understand and deliver effectively to all of these, even more so in the complex and dynamic health environment, that is, the actuality. The context within which this takes place is one of operating in organisations with a diverse, multi-skilled, multilayered workforce requiring a sophisticated approach if followership is to be achieved. Furthermore, a multitude of ever-changing organisational structures from hierarchy to matrix to network to project have implications for leadership. The fact that modern health service organisations are increasingly non-hierarchical requires the devolution or distribution of leadership activity to levels of the organisation below the Board or Executive team. And to be effective requires an understanding of the differences between the term *leader*, that is, an individual with certain traits and competences, and *leadership* which is more concerned with social exchanges that take place at multiple levels. How these terms are defined, overlap, and differ from or interface with what might be referred to as *management* is another important consideration in setting the boundaries of leadership. These concepts will be discussed more in Chaps. 3 and 4.

In conclusion, the environment for health services worldwide is complex and dynamic, which together with pressures on health budgets and a growing demand for a return on investment in health make leadership an increasingly important subject of interest. The fact that health services are vital to national economies in terms of development and growth accentuates this importance. Figure 1.1 summarises some of the key forces affecting health sector leadership. To decide on what is meant by best fit leadership in health in response to these forces, it is important to review current evidence and perspectives about the application of leadership concepts in the sector.

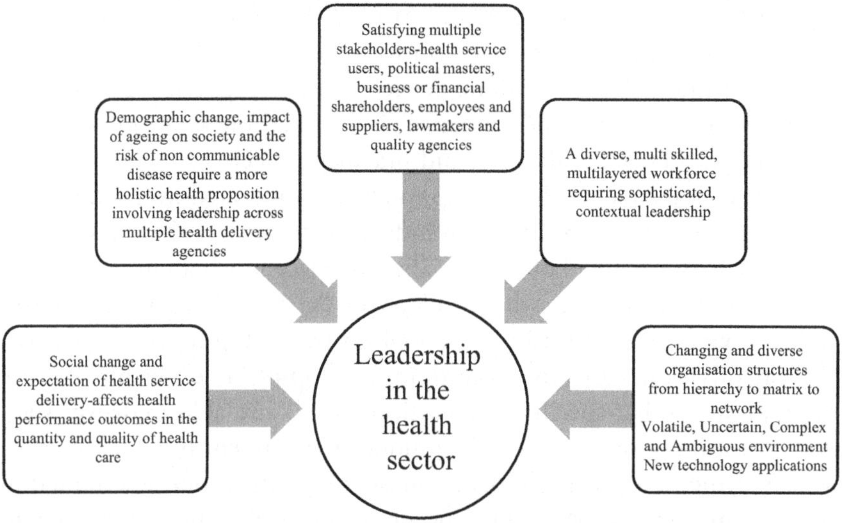

Fig. 1.1 Five forces that impact health sector leadership

Leadership: An Essential Health Sector Practice

Leaders are critical to the success of healthcare systems and to the vision of transforming healthcare (Block and Manning 2007; Mazzoccoli and Wolf 2016). Whilst there are some reservations as to its relative importance (e.g. McDonald (2014) argues that few studies have provided evidence to support the view and the tenets of leadership effectiveness have not been rigorously tested in healthcare), understanding the meaning and nature of leadership is regarded by many as an important foundation on which to build subsequent leadership practice.

Whilst most studies of leadership in the health sector emphasise its importance, therefore, there are a range of interpretations about where it has most impact. In some cases, the task-oriented value of leadership is emphasised focusing on goal achievement, in others on relationships such as team building, and in others still on change orientation (Reichenpfader et al. 2015). And an additional factor in the context of healthcare is the point at which professional health knowledge and skill (such as that acquired by clinicians or nurses) overlaps with generic leadership attributes—a coming together of medical and managerial logics (Zoheir 2012: 261; Love and Ayadi 2015). One conclusion is that as healthcare organisations are transformed, a new type of healthcare leader with new skill sets will be needed. This dialogue inevitably raises questions about what is 'best practice': is it something that can be sought and taught as both an idealised and practical objective?

Whilst 'best practice' leadership might be advocated as a solution to organisational challenges, the conundrum is to answer the questions of 'best practice as defined by whom,' 'best practice in what circumstances,' or 'best practice against which objectives or strategies.' An alternative point of view, put forward in this book, is leadership that is 'best fit' to the organisation, able to succeed in developing a leadership culture appropriate to that specific organisation's need, and able to deliver societal or 'business' outcomes to the unique environment in which it operates. Seeking best practice remains an ongoing target, but it is framed in the assumption that there may be no single, right, 'best' approach to leadership. A transformational style may be appropriate. Or equally inappropriate. Similarly, inclusive leadership, a catch-all phrase that embraces a plethora of popular concepts, may or may not be the leadership that a specific organisation in a specific context requires. Given these multiple scenarios (and there are other configurations of leadership that will be discussed in later chapters), it should be no surprise that even though the subject is one of the 'most-observed concepts, no universally accepted definition or theory of leadership actually exists' (Scully 2015: 439).

In any health sector organisation, ***leadership best fit*** can be an important contributor to providing a vision for the future, long-term strategies for the organisation as a whole, and the efficient execution of those strategies in a way that is suitable, achievable, and sustainable. For this approach to succeed, health sector leaders require insight and an understanding of the specific situation in which they and their organisations are placed to ensure that the leadership style, the diversity of the leadership team (Chisholm-Burns et al. 2017); the culture in which the organisation can flourish, and the depth of the leadership bench strength are best fit to meet objectives in that unique context. Once this is understood, then health sector leaders can have a powerful influence on strategy and operational performance; once they are able to reconcile the sometimes contradictory objectives of 'management and medicine' and once they can combine leadership capability, professional credibility, and an understanding of organisational dynamics, then they will have a chance of achieving the Triple Aim objectives of better care experience, improved population health, and cost-effectiveness, and this will be translated into performance (Farrell 2003: 160; Gulati et al. 2016; Kim and Thompson 2012: 113; Reichenpfader et al. 2015: 299; Denis and van Gestel 2016; Oostra 2016; Storkholm et al. 2017). This means leaders who mobilise intelligence and resources towards the achievement of the organisation's goals. But, because leadership is contextual, it also means that, whilst there may be common elements, each organisation will have its own perspective on what type of leadership is required and what intelligence needs to be mobilised.

Synthesising the many points of view about what it takes to be an effective health sector leader will inevitably lead back to the competences required in any particular organisation at a particular point in time. Most of these will be situation or context dependent, and in this respect, drawing generic conclusions about right or wrong way to lead will be misleading. It is, however, possible to identify certain characteristics that can apply to almost any situation. Chapters 5, 6, 7, and 8 will outline a model for leadership in health and some of its component parts including the competencies identified in the roles. Figure 1.2 introduces the model and its three building blocks.

The Structure of the Book

The focus of this book therefore is to explore theory and practice underpinning the roles of leaders and leadership in the specific context of the world's health sector organisations, examining the impact of significant change on leadership definitions, styles, and traits. The book will take the opportunity to review both academic and practice-based research to identify the knowledge, skills, attitudes, and behaviours of health leaders and the principles of assessing and developing those for succession or leadership roles at all levels. The structure of the book is based on understanding the context of the health sector and likely future challenges, defining what is meant by leaders and leadership from evidence and theory to date, identifying how the concepts have been applied in health, and from these developing a model of health sector leadership that can be adapted to the unique needs of each organisation. Further research into

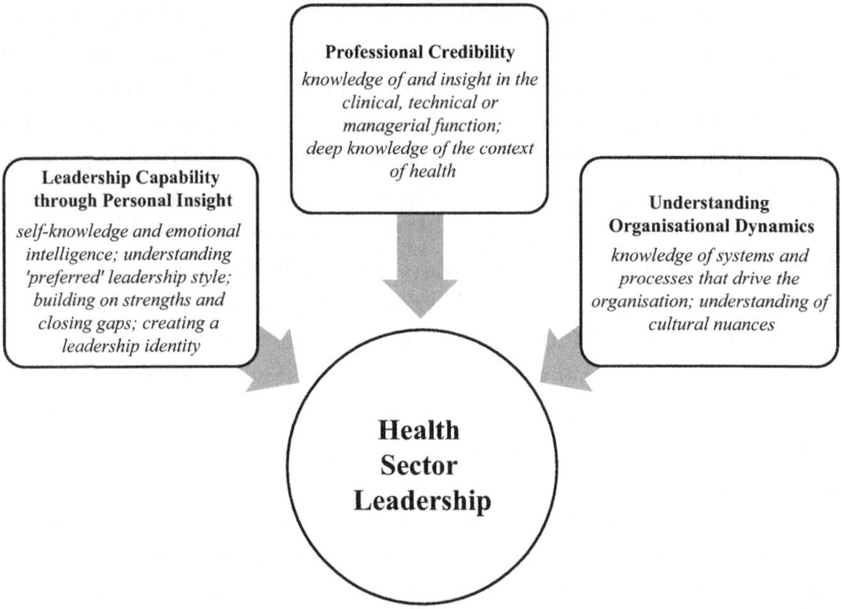

Fig. 1.2 The characteristics of health sector leadership

the assessment and development of leaders or those with leadership potential will be presented in subsequent chapters. The content of each chapter is summarised below.

Chapter 2 identifies the context within which health sector leadership—**the ecology of healthcare**—takes place by discussing some of the key forces which are at work. This narrative covers external forces for change—whether these be social, demographic, or economic—and the structure of health service and its impact on internal organisational dynamics. The chapter will adapt the VUCA concept (volatility, uncertainty, complexity, and ambiguity) and infer the effect of each on leadership requirements.

Chapter 3 investigates **the role of leaders—the importance of leadership** from general theory, its similarities with leadership in health, and the differences between the concepts of leader, leadership, and management. Whereas the former resides in the shape of an individual, the latter are concerned with multiple social interactions. The chapter will investigate the evolution of leadership theory and practice and seek to identify the contexts within which each view or perspective of leadership takes place. It will form the foundation on which the analysis of leadership in the unique situation of the health sector can be analysed.

Chapter 4 looks at the evidence for **leading in the health sector—research and practice**. In the first place, it will analyse high-level leadership and the operation of Board or Executive teams in health sector organisations. In the second it will look at the growing awareness and interest in inclusive and devolved leadership. This chapter includes a timeline for leadership which shows some of the leadership styles that have predominated in the health sector over the past 30 years or so. It will highlight any commonalities in the approaches to leadership that have emerged and whether these can be moulded into a coherent model of leadership that would be relevant to the sector.

Chapter 5 develops the concepts further and proposes a potential **model for health sector leadership** covering three important bases. These are firstly the need to develop leadership capability through personal insight, secondly the importance of professional credibility, and thirdly the necessity of understanding organisational dynamics as a means of crafting strategy and implementation. The model is not put forward as best practice since a best fit leadership approach is advocated. Nor will it present an inflexible point of view about leadership style. Instead it will be based on the need to adapt leadership to suit the circumstances within which leadership is required. A range of competences is included as part of the overall model.

Chapter 6 will look in some detail at the first of these. **Leadership capability through personal insight and leadership identity** means that those who lead organisations at whatever level will require an understanding of their own strengths and weaknesses as a precursor to their leadership approach. It means acknowledging areas in which strong competence or competency is present and those in which development (or delegation) is necessary. Personal insight is intended as an authentic self-assessment of strengths and weaknesses and acknowledgement of the contextual nature of leadership. Once this has taken place, a leadership identity will emerge and will be applied in the specific context of the health organisation in question.

Chapter 7 will investigate the meaning and importance of **professional credibility** to health sector leaders—how this can be defined, established, and developed. It is concerned with the necessity of demonstrating to those who engage with the organisation's strategy, that the strategy has been set with knowledge of clinical, medical, or professional environment within which it is taking place. In such circumstances those in leadership positions will have to demonstrate that they have professional insight into this environment, which in turn will be translated into professional credibility. It is argued that in the context of health, such credibility is critical to the engagement of followers—more so perhaps than in other sectors.

Chapter 8 will be the final part of the model for leadership in health and look at the important ability of a leader of **understanding organisational dynamics** as a way of ensuring that objectives are achieved. These dynamics concern both processes and people. This chapter argues that whilst leadership capability and professional credibility are important, the success of their applicability will be enhanced by an understanding of the dynamics of the organisation within which leadership activity takes place and harnessing or influencing these dynamics to ensure successful outcomes.

Once the model for leadership in health has been defined, it is important that organisations are able to sustain it. One contributor to this will be to ensure that there is succession to leadership roles, wherever they exist. Chapter 9 addresses this subject and covers **linking leadership and succession planning** and its more contemporary derivative **succession management**. In health, there is evidence that these are becoming increasingly devolved to organisational levels other than the Board. What this means for leaders and leadership in practice is an important consideration.

Chapter 10 applies a Leadership Competence Framework for Health in **assessing health professionals for succession and leadership roles**. In this context leadership competences are the skills and behaviours that contribute to leadership performance in the achievement of the organisation's goals and objectives or the underlying characteristics of a person that lead to or contribute to effective outcomes. Assessing leaders against the leadership competence framework is therefore an important part of the leadership process, and this chapter analyses how organisations have undertaken this process particularly for Senior Leaders, Executives, and Managers.

Recognition of the importance of leadership comes the recognition of challenge and complexity in its definition and execution. The challenge of health sector leaders is to make sense of multiple elements in crafting a course through which organisations can thrive and improve. Having insight and understanding about the environment and how the organisation interfaces with it, complemented by organisational and leadership skills, will be essential. Chapter 11 will analyse how effective **leadership development practices** can contribute to the enhancement of these skills.

The objective for presenting the case for leadership in health in this way is to enhance the understanding of the context within which health leadership takes place, the role and responsibilities of health sector leaders, the possible responses to the various organisational structures that are in place, and the ways in which best fit leaders can be assessed and developed. Chapter 12 will pull together the various strands that have been covered in the book into a set of **twenty important conclusions about leadership in the health sector**.

References

Amasawa, F., & Crisp, N. (Eds.). (2014). *African Health Leaders: Making Change and Claiming the Future*. Oxford: Oxford University Press.

Barr, J., & Dowding, L. (2008). *Leadership in Health Care*. London: Sage Publications Ltd.

Block, L., & Manning, L. J. (2007). A Systemic Approach to Developing Frontline Leaders in Healthcare. *Leadership in Health Services, 20*(2), 85–96.

Chisholm-Burns, M. A., Spivey, C. A., Hagemann, T., & Josephson, M. A. (2017). Women in Leadership and the Bewildering Glass Ceiling. *American Journal of Health-System Pharmacy, 74*(5), 312–324. ISSN:1079-2082.

Chobanuk, J., & James, K. (2015). Leadership Special Interest Group: What Is leadership? *Canadian Oncology Nursing Journal, 25*(1), 114–117. ISSN:1181-912X.

Choi, S. L., Goh, C. F., Adam, M. B. H., & Tan, O. K. (2016). Transformational Leadership, Empowerment, and Job Satisfaction: The Mediating Role of Employee Empowerment. *Human Resources for Health, 14*, 73. ISSN:1478-4491.

Collinson, D., & Tourish, D. (2015). Teaching Leadership Critically: New Directions for Leadership Pedagogy. *Academy of Management Learning and Education, 14*(4), 576–594. ISSN:1537-260X.

DaCosta, J. (2012). Leadership Models for Healthcare Improvement. *British Journal of Healthcare Management, 18*(11), 575–580. ISSN:1358-0574.

Delmatoff, J., & Lazarus, I. R. (2014). The Most Effective Leadership Style for the New Landscape of Healthcare. *Journal of Healthcare Management, 59*(4), 245–249. ISSN:1096-9012.

Denis, J. L., & van Gestel, N. (2016). Medical Doctors in Healthcare Leadership: Theoretical and Practical Challenges. *BMC Health Services Research, 16*, S158. ISSN:1472-6963.

Dye, C. F. (2010). *Leadership in Healthcare; Essential Values and Skills*. Chicago: ACHE Management Series.

Ellis, P., & Abbott, J. (2014). Identifying Goals with the NHS Healthcare Leadership Model. *Journal of Renal Nursing, 6*(3), 144–147. ISSN:2041-1448.

Farrell, M. (2003). Health Care Leadership in an Age of Change. *Australian Health Review, 26*(1), 153–164.

Fitzgerald, L., Ferlie, E., McGivern, G., & Buchanan, D. (2013). Distributed Leadership Patterns and Service Improvement: Evidence and Argument from English Healthcare. *The Leadership Quarterly, 24*(1), 227–239. ISSN:1048-9843.

Goffee, R., & Jones, G. (2006). *Why Should Anyone Be Led By You*. Boston, MA: Harvard Business School Press.

Gopee, N., & Galloway, J. (2009). *Leadership and Management in Healthcare*. London: Sage Publications.

Gulati, R., Mikhail, O., Morgan, R. O., & Sittig, D. F. (2016). Vision Statement Quality and Organizational Performance in U.S. Hospitals. *Journal of Healthcare Management, 61*(5), 335–350. ISSN:1096-9012.

Gunderman, R. B. (2009). *Leadership in Healthcare*. London: Springer-Verlag. ISBN:978-1-84800-943-1.

Hicks, R. F. (2014). *Coaching as a Leadership Style: The Art and Science of Coaching Conversations for Healthcare Professionals*. London: Routledge.

Howieson, B., & Thiagarajah, T. (2011). What Is Clinical Leadership? A Journal-Based Meta-Review. *International Journal of Clinical Leadership, 17*(1), 7–18. ISSN:1757-207X.

Kim, T. H., & Thompson, J. M. (2012). Organizational and Market Factors Associated with Leadership Development Programs in Hospitals: A National Study. *Journal of Healthcare Management, 57*(2), 113–131.

Kumar, R. D. C., & Khilijee, N. (2016). Management: Leadership in Healthcare. *Anaesthesia & Intensive Care Medicine, 17*(1), 63. ISSN:1472-0299.

Larkin, H. (2015). The New Health Care CEO: In a Rapidly Changing Field, Effective Leaders Require 'Learning Agility' and 'Emotional Intelligence' as Much – or More – Than Traditional Skills. *H&HN Hospitals & Health Networks, 22*(6).

Levey, S., Hill, J., & Greene, B. (2002). Leadership in Health Care and the Health Literature. *Journal of Ambulatory Care Management, 25*(2), 68–74.

Longenecker, C. O., & Longenecker, P. D. (2014). Why Hospital Improvement Efforts Fail: A View From the Front Line. *Journal of Healthcare Management, 59*(2), 147–157. ISSN:1096-9012.

Love, D. B., & Ayadi, M. F. (2015). Redefining the Core Competencies of Future Healthcare Executives under Healthcare Reform. *Administrative Issues Journal: Education, Practice & Research, 5*(2), 3–16. ISSN:2153-7615.

Maccoby, M., Norman, C. L., Norman, C. J., & Margolies, R. (2013). *Transforming Health Care Leadership: A Systems Guide to Improve Patient Care, Decrease Costs, and Improve Population Health*. San Francisco, CA: Jossey Bass. ISBN:978-1-118-50563-2.

Mazzoccoli, A., & Wolf, G. (2016). Mentoring Through the Leadership Journey: From Novice to Expert. *Nurse Leader, 14*(4), 253–256. ISSN:1541-4612.

McDonald, R. (2014). Leadership and Leadership Development in Healthcare Settings – A Simplistic Solution to Complex Problems. *International Journal of Health Policy and Management, 3*(5), 227–229.

Oostra, R. D. (2016). Physician Leadership: A Central Strategy to Transforming Healthcare. *Frontiers of Health Services Management, 32*(3), 15–26. ISSN:0748-8157.

Putre, L. (2013). Who Will Lead Your Hospital? A Painful Vacuum Looms as Baby Boom Execs Retire Without Preparing a New Generation of Leaders. *H&HN Hospitals & Health Networks, 87*(5), 34–39.

Read, E. A., & Laschinger, H. K. S. (2015). The Influence of Authentic Leadership and Empowerment on Nurses' Relational Social Capital, Mental Health and Job Satisfaction Over the First Year of Practice. *Journal of Advanced Nursing, 71*(7), 1611–1623. ISSN:0309-2402.

Redknap, R., Twigg, D., Rock, D., & Towell, A. (2015). Nursing Practice Environment: A Strategy for Mental Health Nurse Retention? *International Journal of Mental Health Nursing, 24*(3), 262–271. ISSN:1445-8330.

Reed, S. B. (2009). Creating a Leadership Legacy of Caring: A Health Care Leader's Ultimate Journey. *Nurse Leader, 7*(1), 12–15. ISSN:1541-4612.

Reichenpfader, U., Carlfjord, S., & Nilsen, P. (2015). Leadership in Evidence Based Practice: A Systematic Review. *Leadership in Health Services, 28*(4), 298–316. https://doi.org/10.1108/LHS-08-2104-0061.

Rogers, J. K. (2014). Reinventing Shared Leadership to Support Nursing's Evolving Role in Healthcare. *Nurse Leader, 12*(2), 29–43. ISSN:1541-4612.

Sahne, B. S., Arslan, M., & Sar, S. (2015). Concept of Leadership in Healthcare Services and Ethical Leadership. *Medicine and Law, 34*(2), 297–306.

Salomon, J. A., Mathers, C. D., Chatterji, S., Sadana, R., Ustun, T. B., & Murray, C. J. L. (2003). Quantifying Individual Levels of Health: Definitions, Concepts and Measurement Issues. In C. J. L. Murray & D. B. Evans (Eds.), *Health Systems Performance Assessment, Debates, Methods and Empiricism*. Geneva: World Health Organisation.

Saravo, B., Netzel, J., & Kiesewetter, J. (2017). The Need for Strong Clinical Leaders – Transformational and Transactional Leadership as a Framework for Resident Leadership Training. *PLoS One, 12*(8), 1–13. https://doi.org/10.1371/journal.pone.0183019.

Sarto, F., & Veronesi, G. (2016). Clinical Leadership and Hospital Performance: Assessing the Evidence Base. *BMC Health Services Research, 16*, 85–97. ISSN:1472-6963.

Scully, N. J. (2015). Leadership in Nursing: The Importance of Recognising Inherent Values and Attributes to Secure a Positive Future for the Profession. *Collegian, 22*(4), 439–444.

Silva, V. L. d. S., Camelo, S. H. H., Soares, M. I., Resck, Z. M. R., Chaves, L. D. P., Santos, F. C. d., et al. (2017). Leadership Practices in Hospital Nursing: A Self of Manager Nurses. *Revista da Escola de Enfermagem da USP, 51*, e03206. Epub. April 03, 2017. https://doi.org/10.1590/s1980-220x2016099503206.

Storkholm, M. H., Mazzocato, P., Savage, M., & Savage, C. (2017). Money's (Not) on My Mind: A Qualitative Study of How Staff and Managers Understand Health Care's Triple Aim. *BMC Health Services Research, 17*, 1–9. https://doi.org/10.1186/s12913-017-2052-3.

Tropello, P. D., & DeFazio, J. (2014). Servant Leadership in Nursing Administration and Academia Shaping Future Generations of Nurses and Interdisciplinary Team Providers to Transform Healthcare Delivery. *Nurse Leader, 12*(6), 59–61. ISSN:1541-4612.

Weberg, D. (2012). Complexity Leadership: A Healthcare Imperative. *Nursing Forum, 47*(4), 268–277. ISSN:0029-6473.

World Health Organisation. (2014). *A Universal Truth: No Health Without a Workforce*. WHO Press, World Health Organization, 20 Avenue Appia, 1211 Geneva 27. Retrieved from http://www.who.int/workforcealliance/knowledge/resources/GHWA-a_universal_truth_report.pdf?ua=1.

World Health Organisation. (2016). *Health Workforce – High-Level Commission on Health Employment and Economic Growth*. Retrieved from http://www.who.int/hrh/com-heeg/en/.

Zoheir, E. (2012). The Importance of Clinical Leadership in Twenty First Century Health Care. *International Journal of Health Promotion and Education, 50*(5), 261–269.

2

The Ecology of Healthcare

A Transformative Period for Consumers of Health and the Organisations Who Deliver Services

Healthcare is in a state of flux. In fact, it is difficult to identify a sector to which the acronym, VUCA, meaning volatility, uncertainty, complexity, and ambiguity, is more apt. A swell of powerful forces that can be attributed to each of these nomenclatures has created a transformative period for consumers of health and the organisations who deliver services to them (Turner 2017; Vennum 2017). In this context, volatility is the nature of change, its speed, volume, magnitude, and the associated dynamics of change; uncertainty refers to the unpredictability surrounding issues and events; complexity is the confounding of issues and the resultant chaos; and ambiguity is the lack of clarity about reality and the meaning of conditions (Horney et al. 2010). On the one hand, healthcare transformation is producing revolutionary, positive change. On the other VUCA forces are destabilising and chaotic. Health sector leaders have to deal with both scenarios.

P. Turner, *Leadership in Healthcare*, Organizational Behaviour in Health Care,
https://doi.org/10.1007/978-3-030-04387-2_2

The five forces that impact on health leadership outlined in Chap. 1 were indicative of the complexity of the challenges facing the sector, and in which legislative or funding change was likely to occur simultaneously with workforce challenges or shortages of key professional expertise, where social and demographic changes were taking place simultaneously and where multiple stakeholders could hold sometimes contradictory views about what health is and how it should be delivered. Whilst there is a strong case for prevention, societal change, and the application of technology, it is by no means clear as to how this change should take place. So, whilst there is no single driver or burning platform forcing health sector transformation, the UK King's Fund's observation about constraints on funding and a rising demand from a growing and ageing population putting the delivery of health services under enormous pressure would resonate in many geographies. The overall conclusion from their UK insight was equally dramatic stating 'it has been clear for some time that simply working our current hospital-based model of care harder to meet rising demand is not the answer. Rather, the NHS needs to work differently' (Ham 2018). Instead of a single overarching theme or trend, an array of forces—external to health sector organisations—as well as internal dynamics and those based on changing demand and supply are at play. Understanding these forces is a necessary precursor to any strategic or leadership response.

In the first place there has been a restructuring of national healthcare systems to improve efficiency, reduce cost, and improve the quality of care as well as accountability (Peckham 2014; Moen and Prescott 2016). This has occurred at the same time as the development of new business models (and leadership responses) at organisational level. For example, in the USA, due to its sheer size and complexity, it has been argued that healthcare innovation is necessary in every healthcare subsector: health service providers (physicians and hospitals), health service buyers or payers (insurance companies), regulatory agencies (FDA), and suppliers (Kim et al. 2016: 373). Global strategy experts including Professor Michael Porter have advocated a radical approach based on the principle that 'the fundamental goal of health care is to improve value for patients,' but in order to achieve this, redesigning healthcare delivery systems will be needed (Porter 2016). On the other hand, in the UK, a 'wide-ranging program of reforms brought about by the Health and Social Care Act (2012) in England fundamentally changed the operation of the public health system, moving responsibility for the commissioning and delivery of services from the National Health Service to locally elected councils and a new national public health agency' (Gadsby et al. 2017: 1). In China major health system reforms were put in place in 2009 which aimed at achieving 'comprehensive basic healthcare coverage by 2020 and addressing a number of serious problems, including high out-of-pocket payments, inequitable access, overcrowding of hospitals, and misaligned incentive structures that encouraged medical professionals to generate revenues from certain services and medicines' (Munro and Duckett 2016: 656), whilst in India the National Health Policy committed to the ambition of universal health coverage by 2025 (Rao 2017). Significant change is taking place across geographies, at multiple levels, and both within and between healthcare agencies. Throughout all of these, the concept of a smooth 'continuum of care' and achieving the Triple Aim objectives of better care experience, improved population health, and cost-effectiveness are integral threads. In order to deal with many of these challenges, health sector organisations are now composed of a diverse, multi-skilled, multilayered workforce in a wide range of organisational structures. Leaders of health sector organisations have to make sense of this state of affairs.

Sense Making of and Adapting to VUCA

To help in this process, a significant amount of research, analysis, and narrative is available which discusses, in detail, the areas of health which have felt the most impact and possible solutions to some of the challenges, particularly in the areas of leadership and people management. The World Health Organization has produced and continues to produce outstanding research in this area (inter alia WHO 2004, 2006, 2012, 2016, and 2017), and this is complemented by studies commissioned or produced by national health agencies, independent research and insight organisations, and professional representative organisations. There is equally outstanding work on the part of both academics and practitioners (including inter alia Frenk 2010; Czabanowska et al. 2014; Connell and Walton-Roberts 2016; West et al.

2015). To deal with this complex array of issues raised by such insight will require elevated sense making to develop 'a wider and more in-depth view of people, organizations and systems. This part of the process is about the 'so what?' component of reflective practice, it requires the leader to make meaning and sense of her/his own role within the more complex system. Ideally this should lead to identification of learning needs including further… experiences, knowledge and skills' (Till et al. 2016). Sense making on the part of health sector leaders is an understanding of the nature and impact of these forces; and framing leadership responses accordingly will be important contributors to success. Because of the rapid changes, there is significant pressure to lead in new ways that are appropriate to the environment. In organisational terms there are four key considerations as shown in Fig. 2.1.

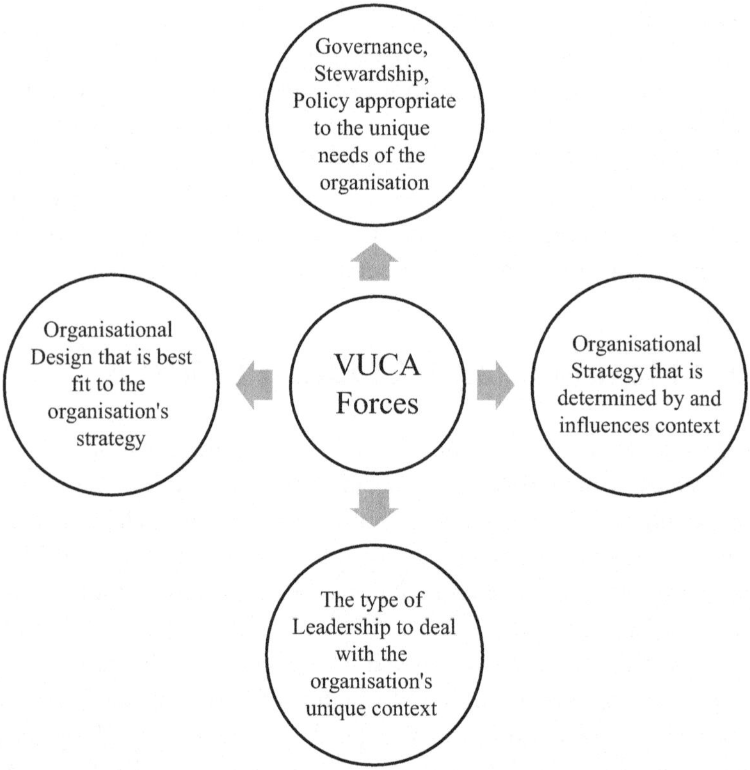

Fig. 2.1 VUCA forces and their impact on health sector organisations

These are the governance, stewardship, and policy decisions it makes to ensure effective delivery of health in the changed environment, the strategy that the organisation adopts in response to the prevailing forces or trends in its area of operation, the design and development of the organisation accordingly and of particular importance to this book, and the style and type of leadership required for success.

Further analysis of the concepts allows a framework for addressing the environmental challenges that leaders face (Till et al. 2016) and may provide cues for such leadership responses, so long as differences between the characteristics are recognised and 'actionable advice' (Bennett and Lemoine 2014: 311) is the outcome. The health sector context lends itself to this as much as any commercial or financial one. There are significant factors in each of the VUCA categories in the health sector which are summarised in Table 2.1.

Volatility Is a Feature of National Healthcare Systems

Volatility has been a feature of many national healthcare systems where 'recession, the credit crunch and reform have increased uncertainty and volatility in the health care industry' (Burik 2010: 1; Boylan and Ho 2017). Macroeconomic indicators and fluctuations in investment continue to provide challenges (Shobert 2015), whilst political change can itself lead to 'root and branch reform of service provision that is based around a model that incorporates a shrinking public sector coupled with an increase in civic participation' (Blakeman and Ford 2011: 482). Using its original conceptualisation, volatility refers to 'sudden, extreme and multi-layered fluctuations in economy, sociopolitics, geopolitics and indicates the difficulty of identifying and describing these changes in a pattern like manner as it used to be the case in a stable world where certainty about the course of events was the salient feature. In this environment, past experience and best practices don't provide enough indicators for identifying solutions for the present, or for the future' (Codreanu

Table 2.1 VUCA factors in the health sector

Volatility	**Uncertainty**
Discontinuity of global or national strategies caused by significant macroeconomic change Variable levels of investment in health due to either economic or political dynamics Changing points of view about the objectives of health and the means to achieve them The pace of change of technology causing disruption to standardised systems and processes and how the Internet of Things might revolutionise the delivery of health services Sudden changes in the supply of the health workforce caused by political influences The fact that past experience is not an indicator for current solutions Changes in organisational structure and the impact on the 'hierarchical' notion of health delivery	Political change and government policy; the incidence of biopolitics Changes in the public/private mix for healthcare delivery Changing national or international organisation of health sector provision Changes to health sector funding; demand for greater return on investment in healthcare from public and private stakeholders Increases in demand for healthcare; incidence of more complex treatments High turnover of health organisation Executives in some geographies Unpredictable pipeline of clinical and medical talent People dynamics, such as talent shortages, and intense competition for skilled health professionals; and the significant levels of human resources for health Uncertainty about the free movement of clinical staff between countries and potential shortages of key practitioners such as nurses or midwives in the UK or primary care doctors in the USA, creating supply challenges A shift in the legislative, regulatory, and financial environment creating uncertain or multiple responses

(*continued*)

Table 2.1 (continued)

Complexity	Ambiguity
The extension of the concept of health—that is, a broader definition of what is understood by the meaning of health, which now goes beyond a biomedical view to one of physical, social, and psychological well-being	Public and private sector provision simultaneously
The challenge of achieving a continuum of care	Changes in definitions and expectations of health sector consumers and providers
Vertically integrated health delivery systems	Ambiguity in clinical practice
Globalisation of supply of and demand for health services	Expectations of more with less, that is, performance improvement and additional services without pro rata budget increases
Demographic change	What is best practice? Best practice in what; defined by whom; to achieve what goals
Diverse, multi-skilled, multigenerational workforce	In which areas to innovate—systems, processes, organisations
Impact of exponential increases in technology capability	The balance of risk versus reward in health business or operational units
Management systems and decision-making processes including long causal supply chains	The incidence of seemingly polarised positions
Multiple layers of decision-making	
Disruptive innovation	
New drugs, new applications	
Impact of organising medical care delivery around patients' needs	
Changes in identity of doctors in transitional health systems from generalist to specialist	

2016: 31). In such an environment, it is difficult to 'read the present through the lenses of past,' which has implications for forecasting and decision-making. These assumptions have significance for identifying critical forces and the effect on leadership demands. Volatility in the health sector arises from both macroeconomic, political, or social change and at the micro level from the rapid changes taking place in individual institutions.

A supply-side challenge, for example, is the shift in the legislative, regulatory, and financial environment meaning that 'VUCA clearly describes circumstances' (Upton and McDonald 2017: 22). This has had an impact on the nature and structure of health sector organisation and funding, further complicated by multiple stakeholders—from politicians and business or financial shareholders and from lawmakers to health quality agencies and sometimes conflicting objectives. At a micro level, people relationships—those with each other, with their organisations, and with their physical or social surroundings, or the move towards patient-centred care in which 'the hierarchical notion of the professional being in charge and the patient being passive does not hold' (Stewart et al. 2014: 4)—contribute further to this transformational scenario. Ever-evolving standards of care as well as growing demands from improvements to quality and safety (Taylor 2014) complicate the dynamic. But an opportunity is the supply-side potential brought about by technological advances. For example, using the Internet of Things concept to support healthcare in rural villages has been explored ranging from remote monitoring to integrated medical devices…. wireless patient monitoring …In Vitro Diagnostics (IVD) Devices, Physiological Monitors, Mobile Medical Apps, Wearable's and Capital-Intensive Devices to identify and potentially solve health issues in rural areas (Prakashan et al. 2017). Forces for change in the health sector are disruptive and problematic on the one hand yet exciting, innovative, and full of potential on the other. Health sector leaders require competence to deal with both scenarios.

It is an important area of consideration given the unprecedented amounts of investment in health, which has created a worldwide sector comprising of a workforce consisting of over 40 million people and spending on healthcare of US$7.2 trillion, equating to 10.6% of global gross domestic product (Deloitte 2015), although there are wide variations of the level of expenditure from country to country. Stemming from these investments, new initiatives appear with the objective of strengthening national health systems (Frenk 2010) and expectations about the outcomes of such investments. Where these are disrupted, influenced by political or social change and differing points of view, there will be volatility in interpretation, the actual implementation of services and the implementation intentions behind these services. Such volatility will inevitably flow down to the micro level—for example, in a hospital—with the effect of the disruption or even discontinuation of services. At operational level this can include such diverse elements as surgeon costs per patient, with implications for quality improvement or the volatility associated with the average bed occupancy for emergency admissions which arises from the interaction between the environment and physiological and immunological processes (Hall et al. 2006; Jones 2011). Hence the concept of volatility will have an effect on health services at global, national, and unit level. How leaders deal with its effect and how wider leadership responds are important considerations.

Uncertainty in Investment, Structural Response, and Strategic Intent

There are uncertainties in healthcare which pervade every activity. Uncertainty is interwoven in daily life and in virtually all clinical situations experienced by patients and health professionals (Han et al. 2011; Hillen et al. 2017). At a macro level this is about the type and scale of investment, the structure and process of health service delivery, and political commitments or intentions. Examples include the effect of political change in the USA in 2017; the timing and logistics of any change and uncertainty about any outcomes; the effect of Britain's decision to leave the European Union and its potential impact on funding, patient's rights, and the free movement of skilled health sector workers; the transformation of the healthcare sector in India and the growth of private healthcare providers; health system dynamics in Nigeria (Emmanuel 2014); or the positive choices facing China regarding access, quality, and affordability in which policy-makers are under pressure to make complex decisions (Paolucci et al. 2015). In each case, uncertainty in the national environment is translated into uncertainty in the organisational environment creating questions about which strategy to pursue and what type of stewardship or governance should be put in place to monitor the strategy and the kinds of policies and processes necessary for its implementation. At a micro level, an emphasis on shared decision-making and patient-centred care has raised the profile of this factor, although it is also recognised that there are a variety of definitions of what uncertainty means in this context. Uncertainty brings with it a set of 'negative or positive psychological responses—cognitive, emotional, and behavioural—provoked by the conscious awareness of ignorance about particular aspects of the world' (Hillen et al. 2017: 63). The role of the leader will be to negotiate a path through such an environment with positive outcomes for the organisation in which she or he leads. This may mean understanding national policy ideas and then undertaking scenario planning around different options (Hegwer 2017) or developing strategy that is flexible and agile enough to track through the continuum of care. In either case, the health sector leader will require the capability to cope with uncertainty and build actionable and defensible strategies accordingly.

Complexity in Health Systems and Management

Complexity theory has been applied to different aspects of healthcare from management to continuity of care to nursing and decision-making. And whilst it is acknowledged that definitions of complexity are ambiguous, context dependent, and subjective, when referring to complexity in healthcare practice, it remains an important consideration for patient safety and quality. In this respect complexity is *the interrelatedness of components of a system…* the influence of system components on each other. It is relative: it increases with number of components in a system, number of relations between them, and uniqueness of those relations (Kannampallil et al. 2011: 944). Undoubtedly, across all disciplines, at all levels, and throughout the world, understanding, defining, and then delivering healthcare are complex (Plsek and Greenhalgh 2001). Indeed, it has been argued that the exponential increase of knowledge in medical science has brought additional levels of complexity which influence decisions and strategy (Ferraz 2015). It is pervasive and as such has been identified as a contributory factor to health sector organisation management, continuity of care, the management of clinical care, nursing decision-making, and complexity in the frame of health system strengthening (Kannampallil et al. 2011; Marchal et al. 2014). Clinical practice, organisation, information management, research, education, and professional development are interdependent and built around multiple, interacting systems (Plsek and Greenhalgh 2001). Whilst it is argued that health systems and organisations can be better understood by recognising their complexity, this is by no means straightforward because of multi-faceted and long causal chains and significant time lags between policy decision, implementation, and outcomes and the consequent risk of mismatch between research and policy time frames (Marchal et al. 2014). On the demand side the forces for change include social change in behaviour and attitude; the extension of the concept of health, that is, a broader definition of what is understood by the meaning of health, which now goes beyond a biomedical view to one of physical, social, and psychological well-being; and the increased demands from these new expectations on health service delivery. In addition, the impact of population ageing and the additional risk of non-communicable diseases both require a more holistic health response.

At a macro level, the dynamics of the sector include the effects of globalisation on both the demand for and supply of health, the 'human ecology' of disease, the importance of culture and its influence on healthcare, the impact of the exponential advances in technology on healthcare analysis and delivery (Skaržauskienė and Juciute-Rotomskienė 2014), and the impact of people-place interactions and the influence of institutions, governance, policy, and biopolitics (Connell and Walton-Roberts 2016; Turner 2017). In addition, the provision of healthcare is increasingly seen as a vital factor in economic development and global security. A combination of these demand-side forces is part of the equation for change in health. In response, health sector organisations recognise that uncertainty is likely to be an ongoing characteristic in the environment, that predicting outcomes with any confidence is a challenge, and most importantly that they have to deal with this situation. These circumstances are additional complicating factors for those who lead. Hence 'leading in complexity requires leaders to accept the complexity, create an adaptive space in which innovation and creativity can flourish and then integrate the successful practices that emerge into the formal organizational structure' (Cohn 2014).

Ambiguity and Change Are the Norm in the Health Sector

The fourth aspect of VUCA is the ambiguity which inevitably arises from environmental change for which there are multiple scenarios or outcomes. For some, the response to ambiguity centres on people, where 'leaders can replace volatility with vision, uncertainty with understanding, complexity with clarity and ambiguity with agility' (Hernandez 2016: 52). For others the response has been about system improvement and adaptation to ensure continuity in spite of ambiguity. For all, the challenges have led to the necessity of those in leadership positions to develop a strategy that is agile enough to deal with changing circumstances over time (Sherman et al. 2014). The responses have been many and diverse. In Poland, for example, the transformation of the health system because of increasing demand and changes to the political system led to competition and private initiatives, but 'systemic limitations to the privatization process have hindered progression. This has resulted in varying rates of privatisation among the distinct health care sectors and an ambiguous relationship between public and private health care provision' (Kaczmarek et al. 2013: 306). In the British NHS, attempts to introduce effective performance management were hampered by ambiguity created by limited resources at the same time as demands to increase activity levels (Conrad and Uslu 2012: 245). Ambiguity in clinical practice, for example, can reduce the likelihood of inconsistent interpretation or practice variation (Codish and Shiffman 2005) and can also impact patient outcomes (Castro-Sanchez et al. 2014). It is for these reasons that clarification is sought to ensure consistency of interpretation and practice. And yet, ambiguity is often the norm rather than the exception in health sector organisations operating in complex environments. Of course, the challenge is to reduce ambiguity and indeed 'high performers know how to prevent problems from producing further consequences once they occur and how to prevent their recurrence. They do this by specifying how work is expected to proceed-who will do what for whom, with what purpose, when, where, and how-before work is actually done' (Spear and Schmidhofer 2005: 627).

There have been proposals for reducing some of the ambiguities. In the UK, the King's Fund (Naylor et al. 2015) has called for more proactive management of chronic disease, the empowerment of patients, and a population-based approach to commissioning and more integrated models of care—from 'virtual' integration through shared protocols to integrated teams and in some cases shared budgets and organisational integration. In his 2018 essay, Leaf raised issues facing the US sector, concerning rigid payment and provider constructs and advocating for self-contained ecosystems with the consumer at the centre and business models (both for-profit and not-for-profit) emerging and evolving around this idea. In addition, he focused on de-hospitalisation arguing that hospitals are large capital assets filled with fixed costs such as CT scanners, MRIs, and other technology and laboratories which were once a strategic advantage, but now, 'because of the liquidity of data and analytics and software, when…all of those capital assets are now actually really constraining' (Leaf 2018). Furthermore the acceleration of technology offers precise treatments based on genetic codes, genetic counselling, editing of genes to repair mutations, using DNA for computing applications, using genetics as a biometric identification system, and 'lifestyle plans and coaching that personalise patient care through the use of genetics' (Vogenberg and Santilli 2018: 51). There are enough wise words and radical ideas from which health sector leaders at all levels can choose. The challenge they face is which will help them to work through the volatility, uncertainty, complexity, and ambiguity which form the daily outlook. Throughout all of this, they are called on to provide direction, to solve problems with insight, and to navigate competently. They do so in a melange of systems and structures for health delivery.

Sense Making of and Adapting to VUCA: Organisational Design and Development

The VUCA analysis, as well as influencing the strategy of the organisation, also has implications for organisation and system design. Both of these impact leadership style and competence and apply in geographies with experience of high levels of health spending per person (the highest being the USA) or government spending per person (the highest being Luxembourg) and others with lower levels as identified by the WHO with spending at US$50 per person or less (WHO 2012). Understanding the systems within which healthcare organisations operate is therefore a necessary precursor to understanding the implications for leadership in health and the ensuing challenges. Indeed, it has been noted that to deal with these forces, some of which are chaotic, a new kind of leadership is needed at every level of the healthcare system (Lee and Hall 2010), from large integrated systems to community hospitals or physician practices. The incidence of the forces covered by the above analysis has an impact on the way in which health is delivered. The volatility of the health sector, uncertainties caused by political or economic upheaval, the complexity inherent in modern health service processes, and the ambiguity caused by both the scale and pace of change can cause discontinuity and disruption to their modus operandi.

The inevitable consequences of external factors are changes in both organisational dynamics and design. The former might refer to the way in which the health sector responds to the demands of stakeholders through new people, systems, and processes; the latter refers to how organisations structure themselves to deliver to the changed environment. The challenge facing those who lead health sector organisations therefore is to respond in a way which ensures the achievement of the overarching objective of a good health system and quality services to all people, when and where they need them. Given the assumption that leadership is contextual, understanding the various forms of health system will provide a further foundation to deriving leadership style and attributes. However, as the World Health Organization has noted, the exact configuration of services varies from country to country (WHO 2017).

Even where the function of healthcare has been defined as providing both preventive diagnostic treatment and emergency care, the physical organisation of the healthcare system varies from a combination of hospitals, outpatient clinics, pharmacies, home healthcare services, long-term care facilities, public health clinics, and other supportive services such as occupational therapy (Anderson Penno 2013). A recognisable organisation of health starts at the **community or primary care** level which is usually the first point of contact for people in need of healthcare, provided by community professionals such as general practitioners, district or community nurses, dentists, and pharmacists. For the WHO (whose driving force is the goal of universal health coverage to ensure that all people obtain the health services they need without suffering financial hardship when paying for them), primary healthcare concerns organising health services around people's needs whilst at the same time increasing stakeholder participation. Primary care is considered to be the cornerstone of most health systems as it provides patients their first contact with professional health care, facilitates access to other health and social services and coordinates care for those with complex needs. Integrated primary care is 'a network of multiple professionals and organisations across the health and social care system provide accessible, comprehensive and coordinated services to a population in a community' (Valentijn et al. 2015). A characteristic is the integration of health services across disciplines and organisations. The implication of this integration is the adept leadership of change, and it has been argued that a model of collective leadership may be appropriate to this setting. Research has shown the 'importance of the distributed change leadership model in contexts where legitimacy, authority, resources, and ability to influence complex change are dispersed across loci. Distributed leadership has both planned and emergent components, and its success in bringing about change is associated with the social capital prevalent in the site' (Chreim et al. 2011).

A conventional way of describing s**econdary and tertiary care** can be derived from that used by the British NHS in which secondary care is referred to as 'hospital and community care' and can either be planned (elective) care or urgent and emergency care (NHS Providers 2017). Included amongst these are a diverse range of health providers such as acute providers (providing largely hospital-based services and ambulance services), community providers (providing services such as district nursing, health visiting), integrated providers (e.g. organisations that provide both acute and community care), and mental health providers and specialist providers (providing services such as specialist eye care or cancer treatment). At the next level, tertiary care concerns specialist treatment or consultative care, such as neurosurgery which usually takes place after referral from those in primary or secondary medical care and is delivered by specialists working in centres with facilities for special treatment.

These traditional definitions of the levels of healthcare are evolving as the health sector moves towards breaking down the barriers between primary care doctors and hospitals, between the areas of physical and mental health, and critically between health and social care. In addition, patient-centred and value-based care act as catalysts in how health services are designed and delivered. The British NHS, for example, predicted in its Five Year Forward View a future in which more care was delivered locally but with some services in specialist centres, organised to support people with multiple health conditions, not just single disease (NHS 2014). Furthermore there is a move towards care coordination through integrated health and social care teams in which 'joint commissioning between health and social care that results in a multi-component approach is likely to achieve better results than those that rely on a single or limited set of strategies.' Amongst the characteristics of this approach are a move to community-based multi-professional teams based around general practices; a focus on intermediate care, case management, and support to home-based care; and joint care planning and coordinated assessments of care needs (Naylor et al. 2015).

Other factors that are influencing the system for health and the impact on the structures of health include recognising that healthcare organisations are 'embedded' in organisational networks (Gopalakrishna-Remani et al. 2016), encouraging greater collaboration with multiple stakeholders and a systems thinking approach (Hoschander et al. 2013), redesigning patient care 'pathways' (Mallinson and King 2013), building what is known as a 'continuum of care' with a focus on 'life care' versus 'sick care' and patient-centred approaches such as shared decision-making (Van Dyke 2016), and interprofessional teamwork as a way of providing holistic healthcare (Hewitt et al. 2015). Technology also has a role to play in ensuring a more integrated proposition. Research in the Brazilian health system assumed that 'there are limitations regarding the development of communication and diffusion of knowledge between health service organizations if they are not effectively connected through social networks' (Francisco José Aragao Pedroza et al. 2016), and in Turkey there is a conscious objective of linking 'macro-level healthcare goals with micro-level system usage behaviours that actualize the macro-level goals' (Findikoglu and Watson-Manheim 2016). There are numerous responses that may be adopted including, as outlined above, mobile health technologies as 'enablers of real system change' (Coughlin et al. 2018) or innovative organisational design using technology as its basis, or the consolidation of services for improved quality and lower costs. However, transformation and change in the health sector will require those in leadership positions to have capability to effect the change, secondly the professional credibility to ensure followership from the multitude of stakeholders, and finally knowledge of the organisations in which they operate and how to best bring about transformation in a way that matches strategy with culture and resources.

Sense Making of and Adapting to VUCA: Organisational Governance, Strategy, and Leadership

As the definition of what constitutes healthcare evolves, so does the definition of what constitutes leadership in healthcare. Whereas once a health sector leader occupied the most senior position in a single physical entity (albeit as part of a wider structure), the contemporary healthcare leader is more likely to be required to operate at multiple levels and across several agencies. Furthermore, the increasing incidence of devolved leadership (discussed in Chaps. 4 and 5) means that more people will find themselves taking leadership actions. The implications on leadership attributes are significant. So, whilst the overall mission of organisations remains, that is, improving health, ensuring fair treatment, and meeting the 'non-health expectations' of the population, how those in leadership roles respond to competitive challenges and the other 'shifting forces' that characterise the contemporary economic or social environment will determine the effectiveness of their organisations in these goals (Bazigos et al. 2016). In this environment, it is argued that 'traditional leadership skills are not sufficient to weather an increasingly volatile, uncertain, complex, and ambiguous (VUCA) world' (Johansen and Voto 2014: 4) and that health sector leaders 'must be able to embrace the rapidly changing environment, be visionary, innovative, adaptive, and learn effective and efficient strategies to minimize risk and maximize opportunities.... in the healthcare environment, the strongest strategic nurse leaders must inspire people to want to follow them, not because of their rank or title, but because of their demonstrated leadership character' (Funari et al. 2015). There is support for the argument that 'today's debate on healthcare leadership, nationally and internationally, is all about integration and system leadership—perhaps a reinvention of consensus management, but this time between organisations rather than within them' (HSJ 2015).

In contemporary analysis (James 2011), health leadership involves multiple actors in the role of leader, some by formal appointment, some informally, who work collaboratively across organisational boundaries supported by practice-oriented organisational interventions. In this context the health leader will have a variety of objectives specific to the organisation but also within diverse health systems. Leadership in this scenario concerns the need to 'craft a common vision and leadership language and collaborating cross functionally' (Becker and Welch 2015: 70) or across agencies, either within the defined organisation (traditional leadership activity) or beyond the organisation (multi-agency leadership). And it has been argued that if the elements of (vertical) leadership can be 'embedded early and systemically into training alongside appropriate horizontal leadership, health-care professionals and organizations should be able to develop tailored personal, professional and collective strategies for improvement' (Till et al. 2016). But this is a significant challenge. There are few benchmarks or examples of external best practice, since health sector leadership is 'distinctive from leadership in other business settings' (Kim et al. 2016: 375). It is framed by unique circumstances against which an organisation has to decide on its strategic direction or operational priorities and to develop a sustainable path for 'creating public value by seeking legitimacy for building and maintaining public trust with patients as social and economic institutions creating value and sustaining both health and wealth for people and communities within society' (Romanelli 2017). The response to this challenge will determine the most effective approach to leadership and the attributes of leaders. On the one hand, there may be a requirement for those who can deliver transformation and change or, on the other, those able to maintain stability and provide consolidation. The question facing the organisation is to determine the type of best fit leadership that is relevant to its specific context. To establish the components of leadership and the styles and attributes that are relevant therefore, it is important to understand the nature and dynamics of the sector. Overlaps and interdependencies in health mean that these dynamics will involve both global and local influences.

Conclusion and Implications for Practice

At a national level there is acknowledgement of the 'contribution the knowledge of, and the practice of leadership' can make to the unique challenges of the health sector (Dickson 2009). At an organisational level, leadership skills have been shown to enhance the performance capability, build up organisational commitment, and increase productivity and effort, as in Thailand (Sriruecha and Buajan 2017), whilst in Denmark, leadership was one instrument to create good and effective patient treatment and care (Thude et al. 2017). In the USA the role of frontline leaders, however designated, was critical to transformation (Morris 2017). There is evidence that leadership in the health sector is a powerful concept across a range of performance indicators. It's possible to conclude that:

- Healthcare is in a state of flux and is subject to a range of forces that might be characterised as 'VUCA,' where volatility is the nature of change, its speed, volume, magnitude, and the associated dynamics of change; uncertainty is the unpredictability surrounding issues and events; complexity is the confounding of issues and the resultant chaos; and ambiguity is the lack of clarity about reality and the meaning of conditions. **Navigating through VUCA forces will require exceptional capability on the part of health sector leaders**.
- For a community or country to achieve universal health coverage, several factors must be in place, including **a strong, efficient, well-run**

health system that meets priority health needs through people-centred integrated care. To achieve this will require programmes that inform and encourage people to stay healthy and prevent illness, detect health conditions early, and have the capacity to treat disease and help patients with rehabilitation (WHO 2014). These objectives will be achieved with a system for financing health services and access to essential medicines and technologies to diagnose and treat medical problems.

- However, it is the third element identified by the World Health Organization to which the subject of leadership is particularly relevant; and this is **a sufficient capacity of well-trained, motivated health workers** to provide the services to meet patients' needs based on the best available evidence.
- **Effective health sector leadership is a vital component of all of these requirements** and will have an impact on creating the vision for health, the strategy to deliver the vision, and the engagement of a skilled workforce in its operationalisation. Leadership is a contextual phenomenon, and its success will depend on the ability of the leader and leadership to navigate their way through external and internal dynamics.
- **Leadership insight into the determinants of health and a depth and breadth of leadership skills will be vital** to organisations as they become more 'responsive to health needs, appropriate in the social and regulatory context, and visionary in balancing both workforce and client needs' (McMurray 2007: 36).

The question raised here is 'what is leadership?' And specifically, 'what is leadership in the health sector?' Chapters 3 and 4 will analyse the evidence to date in response to both.

References

Anderson Penno, E. E. (2013). Health Care Reform. *Magill's Medical Guide* (Online Edition).

Bazigos, M., Gagnon, C., & Schaninger, B. (2016). Leadership in Context. *McKinsey Quarterly*, January.

Becker, E., & Welch, T. A. (2015, September). Establishing a Common Vision Among Healthcare Providers. *Talent Development, 69*, 70–71. Association for Talent Development.

Bennett, N., & Lemoine, J. G. (2014). What a Difference a Word Makes: Understanding Threats to Performance in a VUCA World. *Business Horizons, 57*(3), 311–317.

Blakeman, P., & Ford, L. (2011). Working in the Real World: A Review of Sociological Concepts of Health and Well-Being and Their Relation to Modern Mental Health Nursing. *Journal of Psychiatric and Mental Health Nursing, 19*(6), 482–491. http://dx.doi.org.ezproxy.leedsbeckett.ac.uk/10.1111/j.1365-2850.2011.01818.x.

Boylan, R. T., & Ho, V. (2017). The Most Unkindest Cut of All? State Spending on Health, Education, and Welfare During Recessions. *National Tax Journal, 70*(2), 329–367.

Burik, D. (2010). Survival Strategies for Community Hospitals. *Trustee Magazine, 63*(9), 1–9.

Castro-Sanchez, E., Charani, E., Drumright, L. N., Sevdalis, N., & Holmes, A. H. (2014). Fragmentation of Care Threatens Patient Safety in Peripheral Vascular Catheter Management in Acute Care – A Qualitative Study. *Public Library of Science, 9*, e86167.

Chreim, S., Williams, B. E., Janz, L., & Dastmalchian, A. (2011). Change Agency in a Primary Health Care Context: The Case of Distributed Leadership. *Health Care Management Review, 35*(2), 187–199. https://doi.org/10.1097/HMR.0b013e3181c8b1f8.

Codish, S., & Shiffman, R. N. (2005). A Model of Ambiguity and Vagueness in Clinical Practice Guideline Recommendations. *AMIA Annual Symposium Proceedings, 2005*, pp. 146–150.

Codreanu, A. (2016). A VUCA Action Framework for a VUCA Environment. Leadership Challenges and Solutions. *Journal of Defense Resources Management, 7*(2), 31–38. Retrieved from https://search.proquest.com/docview/1851703435?accountid=12037.

Cohn, J. (2014). Leading Healthcare in Complexity. *Nurse Leadership, 27*(4), 52–64.

Connell, J., & Walton-Roberts, M. (2016). What About the Workers? The Missing Geographies of Health Care. *Progress in Human Geography, 40*(2), 158–176.

Conrad, L., & Uslu, P. G. (2012). UK Health Sector Performance Management: Conflict, Crisis and Unintended Consequences. *Accounting Forum, 36*(4), 231–250. https://doi.org/10.1016/j.accfor.2012.06.001.

Coughlin, S., Roberts, D., O'Neill, K., & Brooks, P. (2018). Looking to Tomorrow's Healthcare Today: A Participatory Health Perspective. *Internal Medicine Journal, 48*(1), 92–96. https://doi.org/10.1111/imj.13661.

Czabanowska, K., Smith, T., Könings, K. D., Sumskas, L., Otok, R., Bjegovic-Mikanovic, V., et al. (2014). In Search for a Public Health Leadership Competency Framework to Support Leadership Curriculum – A Consensus Study. *European Journal of Public Health, 24*(5), 850–856. ISSN:1101-1262.

Deloitte. (2015). *Global Health Care Outlook – Common Goals, Competing Priorities*. https://www2.deloitte.com/content/dam/Deloitte/global/Documents/Life-Sciences-Health-Care/gx-lshc-2015-health-care-outlook-global.pdf.

Dickson, G. (2009). Transformations in Canadian Health Systems Leadership: An Analytical Perspective. *Leadership in Health Services, 22*(4), 292–305.

Emmanuel, A. N. (2014). Challenges of Implementing Sustainable Health Care Delivery in Nigeria Under Environmental Uncertainty. *Journal of Hospital Administration, 3*(6). https://doi.org/10.5430/jha.v3n6p113.

Ferraz, M. B. (2015). Health Care: The Challenge to Deal with Uncertainty and Value Judgment. *Cost Effectiveness and Resource Allocation, 13*(8). https://doi.org/10.1186/s12962-015-0035-y.

Findikoglu, M., & Watson-Manheim, M. (2016). Linking Macro-Level Goals to Micro-Level Routines: EHR-Enabled Transformation of Primary Care Services. *Journal of Information Technology, 31*(4), 382–400.

Francisco José Aragão Pedroza, C., Núbia Moura, R., Roberto Luiz Souza, M., & Hernane Borges de Barros, P. (2016). Social Network Analysis as a Strategy for Monitoring the Dissemination of Information Between Hospitals/Análise de redes sociais como estratégia de monitoramento para a difusão de informações entre hospitais. *Transinformação*, (3), 309. https://doi.org/10.1590/2318-08892016000300006.

Frenk, J. (2010). The Global Health System: Strengthening National Health Systems as the Next Step for Global Progress. *PLoS Medicine, 7*(1), e1000089 Retrieved from www.plosmedicine.org.

Funari, T. S., Feider, L. L., & Schoneboom, B. A. (2015). Build High-Performing Military Nurse Leaders Through Coaching, Sponsorship, and Engagement. *Nurse Leader, 13*, 54–59. https://doi.org/10.1016/j.mnl.2014.07.019.

Gadsby, E. W., Peckham, S., Coleman, A., Bramwell, D., Perkins, N., & Jenkins, L. M. (2017). Commissioning for Health Improvement Following the 2012 Health and Social Care Reforms in England: What Has Changed? *BMC Public Health, 17*, 1–11. https://doi.org/10.1186/s12889-017-4122-1.

Gopalakrishna-Remani, V., Jones, R. P., & Wooldridge, B. R. (2016). Influence of Institutional Forces on Managerial Beliefs and Healthcare Analytics Adoption. *Journal of Managerial Issues*, (3–4), 191.

Hall, B. L., Campbell, D. A., Jr., Phillips, L. R., & Hamilton, B. H. (2006). Evaluating Individual Surgeons Based on Total Hospital Costs: Evidence for Variation in Both Total Costs and Volatility of Costs. *Journal of The American College Of Surgeons, 202*(4), 1072–7515.

Ham, C. (2018). *Making Sense of Integrated Care Systems, Integrated Care Partnerships and Accountable Care Organisations in the NHS in England*. The King's Fund. kingsfund.org.uk.

Han, P. K. J., Klein, W. M. P., & Arora, N. K. (2011). Varieties of Uncertainty in Health Care: A Conceptual Taxonomy. *Medical Decision Making: An International Journal of the Society for Medical Decision Making, 31*(6), 828–838. https://doi.org/10.1177/0272989X11393976.

Hegwer, L. R. (2017). Navigating Uncertainty in Healthcare. *Leadership+*, HFMA.

Hernandez, J. S. (2016). Leading Your Physicians: Perspectives and Perceptions. *Physician Leadership Journal, 3*(6), 50–52.

Hewitt, G., Sims, S., Greenwood, N., Jones, F., Ross, F., & Harris, R. (2015). Inter-professional Teamwork in Stroke Care: Is It Visible or Important to Patients and Carers? *Journal of Interprofessional Care, 29*(4), 331–339. ISSN:1356-1820.

Hillen, M. A., Gutheil, M. C., Strout, T. D., Smets, E. M. A., & Han, P. K. J. (2017). Tolerance of Uncertainty: Conceptual Analysis, Integrative Model, and Implications for Healthcare. *Social Science & Medicine, 80*, 62–75. https://doi.org/10.1016/j.socscimed.2017.03.024.

Horney, N., Pasmore, B., & O'Shea, T. (2010). Leadership Agility: A Business Imperative for a VUCA World. *People & Strategy, 33*(4), 34–41. ISSN:1946-4606.

Hoschander, S., Doyle, J. J., & Istas, A. (2013). A Systems-Thinking Approach for the Health Care Industry: Strategies and Insights for Biopharma, Payers and Providers. *Value in Health, 16*(7), A491–A491.

HSJ. (2015). Ending the Crisis in NHS Leadership: A Plan for Renewal. *Health Service Journal*. Retrieved from www.hsj.co.uk/Journals/2015/06/12/y/m/e/HSJ-Future-of-NHS-Leadership-inquiry-report-June-2015.pdf.

James, K. T. (2011). *Leadership in Context; Lessons from New Leadership Theory and Current Leadership Development Practice*. The King's Fund prepared for the Commission on Leadership and Management in the NHS.

Johansen, B., & Voto, A. (2014). Leadership Skills to Thrive in the Future. *People & Strategy, 36*(4), 4–8. ISSN:1946-4606.

Jones, R. (2011). Volatility in Bed Occupancy for Emergency Admissions. *British Journal of Healthcare Management, 17*(9), 424–430.

Kaczmarek, K., Flynn, H., Letka-Paralusz, E., Krajewski-Siuda, K., & Gericke, C. A. (2013). The Process of Privatization of Health Care Provision in Poland. *Value in Health Regional Issues, 2*(2), 306–311.

Kannampallil, T. G., Cohen, T., & Patel, V. L. (2011). Considering Complexity in Healthcare Systems. *Journal of Biomedical Informatics, 44*, 943–947.

Kim, R. H., Gaukler, G. M., & Lee, C. W. (2016). Improving Healthcare Quality: A Technological and Managerial Innovation Perspective. *Technological Forecasting & Social Change, 113*(Part B), 373–378. https://doi.org/10.1016/j.techfore.2016.09.012.

Leaf, C. (2018). 2 Forces That Will Drive the Health Industry. *Fortune*. Retrieved from http://fortune.com/2018/01/03/health-care-industry-2018/.

Lee, T. H., & Hall, K. W. (2010). Turning Doctors into Leaders. *Harvard Business Review, 88*(4), 50–59. ISSN:0017-8012.

Mallinson, M., & King, P. (2013). Transformation of Services and Care Pathway Re Design in the NHS: Further Reforms in Health Policy. *Value In Health, 16*(3), 8–9.

Marchal, B., Van Belle, S., De Brouwere, V., Witter, S., & Kegels, G. (2014). *Complexity in Health; Consequences for Research & Evaluation*.

McMurray, A. (2007). Leadership in Primary Health Care: An International Perspective. *Contemporary Nurse, 26*(1), 30–36. https://doi.org/10.5172/conu.2007.26.1.30.

Moen, C., & Prescott, P. (2016). A Values-Based Approach to Medical Leadership. *British Journal of Hospital Medicine, 77*(11), 624–629. (London, England: 2005).

Munro, N., & Duckett, J. (2016). Explaining Public Satisfaction with Health Systems. *Health Expect, 19*(3), 654–666.

Morris, B. (2017). Frontline Leadership During Hospital Consolidation. *Radiation Therapist, 26*(2), 200–202. NHS Providers. *The NHS Provider Sector*. Retrieved from https://nhsproviders.org/topics/delivery-and-performance/the-nhs-provider-sector.

Naylor, C., Imison, C., Addicott, R., Buck, D., Goodwin, N., Harrison, T., et al. (2015). *Transforming Our Health Care System*. The King's Fund. Retrieved from https://www.kingsfund.org.uk/publications/articles/transforming-our-health-care-system-ten-priorities-commissioners. This Paper Was Originally Published in March 2011. It Was Last Updated in June 2015 to Reflect Changes in the NHS.

NHS. (2014) *Five Year Forward View*.

Paolucci, F., Mentzakis, E., Defechereux, T., & Niessen, L. W. (2015). Equity and Efficiency Preferences of Health Policy Makers in China – A Stated Preference Analysis. *Health Policy & Planning, 30*(10), 1059–1066. ISSN:0268-1080.

Peckham, S. (2014). Accountability in the UK Healthcare System: An Overview. *Healthcare Policy, 10*, 154–162.

Plsek, P. E., & Greenhalgh, T. (2001). The Challenge of Complexity in Health Care. *BMJ: British Medical Journal, 323*(7313), 625–628.

Porter, M. E. (2016). *Value-Based Health Care and the Role of Outcomes Opportunities for the OECD*. Meeting with OECD Paris 19th May. Retrieved from http://www.oecd.org/els/health-systems/Item-3b-Improving-Health-Care-Value-Porter.pdf.

Prakashan, K., Karthika, A. S., Ankayarkanni, R., & Bright Jose, J. (2017). Transformation of Health Care System Using Internet of Things in Villages. *2017 IEEE International Conference on Industrial Engineering and Engineering Management (IEEM)*. https://doi.org/10.1109/IEEM.2017.8290025.

Rao, K. S. (2017). Challenging Times for Public Health Towards Attaining Sustainable Development Goals. *Indian Journal of Community Medicine, 42*(2), 65–68. https://doi.org/10.4103/0970-0218.205210.

Romanelli, M. (2017). Towards Sustainable Health Care Organizations. *Management Dynamics in the Knowledge Economy*, (3), 377.

Sherman, R. O., Patterson, P., Avitable, T., & Dahle, J. (2014). Perioperative Nurse Leader Perspectives on Succession Planning: A Call to Action. *Nursing Economics, 32*(4), 186.

Shobert, B. (2015). What China's Stock Market Volatility Means for Health Care Investors. *Forbes Asia*, August 25.

Skaržauskienė, A., & Juciute-Rotomskienė, R. (2014). Towards e-health: Information Technologies for Increasing Entrepreneurship. *International Journal of Management Science & Technology Information, 13*(Special Issue), 53–62. ISSN:1923-0265.

Spear, S. J., & Schmidhofer, M. (2005). Ambiguity and Workarounds as Contributors to Medical Error. *Annals of Internal Medicine, 142*(8), 627–630.

Sriruecha, C., & Buajan, S. (2017). Leadership Soft Skills of the Director That Affects the Performance of the Subordinate at Sub District Health Promoting Hospitals. Procedia – Social and Behavioral Sciences, 237, 1341–1346. https://doi.org/10.1016/j.sbspro.2017.02.220. (Education, Health and ICT for a Transcultural World).

Stewart, M., Brown, J. B., Weston, W. W., McWhinney, I. R., McWilliam, C. L., & Freeman, T. R. (2014). *Patient Centred Medicine; Transforming the Clinical Method.* London: Radcliffe Publishing Ltd.

Taylor, D. (2014). Perioperative Leadership: Managing Change with Insights, Priorities and Tools. *AORN Journal, 100*(1), 8–29.

Thude, B. R., Thomsen, S. E., Stenager, E., & Hollnagel, E. (2017). Dual Leadership in a Hospital Practice. *Leadership in Health Services, 30*(1), 101–112.

Till, A., Dutta, N., & McKimm, J. (2016). Vertical Leadership in Highly Complex and Unpredictable Health Systems. *British Journal of Hospital Medicine, 77*(8), 471. ISSN:17508460. https://doi.org/10.12968/hmed.2016.77.8.471.

Turner, P. A. (2017). *Talent Management in Healthcare.* London: Palgrave Macmillan.

Upton, J., & McDonald, C. (2017). 2017 Path of Uncertainty: Pharm Exec's 2017 Industry Forecast. *Pharmaceutical Executive, 37*(1), 20.

Valentijn, P. P., Vrijhoef, H. M., Ruwaard, D., de Bont, A., Arends, R. Y., & Bruijnzeels, M. A. (2015). Exploring the Success of an Integrated Primary Care Partnership: A Longitudinal Study of Collaboration Processes. *BMC Health Services Research, 15*(1), 1. https://doi.org/10.1186/s12913-014-0634-x.

Van Dyke, M. (2016). Leading in an Era of Value 3 Key Strategies for Success. *Healthcare Executive, 31*(6), 20–28. ISSN:0883-5381.

Vennum, K. (2017). *Healthcare in 2017: Amid the Uncertainty, These Changes Are Certain.* Washington, DC: Ernst & Young LLP.

Vogenberg, R., & Santilli, J. (2018). Healthcare Trends for 2018. *American Health & Drug Benefits, 11*(1), 48–54.

West, M., Armit, K., Loewenthal, L., Eckert, R., West, T., & Lee, A. (2015). *Leadership and Leadership Development in Healthcare: The Evidence Base.* London: Faculty of Medical Leadership and Management.

World Health Organisation. (2004). A Glossary of Terms for Community Health Care and Services for Older Persons. *Technical Report Volume 5.* World

Health Organization WHO Centre for Health Development Ageing and Health, WHO/WKC/Tech.Ser./04.2.
World Health Organisation. (2006). *The World Health Report 2006 – Working Together for Health*. Retrieved from www.who.int/whr/2006.
World Health Organisation. (2012). Spending on Health: A Global Overview. Fact Sheet No. 319. Retrieved from http://www.who.int/mediacentre/factsheets/fs319/en/.
World Health Organisation. (2013). *Human Resources for Health: Foundation for Universal Health Coverage and the Post-2015 Development Agenda, Report of the Third Global Forum on Human Resources for Health*, 10–13. November, Recife, Brazil, World Health Organisation and the Global Health Workforce Alliance.
World Health Organisation. (2014). What Is Universal Health Coverage? Retrieved from http://www.who.int/features/qa/universal_health_coverage/en/.
World Health Organisation. (2016). *Global Momentum for Human Resources for Health at the Sixty-Ninth World Health Assembly*. World Health Organisation News Release, May 27.
World Health Organisation. (2017). Health Systems. Retrieved from http://www.who.int/topics/health_systems/en/.

3

The Role of Leaders: The Importance of Leadership

What Needs to Be Done and How Are We Going to Do It?

Analysing leadership is more like looking through the lens of a kaleidoscope rather than that of a microscope because with each turn it changes shape and colour and hue. And as leadership theory evolves, it embraces an ever-increasing range of concepts from behavioural to attitudinal, from social-cognitive to contingency, from social exchange to team (Lord et al. 2017). More recently, leadership research has produced multilevel models and meta-analyses on a range of leadership definitions, styles, and processes. There is no shortage of material for those wishing to understand leaders, leadership, and organisational performance; but those seeking best practice will come away from the subject with conditions, sub-clauses and riders.

This is because there is no universally accepted theory of leadership (Scully 2015: 439). In some cases, leadership definitions (and advice) reflect an individual's perspective or the particular sphere of interest of the person making the definition (Yukl 2010). Those who articulate contingency theories will link leadership style to a particular environment or

P. Turner, *Leadership in Healthcare*, Organizational Behaviour in Health Care,
https://doi.org/10.1007/978-3-030-04387-2_3

situation, whilst those expounding exchange theory will focus on the theme of leader-follower relationships (Kodish 2006: 457). There are plenty of other options from which to choose. The basis of these styles is that such leaders achieve exceptional things through followers who would be deemed to 'go the extra mile.' From one perspective, leadership can be transformational (Burns 1978; Bass 1985); from another it can be framed in terms of an individual's charisma (Conger and Kanungo 1998). Some leaders are iconoclasts who challenge the status quo as a means of achieving innovation. Then there are the high-level leaders who are able to build enduring greatness through a blend of personal humility and professional will (Collins 2001) or those with emotional awareness which allows them to achieve more than those without (i.e. they have high levels of emotional intelligence (Goleman 1996, 1998)). For some, leadership is concerned with authenticity, or inverting the traditional perception to become servant leaders (Greenleaf 1977). Others still will attempt a 'shift' to a new level where purpose, mastery, autonomy, and trust are characteristics of the organisation and whose leaders share aligned values and aspirations. Such leaders see opportunities in challenges and build a strategy for exceptional performance; they are 'powerful but humble,' see leadership in terms of collective action, and lead for change and adaptability (Hlupic 2014). In most cases, leaders will be people who 'mobilise others to want to get extraordinary things done in organisations... transform values into actions, visions into realities, obstacles into innovations, separateness into solidarity, risks into rewards...create a climate in which people turn challenging opportunities into remarkable successes' (Kouzes and Posner 2007: 8). In short, leaders are people who can influence a group to commit willingly to a common goal. But how they do so is open to interpretation.

Amongst the 'vast number of frameworks and theories' (Edger 2012: 115) that have fed into the leadership debate, there has been a tendency to define the leader and the concept of leadership in terms of seniority or as those people at the apex of the organisation responsible for setting strategy and policy. But this approach is being overtaken as acts of leadership are deemed to take place at multiple organisational levels. 'Leadership is no longer about defining moments, taking charge, and acting purely in rational ways. Our current understanding is more nuanced and complex'

(Stackman and Devine 2011: 42). This is important because the reason that there is so much interest in the subject is that when it is defined or shaped to meet a specific context or circumstance, effective leadership can help an organisation to steer a path through the volatility, uncertainty, complexity, and ambiguity that characterise contemporary business and social environments, features of which were outlined in Chap. 2. To cope with complex dynamics, leadership is as an essential practice with the potential for a significant impact on both strategic direction and operational performance. However, for the impact to take place, an organisation will require a leadership style and capability best fit to its specific circumstances, because 'leadership requirements vary by situation and by level. For example, the leadership requirements of a turnaround situation differ from those of sustaining success. The requirements of a start-up differ from requirements to effect a fundamental transformation of an organization's business model. There is an equally profound difference between leadership at the functional and at the enterprise level' (Conger 2004: 138). Clarity about the role of the leader and the type of leadership required is therefore an important consideration. The questions of *what needs to be done and how are we going to do it* will not be answered until the fundamentals of leadership are resolved.

Synthesising Views on Leadership: Context and Possibilities

To help in this quest, theories of leadership have evolved from those which interpreted it as a form of dominance to achieve particular goals or objectives to being the influence which comes about because of the character or personality of an individual leader. In the latter models, the behaviour of the leader was critical to influencing overall effectiveness (Northouse 2016). Several of the theories discussed above followed a tradition of specifying pairs of contrasting leadership functions, behaviours, and styles (Kaiser et al. 2012) such as autocratic to democratic leadership or the distinction between transactional and transformational leadership. Subsequently, interest and research have coalesced around leadership as the ability to get followers to do what the leader wants—the importance of influence as a way of distinguishing leadership from management and leadership as transformation. In addressing the question of what leadership is, Grint (2005) identified four possibilities. Firstly, ***person-based leadership*** resonated with the traits approach pertaining to a leader's character or personality. Such traits included charisma, having a clear vision and strategic objectives, decisiveness, being an inspiring communicator, integrity, trust and delegation, honesty, and consistency (Alimo-Metcalfe and Alban-Metcalfe 2003). In addition, encouraging staff to challenge traditional approaches and having a genuine interest in staff were highly regarded leadership characteristics. Secondly, ***result-based leadership*** is founded on realising potential as a distinguishing feature of the leader's actions. Thirdly, ***process-based leadership*** used the assumption that 'people that we attribute the term leadership to, act differently to non-leaders' (Grint 2005: 27). Finally, ***position-based leadership*** defines the term as a spatial position, that is, where a person sits in the organisation's hierarchy. A complementary approach to this categorisation was also put forward by Yukl (2010) who identified leadership into ***trait***, ***behaviour***, ***power-influence***, ***situational***, ***integrative***, or ***intra-individual*** and Edger (2012) who defined leadership into generic groupings (such as that based on trait or behaviour) and local leadership theories including functional leadership or group and team leadership. These theories sometimes distinguished between a ***leader*** who sits at the head of an organisation, department, or business unit and ***leadership*** which is a social phenomenon that occurs at many organisational levels and points. Kilburg and Donohue's (2011: 15) articulation of a grand unifying theory of leadership concluded that 'leadership is a complex, multidimensional, emergent process in which the leader and followers use their characteristics, capabilities, thoughts, feelings, and behaviours to create mutually influencing relationships that enable them to coevolve strategies, tactics, structures, processes, directions, and other methods of building and managing human enterprises. A synthesis of the many perspectives on leaders and leadership in this grand unifying theory also concluded that in different conditions and situations, leadership can be expressed by virtually any member of such systems, thereby reinforcing a more inclusive perception of leadership.' Furthermore, knowledge, skills, abilities, attitudes, personality, values, ethics, virtues, vices, history, and 'other diverse characteristics of the members of organizational systems have tremendous impact on whether, how, and how effective leadership is expressed'; and the thoughts, feelings, and behaviours of the members of a system create a complex, contingent set of exchanges and mutual influences through which leadership occurs.

As can be deduced from the above narrative, the subject of leadership has produced some brilliant insights, and from academic research it is possible to draw from pointers and clues about leadership in particular contexts. The challenge comes about when leaders apply these insights as they work through 'calculated chaos' or 'controlled disorder' that often accompanies organisational life (Mintzberg 2011: 41).

The Paradoxes of Leadership: Turning Theory into Practice

The complexity of both the environment exacerbated by VUCA forces and the subject itself means that there are significant issues in defining the roles and competences needed to be an effective leader. To put this in context, there is a story in which Aristotle, commenting on the abilities of one of his scholars, proposed that it was necessary for the scholar to have experiences of life before he could be judged as a true leader (something Aristotle was unable to pass on to the person in question, the young Alexander the Great). As a reflection on this point, it was noted that 'if one of the greatest teachers in history had trouble teaching leadership to one of the most successful leaders in history, can we, mere mortals, teach leadership' (Grint 2007: 231). The observation came about in part because of recognition that it was easier to define competence and pass on leadership know-how and understanding (*techne* and *episteme* in Aristotelian terms) than the third important aspect of leadership, practical or prudential wisdom (*phronesis*), which was gained from both action and reflection. Practical wisdom is therefore significant for understanding the complexity of leadership. It includes knowledge, perception, decision-making, purposive action, grasp of the rational and the irrational principles, character, virtue, experience, promotion of one's personal interests, understanding of others, and endorsing their interests and intuition (Kodish 2006: 461). When this is applied, it inspires people to 'become their best selves by reconceputalizing attributes of leadership to reflect and integrate wisdom. Wisdom transcends intelligence; it embraces knowledge, emotion, and moral behavior. It represents the pinnacle of human development' (Valenziano 2015). In the health sector, this can be construed as the tacit know-how that enables health professionals to make ethically sound judgements and take prudent actions in specific situations (Cathcart and Greenspan 2013). However, such a rich list of considerations demonstrates that leadership is not a simple abstract concept and cannot be understood through theoretical constructs alone. Nor is it a concept that can be explained purely through practice experience—the oft and multi attributed quotation of 'leaders do the right things, managers do things right.' To understand leadership better therefore will require dealing with the assumption that it is paradoxical, complex, dynamic, and contextualised (Kodish 2006: 452). In this respect and in much the same was as Mintzberg's (2011) view of management, leadership may be viewed as a mix of art, craft, and science.

To put in place best fit leadership requires an organisation to be aware of the demands of its own unique environment (Longenecker and Longenecker 2014; Redknap et al. 2015: 266; Sarto and Veronesi 2016); it means highlighting the skills and competences required by a leader and the expected outcomes of leadership, identifying the priorities for leaders and leadership, and deciding on what are the constituent parts of leadership and how can they be acquired, improved, or developed. Answers to these questions will provide a platform from which leaders and leadership characteristics can be better understood, from which leader assessment and leadership development will be informed, from which a culture of devolved leadership can be established, and, finally, from which leadership policies and procedures can be set up or organisational structures put in place. A good deal depends on defining the role of the leader and the nature of leadership.

Amongst the wide range of definitions, several have particular resonance for the purpose of understanding the subject in the context of the health sector, fit broadly into contemporary thinking and are applicable to the VUCA scenarios outlined earlier. These are transformational and its counterpart transactional; charismatic; distributed and the leadership 'shift'; and servant leadership. This is not to dismiss other approaches, merely to refine the propositions into concepts that are workable and might be used to formulate leadership responses to the many challenges in the health sector. The following are brief summaries of the most relevant theories to this objective. Their key constructs will be analysed as the basis for developing a model for leadership in subsequent chapters.

Transformational and Transactional Leadership: Satisfying Higher Needs or Contingent Reward

The most popular and enduring leadership concepts are those of transformational and transactional leadership which originated from the work of James MacGregor Burns. In most cases the relationship between leaders and followers was transactional and was based on exchanging one thing for another. This was in contrast to transformational leadership which sought to satisfy higher needs, engaged the full person of the follower, and was deemed to be a more potent form of leadership, a viewpoint that resonated with many during this period and subsequently (Burns 1978). Building on this, the work of Bass et al. (Bass 1985; Bass and Avolio 1993; Bass and Riggio 2006; Bass and Bass 2008) found that 'transformational leaders motivate others to do more than they originally intended and often even more than they thought possible' (Bass and Riggio 2006), and transformational leadership is a style in which followers, through the trust and respect shown to the leader, are motivated to do more than is formally expected of them to achieve organisational goals (Boamah et al. 2017). Such a leadership style was composed of the leader's qualities (e.g. self-efficacy, values, traits, emotional intelligence), organisational features (e.g. organisation fairness), and 'the leader's colleagues' characteristics (e.g., follower's initial developmental level)' (Sun et al. 2017). It has been related to a diverse set of outcomes including, inter alia, business, operational, or job performance (Bellé 2014; Ng 2017); the finding that transformational leadership positively predicts positive measures and negatively predicts negative measures of employee's psychological well-being (Arnold 2017: 382); empowerment of the workforce (Welford 2002); job satisfaction and inspiring or stimulating employees (Babić et al. 2014; Baltaci et al. 2014); team learning, because transformational leadership facilitates psychological safety in the team (Raes et al. 2013); and team effectiveness, when combined with emotional intelligence components such as social skills, motivation, and empathy (Team Performance 2009). In addition, transformational leadership had positive effects on the take-up and application of new technologies or systems (Elkhani et al. 2014), enhancing innovativeness because the transformational style encourages and facilitates the accumulation of tacit knowledge to be used in the development of competitive advantage (Raj and Srivastava 2016), and changing or enhancing organisational cultures and climates (Bass and Avolio 1993; Kaslow et al. 2012) and on values in organisational decision-making (Pandey et al. 2016). Other attributed outcomes of transformational leadership included the ability to change organisations in response to external forces and to achieve higher levels of goal attainment. Given the extent of perceived outcomes, it is no surprise that transformational leadership has remained such an endearing concept.

Transformational leadership has been depicted in multidimensional models such as, first, the Multifactor Leadership Questionnaire, or MLQ; second, the five-factor model which included personal recognition that was closely based on contingent reward behaviours; and third, TFL dimensions, which include core transformational behaviours (Li et al. 2017). In an attempt to isolate the components of transformational leadership and identify the qualities that would be required of a leader to develop the concept, four key areas were also identified, known as the '4 Is':

- ***Idealised influence***—transformational leaders behave in ways that allow them to become role models for followers.
- ***Inspirational motivation***—by providing meaning to work and behaving within the context of this meaning, transformational leaders motivate followers to what might be referred to as 'attractive future states' (Bass and Riggio 2006).

- ***Intellectual stimulation***—transformational leaders encourage questioning of the status quo or the norm through an encouragement to be innovative and creative.
- ***Individual consideration***—finally transformational leaders pay particular attention to individual followers and their need for achievement and growth aspirations. Often this is as coach or mentor.

On the one hand, it was proposed that transformational leadership produced superior performance compared to transactional leadership; 'transformational leadership yields performance beyond expectations, transactional leadership yields expected outcomes' (Alatwi 2017: 19). On the other, transactional leadership with its concept of contingent reward has been shown to be effective in structured contexts such as those surrounding project management. Transactional leadership is based on an exchange process leading to the completion of contractual obligations. It is associated with setting objectives and both monitoring and controlling outcomes and assumes either active or passive management by exception, both of which are involved with corrective transactions—either actively or passively (Aga 2016).

There are strong and well-articulated arguments in favour of an organisation adopting transformational leadership. However, and in spite of the apparent success of the transformational style on a range of indicators, the model has had some critics, with one noting that 'the claim that transformational leadership is a highly effective style of leadership compared to other leadership styles in all kinds of organizations at all managerial levels must be reexamined' (Alatwi 2017: 25). Evidence from research and practice has mitigated this counterview which means that the popularity of transformational leadership has endured. However, in some instances, it was argued that effective leadership required a mix of transactional and transformational leadership skills.

Charismatic Leadership: Larger Than Life and Mysterious

Charismatic leadership is defined as being *value-based*, *symbolic*, and *emotion-laden leader signalling*. In this respect, the term *charisma* describes leaders who, by 'the force of their personal abilities,' have profound and extraordinary effects on followers. Charismatic is the degree to which the leader behaves in ways that can be deemed as praiseworthy and cause followers to identify accordingly (Judge and Piccolo 2004). It is based on the amount of faith, respect, and motivation that the leader can instil. It is also closely related to transformational leadership. Charisma can be an inferential that compares the fit of the person to an ideal or in an attributional way based on the charismatic leader's actual past performance (Jacquart and Antonakis 2015). Since its introduction as a concept, 'the study of charismatic leadership itself has taken on a larger than life and mysterious character in the organisational sciences' (Banks et al. 2017: 508). For some, the charismatic leader has superhuman qualities, and because of this, followers accept unconditionally the leader's mission and directives for action. These leaders represent revolutionary social forces, and they are responsible for significant societal transformations (Conger and Kanungo 1987; Conger et al. 2000; Conger 2008). They are able to inspire their followers to 'throw their heart and soul into creating a better world.'

But the challenge facing organisations who are seeking such visionaries in their leadership cadre is to convert these observations into meaningful findings on which the dimensions of charismatic leadership can be identified and those with the relevant qualities attracted, developed, and retained. When further investigation takes place, it shows that the most heavily cited definitions of charismatic leadership have been based on outcomes or antecedents or 'charisma has been defined as some unknown quality or miraculous ability' (Banks et al. 2017: 508). The distinguishing behaviours of charismatic leadership result from how such leaders solve a problem. Firstly, they show sensitivity to the environmental context; secondly the charismatic leader formulates goals that are aimed at an idealised future and an 'ability to evoke it in the imagination of their followers.' Finally the charismatic leader builds trust through personal example and risk taking. In this respect, it is essential that the followers trust in the leader's vision. In short, the charismatic leader detects deficiencies in the status quo, formulates future visions, articulates them, and then 'devises unconventional means for achieving them' (Conger 2008: 97–99). The results of charismatic leadership are impressive in respect of followership and reverence.

There is a rider on the subject of charismatic leadership. Peter Drucker commented that 'leadership grounded in charisma, which is what so many writers today want to advocate, inevitably becomes misleadership' (Galagan 1998: 24). Drucker believed that 'tomorrow's leader' would not be able to lead by charisma—but that he or she will need to think through the fundamentals so that others can work productively (Bildstein et al. 2013). Such observations add to the arguments of those who are sceptical of the sustainability of the concept over the longer term. However, charismatic leadership remains on the agenda of options because of its perceived relevance to the importance of followership.

Distributed, Shared, Inclusive Leadership and the Leadership 'Shift'

An assumption that is relevant to the debate about leadership and its meaning is that 'organisations have entered an era where there is a sense of urgency to understand shared leadership because of the shift in how work is done' (Hickman 2010: 164). The pace of change in response to, inter alia, external 'VUCA' forces as well as significant changes to the internal dynamics of organisations (from hierarchy to matrix, network, or project) has made it imperative for organisations to be able to respond quickly. 'The kind of responses made have been evident for some considerable time, from structural adaptation to a whole range of workforce strategies, which include job design, motivation and management style, reward… and employee assurances' (Thorpe et al. 2011: 239). This change in point of view requires more collaboration to achieve objectives, 'from an individual recipe of leadership to a collective process throughout networks; from singular theories to complex convergences of diverse methodology, ideas and experience' (Rodriguez and Rodriguez 2015). These adaptations have had implications for the position-based view of leadership and are 'increasingly being viewed within the context of a collective endeavour, where individuals have the ability to contribute to the creation and development of a common purpose or vision' (Thorpe et al. 2011). Whereas transformational leadership might be seen as a vertical leadership style which emanates from a formal leader of a team (Suk et al. 2017), there is a growing awareness of the incidence of a more distributed, shared, or inclusive approach to leadership. Transformational leadership can contribute to team output effectiveness, but distributed or shared leadership can improve the team's organising and planning effectiveness prompting the conclusion that different styles of leadership contribute to different aspects of team effectiveness. In this context, interactions are not dialogues but polylogues which provide inputs from different levels which are then deliberated, analysed, and used in decision-making (Lee-Davies, Kakabadse and Kakabadse 2007; Jha and Bhattacharyya 2017). Leadership becomes a non-hierarchical concept and leaders exist at all organisational levels.

This is a response to what has been identified as a significant leadership challenge, that is, to enable others to act and build leadership capacity by sharing leadership responsibilities 'across different elements of a task…in this model of leadership the dependence of followers on formal leadership figures decreases and the group becomes more empowered' (DaCosta 2012: 576). Hence distributed leadership 'is considered as a social phenomenon with a context integral to its understanding and, indeed, constitutive of the practice of leadership, concerned with thinking and actions in situ. The focus therefore is on conjoint actions rather than role or position. It is the way in which leading is enacted in the performance of tasks that is important' (Thorpe et al. 2011: 240). Rather than deciding on a specific set of traits or behaviours, a more holistic approach towards leadership containing subjective and objective elements and theory supplemented by practice (Kodish 2006) has evolved. Distributed leadership is concerned with how influence is exerted when performance and tasks are stretched over people and variable situations requiring discretionary actions and understanding in 'conjoint' action with others.

A further perspective away from the heroic leadership concept and recognising the wider network within which leaders and leadership are viewed has brought about a shift in approach and a radical rethink of the leadership concept such that 'conventional wisdom about leadership approaches and styles need to be unlearned as it is not serving its purpose anymore' (Hlupic 2014: 33). In this context it is argued that new leaders, at whatever level, should become exemplars in honesty, integrity, and humility. They should embrace transparency and compassion in which leadership should embrace a set of values related to the higher achievements of the human spirit (Grint 2005: 12). It is for these reasons that a traditional command and control style leadership is 'not only unhelpful, it can be counterproductive, causing companies to lose their ability to create value, to innovate and stay competitive' (Hlupic 2014: 33). Devolved leadership and a conjoint approach are complementary to this new situation.

One outcome is the 'emergent leadership model' which advocates that 'leaders lead by letting go, power and authority are distributed, there is a strong teamwork ethos and employees feel purposeful and are passionate about their work' (Hlupic 2014: 89). In order to reach this nirvana, organisations go through several stages in which leadership outcomes can be placed at one of five levels beginning with 'Lifeless' and working through reluctant, controlled, and enthusiastic before reaching the end state of 'Limitless'—limitless potential, collective consciousness, string intuition, and a passion to make a difference. Level 5 leaders are aware of the human environment in which they operate, inspire and energise people to achieve unlimited potential, are connected and develop networks, have a close bonding with their co-workers, and are empathetic and release control (Hlupic 2014: 101).

There is evidence of a shift in leadership style with an emphasis on devolution of power and authority, a recognition of the non-hierarchical nature of organisations, and recognition of the networked, transparent nature of organisational dynamics brought about by amongst other things the changing demographic and the power and utilisation of social media. Leadership by control of activity and information is not effective in such environments. Instead, distributed, devolved, or shared leadership is a more appropriate response.

Servant Leadership Which Focuses on Follower Needs

The servant leader model resonates because 'although attention to organizational outcomes has dominated managerial and leadership theory in the early part of the twentieth century, servant leadership elevates the priority of focusing on follower needs' (Irving and Berndt 2017: 2). Its initiator and champion Robert Greenleaf (1977) observed that a fresh look was being taken at the issues of power and authority and 'people are beginning to learn, however haltingly, to relate one to the other in less coercive and more creatively supporting ways' (Greenleaf, in Hickman 2010: 88). Servant leadership is a shift in emphasis from the guise of an influential individual to the needs of the whole workforce.

This point of view argued that the servant leader had, as a prime motivation, the natural feeling to serve, which provided the antecedent of the desire to lead (not the other way around). The servant leader ensures that other people's highest priority needs are being served by showing the way for others. 'One of the core tenets of servant leadership theory is that servant leaders instil in followers a desire to serve others' (Lacroix and Verdorfer 2017: 2). It is this spirit that is the distinguishing characteristic, the attributes of which are follower focus, leader goal orientation, and leader purposefulness (Irving and Berndt 2017). The goal to be attained through servant leadership is 'the big dream, the visionary concept, the ultimate consummation that one approaches but never really achieves. It is something presently out of reach; it is something to strive for, to move toward, to become' (Greenleaf in Hickman 2010: 91). An outcome demonstrated through research is that servant leadership is instrumental in promoting follower self-actualisation (Lacroix and Verdorfer 2017). In addition, servant leadership was positively related to work engagement, organisational citizenship behaviour, innovative behaviour, organisational commitment, trust, self-efficacy, job satisfaction, person-job fit, person-organisation fit, leader-member exchange, and work-life balance (Coetzer et al. 2017). Servant leaders can 'shape the norms and values of an organisation and can therefore create ethical norms that are able to guide the moral or immoral behavior of the individuals or groups of individuals that they lead' (Burton et al. 2017), with a particular emphasis on ethical behaviour.

The concept of servant leadership has several dimensions such as emotional healing, creating value for the community, conceptual skills, empowering, helping subordinates grow and succeed, putting subordinates first, and behaving ethically (Liden et al. 2014: 1434–1435). Research has demonstrated that servant leadership has significant follower outcomes, including job attitudes, organisational citizenship behaviour, and performance as well as outcomes at the team and organisational levels (Liden et al. 2014; Irving and Berndt 2017: 14). Its attraction is the assumption that when leaders prioritise tangible and emotional support to followers to reach their full potential, followers will positively engage with the work in hand because they want to do so and not through coercive activity. It is a multidimensional leadership theory that in its broadest understanding embraces many aspects of leadership. In reviewing the literature on servant leadership, Coetzer et al. (2017) identified eight distinct characteristics. Further research found competencies (cognitive and technical knowledge, skills, traits, and habits) associated with servant leadership and an additional set of sub-competencies. Developing others to prosper whilst having a transformational influence and transferring responsibility is a marked difference from other leadership styles.

Leadership and Management: The Same or a Different Agenda

The final consideration in this overview is that of how leaders differ from managers and how leadership differs from management. This subject is one of continuing debate in spite of the observations that 'it is obvious that a person can be a leader without being a manager (e.g. an informal leader), and a person can be a manager without leading' (Yukl 2010: 24) and 'leadership is in many instances one of the roles of the manager' (Ellis and Bach 2015: 17). There have been attempts to distinguish between them. Two of the leading thinkers on these subjects had clear points of view in answer to the question. Peter Drucker was extremely forthright in his response: 'as for separating management from leadership, that is nonsense—as much nonsense as separating management from entrepreneurship. Those are part and parcel of the same job. They are different to be sure, but only as different as the right hand from the left or the nose from the mouth. They belong to the same body' (quoted in Galagan 1998), whilst Henry Mintzberg noted that 'leadership cannot simply delegate management; instead of distinguishing managers from leaders, we should see leaders as managers, and leadership as management practiced well'

(Mintzberg 2011: 9). But such statements have not put an end to the debate, and alternative points of view continue to persist from earlier articulations.

Kotter (1990) argued that there were distinct differences between the two. In the first place, there were different agenda. Whilst a leader was responsible for establishing the direction of the organisation, the manager had the task of planning and budgeting to achieve the desired outcomes of the direction. Whilst the leader's role was to align people behind the vision and the strategy, the manager was responsible for organising and staffing and establishing the structure to meet the requirements of the plan. Leaders motivated and inspired; managers controlled and problem-solved. 'People who think of management as being only the implementation part of leadership ignore that fact that leadership has its own implementation processes; aligning people to new directions and then inspiring them to make it happen' (Kotter 1990: 5). This point of view emphasises that leaders produce change whilst managers produce predictability and order. Maccoby also highlighted differences noting that 'managers are principally administrators—they write business plans, set budgets, and monitor progress. Leaders on the other hand, get organizations and people to change. That's true, as far as it goes, but I suggest a more useful distinction between management and leadership: Management is a function that must be exercised in any business, whereas leadership is a relationship between leader and led that can energize an organization' (Maccoby 2000: 57), a perspective articulated by Bennis (1989, 2001) who distinguished the leader's role from that of the manager's, by noting that managers administered whilst leaders innovated; managers maintained the running of the organisation whilst leaders developed new ideas, strategies, and concepts; and managers were mainly concerned with systems and processes whilst leaders with people.

It is possible to reach one of three conclusions in response to the question of difference. In the first, there is a distinction between leaders and managers and leadership and management. In the second, the two overlap to such an extent, especially in the contemporary organisation, that it is difficult to discern any space between them. For example, by describing nurse leaders as leaders and at the same time 'the most senior people in the hospital—the executive and board—are regularly described as the leadership team… consequently, there seems to be little in the way of an easy explanation as to what leadership and management are' (Ellis and Abbott 2015). Or whilst being a manager is a formal position that is conferred by the organisation, being a leader may or may not be the result of such a formalised position (Ellis and Bach 2015: 17). In the third, management searching for an identity.

Whilst several interpretations of the role of the leader versus that of the manager exist, the work of the organisation has a common element that may help to resolve the issue. In this respect 'organisations are sets of ongoing human relationships utilising various technologies in which people cooperate to achieve tasks which would otherwise not be possible either at all or from an equivalent resource base'. To achieve its objectives, the organisation functions through a series of exchanges. At the heart of the managerial role is the task of orchestrating these exchanges with internal and external parties, for the organisation to be successful. In effect, managerial work is organising work. In some instances, this organising work will be in accordance with clear and specified policy systems and processes, and the managerial role will be to enact the objectives within these boundaries. In other instances, there will be less clarity about the objective, which people are designated to perform tasks to achieve the objective, or in extreme instances lack of clarity about the objective to be achieved in the first place. Where a manager acts in this latter situation, he or she is in effect a leader, inspiring others to achieve something they would otherwise not achieve. This happens many times at many levels of the organisation. If Goffee and Jones' (2006) point of view is correct that leadership is non-hierarchical, there will inevitably be an overlap with those roles designated as managerial ones. Similarly, if managers undertake activity outside of strictly designated boundaries (because there may be none or they may have changed—see VUCA above), then this may be interpreted as leadership.

Mintzberg's belief that delineations between leadership and management were wrong because 'managing is controlling and doing and dealing and thinking and leading and deciding and more' (Mintzberg 2011: 44) reinforces Yukl's (2010) view that defining managing and leading into distinctive and specific roles or processes may lead to 'simplistic' theories about leadership. Nevertheless, it is important to note that in many organisations there are differentiations between the two concepts. Where this is the case, and if the best fit model is to be acknowledged, the approach to leadership will need to be adapted accordingly.

Leadership Best Fit and Common Threads

The analysis of research into leadership demonstrates the complexity of the subject. For some, leadership is clearly attributable to those who run the organisation at the highest levels. For others, it is a concept that applies at multiple levels and is undertaken by those who do not have formal leadership roles. But there are some common threads, regardless of which definition is adopted. Firstly, success will depend on the leader's agility, providing guidance and direction to team working and integrating collaboration into the organisation's culture. Such agility can be applied in numerous instances because leadership agility is the capability to be aware of, sense, and respond to changes with fast, flexible actions (Horney et al. 2010). Secondly it will require a response of cognitive readiness, which means the leader will have professional competence and the mental, emotional, and interpersonal preparedness to handle VUCA (Bawany 2016). Thirdly, there is a growing requirement (because of the pace and scale of change and different organisational structural responses to these) for leaders to understand complex organisational dynamics, success within which is 'a collective process must be spread throughout networks of people' (Rodriguez and Rodriguez 2015: 858). There is a sound rationale in applying each of these arguments to several levels of leadership, based on a response to uncertainty by adaptive leadership behaviour.

The above descriptions of the various 'schools' of leadership reflect some of the diversity of opinion on what constitutes leadership in both theory and practice. Furthermore, views about the differences between leadership and management are equally interesting and provide scope for further research—as they have done for many decades. However, even with the contextual nature of this debate, it is a legitimate question to ask if there are any common identifying characteristics of leadership that transcend any specific context and can be used as the basis for a leadership model relevant to the health sector. A synthesis of some of the key points (from Grint 2005; Goffee and Jones 2006; Yukl 2010; Bildstein et al. 2013; Northouse 2016 inter alia) might help to answer this question:

- There is a difference between a *leader*, someone who has an assigned role as such in an organisation and ideally the right level of individual traits to ensure that others will follow her/his personal style and standards, and *leadership* which is about the social exchanges that take place in organisations at multiple levels. A leader is an individual, while leadership is a dynamic set of activities.
- There is also a difference between leadership *in* an organisation and leadership *of* an organisation. Leadership *in* an organisation is concerned with interpersonal or face-to-face relations, whereas leadership *of* an organisation was more concerned with solving organisational problems created by external forces such as those created by VUCA or environmental change or creating internal control through coordination and integration (Kaiser et al. 2012).
- It is difficult to differentiate between the roles of leader and manager in many cases. Sometimes leaders act as managers; sometimes those designated as managers undertake leadership activity. In some instances, in formally structured organisations, for example, with clear lines of authority, it is possible to distinguish between leadership and management; in others, there is a lack of distinction because of the fluidity of the particular context in which the organisation conducts its operations.
- Nevertheless, a leader addresses two important questions: 'what is the organisation going to do and how will it get done?' (Kilburg and Donohue 2011). The responses of the leader will require him or her to understand and practise appreciation, be a connoisseur of talent, act as a curator rather than a creator, understand priorities, and generate and sustain trust (Bennis 1999).
- Some people are leaders because of their formal positions, but others are leaders because people respond to their ideas or wishes. Mintzberg distinguished between the two by noting that on the one hand leadership referred to the leader and the led: 'the leaders is in charge, motivates and inspires, elicits shock and awe' (Mintzberg 2011: 65). On

the other hand, leadership goes beyond formal authority, and in this context a leader is anyone who sets a direction that shows others the way and who subsequently follows that direction.

- Leadership involves people who have a common purpose towards the achievement of common goals. But leadership is a process, not a trait or characteristic that resides in a leader; it does not necessarily reside with any one person who has been formally designated as leader; leadership is situational and non-hierarchical.
- Leadership is multi-faceted and involves 'aspects of the leader, the follower, and the dyadic relationship between the two' (Bildstein et al. 2013: 789).

These broad conclusions support the contextual view of leadership in that it resides in the roles of those who are in assigned positions of leadership (Executives, Directors, Heads of Department) but also in the everyday activity of many other organisational members who do not have the designated leadership title. A leader is a human being who undertakes activities to persuade others to achieve a goal. Leadership is a social exchange to the same end.

Case Study: Systemic Leadership Within the NHS

Adam Turner, Leadership Programme Lead, NHS Leadership Academy, UK

The Context for Systemic Leadership in the NHS

The UK NHS operates as a complex ecosystem, made up of many interconnected services, regulators, and wider care partners and subject to conditions of volatility, uncertainty, complexity, and ambiguity (VUCA). These forces combine to drive the need for systemic ways of working. For example, service user needs are growing and their requirements are increasingly complex with multiple long-term conditions, compounded with an ageing population. This means that service users that are interfacing with healthcare naturally span across multiple services and organisations. To offer optimum and tailored care, healthcare services now need to work collaboratively in the best interest of the service user.

The NHS Five Year Forward View (NHS England 2014) was developed to address this and outline ways for NHS and wider care organisations to work together on common challenges to become sustainable. Sustainability and Transformation Partnerships (STPs) were developed to enable local geographical systems of NHS and wider care organisations to collaborate to understand their local population needs and seek innovative ways to collectively address these. This collaborative way of working has recently begun to transform into Integrated Care Systems where NHS organisations, in partnership with wider care services, take collective responsibility for managing resources, delivering care standards, and improving the health of the diverse populations they serve (NHS England 2017).

As a result of this change in how services need to be delivered, leaders of healthcare services are increasingly required to work systemically, collaboratively, and innovatively to find collective ways to improve services, improve quality, and innovatively meet these key challenges. There is a call for the NHS to move beyond traditional bureaucratic and heroic leadership styles and embrace shared, collective, distributed, and adaptive styles of leadership (The King's Fund 2011; West et al. 2014). This has been acknowledged within the current NHS leadership framework, Developing People, Improving Care (NHS Improvement 2016).

Embracing Systemic Leadership

To assist NHS leaders working in this increasingly complex and interconnected environment, there has been a strong pull to develop the capability and capacity for systemic leadership at all levels of the NHS.

System leadership is seen as a collaborative and collective form of leadership. It involves a concentrated effort of many people working together in different places and at different levels of the system to create a shared endeavour to bring about significant change in culture and ways of working for the greater good (Ghate et al. 2013; NHS Education for Scotland 2016).

This poses a conundrum for current NHS leaders. Traditional styles of leadership are still required to manage organisations who are currently regulated in isolation. At the same time, these new styles of collective and systemic leadership are required to enable organisations and services to work together as one system to meet increasing demands (Timmins 2015). Western (2008) articulates this challenge within his model of eco-leadership. He acknowledges that as the evolution of society is starting to change the predominant discourse of leadership towards leaders leading across a complex 'ecosystems,' traditional forms of leadership are still valid and needed. This means that the leader's role is identifying and applying the best leadership style to the context that they are operating within.

Senge (2006) introduces the concept of systems thinking for leaders by promoting that leaders of the future need to embrace the bigger picture by seeking out how interconnected relationships operate dynamically, rather than simply focusing on cause-and-effect relationships. He argues that leaders of systems can no longer implement simple solutions, as the complex system will push back against this simplicity. Leaders need to be slower at implementing solutions to ambiguous problems by taking time to appreciate the complex multiple cause-and-effect relationships as they implement change.

Grint (2010) sees that system leaders must embrace the art of working in ambiguity. He refers to this as dealing with 'wicked problems' where it is acceptable and expected to have clumsy solutions to ambiguous problems. He sees that system leaders need to become at ease with multiple uncertainties and appreciate that any change in a system will only have a slightly positive or slightly negative impact. He sees that the system leader's role is to ask the right questions, not to provide the right solutions.

In exploring what leaders did to implement change at different levels across systems in the public sector, Timmins (2015) identified how system leadership needs to start with a coalition of willing leaders who have a shared purpose and vision and are willing to collaborate flexibly to achieve this. They need to embrace being outcome focused, rather than target driven. They must also embrace a large degree of altruism. Anything can be achieved if the leaders are happy to discharge power, feel no need to take credit for the change, and also appreciate that the vision and outcome is more important than winners, losers, and their own role in the system.

At the heart of system leadership is the focus on enabling trusting relationships through promoting a culture for collective leadership where everyone must take responsibility for improving the system (West et al. 2014). System leaders must draw on influence over individual authority and become expert at developing strong trusting relationships by authentically role modelling that enhancing the system is at the heart of what they do.

Conclusion and Implications for Practice

It is possible however to lay out some underlying principles whether these apply to transformational, transactional, charismatic, servant, or devolved leadership styles or whether these reside in the person who is an assigned leader or someone who assumes leadership activity without the formal designation. It is these principles that may be most beneficial when considering the subject of leadership in the specificity of the health sector. Some of these are outlined below:

- Firstly, **it is important for the leader to be clear about their own position, what is expected by the organisation, and what is expected by followers**. But this is only one part of the equation, for in order to achieve best fit, the leader will need clarity about their own strengths and weaknesses and what they need to do to achieve their specific organisational context. They will be able to do so because of personal reflection and insight. A theme which runs through many contemporary views of leadership is that of emotional intelligence and awareness, not in some abstract way but demonstrated by a leader being aware of her or his own preferred style of leadership, whether this needs to be adapted to the context, and the impact that she or he has on others—followers. The leader of the future is a person with a high level of emotional intelligence.

- Secondly, it is clear that Drucker's observation that '**leadership** has to be grounded in responsibility; it has to be grounded in a Constitution. It has to be grounded in accountability. Otherwise, it will lead to tyranny' (Drucker from Galagan 1998) resonates once again across the leadership styles discussed above.
- Thirdly, **leaders have credibility**—there is a sense that leadership is about doing or enabling others to do things in the quest for a common vision or goal. To do so will require followers to trust and accept the decisions of those in leadership positions and to act accordingly. They are less likely to do so if they feel that the leader lacks credibility to make such decisions.
- And finally, **leaders know their way around organisations**. Given the contextual nature of leadership, the ability to read and sense how to achieve goals and the willingness and engagement of followers will be critical at whatever level the leadership activity takes place.

Within the multitude of interpretations of the terms leader and leadership, there is a tacit understanding that a leader somehow inspires others to achieve things they may not have done if left to their own devices and that leadership at several organisational levels contrives to do this in the context of a department or business unit. The question of relevance to the health and other sectors is: why are there so many different interpretations? Understanding the implications of this question is important, and the answers will inspire decisions about leadership style or competences which will influence both strategy and operational continuity.

These conclusions have implications for the subject of leadership in the health sector where clarity in leadership has been identified as an important criterion and associated with clear team objectives, high levels of participation, commitment to excellence, and support for innovation

(West et al. 2003). This reinforces the need for health sector to establish how leadership is defined. Does leadership refer to those at the very top of the organisation or does it have a more inclusive, distributed interpretation? It is important for organisations to have an understanding of what they require from leaders and leadership and there are models to support them in so doing. These issues are as relevant to health as to any other sector and will determine the position from which leadership best fit for health can be developed.

References

Aga, D. A. (2016). Transactional Leadership and Project Success: The Moderating Role of Goal Clarity. *Procedia Computer Science, 100* (International Conference on ENTERprise Information Systems/International Conference on Project MANagement/International Conference on Health and Social Care Information Systems and Technologies, CENTERIS/ProjMAN/HCist 2016), 517–525. https://doi.org/10.1016/j.procs.2016.09.190.

Alatwi, M. A. (2017). The Myth of the Additive Effect of the Transformational Leadership Model. *Contemporary Management Research, 13*(1), 19–29. ISSN:1813-5498.

Alimo-Metcalfe, B., & Alban-Metcalfe, J. (2003, March 16). Under the Influence. *People Management, 9*, 32–35.

Arnold, K. A. (2017). Transformational Leadership and Employee Psychological Well-Being: A Review and Directions for Future Research. *Journal of Occupational Health Psychology, 22*(3), 381–393. ISSN:1076-8998.

Babić, V. M., Savović, S. D., & Domanović, V. M. (2014). Transformational Leadership and Post-acquisition Performance in Transitional Economies. *Journal of Organizational Change Management, 27*(6), 856. https://doi.org/10.1108/JOCM-02-2014-0028.

Baltaci, F., Kavacik, M., Şentürk, F. K., & Kurare, I. (2014). The Effect of Leadership Behaviors on Job Satisfaction: A Research on Four and Five Stars Hotels Employees in Alanya. *Abant Izzet Baysal University Journal of Social Sciences/Sosyal Bilimler Enstitüsü Dergisi, 14*(2), 59. ISSN:1303-0035.

Banks, G. C., Engemann, K. N.,Williams, E., Gooty, J., McCauly, K. D., & Medaugh, M. R. (2017). A Meta-analytic Review and Future Research Agenda of Charismatic Leadership. *The Leadership Quarterly, 28*(4), 508–529. https://doi.org/10.1016/j.leaqua.2016.12.003.

Bass, B. M. (1985). *Leadership and Performance Beyond Expectations*. New York: The Free Press.

Bass, B. M., & Avolio, B. J. (1993). Transformational Leadership and Organisational Culture. *Public Administration Quarterly, 1*(17), 112–121.

Bass, B. M., & Bass, R. (2008). *The Bass Handbook of Leadership: Theory, Research, and Managerial Applications* (4th ed.). New York: The Free Press.

Bass, B. M., & Riggio, R. E. (2006). The Transformational Model of Leadership. In G. R. Hickman (Ed.) (2010). *Leading Organisations-Perspectives for a New Era*. London: Sage Publications Ltd.

Bawany, S. (2016). Leading in A VUCA Business Environment. *Leadership Excellence Essentials, 33*(7), 39–40.

Bellé, N. (2014). Leading to Make a Difference: A Field Experiment on the Performance Effects of Transformational Leadership, Perceived Social Impact, and Public Service Motivation. *Journal of Public Administration Research & Theory, 24*(1), 109.

Bennis, W. (1989). *On Becoming a Leader*. Reading, MA: Addison Wesley.

Bennis, W. (1999). The End of Leadership: Exemplary Leadership Is Impossible Without Full Inclusion, Initiatives, and Cooperation of Followers. *Organizational Dynamics, 28*(1), 71–79. ISSN:0090-2616.

Bennis, W. (2001). The New Leadership. In S. Crainer & D. Dearlove (Eds.), *Financial Times Handbook of Management* (2nd ed.). London: Prentice Hall.

Bildstein, I., Gueldenberg, S., & Tjitra, H. (2013). Effective Leadership of Knowledge Workers: Results of an Intercultural Business Study. *Management Research Review, 36*(8), 788–804. ISSN:2040-8277.

Boamah, S. A., Spence Laschinger, H. K., Wong, C., & Clarke, S. (2017). Effect of Transformational Leadership on Job Satisfaction and Patient Safety Outcomes. *Nursing Outlook*. https://doi.org/10.1016/j.outlook.2017.10.004.

Burns, J. M. (1978). *Leadership*. New York: Harper and Row.

Burton, L. J., Welty P. J., & Wells, J. E. (2017). The Role of Servant Leadership in Developing an Ethical Climate in Sport Organizations. *Journal of Sport Management, 31*(3), 229–240. ISSN:0888-4773, 2017-0501.

Cathcart, E. B., & Greenspan, M. (2013). The Role of Practical Wisdom in Nurse Manager Practice: Why Experience Matters. *Journal of Nursing Management, 21*(7), 964–970.

Coetzer, M. F., Bussin, M., & Geldenhuys, M. (2017). The Functions of a Servant Leader. *Administrative Sciences, 7*(1), 5. ISSN:2076-3387.

Collins, J. (2001). *Good to Great*. New York: Harper Business.

Conger, J. A. (2004). Developing Leadership Capability: What's Inside the Black Box? *The Academy of Management Executive (1993–2005)* [Serial Online], *18*(3), 136.

Conger, J. A. (2008). In G. R. Hickman (Ed.) (2010). *Leading Organisations – Perspectives for a New Era*. London: Sage Publications Ltd.

Conger, J. A., & Kanungo, R. N. (1987). Toward a Behavioral Theory of Charismatic Leadership in Organizational Settings. *Academy of Management Review, 12*(4), 637–647. https://doi.org/10.5465/AMR.1987.4306715.

Conger, J. A., & Kanungo, R. N. (1998). *Charismatic Leadership in Organisations*. London: Sage Publications.

Conger, J. A., Kanungo, R. N., & Menon, S. T. (2000). Charismatic Leadership and Follower Effects. *Journal of Organizational Behavior, 21*(7), 747.

DaCosta, J. (2012). Leadership Models for Healthcare Improvement. *British Journal of Healthcare Management, 18*(11), 575–580. ISSN:1358-0574.

Edger, C. (2012). *Effective Multi-Unit Leadership: Local Leadership in Multi-Site Situations*. Farnham: Gower Applied Research Press.

Elkhani, N., Soltani, S., & Ahmad, M. N. (2014). The Effects of Transformational Leadership and ERP System Self-Efficacy on ERP System Usage. *Journal of Enterprise Information Management, 27*(6), 1.

Ellis, P., & Abbott, J. (2015). Exploring the Differences Between Leaders and Managers. *Journal of Renal Nursing, 7*(2), 2041–1448.

Ellis, P., & Bach, S. (2015). *Leadership, Management and Team Working*. London: Sage Publications.

Galagan, P. A. (1998). Peter Drucker. *Training & Development, 52*(9), 22–29. ISSN:1055-9760.

Ghate, D., Lewis, J., & Welbourn, D. (2013). Systems Leadership: Exceptional Leadership for Exceptional Times Synthesis Paper. ADCS Virtual Staff College. Retrieved from https://www.scie-socialcareonline.org.uk/systems-leadership-exceptional-leadership-for-exceptional-times-synthesis-paper/r/a11G000000537cDIAQ.

Goffee, R., & Jones, G. (2006). *Why Should Anyone Be Led By You*. Boston, MA: Harvard Business School Press.

Goleman, D. (1996). *Emotional Intelligence*. New York: Bloomsbury.

Goleman, D. (1998). *Working with Emotional Intelligence*. New York: Bantam Books.

Greenleaf, R. K. (1977). Servant Leadership. In G. R. Hickman (Ed.) (2010). *Leading Organisations – Perspectives for a New Era*. London: Sage Publications Ltd.

Grint, K. (2005). *Leadership: Limits and Possibilities.* Basingstoke, UK: Palgrave Macmillan.

Grint, K. (2007). Learning to Lead; Can Aristotle Help Us Find the Road to Wisdom? *Leadership, 3*(2), 231–246.

Grint, K. (2010). Wicked Problems and Clumsy Solutions: The Role of Leadership. In S. Brookes & K. Grint (Eds.), *The New Public Leadership Challenge* (pp. 169–186). Basingstoke: Palgrave Macmillan.

Hickman, G. R. (Ed.). (2010). *Leading Organisations, Perspectives for a New Era.* Thousand Oaks, CA: Sage Publications.

Hlupic, V. (2014). *The Management Shift.* Basingstoke, UK: Palgrave Macmillan.

Horney, N., Pasmore, B., & O'shea, T. (2010). Leadership Agility: A Business Imperative for a Vuca World. *People & Strategy, 31*, 32–38.

Irving, J. A., & Berndt, J. (2017). Leader Purposefulness Within Servant Leadership: Examining the Effect of Servant Leadership, Leader Follower-Focus, Leader Goal-Orientation, and Leader Purposefulness in a Large U.S. Healthcare Organization. *Administrative Sciences, 7*(2), 10. ISSN:(2076-3387), 2076-3387.

Jacquart, P., & Antonakis, J. (2015). When Does Charisma Matter for Top Level Leaders? Effect of Attributional Ambiguity. *Academy of Management Journal, 58*(4), 1051–1074.

Jha, S., & Bhattacharyya, S. (2017). Development of a Firm Level Strategic Shared Leadership Scale. *Indian Journal of Industrial Relations, 52*(3), 499–515. ISSN:0019-5286.

Judge, T. A., & Piccolo, R. F. (2004). Transformational and Transactional Leadership: A Meta-analytic Test of Their Relative Validity. *Journal of Applied Psychology, 89*(5), 755–768.

Kaiser, R. B., McGinnis, J. L., & Overfield, D. V. (2012). The How and the What of Leadership. *Consulting Psychology Journal: Practice and Research, 64*(2), 119–135. ISSN:1065-9293.

Kaslow, N., Falender, C., & Grus, C. (2012). Valuing and Practicing Competency-Based Supervision: A Transformational Leadership Perspective. *Training and Education in Professional Psychology, 6*(1), 47–54.

Kilburg, R. R., & Donohue, M. D. (2011). Toward a 'Grand Unifying Theory' of Leadership: Implications for Consulting Psychology. *Consulting Psychology Journal: Practice and Research, 63*(1), 6–25. https://doi.org/10.1037/a0023053.

Kodish, S. (2006). The Paradoxes of Leadership: The Contribution of Aristotle. *Leadership, 2*(4), 451–468. https://doi.org/10.1177/1742715006069175.

Kotter, J. (1990). *A Force for Change: How Leadership Differs from Management*. New York: The Free Press.

Kouzes, J. M., & Posner, B. Z. (2007). *The Leadership Challenge*. San Francisco: Jossey Bass.

Lacroix, M., & Verdorfer, A. P. (2017). Can Servant Leaders Fuel the Leadership Fire? The Relationship Between Servant Leadership and Followers' Leadership Avoidance. *Administrative Sciences, 7*(1), 6. ISSN:2076-3387, 2076-3387.

Lee-Davies, L., Kakabadse, N. K., & Kakabadse, A. (2007). Shared Leadership: Leading Through Polylogue. *Business Strategy Series, 8*(4), 246–253.

Li, J., Furst-Holloway, S., Gales, L., Masterson, S. S., & Blume, B. D. (2017). Not All Transformational Leadership Behaviors Are Equal: The Impact of Followers' Identification with Leader and Modernity on Taking Charge. *Journal of Leadership & Organizational Studies, 24*(3), 318–334.

Liden, R., Wayne, S. J., Chenwei, L., & Meuser, J. D. (2014). Servant Leadership and Serving Culture: Influence on Individual and Unit Performance. *Academy of Management Journal, 57*(5), 1434–1452. ISSN:0001-4273.

Longenecker, C. O., & Longenecker, P. D. (2014). Why Hospital Improvement Efforts Fail: A View from the Front Line. *Journal of Healthcare Management, 59*(2), 147–157. ISSN:1096-9012.

Lord, R. G., Day, D. V., Zaccaro, S. J., Avolio, B. J., & Eagly, A. H. (2017). Leadership in Applied Psychology: Three Waves of Theory and Research. *Journal of Applied Psychology, 102*(3), 434–451. https://doi.org/10.1037/apl0000089.

Maccoby, M. (2000). Understanding the Difference Between Management and Leadership. *Research Technology Management, 43*(1), 57.

Mintzberg, H. (2011). *Managing*. London: Prentice Hall.

Ng, T. W. H. (2017). Transformational Leadership and Performance Outcomes: Analyses of Multiple Mediation Pathways. *The Leadership Quarterly, 28*(3), 385–417. ISSN:1048-9843, 2017-0601.

NHS Education for Scotland. (2016). *Systems Thinking and Systems Leadership*. Retrieved from http://www.central.knowledge.scot.nhs.uk/Leadership/systems.html.

NHS England. (2014). *Five Year Forward View*. Retrieved from https://www.england.nhs.uk/five-year-forward-view.

NHS England. (2017). *Next Steps on the NHS Five Year Forward View*. Retrieved from https://www.england.nhs.uk/publication/next-steps-on-the-nhs-five-year-forward-view.

NHS Improvement. (2016). *Developing People; Improving Care*. Retrieved from https://improvement.nhs.uk/resources/developing-people-improving-care.

Northouse, P. G. (2016). *Leadership, Theory and Practice* (7th ed.). Thousand Oaks, CA: Sage Publications Inc.

Pandey, S. K., Davis, R. S., Pandey, S., & Peng, S. (2016). Transformational Leadership and the Use of Normative Public Values: Can Employees Be Inspired to Serve Larger Public Purposes? *Public Administration, 94*(1), 204–222. ISSN:0033-3298.

Raes, E., Decuyper, S., Lismont, B., den Bossche, P., Kyndt, E., Demeyere, S., et al. (2013). Facilitating Team Learning Through Transformational Leadership. *Instructional Science, 41*(2), 287. https://doi.org/10.1007/s11251-012-9228-3.

Raj, R., & Srivastava, K. B. L. (2016). Transformational Leadership and Innovativeness: The Mediating Role of Organizational Learning. *Journal of Management Research, 16*(4), 201–219. ISSN:0972-5814.

Redknap, R., Twigg, D., Rock, D., & Towell, A. (2015). Nursing Practice Environment: A Strategy for Mental Health Nurse Retention? *International Journal of Mental Health Nursing, 24*(3), 262–271. ISSN:1445-8330.

Rodriguez, A., & Rodriguez, Y. (2015). Metaphors for Today's Leadership: VUCA World, Millennial and 'Cloud Leaders'. *Journal of Management Development, 34*(7), 854–866. ISSN:0262-1711, 2015-0101.

Sarto, F., & Veronesi, G. (2016). Clinical Leadership and Hospital Performance: Assessing the Evidence Base. *BMC Health Services Research, 16*, 85–97. ISSN:1472-6963.

Scully, N. J. (2015). Leadership in Nursing: The Importance of Recognising Inherent Values and Attributes to Secure a Positive Future for the Profession. *Collegian, 22*(4), 439–444. ISSN:1322-7696.

Senge, P. (2006). *The Fifth Discipline: The Art and Practice of the Learning Organisation* (2nd ed.). London: Random House Business Books.

Stackman, R. W., & Devine, K. (2011). Leadership and "Emotional-Rational" Coherence: A Start? Editor's Introduction. *Academy of Management Perspectives, 25*(1), 42–44. https://doi.org/10.5465/AMP.2011.59198448.

Suk, Bong Choi, Kihwan Kim, & Seung-Wan Kang. (2017). Effects of Transformational and Shared Leadership Styles on Employees' Perception of Team Effectiveness. *Social Behavior & Personality: An International Journal, 45*(3), 377–386. ISSN:0301-2212, 2017-0301.

Sun, J., Chen, X., & Zhang, S. (2017). A Review of Research Evidence on the Antecedents of Transformational Leadership. *Education Sciences, 7*, 15. ISSN:2017-0101.

Team Performance. (2009). Relationship Between Emotional Intelligence and Transformational Leadership of Supervisors: The Impact on Team

Effectiveness. *Team Performance Management, 15*(7/8), 343–356. ISSN:1352-7592.

The King's Fund. (2011). *The Future of Leadership and Management in the NHS: No More Heroes.* Retrieved from https://www.kingsfund.org.uk/blog/2011/05/no-more-heroes-lesson-our-future-leaders.

Thorpe, R., Gold, J., & Lawler, J. (2011). Locating Distributed Leadership. *International Journal of Management Reviews, 13*(3), 239–250. https://doi.org/10.1111/j.1468-2370.2011.00303.x.

Timmins, N. (2015). *The Practice of System Leadership: Being Comfortable with Chaos.* The Kings Fund. Retrieved from https://www.kingsfund.org.uk/publications/practice-system-leadership.

Valenziano, K. B. (2015). Wisdom Leadership in Academic Health Science Centers: Leading Positive Change. *Journal of Interprofessional Care, 29*(1), 87. https://doi.org/10.3109/13561820.2014.948317.

Welford, C. (2002). Transformational Leadership in Nursing: Matching Theory to Practice. *Nursing Management – UK, 9*(4), 7–11. ISSN:1354-5760.

West, M. A., Borrill, C. S., Dawson, J. F., Brodbeck, F., Shapiro, D. A., & Haward, B. (2003). Leadership Clarity and Team Innovation in Health Care. *The Leadership Quarterly, 14*(4–5), 393–410. https://doi.org/10.1016/S1048-9843(03)00044-4.

West, M., Eckert, R., Steward, K., & Pasmore, B. (2014). *Developing Collective Leadership for Health Care.* The Kings Fund. Retrieved from https://www.kingsfund.org.uk/publications/developing-collective-leadership-health-care.

Western, S. (2008). *Leadership, a Critical Text.* London: Sage Publications Ltd.

Yukl, G. (2010). *Leadership in Organisations.* London: Pearson.

4

Leading in the Health Sector: Research and Practice

The Evolution of Health Sector Organisations Means the Evolution of Health Sector Leadership

Effective leadership can make a difference as to how organisations in the sector are run and how they deliver services. Health sector leaders can influence organisational culture and performance. They can have positive outcomes across a range of patient-oriented, staff-oriented, or organisational measures including patient care quality and patient satisfaction and employee satisfaction and organisational commitment, on organisational productivity and team working, and on interprofessional collaboration. Effective leadership is important to the achievement of high-quality, safe, compassionate healthcare through setting clear team objectives, high levels of participation, commitment to excellence, and support for innovation (West et al. 2003; Reichenpfader et al. 2015: 299; McSherry and Pearce 2016; Gauld 2017; Jeyaraman et al. 2018: 84). But it is argued that leaders in the health sector 'need to continuously develop and refine their capacity to stay in the know' (Korica 2018: 9). It is no surprise therefore that the subject is attracting international attention with

P. Turner, *Leadership in Healthcare*, Organizational Behaviour in Health Care,
https://doi.org/10.1007/978-3-030-04387-2_4

significant focus on leadership style and the development of skills and competences (Till et al. 2015: 139). But achieving these desired outcomes is far from straightforward because contemporary health sector organisations are faced with a range of influencing factors, in a world of maximum surprise (Schwartz 2010: 5), that can inhibit their delivery.

The 'ecology of healthcare' presented in Chap. 2 covered, inter alia, dynamic and changeable economies which have disrupted health sector operating parameters including finance. And even though unprecedented amounts of investment are flowing into the sector, the demand for health often exceeds the capacity of those who can provide it, leading to pressures to improve quality and efficiency whilst, at the same time, undergoing cost reviews (Kjeld and Rapsaniotis 2017). Furthermore, technology developments are changing the nature of how and where health is delivered; and people dynamics such as talent shortages, intense competition for skilled health professionals, and the significant levels of human resources for health have precipitated wide-ranging health process reengineering. The pace, scale, and scope of change, epitomised by VUCA forces, therefore, have created a need for leadership in business or change management as well as in professional or clinical areas to ensure the efficient deployment of resources to each level of care (Turner 2017). This is important because, as healthcare becomes more complex, patient outcomes are 'no longer just dependent upon excellent clinical management at the individual clinician–patient level. There are now tiers of supporting processes, microsystems and organisations that can determine the provision of good quality care' (Johnston et al. 2016: 205). Nevertheless, there is no single unifying model of health sector organisation either at system level or within the systems themselves. Instead, the size, shape, and scale of the organisation's response within a country, region, or community are likely to have evolved through a combination of community and stakeholder need, history, positive and negative experiences, political pressure, changes in financial targets or demands, and happenstance. For some organisations, coping with the new environment has meant tactical adjustment, for others a radical, strategic response with step change in business or service models. The result is a multiplicity of organisational designs each with its own particular set of objectives, strategies, systems, and processes. This chapter will consider how health sector organisations have adapted their leadership responses accordingly and whether a model for health sector leadership can be created which allows for the many and different leadership challenges. Unsurprisingly, organisations seek to find effective leadership models in response to a dramatically changing environment, a 'new landscape for healthcare,' and leadership in innovative healthcare models or processes (DaCosta 2012; Delmatoff and Lazarus 2014). How to do so remains ambiguous.

A Paradigm Shift in Health Sector Leadership: Theory and Practice

In an attempt to provide clarity, significant research and practice experience have created a rich vein of insight. The 'schools' of leadership outlined in Chap. 3 and a wide range of studies have been conducted to test or evaluate leadership models in the sector (Maccoby et al. 2013; Sang Long Choi et al. 2016; Hillen et al. 2017). For some organisations, change has led to a call for a paradigm shift involving a transition from what might be referred to as industrial age leadership to that of 'relationship age' leadership (Marquis and Huston 2012). To facilitate this shift, there is an emphasis on identifying the leadership competences required. Efforts to do so range from continent-wide studies (Czabanowska et al. 2014) to the application of multidimensional models of leadership (Hartley 2015) or to identifying what is required for the successful transition to new practices (Reichenpfader et al. 2015). Nevertheless, and in spite of the vast amount of research in the sector, interpretations as to what is meant by the term leadership and what a 'paradigm shift' means in practice vary considerably. For some, leadership means the creation of leader superheroes (Day et al. 2014), for others, the complete opposite and 'the abandonment of individualistic, heroic models of leadership to one of shared, distributive, and adaptive leadership' (de Zulueta 2016: 1). But, in all examples, 'forming and sustaining productive relationships' is at leadership's heart (Gray et al. 2010: 16).

The analysis of leadership in the health sector is both deep and wide ranging. Leadership has been defined in its broadest sense or through its 'inherent values' or how best to deliver effective strategy and its implementation (Barr and Dowding 2008; Gopee and Galloway 2008; Gunderman 2009; Dye 2010; Scully 2015). Transformational leadership has been analysed in several contexts, including in the USA, where it had been applied to different leadership roles in clinical, financial, and operational areas (Larkin 2015; Manss 2017). Shared, distributed, servant, and devolved leadership have become increasingly popular areas of study as emphasis shifts to a more inclusive approach and the impact of such an approach on a range of indicators (Vanderpyl 2011; Fitzgerald et al. 2013; Rogers 2014; Trastek et al. 2014; Tropello and DeFazio 2014; Lorber et al. 2016; Saravo et al. 2017). Leadership studies have focused on specific areas such as the role of women in leadership in health and its 'bewildering glass ceiling' (Chisholm-Burns et al. 2017) and the necessity of 'achieving gender parity in global health leadership at all levels of health systems' in order to tap into the potential of the global health community (Dhatt et al. 2017). Evolving leadership (Evans 2014), complexity leadership (Weberg 2012), coaching as a leadership style (Hicks 2014), and leadership as it relates to organisational theory (McKimm and Phillips 2009) provide additional material from which to consider the leader's role and leadership style. A study of collective leadership in Chinese healthcare concluded that 'fostering collective leadership across health care organizations would highlight the continued growth of the whole team. Ideally, collective leadership will adapt to change along with the team to bridge the gaps' (Lv and Zhang 2017). The constant and rapid change that is a feature of the healthcare sector highlights the need for such leadership at the top of the organisation. The implication is that the presence of transformative leadership will facilitate the organisation's ability to deal with such change. Indeed, transformational leadership was correlated significantly with leader outcomes of workforce participation, effectiveness, satisfaction, and extra effort with results on staff, satisfaction, staff retention, and patient satisfaction (Zvi 2001; Robbins 2007; Hillen et al. 2017).

However, the scale and scope of some health sector organisations makes generalising about leadership a difficult task—'with an organisation as large and complex as the National Health Service (NHS) there is always a risk in attempting to summarise aspects of its history. Indeed drawing any general conclusions about its leadership and management is fraught with difficulty because there are so many factors to take into account including tradition, the power of the professions, the legacy of structural changes, successive reforms, and different ideologies' (Hewison and Morrell 2014).

There is an abundance of leadership models in the health sector. Each is open to interpretation, acceptance, or rejection.

Cultural Insights into Leadership in the Health Sector

Research in specific geographies have added to this diversity with cultural perspectives including global insights from the World Health Organization as it reflects on participatory leadership as an important contributor to fulfilling sustainable development goals (WHO 2017). Developing leaders has been a key subject in geographies as far apart as the Pacific region (Pacific Association 2016) and European health services (Ellis and Abbott 2014; Martin et al. 2015; Kjeld and Rapsaniotis 2017). In Europe, for example, studies of transformational leadership in German hospitals (Hillen et al. 2017) added to the richness of evidence about the effectiveness of different approaches to leadership in different contexts. Work in the USA includes a long-range study of the characteristics of leaders in hospitals (Westphal 2012) and of improving medical leadership (Smits et al. 2014) to that of unit-based leadership (Kim et al. 2014; Parnell 2014). In Africa, a broad range of studies (inter alia Curry et al. 2012; Amasawa and Crisp 2014; Olu-Abiodun and Abiodun 2017) found that, amongst other things, the key themes of leadership were an aspirational, value-based vision for improving future health (a transformational quality in the case of nurse leaders), being self-aware and having the ability to identify and use complementary skills of others, tending to relationships, using data in decision-making, and sustaining a commitment to learning. In India, there was a focus on strategic management and leadership in pursuit of health goals (Kumar et al. 2015), and in Korea, conceptual analyses of health sector leadership were presented (Korean Academy of

Nursing 2015). In the Australian context, Farrell (2003) identified four components of the leadership frame, and, as cited above, Lv and Zhang's (2017) study in China focused on collective leadership. These studies reflect both breadth and depth in knowledge of leadership in the world's health sector organisations. They also show the importance of context to leadership and the diverse responses that inevitably accompany this.

To complete a holistic picture of leadership in the world's health sector, research has been undertaken on specific professional groupings from medical directors and medical doctors to physicians, to medical leadership in perioperative practice, from dietitians to administrative leaders (Zohier 2012; Sahne et al. 2015; Denis and van Gestel 2016; Ohta et al. 2015; Johnston et al. 2016; Oostra 2016; Cox and Westbrook 2017; Hillen et al. 2017). And the range of studies of nurse leadership is extensive. Nurse leadership is regarded as pivotal because it is one of the most extensive disciplines in healthcare, and studies have covered transformational leadership in general hospital nursing (Olu-Abiodun and Abiodun 2017) to 'new' nurse leaders (Dolamo 2015), from conceptual analyses (Korean Academy of Nursing 2015; Scully 2015; Pacific Association 2016) to nurse leadership in primary healthcare (de Melo Lanzoni et al. 2016), and from studies relating to the role of nurses in the leadership of healthcare promotion (Maijala et al. 2016) to clinical nurse leadership (Murphy et al. 2009) or nurse leadership in health policy (Clarke et al. 2013). Lorber et al.'s study (2016) found that although nursing leaders perceived themselves as transformational more often than as transactional, the leaders most widely use the transactional leadership style. The reason for this was that 'hospitals and other health care institutions, by nature, tend to be bureaucratic organizations in which the transformational leadership may not be fostered to the greatest possible degree.'

Studies of leadership in health abound from the conceptual understanding of leadership and its application in the sector (Ewens 2002) to the practice of leadership (Bishop 2009; McKimm and Phillips 2009; Gray et al. 2010), to team working with an emphasis on creating a vision, and 'the passion and intellect to sell it to your peers' (Bishop 2009: 29). It is fair to conclude that the resources which emanate from the many studies of leadership in health add significant value to a plethora of specific environments or contexts; but they also give rise to a multitude of points of view. There is support for the generic conclusion that 'a leader's behaviour needs to vary from situation to situation' (Gray et al. 2010: 32). Nevertheless a theme is emerging in which it is essential for health sector leadership to combine both compassion and collaboration (West 2014) to ensure its successful delivery.

Interpretations of Leadership Over Time

The ebbs and flows of leadership theory as applied to the health sector mirror roughly those that pertain to other sectors and a range of leadership styles have been identified. Reflecting the primary foci of the business and management literature, transformational and charismatic leadership occupy the space at one end of the spectrum, whilst servant, participative, and distributed leadership reside at the other. Thus, the early twentieth century has been identified as the 'Great Man' or hero period, with leadership emphasising individual outstanding characteristics such as charisma, intelligence, and energy. Subsequently 'these theories were superseded by the influential transformational leadership' (Parker 2013: 391). Variations on the theme, taking account of the dynamic nature of the external environments and the systems which operate in them, include complex adaptive leadership in which 'leaders are seen as catalysts for complex, emergent change within interactive networks, of which they form a part' (Hill and Stephens 2005: 145). The analysis reveals some important clues as to the nature of leadership in health. Firstly, it appears to respond to external environmental changes or pressures, whether these be political, resulting in a different perspective on the meaning and availability of health, or socio-economic forces such as increases in demand for health because of demographic change or in the supply of health service caused by the effects of economic fluctuations. The leadership capabilities needed will be influenced by and adapted to the specific needs of the health sector organisation. In this respect leadership in the health sector is contextual. Secondly, leadership both reflects and influences the organisational culture or structure. Leadership in a hierarchy will call for different emphases and approaches to that in a matrix or network. And thirdly, leadership is influenced by

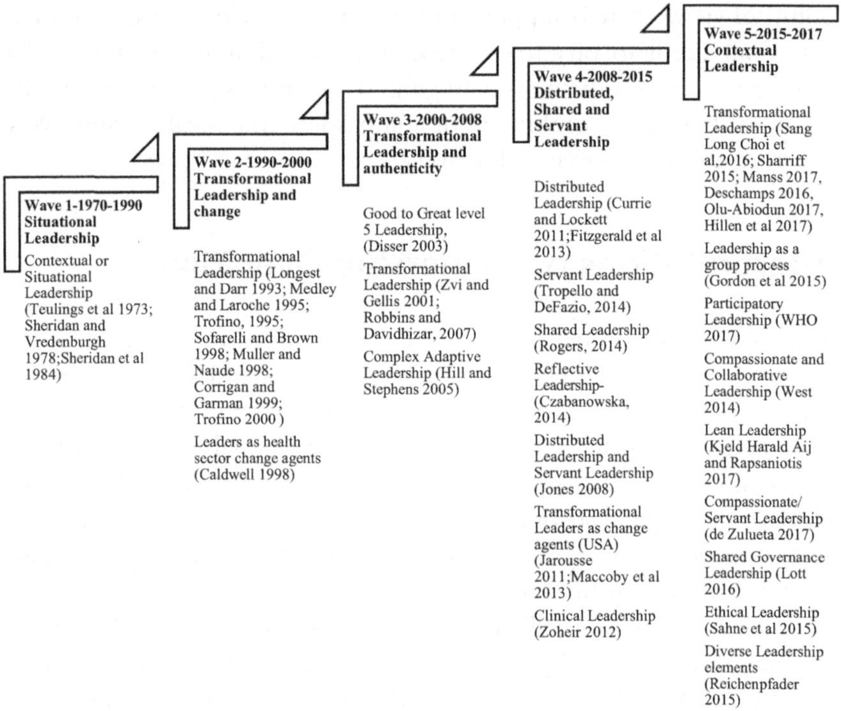

Fig. 4.1 Waves of leadership theory in health sector organisations: a timeline

internal organisational dynamics, such as changing expectations of the workforce in respect of inclusion in decision-making or career management. Having credibility within the organisation to apply relevant and insightful knowledge to leadership decisions would appear to be an important aspect of this.

Figure 4.1 maps some of the different approaches to leadership in health over recent years. This timeline shows how the generic concepts of leadership have been adapted for application and that leadership theory in health has mirrored that which has taken place in other sectors. With each piece of research or practice insight, the understanding of the nature of leadership in health has increased, and the application of theories or models has evolved to reflect circumstances. But, after the Great Man approach to leadership was transcended in the middle of the last century, there is not a straightforward attribution of a particular type of leadership style to each era or generation. Most recently, a range of health sector leadership styles can be identified from transformational to adaptive or devolved. This suggests that approaches to leadership in healthcare have evolved, and the following are some of the conclusions that can be drawn from this analysis.

Health Sector Leadership Means a Transformational Style at the Top of Organisations

Whilst there are many definitions and applications of leadership in evidence in the sector, the transformational model 'has persisted in many organizations and training courses, including health organizations and health-care training institutions, based on the idea that different situations require different dynamic relationships and roles, and hence different people may emerge as leaders for different purposes' (Parker 2013: 391). This is because in health sector organisations, leadership has often been associated with change management activity which is initiated at the highest levels, and hence transformational leadership has been popular from the 1990s involving studies across a range of health and social care environments. In this view, health executives manage 'the gap between the former traditional model of healthcare and a future emerging model that remains shrouded in the mist,' by examining 'the scope and nature of the change we are facing during this period of turmoil and ambiguity, in order to develop effective strategies for leading organizations and the profession into the future' (Fitzsimmons and Rose 2015: 34). Transformational leaders are responsible for overall direction and strategy or producing a positive impact through their abilities to mobilise resources in a powerful way (Gabel 2012). They will try to create a unifying vision around which the workforce can mobilise (Turner 2017) and are 'people who can guide others to achieve a desired goal and demonstrate the ability to augment productivity, create sustainable change, and inspire others to engage in professional development' (Chan et al. 2015: 342). Such abilities can be critical to the achievement of positive clinical outcomes or business and operational performance.

Health Sector Leadership Has Increasingly Embraced the Concept of Devolution 'from Board to Ward—from Ward to Community'

The recognition that leadership in health can be effective when it is inclusive and collaborative (West 2014) perhaps explains the shift of leadership emphasis from Board to Ward, from Ward to Community—distributed, devolved, inclusive leadership; and there is a growing emphasis on leadership with a wide range of professionals, such as doctors in all specialties, expected to undertake leadership roles (Gordon et al. 2015). 'Within this perspective, leadership processes cannot be understood apart from the social system in which they are embedded, and the behaviors of any one individual are less important than the combined behaviors of the collective whole' (Gifford et al. 2013: 62). The recognition for more devolved leadership in health, facilitating leadership at all levels, has been brought about, in part, because health sector organisations are inundated with change caused by 'multifaceted developments in the technological, political, financial, professional, scientific, and social realms are rapidly redefining the nature of healthcare and healthcare delivery' (Fitzsimmons and Rose 2015: 33). In this context leadership will be essential at multiple levels if organisations are to perform effectively.

The growing interest in both devolved and distributed leadership has come about for three possible reasons. In the first instance, there is a belief in some quarters that an organisational response to a volatile or uncertain external environment is improved where more independent units take responsibility for their own strategy and operations. To do so requires a faster pace of decision-making and a devolution of leadership authority, which in turn means leadership driven down to levels other than the Boardroom or Executive Suite, creating a more participatory perspective (WHO 2017). Secondly, there is the recognition that strict lines of demarcation between those with the denomination of leader and those with the denomination of manager are becoming increasingly blurred by the pace of change and the nature of both organisational structure and decision-making. And third, the availability, scale, and transparency of information, more of which is available readily to more people, means that knowledge and insight don't necessarily reside only in the brains (and hands) of a few. The environment for devolving leadership responsibility to managers and others is a positive one.

There is evidence for the benefits of so doing. On the one hand, Fitzgerald et al. (2013) found that widely distributed change leadership was linked to improvements in service outcomes and that 'professional/managerial hybrids' were adaptable to the organisational context. On the other, shared governance structures were shown to have a clear impact with the outcomes of increased staff engagement, staff satisfaction, professional accountability, and improved patient care outcomes (Lott 2016). This devolution of leadership has been one of the themes in the British NHS, with leadership and managerial activity overlapping at multiple levels embracing smaller clinical units and multidisciplinary teams, and to those leaders who are skilled at working across systems and boundaries (Department of Health 2009). The National Leadership Council noted that that 'world-class leadership talent and leadership development will exist at every level in the health system to ensure high quality care for all' ('The changing role of managers in the NHS' 2011). It is important for the health sector because of the source of its future leaders include a growing number of clinical specialists who are moving to senior healthcare leadership positions (Henson 2016). And anyway nursing leaders are highly independent regarding their role as leaders (Nilsen et al. 2016) creating de facto devolved leadership.

But devolving leadership in health is inevitably bound up with the structures and processes inherent in health sector organisation, and there is a caveat which concerns how distributed leadership is put into effect, with the risk that if it does not encompass conjoint agency, it will tend more towards 'nobody in charge' (Currie and Lockett 2011) which would be the worst possible outcome of a laudable objective.

Health Sector Leadership Is Complex: Sometimes Inclusive, Always Diverse

But this is not to say that there is a binary choice between transformational and transactional or centralised against devolved leadership. The diverse nature of health sector organisations mitigates against such singularity. Hence the third conclusion is that leadership in the health sector is a melange of transformation, transaction, and inclusion. This complexity occurs because of demands across a broad range of areas. A recent European study identified 52 competences in 8 domains for health leaders including most importantly professional credibility by understanding health issues and synthesising divergent viewpoints. In addition, there was reference to reflective leadership, servant leadership, adaptive leadership, and the application of emotional leadership (Czabanowska et al. 2014). The complexity of the subject was reinforced by further studies in whose health leaders required technical competences, as well as cognitive and emotional competences including being sympathetic to individual differences (Kumar et al. 2015: 161; Silva et al. 2017) and the need for public advocacy, networking, and negotiation. In the USA, 'effective leaders at the frontline' (Kim et al. 2014: 545) had the task of negotiating through the complexity and providing strategic direction which embraced a range of competences. These experiences suggest that leadership in the health sector is multidimensional, multilayered, and contextual. No single leadership style or best practice exists or is indeed possible. The closest to best practice is not in style but in approach which might be referred to as dynamic adaptive.

Health Sector Leadership Has Different Emphases to Leadership in Other Sectors

Whilst there is an ongoing dialogue in the sector about the nature of leadership and its expected outcomes, there is a growing consensus on the role of high-performing leaders in the transformation of healthcare organisations. Health sector leaders establish direction, align people, and motivate and inspire colleagues towards a common goal, and effective leadership is essential to an effective healthcare strategy. Health sector leaders articulate the vision of the future to which the organisation aspires and which enables business decisions, plans, and activities to be directed accordingly in the same way as leaders would in organisations in any industry or commercial sector. In addition, health sector leaders participate in setting strategy, policy, and stewardship to create a culture in which talented individuals can deliver these objectives whilst at the same time achieving their full potential, once again a role commonly held. The various theories of leadership also hold true in health, with research shown in the above narrative and reflected in the timeline mirroring the terminology and approach of leadership study in commercial or industrial sectors. And even though no universally accepted definition or theory of leadership exists, most recognise the importance of leadership in one of its many forms. These points of view would make health leadership comparable to that in any other sector. However, a further conclusion is the difference in some areas of health leadership from that advocated in business or management literature and practice.

Firstly, the massively different context creates additional factors. In particular 'it is essential that leaders in health care bring an understanding of both the clinical world and the organisational world' (Baldwin et al. 2011: 66) to their activity. Secondly, the emphasis on leaders' and leadership's role in achieving care, compassion, courage, commitment, communication, and competency that are enshrined in healthcare organisations adds an extra dimension to health sector leadership. The significant human responsibility and the effect of a health leader's actions on countless lives (Reed 2009) create a particularly intense level of scrutiny for those who lead in health. The ability to understand the implications and deal with it as expectations rise is a key differentiator. So, whilst it is possible to synthesise some of the characteristics of leadership as it applies in other sectors into the unique environment of health, there are also significant differences, particularly at the level of output, which not only include those relating to shareholder value but also relating to genuine life-changing decisions, the human and humanity element of a health sector leader's role.

Health Sector Leadership Embraces a Multiplicity of Professional and Managerial Fields

There is as much emphasis on leadership in clinical, professional, and technical leadership as there is in roles that are mainly focused on business and management issues. This is important because 'clinically led structures may look different from management led structures' (Gauld 2017: 7). Whilst leadership research has provided 'an essentially descriptive-historical account of leadership models,' it has more recently come to focus on the participation of the whole of the workforce in the achievement of organisational goals and values and a more devolved leadership model as opposed to the traditional hierarchical approach (Parker 2013). Indeed, it has been noted that as members of health organisations, physicians, amongst others, 'must also learn to think in additional, different ways to the clinical and the pathophysiological'. Clinical skills, it is argued, do not always translate directly into the capacities required of system players, managers, and leaders; there is evidence of the need for increased exposure to the managerial sciences in the organisation and delivery of healthcare in complex settings (Parker 2013). In this context, clinical leadership means 'health professional leadership' and may be deemed to encompass a broad range of health sector professionals including doctors, nurses, and allied care providers working in hospitals and primary care (Gauld 2017). If this can be achieved, then clinical leaders can be effective in facilitating innovation and change. This will happen by 'recognising, influencing, and empowering individuals through effective communication in order to share and learn from and with each other in practice' (McSherry and Pearce 2016: 11). Clinical leadership means clinical healthcare staff undertaking the roles of leadership and involves both promoting the organisation's strategy, its values, and vision and using clinical experience and ensuring that patient needs are at the core of the strategy and delivery (Taylor and Martindale 2013). This is one of the reasons behind the increase, in some areas, of the Doctor of Medicine or physician as CEO (Cohen 2013), and having clinicians in leadership positions can better address health sector challenges (Erol et al. 2015).

Leadership in health covers a wide range of roles and situations. It can relate to those responsible for clinical excellence and the application of evidence-based nursing practice, professional health technical leaders, business managers, and client relationship managers. Leaders can operate in a local area, across communities, or internationally. They can be transformational or transactional, exclusive or inclusive. In many cases they will operate in an environment which is increasingly complex and expensive and in which 'the search for reliable, safe and high value care goes on' (Zohier 2012: 261). Indeed because of the dramatic, rapid change outlined in Chap. 2, it has grown increasingly important for clinical, medical, and professional staff to develop skills in both leadership roles and management functions such that the two become integrated (Marquis and Huston 2012: 44). For some 'this context reinforces an ideology of bureaucratic rationalism, with scientific management being given more power to ensure that hospitals are better controlled and more predictable' (Correia 2013: 255). Similarly, effective clinical leadership comprises of a series of 'ingredients' which included setting a vision, inspiring values, giving strategic guidance, and motivating a team. It was argued that the range of skills covered human, technical, and conceptual and 'must be obtained by identifying and learning them through practice.' Most importantly it was argued that the leader should have inner skills to ensure that they were self-led. This was the acquisition of personal insight that would help the leader to adopt the most appropriate leadership style to the context of the organisation. Amongst the individual attributes were self-awareness, social skills (communication and conflict management), self-regulation (self-control and adaptability), and social awareness (Zohier 2012: 262–263). It is in this regard that health sector leadership crosses the line between business and management on the one hand and specialist health knowledge on the other.

Health Sector Leadership Often Overlaps with Health Sector Management and Vice Versa

The ongoing debate about whether leadership is different from management outlined in the previous chapter is also prevalent in health with references to leadership and management as distinct concepts, but often present in the same role. An early study noted that 'the head nurse's leadership behaviour represents daily activities in three managerial roles' including, firstly, the decision-making role which involves activities in allocating resources, assertiveness in handling work problems, and delegation or collaboration. Secondly, the informational role encompassed monitoring the care in the unit and providing feedback to the professional workforce. Thirdly is the interpersonal role described being sensitive to the feelings and needs of staff as well as in providing liaison activities between the unit and the hospital administration and other related service units (Sheridan et al. 1984: 60). But often, the terms leader and manager are used interchangeably (Reichenpfader et al. 2015: 305) particularly when the leadership scenario in question is task or relationship oriented.

On this subject, some have been stridently clear in concluding that leadership and management are different (Bishop 2009: 49) and that 'misunderstanding the difference can lead to conflict.' And 'management and leadership function embodied in the same person or within the same post lead to confusion, conflict and diminished clinical and management effectiveness.' Ewens (2002: 76) also pointed to research which differentiated between the roles of managers and leaders. On the one hand, managers created stability, took control, accomplished tasks, and took responsibility for planning, organising, and controlling human and material resources. On the other hand, leaders inspired followers, had a vision, and empowered others to deliver that vision. Furthermore, it is argued that leadership and management are both needed to administer and develop health services. Leadership roles that have a significant administrative burden can distract from important leadership functions and make leadership roles unappealing. The terms are often used interchangeably but require different skills and focus (Johnston et al. 2016). The differences are played out in practice since there is a constant struggle for control between organised stakeholders—on one side the managerial group, and on the other the health care professionals who tend to have a 'tribal' nature. These influences make leadership more difficult in the health unit, especially from the political and symbolic perspective (Farrell 2003: 169). However, whereas leadership and management experts such as Kotter (1990) or Bennis (1989, 2001) have put forward clear delineations between management and leadership, there are arguments against distinction between the two. A view that leadership is one of the roles of the manager or that effective leadership required an understanding of management principles and vice versa led to the important conclusion that 'successful organisations and teams need both sets of roles and one is not superior to the other' (McKimm and Phillips 2009: 4; Ellis and Bach 2015: 17). In several studies, health sector management and leadership are regarded as one and the same or at least so closely related as to require minimum distinction. This is especially true as leadership activity is devolved through the organisation (Tomey 2008). Hence the observations that 'nurse managers can provide the necessary leadership' or the description of 'the management function of leading and or directing' (Swansburg 2002). In other instances, leadership was seen as the addition of business knowledge to managerial, technical, or professional skills (Kleinman 2003). And in another still the conventional wisdom of leaders taking on management activity as part of their implementation responsibility was turned on its head with the perspective of 'nurse managers as transformational and transactional leaders' (McGuire and Kennerly 2006).

In trying to bridge the divide, Marquis and Huston put forward the innovative concept of integrated leader-managers with six distinguishing traits including longer-term thinking, looking outward towards the larger organisation, influencing others beyond their immediate areas of responsibility, emphasising vision and values, being politically astute, and 'they think in terms of change and renewal' (Marquis and Huston 2012: 44).

Health Sector Leadership Is Related to Organisation Strategy, Stewardship, Policy, Governance, and Structure

The final conclusion is that leadership in the health sector is influenced not only by the governance process but also by the type of organisational structure in place to respond to social and community needs. This is in itself a complex process. In Canada, 36 frameworks were identified that brought together integrated views of what causes health and which could be used to distinguish between sectoral determinants, governance arrangements, belief systems, social connectedness, and capital (de Leeuw 2017). The different levels of causation of health have an impact on the engagement for health and hence on the type of organisation structure put in place at multiple levels. In this respect, research has shown that 'the debates involving health professions, organisation studies, and hospital governance should pay more attention to the professionals' actions in relation to structural configurations' because 'among the medical profession in general and physicians and surgeons in particular, there is no uniform response in relation to managerial expectations' (Correia 2013: 264). Nevertheless, three variants of health sector organisation structure and their implications for leadership scope and style are traditional hierarchy, leadership in a network (or cross agency), and leadership in a matrix.

The first level, that of a hierarchically structured health sector organisation, is the most identifiable. In a representative structure, there would typically be three leadership levels. It refers to Executive Leadership and would include those who sat on an Executive team or on the Board. Classically these would be responsible for strategy, stewardship, policy, and governance. At the second level of the hierarchy, leaders would be those responsible for a business or operational unit and Heads of Department. Operational leadership would ensure that the departmental or unit strategy was aligned to organisational strategy, that it was operationalised effectively, that this took place by the engagement and motivation of the workforce and the creation of effective teams, and that 'success' was measured against strategy or key performance indicators. Those in such leadership positions have an input into strategy setting. An additional level of leadership would occur within the confines of those roles identified as management. The discussion about the differences or otherwise between the two concepts is covered above with the conclusion that it is highly likely that those identified as managers would undertake leadership activity. In the organisational hierarchy, there are theoretically clear lines of authority, either through business or operational management or through clinical or medical lines (although as Correia (2013) has shown the lines in the health sector are sometimes blurred and open to interpretation). Nevertheless, in most cases, the clarity offered by the hierarchy facilitates the role of the leader and the activities of leadership which will be to direct the organisation's resources towards a common organisational goal or objective.

A second type of organisation is a multi-agency structure that spans one or more different providers. The increasing differentiation of organisations involved in the health sector has created a need for inter-organisational integration (Axelsson and Axelsson 2006). Principal agent theory addresses the requirements for leadership success in this context and is described as 'where one party (the principal) needs another party (the agent) to deliver the first party's objectives, although the principal cannot fully control or even observe the agent's activity' (Rogan and Boaden 2017: 4). In this instance the leader will have the responsibility to influence others outside of her or his immediate sphere of operations and as such will have to ensure that goal alignment between the two agencies is present and the relationship between the principal and the agent affects several dimensions that influence goal alignment including the stakeholders' ability to overcome divisions between managers as principals and clinicians as agents; 'the level at which principals and agents agree with the overall vision and objectives; attaining the right balance between financial and clinical accountability with clinical autonomy and the flexibility to innovate; and ensuring information is: accurate, up-to-date, responsive and adequately explained prior to use or release into the public domain' (Rogen and Boaden 2017: 14). This type of context adds a dimension to leadership requirements. The Executive Leader will have overall responsibility for her or his agency or unit, but success will depend on engaging the leadership and workforce from other agencies or units and that requirement has some additional challenges. In this example, the leader will have to achieve a balance between accountability and clinical autonomy.

The third structure to be considered in respect of leadership in health is that of the organisational matrix. The outliers of the structure represent executive, professional or functional, political or external agency, and clinical or medical leadership. In each of these compartments, leadership will be concerned with delivering specific functional or unit objectives, but there will be a further 'matrix role' in which a specific leader will act as lead on a specialist area or function. This involves separate units or departments coming together to deliver additional objectives of strategy, policy, stewardship, and ethics with each functional leader providing or taking responsibility for one of these areas overall in addition to the 'line' leadership role. Structures such as the matrix have arisen because of evidence that 'few organisations can be successful today with a pure functional structure because the resulting functions or silos inhibit the amount of coordination needed' in a volatile and uncertain environment (Anand and Daft 2010: 307). In the contemporary health sector, there is an inevitable interface between managerialism and medical professionalism and evidence from medical sociology and the sociology of organisations reflects the challenges when the two come together in particular 'the role of the autonomy and discretion attached to medical knowledge, when doctors are allowed to act more freely within hospital settings' (Correia 2013: 255). Where a hospital's dual line of authority places medicine and management separately, there is the possibility for each to follow different objectives, hence the appearance of a hybridisation of medicine and management which is one interpretation of a matrix structure. In the matrix organisation, specialists from different functions or specialisms combine in an 'interdisciplinary team led by a project leader.' Matrices are put in place when there is a need to bring functional centers of excellence together with business or operational people and processes (Huczynski and Buchanan 1991: 424; Bazigos and Harter 2016). One advantage of this is that it allows competing perspectives to be articulated without one point of view being subordinated. The success of this will depend on the maintenance of a balance of power between the perspectives, a critical role for the leader of a matrix organisation. However, a strength for matrix organisations is in the facilitation of collaboration.

Case Study: The Practice of Leadership in Indian Health Sector Organisations

The Indian health sector is undergoing significant change. Total healthcare spending is projected to rise at an annual rate of over 12%, from an estimated US$96.3 billion in 2013 to around US$200 billion in 2018 (Deloitte 2015). And whilst India's healthcare sector continues to face complex challenges, they are being addressed by recognising the system's gaps and introducing healthcare schemes to bridge them, with patient needs the focus of policy decisions and patient feedback as an important input (Ghosh et al. 2018). Innovative public-private partnerships, leveraging information technology in patient-centric healthcare systems, investing in preventive and social medicine, and establishing more medical colleges and training institutes should contribute to further improvement towards achieving the objective of affordable, universal healthcare. Whilst there has been considerable progress, there is some way to go, and the scale of the transition means that, as shown by the publication of the *India Healthcare Roadmap for 2025*, there is work to do in infrastructure and people-related issues as well as regional variations in the accessibility of health (Singh et al. 2015). To meet these challenges, a variety of stakeholders from government through to the private sector, health insurance, and pharmaceutical companies are engaged in the process of improving national healthcare access (McKinsey 2012; Nath 2017).

At local, organisational level, the challenges are equally formidable, and having the right amount of leadership talent to take responsibility and manage through health change and transformation is critical (Turner 2017). This won't be straightforward because behaviour change is in many cases a significant challenge during any transformation programme. Organisational leaders who start a transformation initiative are 'advised to focus on change management to realise its value. Early alignment on a bold vision ensures leadership commitment. Additionally, creating clear sponsorship across the organisation, co-creating solutions with the team and ensuring appropriate incentives helps make change stick' (Ghosh et al. 2018). Within these guidelines, it is possible to identify the leadership challenges as being *organisational*, which relate to having clarity of mission and strategy and ensuring that there is sufficient capital to deliver the desired outcomes, and *human resources* related to the need to attract, retain, and develop talented health professionals and deploy them in a way that is aligned to the organisation's strategy. There is evidence of progress in each of these areas.

At organisational level, some Indian hospitals are exemplars and provide world-class healthcare cost effectively. Effective leadership contributes to this by providing a mix of capability in strategic decision-making and coherence in implementation—for example, the establishment of urban hubs in which high-quality talent and sophisticated equipment were concentrated (Govindarajan and Ramamurti 2018). Where leadership in Indian organisations has been analysed, a combination of factors is evident, although multiple leadership styles and approaches have been adopted to suit the context of the organisation in question. Many of the leading innovative healthcare organisations in India are led by 'dynamic physician-executives,' for example, using a servant leadership model that empowers physician-led initiatives and hence innovation (Richman et al. 2008). Other parts of the sector have applied an adaptive or authentic leadership model (Malik et al. 2016; Mantha et al. 2016). Amongst the leadership characteristics of organisational leaders are that they assume the Chief input role for business strategy; are keepers of organisational culture; act as guides, teachers, and role models for the workforce; and ensure that they are mindful of the needs of external stakeholders (Cappelli et al. 2010). This is a complex process in the health sector where leaders have to 'juggle multiple hats' to drive improvements including being simultaneously an innovator and integrator, a strategic partner, a change champion, and a capability builder (Jacob 2014). But it is not only in strategy setting that leadership in the Indian health sector is notable.

At a *human resource* level, ensuring that there is a sufficient supply of qualified and competent health professionals is a challenge facing leaders in all health sector organisations across the world (Turner 2017). In India, to meet the demand means at organisational level, there are innovative approaches to the recruitment, development, and retention of health workers (Srinivasan and Chandwani 2014). From a people-related perspective, attracting and retaining doctors seeking to improve their skills rapidly is seen as a priority for leaders in Indian health. And finally, ensuring the right level of leadership talent to manage health transformation is critical because of the effects of globalisation, technology developments, and the increasing focus on performance (Turner 2017).

The challenges facing leaders of healthcare organisations in India are formidable. The sheer scale of the demand for health means that there is an urgency in response, requiring national, government-coordinated actions on the one hand, backed up by efficient modern health sector organisations. In all of these, leaders will have the dual responsibility of creating dynamic organisations in which talented human resource professionals deliver a caring and efficient health service.

Conclusion and Implications for Practice

Leadership theory and practice in the health sector are contextual and emergent as the environment in which health services are delivered changes. Issues have been raised about its teachability, relevance to the doctor-patient relationship, and possible erosion of medical roles and status (Parker 2013). Nevertheless, a convergence of powerful forces and their impact on health service structure and delivery have raised the profile of clinical, medical, or professional leadership in healthcare organisations and in some cases have led to calls for a paradigm shift in leadership. There is considerable emphasis on identifying the leadership competences required, and the results show a rich vein of leadership theory and practice in health, much of which mirrors that which occurs in other commercial or industrial sectors. For example, the long-term popularity of transformational leadership as a driving force for change is common as is the increasing move towards inclusion and devolution of leadership to more agile and responsive units. However, there are also unique distinguishing factors for health sector leaders and leadership. In this respect, it is possible to conclude that:

- Leadership theory and practice in health reflect a complex and diverse environment with a wide range of interpretations. In most, there is an attempt to **adapt leadership style or competences to be appropriate to the context within which the leadership activity takes place**. Health sector leadership is related to organisation strategy, stewardship, policy, governance, and structure.
- There is no single, all-encompassing definition of leadership in health but that definitions embrace both **transformation at the top and devolution 'from Board to Ward—from Ward to Community**.' Increasingly there is recognition that the concept of leadership has greater scope than only the most senior members of the organisation and other leadership positions extend to the level of point of care. As it does so, health sector leadership often overlaps with health sector management and vice versa. Nevertheless it is important to identify aspects of leadership capability that are specific to the sector and will contribute to the effectiveness of its leaders, wherever they reside within the organisation.
- Health sector leadership takes place in often complex organisational entities, and even within a single unit, there is the possibility of transformation, transaction, and inclusion in leadership style. In addition health sector leadership embraces a multiplicity of professional and managerial fields. In this respect an understanding of the complexities and dynamics of the organisation will be an important complemen-

tary aspect of any leadership approach. Similarly the clinical or medical environment demands an understanding of professional mores and ethics if leadership decisions are to be seen as credible.

- The analysis suggests that leadership in the health service is characterised by such diversity that it is not possible to derive a single dominant leadership style which could be applied in all situations. It is possible however to highlight some characteristics that have the potential to be transportable between roles and organisations.

The following chapters will identify some of the commonalities that have so far been alluded to but which may form the basis of a model for leadership in health.

References

Amasawa, F., & Crisp, N. (Eds.). (2014). *African Health Leaders: Making Change and Claiming the Future*. Oxford: Oxford University Press.

Anand, N., & Daft, R. (2010). What Is the Right Organisation Design. In G. R. Hickman (Ed.) (2010). *Leading Organisations, Perspectives for a New Era*. Thousand Oaks, CA: Sage Publications.

Axelsson, R., & Axelsson, S. B. (2006). Integration and Collaboration in Public Health – A Conceptual Framework. *International Journal of Health Planning and Management, 21*, 75–88. https://doi.org/10.1002/hpm.826.

Baldwin, K. S., Dimunation, N., & Alexander, J. (2011). Health Care Leadership and the Dyad Model. *Physician Executive, 37*(4), 66–70.

Barr, J., & Dowding, L. (2008). *Leadership in Health Care*. London: Sage Publications Ltd.

Bazigos, M., & Harter, J. (2016). Revisiting the Matrix Organisation. *McKinsey Quarterly*, January.

Bennis, W. (1989). *On Becoming a Leader*. Reading, MA: Addison Wesley.

Bennis, W. (2001). The New Leadership. In S. Crainer & D. Dearlove (Eds.), *Financial Times Handbook of Management* (2nd ed.). London: Prentice Hall.

Bishop, V. (2009). *Leadership for Nursing and Allied Healthcare Professionals*. Maidenhead, UK: McGraw Hill.

Cappelli, P., Singh, H., Singh, J. V., & Useem, M. (2010). Leadership Lessons from India. *Harvard Business Review*, March.

Chan, Z., Bruxer, A., Lee, J., Sims, K., Wainwright, M., Brooks, D., et al. (2015). What Makes a Leader: Identifying the Strengths of Canadian Physical Therapists. *Physiotherapy Canada, 67*(4), 341–348. ISSN:0300-0508.
Chisholm-Burns, M. A., Spivey, C. A., Hagemann, T., & Josephson, M. (2017). A Women in Leadership and the Bewildering Glass Ceiling. *American Journal of Health-System Pharmacy, 74*(5), 312–324. ISSN:1079-2082.
Choi, S. L., Goh, C. F., Adam, M. B. H., & Tan, O. K. (2016). Transformational Leadership, Empowerment, and Job Satisfaction: The Mediating Role of Employee Empowerment. *Human Resources for Health, 14*, 73.
Clarke, P., Swider, S., & Bigley, M. (2013). Nursing Leadership and Health Policy: A Dialogue with Nurse Leaders. *Nursing Science Quarterly, 26*(2), 136–142.
Cohen, E. (2013). The Rise of the MD CEO. *Business NH Magazine, 30*(6), 18.
Correia, T. (2013). The Interplay Between Managerialism and Medical Professionalism in Hospital Organisations from the Doctors' Perspective: A Comparison of Two Distinctive Medical Units. *Health Sociology Review, 22*(3), 255–267. https://doi.org/10.5172/hesr.2013.22.3.255.
Corrigan, P., & Garman, A. N. (1999). Transformational and Transactional Leadership Skills for Mental Health Teams. *Community Mental Health Journal, 35*(4), 301–312. ISSN:0010-3853.
Cox, K., & Westbrook, D. H. (2017). Hospital Leadership Recognizes Need to Create Partnerships to Treat Consequences of Poverty. *Current Problems in Pediatric and Adolescent Health Care*. https://doi.org/10.1016/j.cppeds.2017.07.009.
Currie, G., & Lockett, A. (2011). Distributing Leadership in Health and Social Care: Concertive, Conjoint or Collective? *International Journal of Management Reviews, 13*, 286–300. https://doi.org/10.1111/j.1468-2370.2011.00308.x.
Curry, L., Taylor, L., Guey-Chi Chen, P., & Bradley, E. (2012). Experiences of Leadership in Health Care in Sub-Saharan Africa. *Human Resources for Health, 10*(1), 33. ISSN:1478-4491.
Czabanowska, K., Smith, T., Könings, K. D., Sumskas, L., Otok, R., Bjegovic-Mikanovic, V., et al. (2014). In Search for a Public Health Leadership Competency Framework to Support Leadership Curriculum – A Consensus Study. *European Journal of Public Health, 24*(5), 850–856. ISSN:1101-1262.
DaCosta, J. (2012). Leadership Models for Healthcare Improvement. *British Journal of Healthcare Management, 18*(11), 575–580. ISSN:1358-0574.

Day, M., Shickle, D., Smith, K., Zakariasen, K., Moskol, J., & Oliver, T. (2014). Training Public Health Superheroes: Five Talents for Public Health Leadership. *Journal of Public Health, 36*(4), 552–561. ISSN:1741-3842.

De Leeuw, E. (2017). Engagement of Sectors Other Than Health in Integrated Health Governance, Policy, and Action. *Annual Review of Public Health, 38*, 329–349. https://doi.org/10.1146/annurev-publhealth031816-044309.

De Zulueta, P. C. (2016). Developing Compassionate Leadership in Health Care: An Integrative Review. *Journal of Healthcare Leadership, 8*, 1–10.

Delmatoff, J., & Lazarus, I. R. (2014). The Most Effective Leadership Style for the New Landscape of Healthcare. *Journal of Healthcare Management, 59*(4), 245–249. ISSN:1096-9012.

Deloitte. (2015). 2015 Health Care Outlook-India. Retrieved from https://www2.deloitte.com/content/dam/Deloitte/global/Documents/Life-Sciences-Health-Care/gx-lshc-2015-health-care-outlook-india.pdf.

Denis, J. L., & van Gestel, N. (2016). Medical Doctors in Healthcare Leadership: Theoretical and Practical Challenges. *BMC Health Services Research, 16*, S158. ISSN:1472-6963.

Department of Health. (2009). Inspiring Leaders: Leadership for Quality; Guidance for NHS Talent and Leadership Plans, Department of Health Workforce Directorate, Publication date 22 January.

Dhatt, R., Theobald, S., Buzuzi, S., Ros, B., Vong, S., Muraya, K., et al. (2017). The Role of Women's Leadership and Gender Equity in Leadership and Health System Strengthening. *Global Health, Epidemiology & Genomics, 2*(1). Complementary Index.

Dolamo, B. L. (2015). Preparing the New Nurse Leader for Health Care Delivery in South Africa in the Twenty-First Century. *African Journal for Physical, Health Education, Recreation & Dance, 21*, 485–497.

Dye, C. F. (2010). *Leadership in Healthcare: Essential Values and Skills* (3rd ed.). Chicago: Health Administration Press. ISBN: 978-1567938463.

Ellis, P., & Abbott, J. (2014). Identifying Goals with the NHS Healthcare Leadership Model. *Journal of Renal Nursing, 6*(3), 144–147. ISSN:2041-1448.

Ellis, P., & Bach, S. (2015). *Leadership, Management and Team Working in Nursing*. London: Sage.

Erol, R., Upton, P., Mackenzie, H., Donnelly, P., & Upton, D. (2015). Delivering the Future: An Evaluation of a Multidisciplinary Clinical Leadership Programme. *British Journal of Healthcare Management, 21*(1), 29–35.

Evans, J. (2014). Evolving Leadership in Healthcare Design. *Health Environments Research & Design Journal (HERD)), 7*(4), 9–12. ISSN:1937-5867.

Ewens, A. (2002). The Nature and Purpose of Leadership. In E. Howkins & C. Thornton (Eds.) (2002). *Managing and Leading Innovation in Healthcare*. London: Elsevier Science.

Farrell, M. (2003). Health Care Leadership in an Age of Change. *Australian Health Review, 26*(1), 153–164.

Fitzgerald, L., Ferlie, E., McGivern, G., & Buchanan, D. (2013). Distributed Leadership Patterns and Service Improvement: Evidence and Argument from English Healthcare. *The Leadership Quarterly, 24*(1), 227–239. ISSN:1048-9843.

Fitzsimmons, M. J., & Rose, R. (2015). Designing Structure to Meet Demands, and Recruiting Talent to Achieve Results. *Nurse Leader, 13*(1), 33–36. ISSN:1541-4612.

Gabel, S. (2012). Power, Leadership and Transformation: The Doctor's Potential for Influence. *Medical Educator, 46*, 1152–1160.

Gauld, R. (2017). Clinical Leadership: What Is It and How Do We Facilitate It? *Journal of Primary Health Care, 9*(1), 5–8. https://doi.org/10.1071/HC16041.

Ghosh, P., Mehra, S., & Arunave, S. D. (2018). Operational Excellence in Healthcare Delivery in India; A Critical Imperative During a Painful Transition. Retrieved from https://www.bain.com/insights/operational-excellence-in-healthcare-delivery-in-india/.

Gifford, W. A., Davies, B. L., Graham, I. D., Tourangeau, A., Woodend, A. K., & Lefebre, N. (2013). Developing Leadership Capacity for Guideline Use: A Pilot Cluster Randomized Control Trial. *Worldviews on Evidence-Based Nursing, 10*(1), 51–65. https://doi.org/10.1111/j.1741-6787.2012.00254.

Gopee, N., & Galloway, J. (2008). *Leadership and Management in Healthcare*. London: Sage Publications.

Gordon, L. J., Rees, C. E., Ker, J. S., & Cleland, J. (2015). Dimensions, Discourses and Differences: Trainees Conceptualising Health Care Leadership and Followership. *Medical Education, 49*(12), 1248–1262. ISSN:0308-0110.

Govindarajan, V., & Ramamurti, R. (2018). Transforming Health Care from the Ground Up. *Harvard Business Review, 96*(4), 96–104.

Gray, I., Field, R., & Brown, K. (2010). *Effective Leadership, Management and Supervision in Health and Social Care*. Exeter, UK: Learning Matters.

Gunderman, R. B. (2009). *Leadership in Healthcare*. London: Springer-Verlag.

Hartley, V. (2015). Transforming Community Services Through the Use of a Multidimensional Model of Clinical Leadership. *Journal of Clinical Nursing, 24*(5/6), 749–760. ISSN:0962-1067.

Henson, J. W. (2016). Five Ideas for the Development of Successful Physician Leaders. *Journal of Healthcare Management, 61*(3), 171–175. ISSN:1096-9012.

Hewison, A., & Morrell, K. (2014). Leadership Development in the English National Health Service: A Counter Narrative to Inform Policy. *International Journal of Nursing Studies, 51*(4), 677–688. https://doi.org/10.1016/j.ijnurstu.2013.08.004.

Hicks, R. F. (2014). *Coaching as a Leadership Style: The Art and Science of Coaching Conversations for Healthcare Professionals*. London: Routledge.

Hill, F., & Stephens, C. (2005). Building Leadership Capacity in Medical Education: Developing the Potential of Course Coordinators. *Medical Teacher, 27*(2), 145–149. https://doi.org/10.1080/01421590400029731.

Hillen, H., Pfaff, H., & Hammer, A. (2017). The Association Between Transformational Leadership in German Hospitals and the Frequency of Events Reported as Perceived by Medical Directors. *Journal of Risk Research, 20*(4), 499–515. https://doi.org/10.1080/13669877.2015.1074935.

Huczynski, A., & Buchanan, D. (1991). *Organisational Behaviour*. New York: Prentice Hall.

Jacob, J. (2014). Steering India's Healthcare Sector. *The Hindu Business Line*. Retrieved from https://www.thehindubusinessline.com/specials/new-manager/steering-indias-healthcare-sector/article20841837.ece.

Jeyaraman, M. M., Qadar, S. Z., Wierzbowski, A., Farshidfar, F., Lys, J., Dickson, G., et al. (2018). Return on Investment in Healthcare Leadership Development Programs. *Leadership in Health Services (1751–1879), 31*(1), 77–97. https://doi.org/10.1108/LHS-02-2017-0005.

Johnston, C., Turpin, N., & Wynn-Jones, W. (2016). Medical Leadership in Perioperative Practice. *BJA Education, 16*(6), 203–208. https://doi.org/10.1093/bjaed/mkv041.

Kim, C. S., King, E., Stein, J., Robinson, E., Salameh, M., & O'Leary, K. J. (2014). Unit-Based Inter-professional Leadership Models in Six US Hospitals. *Journal of Hospital Medicine, 9*(8), 545–550.

Kjeld, H. A., & Rapsaniotis, S. (2017). Leadership Requirements for Lean Versus Servant Leadership in Health Care: A Systematic Review of the Literature. *Journal of Healthcare Leadership, 9*, 1–14.

Kleinman, C. S. (2003). Leadership Roles, Competencies and Education: How Prepared Are Our Nurse Managers? *Journal of Nursing Administration, 33*, 451–456.

Korean Academy of Nursing Administration. (2015). Concept Analysis of Nursing Leadership. *Journal of Korean Academy of Nursing Administration, 21*(5), 575–586. https://doi.org/10.11111/jkana.2015.21.5.575.

Korica, M. (2018). *How Leaders Stay in the Know, Work*. London: Chartered Institute of Personnel and Development.

Kotter, J. (1990). *A Force for Change: How Leadership Differs from Management*. New York: The Free Press.

Kumar, S., Kumar, N., Adhish, V. S., & Reddy, R. S. (2015). Strategic Management and Leadership for Health Professionals – Skills to Leverage Resources to Achieve Health Goals. *Indian Journal of Community Medicine, 40*(3), 158–162. ISSN:0970-0218.

Larkin, H. (2015). The New Health Care CEO: In a Rapidly Changing Field, Effective Leaders Require 'Learning Agility' and 'Emotional Intelligence' as Much – or More – Than Traditional Skills. *H&HN Hospitals & Health Networks, 22*(6).

Longest, B. B., Jr., & Darr, K. (1993). Organizational Leadership in Hospitals. *Hospital Topics, 71*(3), 11.

Lorber, M., Treven, S., & Mumel, D. (2016). The Examination of Factors Relating to the Leadership Style of Nursing Leaders in Hospitals. *Naše Gospodarstvo, 62*(1), 27–36. https://doi.org/10.1515/ngoe-2016-0003.

Lott, T. F. (2016). Preparing Clinical Nurses for Shared Governance Leadership Roles. *Nurse Leader, 14*(6), 403–408. ISSN:1541-4612.

Lv, C.-M., & Zhang, L. (2017). How Can Collective Leadership Influence the Implementation of Change in Health Care? *Chinese Nursing Research, 4*(4), 182–185. ISSN:2095-7718.

Maccoby, M., Norman, C. L., Norman, C. J., & Margolies, R. (2013). *Transforming Health Care Leadership: A Systems Guide to Improve Patient Care, Decrease Costs, and Improve Population Health*. San Francisco, CA: Jossey Bass. ISBN: 978-1-118-50563-2.

Maijala, V., Tossavainen, K., & Turunen, H. (2016). Original Article: Health Promotion Practices Delivered by Primary Health Care Nurses: Elements for Success in Finland. *Applied Nursing Research, 30*, 45–51. https://doi.org/10.1016/j.apnr.2015.11.002.

Malik, N., Dhar, R. L., & Handa, S. C. (2016). Authentic Leadership and Its Impact on Creativity of Nursing Staff: A Cross Sectional Questionnaire Survey of Indian Nurses and Their Supervisors. *International Journal of Nursing Studies, 63*, 28–36. https://doi.org/10.1016/j.ijnurstu.2016.08.004.

Manss, G. (2017). Implementation of Daily Senior Leader Rounds Using a Transformational Leadership Approach. *Nurse Leader, 15*(1), 65–69. ISSN:1541-4612.

Mantha, A., Coggins, N. L., Mahadevan, A., Strehlow, R. N., Strehlow, M. C., & Mahadevan, S. V. (2016). Adaptive Leadership Curriculum for Indian Paramedic Trainees. *International Journal of Emergency Medicine, 9*, 1–7. https://doi.org/10.1186/s12245-016-0103-x.

Marquis, B. L., & Huston, C. J. (2012). *Effective Leadership, Management and Supervision in Health and Social Care*. Exeter, UK: Learning Matters.

Martin, G., Beech, N., MacIntosh, R., & Bushfield, S. (2015). Potential Challenges Facing Distributed Leadership in Health Care: Evidence from the UK National Health Service. *Sociology of Health & Illness, 37*(1), 14–29. https://doi.org/10.1111/1467-9566.12171.

McDonald, R. (2014). Leadership and Leadership Development in Healthcare Settings – A Simplistic Solution to Complex Problems. *International Journal of Health Policy and Management, 3*(5), 227–229.

McGuire, E., & Kennerly, S. M. (2006). Nurse Managers as Transformational and Transactional Leaders. *Nursing Economics, the journal for Health Care Leaders, 24*(4), 179–185.

McKimm, J., & Phillips, K. (2009). *Leadership and Management in Integrated Services*. Exeter, UK: Learning Matters.

McKinsey. (2012). India Healthcare: Inspiring Possibilities, Challenging Journey. Retrieved March 10, 2017, from www.mckinsey.com.

McSherry, R., & Pearce, P. (2016). What Are the Effective Ways to Translate Clinical Leadership into Health Care Quality Improvement? *Journal of Healthcare Leadership, 2016*(1), 11–17.

Medley, F., & Larochelle, D. (1995). Transformational Leadership and Job Satisfaction. *Nursing Management, 26*(9), 64–65. ISSN:64JJ-64NN.

de Melo Lanzoni, G. M., Schlindwein Meirelles, B. H., & Cummings, G. (2016). Nurse Leadership Practices in Primary Health Care: A Grounded Theory. *Texto & Contexto Enfermagem, 25*(4), 1–9. https://doi.org/10.1590/0104-07072016004190015.

Muller, M., & Naude, M. (1998). A Model for Transformational Leadership by Nursing Unit Managers. *Health SA Gesondheid: Journal of Interdisciplinary Health Sciences, 3*(3), 31–38.

Murphy, J., Quillinan, B., & Carolan, M. (2009). Role of Clinical Nurse Leadership in Improving Patient Care. *Nursing Management – UK, 16*(8), 26–28.

Nath, P. (2017). Talent Management Challenges in the Indian Health Sector. In Turner, P. A. (2017). *Talent Management in Healthcare*. Palgrave Macmillan.

Nilsen, E. R., Olafsen, A. H., Steinsvag, A. G., Halvari, H., & Grov, E. K. (2016). Stuck Between a Rock and a Hard Place: The Work Situation for Nurses as Leaders in Municipal Health Care. *Journal of Multidisciplinary Healthcare, 2016*(1), 153–161.

Ohta, J., Kuwabara, A., Fujii, A., & Tanaka, K. (2015). Leadership Style of Registered Dietitians in Hospitals or Facilities for the Elderly. *Journal of Japanese Society of Nutrition and Food Science* (Nippon Eiyo Shokuryo Gakkaishi), *68*(4), 165–173. https://doi.org/10.4327/jsnfs.68.165.

Olu-Abiodun, O., & Abiodun, O. (2017). Perception of Transformational Leadership Behaviour Among General Hospital Nurses in Ogun State, Nigeria. *International Journal of Africa Nursing Sciences, 6*, 22–27. ISSN:2214-1391.

Oostra, R. D. (2016). Physician Leadership: A Central Strategy to Transforming Healthcare. *Frontiers of Health Services Management, 32*, 15–26. ISSN:0748-8157.

Pacific Association. (2016). Pacific Association: Building Nurse Leadership. *Kai Tiaki Nursing New Zealand, 22*(5), 43.

Parker, M. (2013). Misconceiving Medical Leadership. *Perspectives in Biology and Medicine, 56*(3), 387–406. https://doi.org/10.1353/pbm.2013.0027.

Parnell, T. A. (2014). Nursing Leadership Strategies, Health Literacy, and Patient Outcomes. *Nurse Leader, 12*, 49–52. https://doi.org/10.1016/j.mnl.2014.09.005.

Reed, S. B. (2009). Creating a Leadership Legacy of Caring: A Health Care Leader's Ultimate Journey. *Nurse Leader, 7*(1), 12–15. ISSN:1541-4612.

Reichenpfader, U., Carlfjord, S., & Nilsen, P. (2015). Leadership in Evidence-Based Practice: A Systematic Review. *Leadership in Health Services, 28*(4), 298–316.

Richman, B. D., Udayakumar, K., Mitchell, W., & Schulman, K. A. (2008). Lessons from India in Organizational Innovation: A Tale of Two Heart Hospitals. *Health Affairs, 27*(5), 1260–1270. https://doi.org/10.1377/hlthaff.27.5.1260.

Robbins, B. (2007). Transformational Leadership in Health Care Today. *The Health Care Manager, 26*(3), 234–239. https://doi.org/10.1097/01.HCM.0000285014.26397.e7.

Rogan, L., & Boaden, R. (2017). Understanding Performance Management in Primary Care. *International Journal of Health Care Quality Assurance, 30*(1), 4–15. https://doi.org/10.1108/IJHCQA-10-2015-0128.

Rogers, J. K. (2014). Reinventing Shared Leadership to Support Nursing's Evolving Role in Healthcare. *Nurse Leader, 12*, 29–43. ISSN:1541-4612.

Sahne, B. S., Arslan, M., & Sar, S. (2015). Concept of Leadership in Healthcare Services and Ethical Leadership. *Medicine and Law, 34*(2), 297–306.

Saravo, B., Netzel, J., & Kiesewetter, J. (2017). The Need for Strong Clinical Leaders – Transformational and Transactional Leadership as a Framework for Resident Leadership Training. *PLoS One, 12*(8), 1–13. https://doi.org/10.1371/journal.pone.0183019.

Schwartz, P. (2010). Inevitable Strategies. In G. R. Hickman (Ed.), *Leading Organisations, Perspectives for a New Era.* Thousand Oaks, CA: Sage Publications.

Scully, N. J. (2015). Leadership in Nursing: The Importance of Recognising Inherent Values and Attributes to Secure a Positive Future for the Profession. *Collegian, 22*(4), 439–444. ISSN:1322-7696.

Sheridan, J. E., & Vredenburgh, D. J. (1978). Predicting Leadership Behavior in a Hospital Organization. *Academy of Management Journal, 21*(4), 679–689. https://doi.org/10.2307/255708.

Sheridan, J. E., Vredenburgh, D. J., & Abelson, M. A. (1984). Contextual Model of Leadership Influence in Hospital Units. *Academy of Management Journal, 27*(1), 57–78. ISSN:0001-4273.

Silva, V. L. S., Camelo, S. H. H., Soares, M. I., Resck, Z. M. R., Chaves, L. D. P., Santos, F. C., et al. (2017). Leadership Practices in Hospital Nursing: A Self of Manager Nurses. *Revista da Escola de Enfermagem da USP, 51*, e03206. Epub April 03, 2017. https://doi.org/10.1590/s1980-220x2016099503206.

Singh, K., Ghosh, P., & Talukdar, D. (2015). India Healthcare Roadmap for 2025. Bain Brief. Retrieved from http://www.bain.com/publications/articles/india-healthcare-roadmap-for-2025-brief.aspx.

Smits, S. J., Bowden, D., Falconer, J. A., & Strasser, D. C. (2014). Improving Medical Leadership and Teamwork: An Iterative Process. *Leadership in Health Services, 27*(4), 299.

Srinivasan, V., & Chandwani, R. (2014). HRM Innovations in Rapid Growth Contexts: The Healthcare Sector in India. *International Journal of Human Resource Management, 25*(10), 1505–1525. ISSN:0958-5192.

Swansburg, R. (2002). *Introduction to Management and Leadership for Nurse Managers*. Sudbury, MA: Jones and Bartlett Publishers Inc.

Taylor, R., & Martindale, S. (2013). Clinical Leadership in Primary Care. *Primary Health Care, 23*(5), 32–38.

Teulings, A. M., Jansen, L. O., & Verhoeven, W. G. (1973). Growth, Power Structure and Leadership Functions in the Hospital Organization. *British Journal of Sociology, 24*(4), 490.

Till, A., Jones, P., & McKimm, J. (2015). Medical Leadership and Management: An International Revolution. *Journal of Health Specialties, 3*(3), 139–143.

Tomey, A. M. (2008). *Nursing Management and Leadership*. St. Louis, MO: Mosby Elsevier.

Trastek, V. F., Hamilton, N. W., & Niles, E. E. (2014). Leadership Models in Health Care – A Case for Servant Leadership. *Mayo Clinic Proceedings, 89*(3), 374–381. https://doi.org/10.1016/j.mayocp.2013.10.012.

Tropello, P. D., & DeFazio, J. (2014). Servant Leadership in Nursing Administration and Academia Shaping Future Generations of Nurses and Interdisciplinary Team Providers to Transform Healthcare Delivery. *Nurse Leader, 12*(6), 59–61. ISSN:1541-4612.

Turner, P. A. (2017). *Talent Management in Healthcare*. Basingstoke: Palgrave Macmillan.

Vanderpyl, T. H. (2011). Servant Leadership: A Case Study of a Canadian Health Care Innovator. *Journal of Healthcare Leadership, 4*, 9–16. https://doi.org/10.2147/JHL.S28810.

Weberg, D. (2012). Complexity Leadership: A Healthcare Imperative. *Nursing Forum, 47*(4), 268–277. ISSN:0029-6473.

West, M. (2014). Leadership for Cultures of High-Quality Care. *British Journal of Healthcare Management, 20*(6), 260–261.

West, M. A., Borrill, C. S., Dawson, J. F., Brodbeck, F., Shapiro, D. A., & Haward, B. (2003). Leadership Clarity and Team Innovation in Health Care. *The Leadership Quarterly, 14*(4–5), 393–410. https://doi.org/10.1016/S1048-9843(03)00044-4.

Westphal, J. A. (2012). Characteristics of Nurse Leaders in Hospitals in the USA from 1992 to 2008. *Journal of Nursing Management, 20*(7), 928–937. https://doi.org/10.1111/j.1365-2834.2012.01403.

WHO. (2017). Participatory Leadership. *Bulletin of the World Health Organization, 95*(1), 5.

Zohier, E. (2012). The Importance of Clinical Leadership in Twenty First Century Health Care. *International Journal of Health Promotion and Education, 50*(5), 261–269.

Zvi, D. G. (2001). Social Work Perceptions of Transformational and Transactional Leadership in Health Care. *Social Work Research, 25*(1), 17–25. https://doi.org/10.1093/swr/25.1.17.

5

A Model for Health Sector Leadership

The Formalities of Formal Leadership

High-performing health sector organisations have a vision of quality and compassionate care as their core purpose, which in turn is communicated from the top to the front line (West et al. 2015: 5). For some, stakeholder engagement with this vision will be facilitated by transformational or charismatic leadership. For others, engagement will be via a more devolved or distributed leadership style, where this fits the organisation's culture or business model. However, in most cases, there isn't a simple binary formula which favours one leadership style over another and 'a combination of horizontal, vertical, transformational and collective leadership and followership development may provide a blueprint against which to develop strong leadership within organizations' (Till et al. 2016). When leadership theory is converted into practice, there are multiple approaches, many variants, and a wide range of leadership frameworks (Kim et al. 2014; Kumar et al. 2015; Chan et al. 2015; Elwell 2015; Reichenpfader et al. 2015; Scully 2015; Dye 2017; Johnston et al. 2016). Given the broad spread of experience, the questions addressed by this chapter are about common underlying characteristics that are present

P. Turner, *Leadership in Healthcare*, Organizational Behaviour in Health Care,
https://doi.org/10.1007/978-3-030-04387-2_5

in the many leadership styles in health sector organisations and whether these can be crafted into a model adaptable to the different scenarios and contexts in which leadership is required and enacted.

In the first place, there is the consideration of those who are formally designated as leaders through their position and defined responsibilities. In the commercial health sector, for example, an organisation may be a corporation, company, partnership, or trust and will be overseen by a leadership team usually consisting of a Board of Directors, who provide the external link to shareholder/stakeholder interests whilst at the same time approving direction and strategy, complemented by Executive Leaders who are responsible for setting and implementing strategy and delivering performance through day-to-day operations. (McAlearney 2010) Executives hold formal leadership positions but are supported by other leaders who are not Board or Executive team members such as senior professionals in patient care, as well as those in managerial, technical, and administrative leadership roles. Similar principles apply to health sector organisations which are not-for-profit or public sector. In all cases, the organisation, a hierarchy, multi-agency, or matrix, will have processes in place to ensure that the levels of authority for policy decisions, people management, and financial control and authority are understood and practised in line with formal governance 'rules.' These are the formalities of formal leadership.

However, as outlined in previous chapters, there will also be devolved or informal practice whereby particular circumstances will require leadership action from someone who is not formally designated in a leadership role. Hence, in place of the formality, there will be tacit, devolved, or informal leadership. The implication here is that individuals who find themselves in situations requiring leadership action have both willingness and a skill set that allows them to make leadership decisions and a confidence that the organisation will back them once made. The diverse circumstances within which this kind of scenario could take place means that leaders, either through formal or informal positions, are likely to have a fusion of characteristics, behaviours, and skills. Furthermore, the obfuscation that exists between leadership and managerial roles, since the unresolved debate means that distinctions between management and leadership at levels other than Board or Executive remain blurred (Reichenpfader et al. 2015), adds to this fusion—and also confusion.

However, the environment that facilitates effective leadership action will be one of shared understanding and values, a sense of purpose and trusting relationships in a framework of structure (vision and goals), people (investing and empowering), political considerations, and symbolism (Farrell 2003; Moen and Prescott 2016; Popescu and Predescu 2016: 273). These are constant leadership aspirations.

To understand better how the various models and layers of leadership work, four possible situations might be considered. These are leadership at Board level, Executive Leadership, Clinical Leadership, and Leadership in devolved or distributed situations.

Leadership at Board Level: Governance, Strategy, Stewardship, and Policy

Complexity in the health sector environment, increasing scrutiny on improving performance in quality and patient outcomes, and market and regulatory forces precipitating higher levels of accountability (Curran and Totten 2010; Prybil et al. 2014) have reinforced the need for effective governance in health sector organisations. Numerous international frameworks have been proposed for ensuring this in health systems by the WHO's domains of stewardship, Pan American Health Organization's essential public health functions, the World Bank's six basic aspects of governance, and the United Nations Development Programme's principles of good governance (Siddiqi et al. 2009). There is a similar focus at organisational or health sector operating at unit level, because effective governance has been positively associated with better performance. The governance entity in the operating unit will also be the Board, the leaders of which will have responsibility for setting and delivering to objectives in a way that sustains integrity in the delivery of high-quality care in an environment in which strategic and operational performance is backed up by clinical excellence and in which diversity flourishes (Langabeer and Galeener 2008; Carol et al. 2013: 667; McBride 2017: 373). Whatever the governance framework, the Board is most effective when those in leadership positions bring to life the organisation's vision and values through their actions;

> when they listen to patient voices as the most important sources of feedback on organisational performance; and when they listen to staff voices to discover how they can best support and enable staff to provide high quality patient care. Effective boards ensure a positive culture; sense problems before they happen and improve organisational functioning; promote staff participation and proactivity; enable and encourage responsible innovation by staff; and engage external stakeholders effectively to develop cooperative relationships across boundaries. (West et al. 2015: 3)

Hence the leadership role of those on health sector Boards has both high-level policy ('viewing the organisation from the balcony is essential in order to see what is going on' (Deffenbaugh 2015: 308)) and practice elements which will be adapted and fit to the organisation's context.

There are a range of governance ideologies based on different internal dynamics, business and operational processes, and levels of engagement. Governance Boards are set up to ensure positive values and a positive culture of safety in which success depends on effective cooperation between the Board of Directors, the CEO or management, and the hospital's medical staff. In addition, Health Boards facilitate the creation of effectiveness through performance, conformance, and a responsible approach between key groups that comprise the internal organisation of specific units such as hospitals, that is, physicians, nurses, management, and trustees, who have the same overall goal of compassionate and effective care, but they may have diverse views about resource management and allocation to achieve this goal (Glouberman and Mintzberg 2001a, b; Veronesi and Keasey 2012; Cardinaels and Soderstrom 2013; MacLeod 2015; Deschamps et al. 2016). The solution to the complexity will be coordination and collaboration, both of which can be facilitated by effective Board-level leadership in a cooperative, trusting environment (Veronesi and Keasey 2012). Where Board-level governance and leadership are effective, there are positive 'operational' outcomes and results (Veronesi and Keasey 2012; Pirozek et al. 2015: 1093). Health Boards hold these assumptions in common with other sectors, but there are added dimensions which stem from different stakeholder expectations and legislative frameworks and because of the complexity of the sector's organisations and social systems (Kirkpatrick et al. 2013). Such governance may include shareholder financial interests but also the interests of the state or wider stakeholder needs. Those in Board and Executive positions will require leadership capability related to the dynamics of the organisation for which they have oversight and the ability to apply these to enhance this environment.

Executive Leadership: Vision, Strategy, Prioritisation, and Resource Allocation

Amongst the key challenges of health sector Executives are clarifying objectives, agreeing strategies to meet them, engaging the workforce in their delivery by encouraging individual accountability, and finally allocating sufficient resources for the achievement of the strategy. Executive Leaders are responsible for the culture within which these will be delivered including 'inspiring visions operationalised at every level; clear, aligned objectives for all teams, departments and individual staff; supportive and enabling people management and high levels of staff engagement; learning, innovation and quality improvement embedded in the practice of all staff; (and) effective team working' (West et al. 2015: 5). Effective leadership equates to effective people management which in turn has a positive effect on employee perceptions and interpretations and will facilitate the alignment of the workforce to the organisation's strategic outcomes (Choo et al. 2010; Pereira and Gomes 2012: 4301; West et al. 2015).

This is especially appropriate to the health sector environment because health units are complex organisations and Executive decisions can have significant implications for patient care and safety, innovativeness in responding to health sector challenges, and financial well-being (Alam et al. 2016; Hawkins 2016). Executive Leader responsibilities are a balancing act in allocating resource between clinical priorities and broader organisational ones. One of the important roles of the health sector Executive Leader therefore is to bring together the 'logics of management and medicine' to ensure that Triple Aim objectives, that is, the provision of better care experience and improved population health at a lower cost, are met efficiently. If the leader can articulate a vision for the organisation, clarity about role and purpose to achieve it, and an alignment of the leadership practices of health managers behind it, this will have a positive impact on a range of performance indicators (Gulati et al. 2016; Kim and Thompson 2012: 113). However, whilst the logic may be sound, the paradoxes contained when it is converted into practice bring challenges brought about by the 'classic professional divides' (Storkholm et al. 2017). In this respect, Executive Leaders face the challenge of allocating their limited resources in a way that ensures high quality of care is given equitably and efficiently, which means that the management of healthcare facilities is multidisciplinary, requiring the involvement of clinicians, nurses, allied health professionals, and those responsible for providing support services such as from finance to HR and IT, all focused on performance excellence (Levey et al. 2002; Dalmas 2012).

Executives will be in a better position to deliver to their objectives if they have an understanding of the particular context and dynamics of the organisation for which they have responsibility. In addition, and because of the intensely professional nature of the sector in which they operate, health sector Executives will also need to have credibility in the eyes of clinical, managerial, and technical colleagues. They hold these requirements in common with those at Board level.

Clinical Leadership: The Patient at the Centre

A specific challenge in the health sector is to balance clinical and operational (business, cost management, administrative or technical process) needs, and it is this aspect of leadership that separates the sector from others. Indeed, it has been argued that it is important that leaders in healthcare bring an understanding of both the clinical and organisational world. In this respect, all clinicians take on leadership responsibilities when delivering care and will be expected to act as stewards of the healthcare system (Baldwin et al. 2011: 66; Blumenthal et al. 2012; Gauld 2017), and clinical leadership 'at the point of service is now recognised as a central professional competency to ensure quality patient care and patient safety' (Grindel 2016: 9). Clinical leadership is putting physicians at the heart of shaping and running clinical services so as to deliver excellent outcomes for patients and populations, not as a one-off task or project, but as a core part of a clinician's professional identity. It may be interpreted in its broadest form to include all professionals: doctors, nurses, and allied care providers. There is a defined need for clinical leaders to demonstrate the versatility to work with diverse disciplines and respond to changing environments (Ezziane 2012; Khoshal and Guraya 2016; Gauld 2017; Saravo et al. 2017). The challenge here is to clarify the role of the clinical leader, identifying appropriate concepts and adjusting them to the clinical environment.

Clinical leadership occurs where clinical professionals take on the roles of leadership including 'setting, inspiring and promoting values and vision, and using their clinical experience and skills to ensure the needs of the patient are the central focus to the organisation's aims and delivery' (Taylor and Martindale 2013). Recognising, however, that rather than a set of scientific procedures, leadership is context dependent (Gauld 2017: 5). Nevertheless clinical leaders operate most effectively in a system of collegiality identified with other professional organisations (Ham 2003). How does this manifest in practice and how to ensure role clarity for clinical leaders?

A comprehensive review concluded that most studies did not explicitly define the concept of medical or clinical leadership. Implicitly, these leaders were described as champions, key physicians, team-oriented change agents, and visionaries. In the study, physicians had multiple functions in addition to their clinical roles,

> committed to hospital success and able to influence and inspire their colleagues. Only two studies provided an explicit definition of medical leadership, describing it as embodied by a practitioner who operates as an opinion—leader or even as a particular school of thought within medicine and physicians in leading positions. Although many researchers did not define medical leadership, they *did* underscore the need for a clear definition. (Berghout et al. 2017: 8)

Nevertheless, the study identified two types of medical leadership definitions or conceptualisations. These were, firstly, medical leadership which included physicians working in formal leadership roles, defined as medical managers who work at either the management or executive level in addition to or instead of their clinical practice. The second type were those including physicians in informal leadership roles at the clinical level, that is, those who acted as leaders within their daily clinical practice. The research also found that irrespective of which type of role, there were two activity 'sets'—on the one hand, a broad range of general management and leadership activities, but on the other activities that balanced between management and medical objectives.

The ambiguity in the role raises issues about the scope of clinical leadership, its core competences, and how it interfaces or overlaps with other leadership theories in both concept and practice. For some, this means 'physicians are expected to formulate clear expectations, set high standards and motivate team members to make strides to meet specific requirements' (Saravo et al. 2017: 3). They not only act as clinical experts but must also demonstrate emotional intelligence and engage others to act. Their core knowledge not only includes an understanding of patient safety goals and the critical appraisal of clinical evidence but an understanding of how to work through organisational systems and processes in the creation of healthy practice environments. The '3 C's of communication, collaboration and coordination rank highly in the ability to be a clinical leader'. Amongst the competences are emotional intelligence, coaching and mentoring, resolving conflict collaborating, managing change and leading teams (Grindel 2016: 9–13), which may be regarded as fundamental leadership skills. A New Zealand-based study concluded that 'clinical leadership requires the ability to work with professional colleagues from across the organisation and its different disciplines' (Gauld 2017: 5). These findings imply that clinical leadership is a combination of excellence and professionalism in a clinical or medical specialism but also the ability to engage with wider non-clinical organisational activities. Those in clinical leadership positions build on technical strengths and develop competences.

Case Study: Clinical Leadership in the European Health Sector

Dr Niki Kyriakidou, Senior Lecturer in HRM, Senior Lecturer, Leeds Business School; Research Chair, International HRM; EuroMed Research Business Institute

Mr Kostas Papagiannopoulos, mmed thorax, md (cth)

The European health sector is undergoing significant transformation (Enock and Markwell 2010; Veronesi et al. 2013), and the resulting complexity has led to an increased focus on leadership at all levels.

Health sector leaders can have a positive effect on a range of outcomes relating to communities as a whole, patients, and employees (Kirkpatrick et al. 2016; Mountford and Webb 2009). But the definition of health sector leadership has many interpretations. There are those in business, operational, or managerial roles and those who lead health professionals in the delivery of care. The latter area is one of clinical leadership, and it is important to have both role clarity and the right set of competences if those in such leadership positions are going to deliver their objectives. However, empirical evidence shows that the engagement of clinicians in hospital management and leadership in terms of hospital performance varies across countries: 26.03% of Board members in the UK have clinical background and 22% of Chief Executive Officers in hospitals have clinical background (Veronesi et al. 2013).

A comparative European research conducted in 2010 in regard to the role of doctors in senior management demonstrates that doctors represent a majority of the senior managers in the European health system with 50% in Italy, 63% in France, and 71% in Germany. Engaging more doctors in leadership positions has been found to improve effectiveness and efficiency of hospitals along some performance indicators (Veronesi et al. 2013, 2018; The King's Fund 2011; Hamilton et al. 2008).

The European clinical leadership case shows the impact of doctors may have in their medical practice when they exercise their qualities in leading their staff as part of their practice and promoting change within their health organisations. A clinical leader may become a potent force and holds wide appeal in reforming policy-makers. The majority of hospitals globally have taken into consideration the role of Clinical Director; in such managerial responsibilities relating to financial and human resources are given to a clinician, who is also accountable for the performance of the Directorate (Kirkpatrick et al. 2016). A common assumption across various healthcare systems is that the greater involvement of clinicians in the roles of management and governance would enhance effectiveness and efficiency of healthcare organisations (Veronesi et al. 2018).

Additionally, clinical leaders' innovative practices may result in a great cultural shift of main stakeholders involved in managing health conditions, developing services, and helping to shape learning and development, as clinicians, managers, and commissioners. As such, clinical leaders can exercise leadership qualities, manage talent within the hospital, and make informed decisions since they have expert knowledge at the core of the health organisation they are operating.

Most recruiters when they try to identify talented managers to lead traditionally focus on competencies, knowledge, skills, and qualifications as these are generally easier to articulate, identify, and measure. Some qualitative studies have pointed out that the major factors that are related to the improvement of hospital performance are physician engagement, leadership, culture, strategy, structure, good communication, training, skills, and information (Brand et al. 2012). However, values, personality traits, organisational behaviours, and motivational drivers are equally of value to identify talents. As complexity in healthcare increases, European Health Management Systems require leaders who can identify needs and current challenges in their practice, shift and adapt quickly, are resourceful and effective, thrive on organisational change, inspire others, and can make sense out of uncertainty and resistance to change for those they lead.

A clinical leader needs to possess several skills and attitudes in order to be effective.

Clinical skills are of paramount importance combined with the ability to exercise such with elegance and common sense. We need to remember that the ability to persuade others to follow 'visions' requires a raw model.

Empathy and emotional intelligence are important values. It is the ability to communicate with colleagues, key stakeholders, and end users who are the patients. A developed emotional intelligence allows effectiveness in difficult financial and organisational circumstances. It protects from irrational decisions and buffers emotional outbursts from team members steering the Directorate into the right direction while keeping the satisfaction levels adequate for members to perform.

The charismatic leader has the ability to identify good values within members of the team, promote such for the benefit of the whole unit and service, and cultivate such in a constant and progressive manner.

Communication skills remain of paramount importance. But these go further than simply been pleasant. It is the ability to 'read' humans, engage in multiple levels, and have the charisma to diversify depending on individual circumstances and situations.

Effective Clinical Directors have the ability to see the 'big picture,' look deep in the future, and even shape it but been able to be flexible at the same time.

This specific attitude separates those who simply succeed in developing a service element from those who succeed in giving life to an ever-expanding service; a service which adapts to the local needs of the patients, has the ability to continue to expand, draws constant interest from key stakeholders, remains attractive for new employees, and highlights everyone's good values hence encourages all to contribute and work smarter.

The need for a modern clinical leader is more than obvious in all healthcare systems. Such need will only be satisfied if modern healthcare systems have the ability to:

1. identify future leaders at undergraduate level
2. provide training opportunities for future clinical leaders
3. empower such leaders within health organisations and most of all
4. encourage such to perform with genuine support

Devolved Leadership: Distribution of Leadership Responsibility

The lack of a precise definition of leadership and the overlaps with more traditional definitions of management present a 'conceptual inconsistency' (Reichenpfader et al. 2015: 309) which has to be dealt with in any overview of the subject. However, there is increasing acceptance that leadership is not only based on the actions of a few people at the top of organisations. Instead, leadership may be viewed as a non-hierarchical activity. Indeed, 'contemporary leadership models … in health care organisations have shifted from hierarchical command and control models to those based on influential relationships that require different interactions between the nurse manager and members of the team' (Gilbert et al. 2017: 699). Such an assumption provides the foundation for the incidence of devolved or distributed leadership. The changing nature of organisational structures such as the replacement of hierarchy with matrices or networks, as outlined earlier, means that leadership activity will exist at several levels or at different nodes on the network. Formally acknowledging this fact by extending the nomination of leaders beyond the Board or Executive team creates a new type of leadership situation. Such a view is the antithesis to the 'preoccupation of most Western writers about leadership, with the position reified in single individuals—usually those at the top of the organisation' (Thorpe et al. 2011: 239). Devolved leadership can take place in a formal context by extending the scope of those covered by the leadership nomenclature or policy; or it can take place informally by dint of the fact that leadership is a response to a circumstance or situation regardless of job role or title.

The type of devolved leadership is recognition that any person can commit an act of leadership, and the sum total of leadership in a unit is the aggregation of such acts. The second recognises emergent and holistic patterns of leadership whereby in some cases leadership passes from one individual to another and as such becomes stretched across several contexts. 'There can be little planning for such practices' (Thorpe et al. 2011: 245). In these situations, individuals at multiple levels will have leadership inclination, willingness, and capability which will include, in addition to the expected professionalism or technical competence, the skills of motivation, innovation, the ability to communicate, resilience, and the utilisation of networks of supporters and affiliates—which adds legitimacy to the leadership role. High-performance leadership requires both technical and behavioural skills from clinical care to delivering the service and managing people, and where leadership teams are in place, there will be a range of skills to complement these from technical and administrative to health professionalism (Vinot 2014; Wang et al. 2014; Valori and Johnston 2016; Green et al. 2016). These will include the creation of a shared purpose, role clarity; communication as to why the leadership activity has taken place—perhaps in the absence of formal policy; and flexibility and adaptability to the situation, a point which was reinforced by a study in France, amongst others, which noted that there had been a shift from a model emphasising the position of an individual leader holding power over a team 'towards one emphasising a network in which responsibilities and decision making are distributed more widely and are subject to negotiation' (Vinot 2014: 408). Such distribution requires more people in the organisation to be prepared to take on leadership responsibilities. Their legitimacy in such situations will come from relationships with the organisation's communities, credibility because of prior (clinical or technical) performance, or a level of respect amongst the workforce that precipitates engagement with the direction or goals identified.

Common Elements in Health Sector Leadership: 'An Intricate Fusion of Characteristics, Conducts and Skills'

The above examples reinforce the point of view that 'to be a successful leader demands an intricate fusion of characteristics, conducts and skills' based on forming and sustaining productive relationships regardless of roles and status (Popescu and Predescu 2016: 273). But throughout this complexity, it is also possible to identify common threads or strains that permeate leadership styles. Self-knowledge and awareness, for example, is

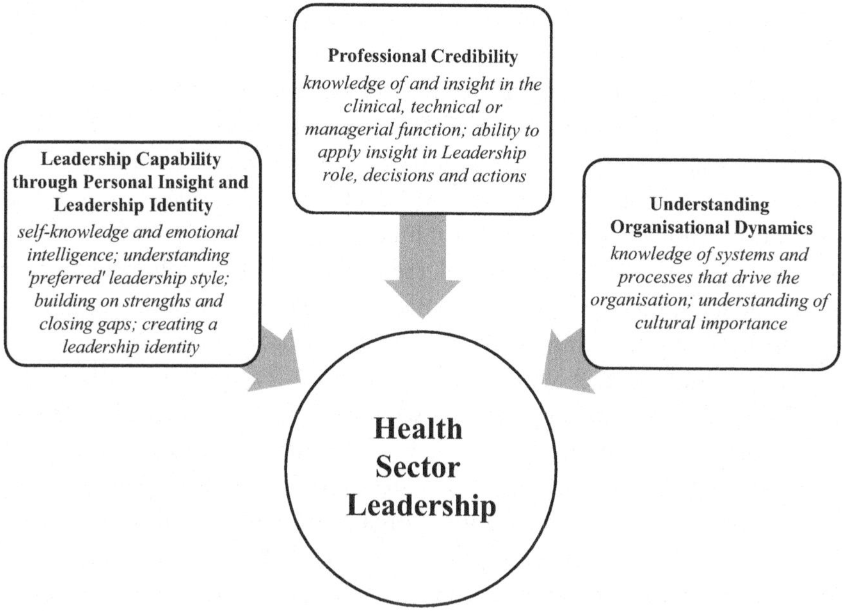

Fig. 5.1 The characteristics of health sector leadership

something that has featured in leadership narratives: the need for ability of the leader to take account of the unique context of health in decision-making and an ability to work within an organisation; understanding its forces and power bases would appear to be further criteria for successful leadership in health. The interpretation of the precise requirements of each would of course depend on the context of the organisation within which leadership activity was taking place. Figure 5.1 shows three areas which are important in understanding leadership requirements and a broad definition of some of their characteristics. It remains to develop these concepts more with a view to providing insights as to how leaders in the sector can be assessed and developed. The following narrative summarises the areas and subsequent chapters will provide more detail on the requirements in each.

The first is developing leadership capability through personal insight and the creation of a 'leadership identity.' This begins with an understanding, on the part of the leader, of the requirements of leadership, her or his abilities to meet these, and areas in which further professional leadership development will be required. Amongst the important aspects of this will be emotional intelligence and awareness, empathy, and the ability to engage and communicate. The second common thread that runs through health sector leadership is that of professional credibility which will need to be demonstrated in whichever leadership role is undertaken (medical, clinical, professional, or managerial) if followership is to be secured. The level of professional credibility, whilst applying in other commercial or business sectors, is a particular aspect of health sector leadership that requires emphasis. The third common thread is that of an understanding of the organisation's dynamics, a leadership skill that applies across all leadership activity, whatever the sector. If the health sector leader is to negotiate her or his way through organisational systems and processes in order to secure resource to deliver unit or departmental objectives, then an understanding of organisational dynamics and behaviour is critical. This isn't to say that the knowledge will be used to perpetuate the status quo but to ensure the best ways of delivering objectives in what are mostly complex and dynamic structures.

Leadership Capability Through Personal Insight and the Creation of a Leadership Identity

Marshall Goldsmith's (2008: 13) 'simple but brutal regime' for improving the effectiveness of leaders in the workplace began with individuals gaining a comprehensive assessment of their strengths and weaknesses by eliciting feedback (normally through 360-degree processes). 'For us to have integrity as leaders, we have to continue to work to know who we are as we relate to our work' (Size 2006: 73). The accumulation of self-knowledge, interpreting the implications of the findings on leadership behaviour and understanding how these can be applied, is the starting point in developing a model for leadership, and personal insight is common to all leadership styles. In practice, this means that leaders are aware of their personal impact on others and how their beliefs, values, and behaviours affect the perception (and performance) of others. They will have understanding about where they have strengths and will build on these but will also recognise limitations and either work to improve these or facilitate others to fill the gaps. Whilst desired leadership traits might be articulated as honesty, the ability to motivate others, a positive attitude, effective communication skills, the ability to work effectively in a team, social skills and emotional intelligence are also critical. This means effective interpersonal skills and to be able to build good working relationships with colleagues and others within and outside the professional area at all levels (Yielder 2006; Shariff 2015). Personal insight as to the reality of an individual's capability and the willingness to utilise and develop this through the creation of a leadership identity are important foundations on which to build effective leadership.

Much of this requirement is contained within the concept of emotional intelligence and is mostly used to describe the ability or skill to understand and manage emotions in oneself and, in the case of health sector leaders, to use this in the direction of others. Emotional intelligence has been identified as a core competence and includes self-awareness, social skills, self-regulation, and social awareness (Ezziane 2012; Ohlson and Anderson 2015; Foster et al. 2017). The outcome of such intelligence is an empathetic approach which is incorporated into the leadership style and used in relationships within the sphere of responsibility and with people outside, such as in networks or supply chains. Emotional intelligence will also help the leader to be sensitive across to the requirements and nuances of different cultures. A recent study of nurse leadership concluded that leaders had to be 'sympathetic to individual differences and use communication as an essential tool in the work process so that the members of the team feel a balance of power, being cared for instead of controlled or manipulated' (Silva et al. 2017: 5). It follows that personal insight, leading to greater emotional intelligence, will contribute to a leadership style that is appropriate to the context. But personal insight goes beyond the single attribute of emotional intelligence. It is a fundamental process of an individual in a leadership position understanding their own strengths and weaknesses and in so doing responding in a way which utilises the strengths that are right for the context or fills any gaps in leadership capability through the strengths of others or through self-development.

Professional Credibility: *Knowledge of the Clinical, Technical, or Managerial Function*

The importance of professional credibility to the health sector leader is the second 'common' thread. In a general sense, leadership of extremely skilled and clever people requires different leadership approaches and a different psychological relationship (Goffee and Jones 2007) in creating an environment in which people are inspired to achieve their fullest potential in a way that produces value for stakeholders. This assumption resonates in health. Studies of professional leaders (in, e.g. East Africa, Australia, and Finland) included competences such as being able to influence, being visionary and inspiring a shared vision, having negotiation skills that generate win-win solutions, and being politically astute—but also, in a policy setting environment, being able to articulate health issues of concern in respect of policy development and to be effective communicators who could articulate health policy-related issues. In addition, expert knowledge could be used to influence strategy in an effective way because of a professional perspective on the operating environment; it could be used to create an optimal work environment because goal setting, evaluation, and support would be based on professional insights including 'clinical and scientific dispositions that was manifested through an investigative, non-judging, analytic stance' and a focus on evidence-based practice to the overall leadership role. Professional credibility would combine competence areas such as communication and influencing skills and competences in research, political, and legal issues (Shariff 2015; Goodall 2016; Lalleman et al. 2016; Kantanen et al. 2017). Professional credibility can add to the process of defining a vision, as well as facilitating collaboration and influence during this process (Kelly et al. 2008; Bussières et al. 2017). There are challenges of course in balancing the professional role with that of other leadership demands, and a study in the UK found that professional self-identification was strong in the transition to a leadership role (Divall 2015).

Professional credibility is an important characteristic when considering ethical and legal issues in health or understanding and interpreting specific issues as they relate to the sector or translating complex requirements into the specific needs of the department or unit. Professional understanding is often essential in inspiring or influencing others in the professional area. As Henry Mintzberg has written:

> Look to the people on the ground, not outside experts, for ideas for real improvements. Administrators, economists, and consultants who believe they understand problems conceptually should not be imposing solutions on the clinicians of all kinds who have to deal with problems tangibly. The latter must often take the lead—working with the former—on developing solutions. (Mintzberg 2011)

There is a compelling case for professional credibility in the leadership role in health sector organisations. This applies to those in clinical leadership, those in business or operational leadership roles, and those in specialist professional or technical roles. The concept spans a broad range of 'managerial' and 'medical' roles and situations.

Understanding Organisational Dynamics

The efforts of individuals in leadership positions to influence the psychosocial, technical, political, economic, and other features of the organization are often multidimensional and multidirectional (Kilburg and Donohue 2011: 12); and health sector organisations provide dynamics and challenges that need to be both understood and managed within this context if wider objectives are to be achieved. These dynamics can be structural (complex organisational design; lack of clear accountability across functions for common objectives) or social in the form of 'social defences' as individuals 'negotiate dominant discourses in the construction of identity and self' (Doolin 2002: 369; Stevenson 2015). In order to craft a way through these and ultimately harness them to a desired end state, understanding organisational dynamics will be a critical component of health sector leadership. High levels of charisma or transformational visions, or a deep understanding of professional matters, may not, alone, be able to deliver. This is because of the complexity of human relationships across psychological, social, political, and economic features, an assumption that applies equally to leadership at Board or Executive level and in devolved or distributed leadership activities on the other. There are numerous examples to illustrate the point.

For example, the role of transformational leadership in continuous quality improvement (CQI) was enhanced when leadership was accompanied by the ability to align the organisation's strategy and structure to create the organisational learning necessary to achieve the paradigm shift. An organisational structure with specialist departments and internal processes designed to support one professional group was less effective than a programme-based structure which facilitated working between departments and diminished 'the discipline-based constraints that are characteristic of the traditional hospital structure. Since CQI was more compatible with a program-based structure, its implementation has a more favourable prognosis in hospitals where functional walls were removed' (LeBrasseur et al. 2002: 146). To move from one position to a new ideal required not only the traditional attributes of leaders, such as effective communication and engagement skills, but an understanding of the dynamics of organisational structures, how these worked for or against a particular health project, and how leadership could read the organisation, identify what was necessary for change, and craft new ideas accordingly. Furthermore, a study to define globally relevant competences specific to health professionals concluded that, in addition to resource deployment, personal and team development skills, 'professionals must be equipped with the tools and knowledge around quality improvement process and a perspective across wider healthcare systems' (Turner et al. 2017: 331). Amongst the 'essential components' that are needed to develop a model of leadership for health is an understanding of 'the organizational systems—structures, processes, contents, and internal situations—of the organization' (Kilburg and Donohue 2011: 15). Recognising this is an important characteristic that can be identified as a theme that runs through much of the research into health sector leadership. Understanding organisational dynamics is a critical factor for success. It will allow the leader to influence both ideology and policy; it will allow her or him to contribute a vision in a way and language that will be understood; and it will allow the leader to ensure that as the strategy flows out it will match and steer the culture of the organisation, embracing and engaging multiple stakeholders along the way.

A Leadership Competency Framework for Senior Leaders, Executives, and Managers in Health Sector Organisations

Although competency frameworks have been subject to some criticism based on the observation that they don't take enough account of contextual factors, they remain a dominant method in leadership assessment and development. Recognising that such frameworks are 'flexible and complex and vary according to the demands of a particular business strategy of an organisation' (Kovačič and Rus 2015: 12) will allow an organisation to develop ones that are best fit. For example, there are a number of competence frameworks in use in the British healthcare sector which cover a range of applications with the benefits outweighing any challenges as long as the 'framework demonstrates the benefits of integrating the competences with other measures to deliver a new service' (Mitchell and Boak 2009: 701). A comprehensive study of leadership competences in a health context across Europe (Czabanowska et al. 2014) demonstrated the diversity of views about leadership, the potential complexity of identifying relevant competences against which leaders might be assessed, and the criticality of synthesising the diverse views into competences that were relevant to a specific organisation in its unique context. In Finland, leadership competences were categorised as healthcare context-related, operational, and general (Pihlainen et al. 2016). And studies of leadership competency frameworks have been undertaken in a wide range of geographies (see inter alia Garman and Scribner 2011; Rick 2014; American Medical Association 2015). The Health Leadership Competency Model (HLCM) was adopted in the USA as an 'evidence-based and behaviourally focused approach for evaluating leadership skills across the professions, including health management, medicine, and nursing, and across career stages' (Calhoun et al. 2008). Adapting a competency framework to fit the proposed model for leadership in health means using the generic groupings of competences around the three areas of the model as follows.

The first such grouping concerns leadership capability. This aspect of health leadership will require the leader to reflect on her or his particular leadership style and either use this to the advantage of the organisation where it is aligned to the organisation's strategy or to adapt it in response to the factors that prevail. Hence the need for competences that are concerned with the ability to reflect, to demonstrate emotional intelligence, and to have a flexible approach to the environment is important. Indeed, some have argued that

> organizations that avoid open meaningful dialogue and lack supportive infrastructure need to be transformed. To advocate for safe patient care, interactional justice needs to be part of leadership practices and decisions. This along with incorporating resonant skills of empathy, relating, listening and responding to concerns, will create an atmosphere of trust and respect which facilitates open dialogue. (Squires et al. 2010: 922)

These are precursors to the more established leadership competences of having a vision and creating a purpose for the organisation, of the ability to develop and deliver strategy, and of the ability to mobilise and engage a health sector workforce. The second group of competences relates to professional credibility which is increasingly important with the adoption of integrated healthcare and its adjunct integrated leadership. In bridging the managerial and medical logics outlined earlier, professional credibility improves the chances of the leader of the health organisation to create value by combining these different logics. So, whilst professional credibility might mean acting as an authoritative source of knowledge on medical professionalism, it also means applying this leverage to broader strategic questions. Finally, neither leadership capability nor professional credibility will be useful unless the leader is able to put these into effect for the overall good of the organisation's stakeholders. It is these areas that an understanding organisational dynamics is an important competence ranging from an understanding of the requirements of the Board of Directors to the nature of the organisation's politics to the ability to mobilise human and practical resources. There are a wide range of sources that can provide insights into each of these areas, and these have been used in compiling the competency framework in Table 5.1.

Table 5.1 A leadership competency framework for Senior Leaders, Executives, and Managers in health sector organisations

Leadership criteria	Competency
Leadership capability through personal insight and leadership identity	1. Creates meaning for the organisation, its strategy, and individual roles 2. Translates broad strategy into practical actions; has ability in 'knowing-interpreting' 3. Develops and implements 'strategies to align stakeholders to organizational mission and vision' 4. Operates effectively across networks and boundaries 5. Identifies opportunities for growth and development of the organisation—drives for results 6. Acts as a force for change and understands the dynamics of change 7. Shapes and engages actively to generate situations and opportunities for change 8. Mobilises the potential and capacities of members of the organisation as a whole or individual departments/teams 9. Engages and motivates a broad section of the health workforce—understands the importance of followership 10. Assesses and acts on factors that 'contribute to or impede individual, team, or organizational success' 11. Acts as advocate, influences policy, and negotiates resources to deliver strategy 12. Performs well in a VUCA environment—able to take decisions, in spite of ambiguity 13. Anticipates impact of decisions and plans accordingly 14. Prioritises clinical outcomes amongst competing objectives 15. Empowers others; develops and mentors to 'create a strong team with diverse skills and perspectives' 16. Develops successors to ensure either continuity or change of strategy, stewardship, and policy 17. Shares critical information and seek input from employees 18. Acts as a role model for multicultural and diversity leadership 19. Demonstrates emotional intelligence and impact of actions on others 20. Awareness of existing perceived leadership 'style' and the perceived required leadership style determined by the context of the organisation 21. Able to mediate leadership identity using insight and hindsight to adapt leadership behaviour 22. Acts with integrity; is authentic, reliable, truthful, and transparent as a means of earning trust and respect 23. Adopts a collaborative style

(*continued*)

Table 5.1 (continued)

Leadership criteria	Competency
Professional credibility	24. Creates an integrated leadership model and shares management responsibilities and accountabilities across clinical and business or administrative decision-making 25. Establishes professional contacts and networks with experts outside the organisation 26. Provides an authoritative source of advice to professional colleagues 27. Encourages a high level of ethical behaviour and commitment to the professional values of the organisation 28. Balances the ethics of care to the individual with care to the community 29. Acts as role model for professional leadership in clinical and medical disciplines 30. Understands the core elements of medical professionalism 31. Understands the fundamentals of the care delivery process including how physicians make clinical decisions 32. Practises and promotes professional accountability and responsibility 33. Demonstrates commitment to professional welfare in the form of 'mentoring-nurturing' colleagues 34. Identifies innovations, new methods, technologies, or opportunities for the delivery of healthcare 35. Provides collaborative leadership and builds interdisciplinary teams—works collaboratively to maximise patient care 36. Actively seeks and is able to acquire new knowledge 37. Creates value by combining clinical, medical, and managerial logics 38. Achieves unity of purpose by integrating performance and interprofessional collaboration 39. Builds alliances and partnerships with clinical, medical, and managerial colleagues to ensure effective outcomes 40. Understands patient and consumer healthcare expectations and requirements 41. Understands the importance of clinical integration and coordination of care 42. Uses both professional intuition and evidence-based outcomes in decision-making 43. Applies both professional or managerial competence to organisational challenges

(continued)

Table 5.1 (continued)

Leadership criteria	Competency
Understanding organisational dynamics	44. Understands and is able to inspire a vision that is operationalised at every level 45. Works across organisations and agencies in the achievement of own organisation's objectives 46. Understands implications of working with boards and within governance structures 47. Aligns strategy to organisation and organisation to strategy 48. Sets 'clear, aligned objectives for all teams, departments and individual staff' 49. Promotes a sense of common ownership of the organisation and its reputation 50. Identifies strategies for initiating, sustaining, and organising change—fosters positive change 51. Manages the processes of influence that can impact on the change including organisational politics 52. Creates a work environment that supports innovation, risk taking, and ownership of professional practice 53. Collaborates to drive system change and is resilient in its delivery 54. Sets a positive team climate 55. Engages in dialogue to solve disputes and to solve critical problems 56. Integrates divergent viewpoints for the good of the organisation as a whole 57. Understands that collective action is a critical success factor 58. Understands the need for connection, as well as sharing of information in an uncertain (VUCA) environment 59. Provides leadership to multiple groupings simultaneously—organisation as a whole, teams, and individuals 60. Provides leadership across interdisciplinary teams 61. Is sensitive to and understands leadership of diverse cultures and disciplines—acts as cultural role model 62. Ensures that plans and actions remain flexible to take account of the needs and work commitments of others 63. Understands and explains financial, accounting, and other performance or business measures

Sources: Wolf 2008; Mitchell and Boak 2009; NHS 2010; Garman and Scribner 2011; Lehr et al. 2011; Hatler and Sturgeon 2013; Stempniak 2013; Czabanowska et al. 2014; Day et al. 2014; Hlupic 2014; Poikkeus et al. 2014; Rick 2014; Dauvrin and Lorant 2015; American Medical Association 2015; Fernandez et al. 2015; Humphreys et al. 2015; Kantanen et al. 2017; Kovačič and Rus 2015; Love and Ayadi 2015; Rosenman et al. 2015; West et al. 2015; Ang et al. 2016; Leenstra et al. 2016; White et al. 2016; Patnaik et al. 2017

The application of this framework will depend on the unique context of a health sector organisation and the strategy that it has adopted. For some there will be an emphasis on leadership capability. An example of this might occur because of the succession plan at Board level and the need for replacements over time. If the 'preferred' candidates are from a professional background with little experience working at Board level, then the emphasis will be on leadership skills. On the other hand, if the candidate has both leadership potential and capability and has the credibility from within a professional specialism, then the emphasis will be on developing organisational skills. There is no best practice combination of which competences are required but a best fit of competences to match the uniqueness of the organisation and its environment.

Conclusion and Implications for Practice

There are a large number of theories of leadership, and in the health sector (as others), the lens of leadership is kaleidoscopic in which fragments of colour come together in different forms depending on the angle and trajectory of the leadership lens. Making sense out of such fragmentation and trying to derive a 'grand unifying theory' is a complex task. The contextual nature of leadership adds to the challenge, and in the health sector with its multivariate organisational forms and occasionally Byzantine processes, the challenge is doubly difficult. Leadership is serious and critical to the success of health sector organisations, and hence this chapter has tried to make some sense out of the multiplicity of ideas. In this respect three messages stand out and these have gone to form the model for leadership outlined above.

- Firstly, **it is incumbent on those in leadership positions to be very clear about their own strengths and weaknesses**. This is the foundation upon which all leadership activity rests. The transformational or charismatic leader will complement motivation and engagement skills with analytic capability. The transactional leader who deals in trade-offs to achieve change will recognise that communication and engagement are more than a series of give-and-take transactions. In some cases, this will mean leader or leadership development. In others it will be appointing teams which are multi-faceted and skilled. This self-analysis will be necessary at all levels of the organisation because leadership is contextual. Those not appointed into formal leadership roles will have as much need for personal insight as the Chief Executive.

- Secondly, **those in leadership positions in health sector organisations will require professional credibility if they are to be successful**. Professional credibility means that policy contributions or decisions will be informed by the unique contexts of health and that followers will be more inclined to undertake actions to meet the organisation's objectives, believing that they have been set by people with the knowledge, skills, and attitudes to do so. Professional credibility will be necessary in the dialogue with external stakeholders whether these be shareholders, trustees, or regional or national governments.
- Finally, **understanding and working with the dynamics of the organisation is a characteristic that will apply to most leadership styles or models**. Complex organisational structures in which multi-dimensional processes are made effective by diverse professions with different expectations and outcomes and in which external expectations are those of the highest levels of excellence and performance will in turn require leadership of the highest standard. Understanding such dynamics is a prerequisite of health sector leaders.

These three characteristics can be identified in many of the leadership theories that apply to health sector organisations, and understanding them in more detail will be of value in building the model of leadership.

References

Alam, M. G. R., Masum, A. K. M., Beh, L.-S., & Hong, C. S. (2016). Critical Factors Influencing Decision to Adopt Human Resource Information System (HRIS) in Hospitals. *PLoS One, 11*(8), e0160366. ISSN:1932-6203.

American Medical Association. (2015). *Integrated Leadership for Hospitals and Health Systems: Principles for Success*. Retrieved from https://www.ama-assn.org/sites/default/files/media-browser/public/about-ama/ama-aha-integrated-leadership-principles_0.pdf.

Ang, H.-G., Koh, J. M.-Y., Lee, J., & Pua, Y.-H. (2016). Development and Preliminary Validation of a Leadership Competency Instrument for Existing and Emerging Allied Health Professional Leaders. *BMC Health Services Research, 16*, 64. ISSN:1472-6963.

Baldwin, K. S., Dimunation, N., & Alexander, J. (2011). Health Care Leadership and the Dyad Model. *Physician Executive Journal, 37*(4), 66–70.

Berghout, M. A., Fabbricotti, I. N., Buljac-Samardzic, M., & Hilders, C. M. (2017). Medical Leaders or Masters?—A Systematic Review of Medical Leadership in Hospital Settings. *PLoS One, 12*(9), e0184522. https://doi.org/10.1371/journal.pone.0184522.

Blumenthal, D., Bernard, K., Bohnen, J., & Bohmer, R. (2012). Addressing the Leadership Gap in Medicine: Residents' Need for Systematic Leadership Development Training. *Academic Medicine, 87*(4), 513–522.

Brand, C. A., Baker, A. L., Morello, R. T., Vitale, M. R., Evans, S. M., Scott, I. A., et al. (2012). A Review of Hospital Characteristics Associated with Improved. *International Journal for Quality in Health Care, 24*(5), 483–494.

Bussières, A. E., Maiers, M., Grondin, D., & Brockhusen, S. (2017). Selecting and Training Opinion Leaders and Best Practice Collaborators: Experience from the Canadian Chiropractic Guideline Initiative. *Journal of the Canadian Chiropractic Association, 61*(1), 53–64.

Calhoun, J., Dollett, L., Sinioris, M. E., Wainio, J. A., Butler, P. W., Griffith, J. R., et al. (2008). Development of an Interprofessional Competency Model for Healthcare Leadership. *Journal of Healthcare Management, 53*(6), 375–389.

Cardinaels, E., & Soderstrom, N. (2013). Managing in a Complex World: Accounting and Governance Choices in Hospitals. *European Accounting Review, 22*(4), 647–684.

Carol, C., Mark, H., & Matthew, F. (2013). Clinical Governance, Performance Appraisal and Interactional and Procedural Fairness at a New Zealand Public Hospital. *Journal of Business Ethics, 117*(3), 667–678. https://doi.org/10.1007/s10551-012-1550-9.

Chan, Z., Bruxer, A., Lee, J., Sims, K., Wainwright, M., Brooks, D., et al. (2015). What Makes a Leader: Identifying the Strengths of Canadian Physical Therapists. *Physiotherapy Canada, 67*(4), 341–348. ISSN:0300-0508.

Choo, S. S., Halim, H., & Keng-Howe, I. C. (2010). The Impact of Globalisation on Strategic Human Resources Management: The Mediating Role of Ceo in HR. *International Journal of Business Studies, 18*(1), 101–124. ISSN: 1320-7156.

Curran, C. R., & Totten, M. K. (2010). Enhancing Board Effectiveness. *Nursing Economic$, 28*(6), 420–422.

Czabanowska, K., Smith, T., Könings, K. D., Sumskas, L., Otok, R., Bjegovic-Mikanovic, V., et al. (2014). In Search for a Public Health Leadership Competency Framework to Support Leadership Curriculum-a Consensus Study. *European Journal of Public Health, 24*(5), 850–856. ISSN:1101-1262.

Dalmas, M. (2012). Involving Clinicians in Hospital Management Roles: Towards a Functional Integrative Approach. *International Journal of Clinical Leadership, 17*(3), 139–145.

Dauvrin, M., & Lorant, V. (2015). Leadership and Cultural Competence of Healthcare Professionals: A Social Network Analysis. *Nursing Research, 64*(3), 200–210. https://doi.org/10.1097/NNR.0000000000000092.

Day, M., Shickle, D., Smith, K., Zakariasen, K., Moskol, J., & Oliver, T. (2014). Training Public Health Superheroes: Five Talents for Public Health Leadership. *Journal of Public Health, 36*(4), 552–561. ISSN:1741-3842.

Deffenbaugh, J. (2015). Houston, We've Had a Problem Here: Tackling Board Governance. *British Journal of Healthcare Management, 21*(7), 304–309.

Deschamps, C., Rinfret, N., Lagacé, M. C., & Privé, C. (2016). Transformational Leadership and Change: How Leaders Influence Their Followers' Motivation Through Organizational Justice. *Journal of Healthcare Management, 61*(3), 194–213. ISSN:1096-9012.

Divall, B. (2015). Negotiating Competing Discourses in Narratives of Midwifery Leadership in the English NHS. *Midwifery, 31*, 1060–1066. https://doi.org/10.1016/j.midw.2015.07.006.

Doolin, B. (2002). Enterprise Discourse, Professional Identity and the Organizational Control of Hospital Clinicians. *Organization Studies, 23*(3), 369–390.

Dye, C. F. (2017). *Leadership in Healthcare; Essential Values and Skills* (ACHE Management Series). Chicago: Health Administration Press.

Elwell, S. M. (2015). Defining Leadership in a Changing Time. *Journal of Trauma Nursing, 22*(6), 312–314. ISSN:1078-7496.

Enock, K., & Markwell, S. (2010). *Interactions Between Managers, Doctors and Others: Understanding Individuals*. Retrieved from https://www.healthknowledge.org.uk/public-health-textbook/organisation-management/5a-understanding-itd/interactions.

Ezziane, Z. (2012). The Importance of Clinical Leadership in Twenty First Century Healthcare. *International Journal of Health Promotion and Education, 50*(5), 261–269.

Farrell, M. (2003). Health Care Leadership in an Age of Change. *Australian Health Review, 26*(1), 153–164.

Fernandez, C. P., Noble, C. C., Jensen, E., & Steffen, D. (2015). Moving the Needle: A Retrospective Pre- and Post-Analysis of Improving Perceived Abilities Across 20 Leadership Skills. *Maternal and Child Health Journal, 19*(2), 343–352. https://doi.org/10.1007/s10995-014-1573-1.

Foster, K., Fethney, J., McKenzie, H., Fisher, M., Harkness, E., & Kozlowski, D. (2017). Emotional Intelligence Increases Over Time: A Longitudinal Study of Australian Pre-Registration Nursing Students. *Nurse Education Today, 55*, 65–70. https://doi.org/10.1016/j.nedt.2017.05.008.

Garman, A., & Scribner, L. (2011). Leading for Quality in Healthcare: Development and Validation of a Competency Model. *Journal of Healthcare Management, 56*(6), 373–382. ISSN:1096-9012.

Gauld, R. (2017). Clinical Leadership: What Is It and How Do We Facilitate It? *Journal of Primary Health Care, 9*(1), 5–8.

Gilbert, J. H., Von Ah, D., & Broome, M. E. (2017). Organizational Intellectual Capital and the Role of the Nurse Manager: A Proposed Conceptual Model. *Nursing Outlook, 65*(6), 697–710. https://doi.org/10.1016/j.outlook.2017.04.005.

Glouberman, S., & Mintzberg, H. (2001a). Managing the Care of Health and the Cure of Disease–Part I: Differentiation. *Health Care Management Review, 26*(1), 56–69; discussion 87–9.

Glouberman, S., & Mintzberg, H. (2001b). Managing the Care of Health and the Cure of Disease–Part II: Differentiation. *Health Care Management Review, 26*(1), 70–84; discussion 87–9.

Goffee, R., & Jones, G. (2007). Leading Clever People. *Harvard Business Review, 85*(3), 72–79. https://hbr.org/2007/03/leading-clever-people.

Goldsmith, M. (2008). *What Got You Here Won't Get You There*. London: Profile Books.

Goodall, A. H. (2016). A Theory of Expert Leadership (TEL) in Psychiatry. *Australasian Psychiatry, 24*(3), 231–234. https://doi.org/10.1177/1039856215609760.

Green, B., Mitchell, D., Stevenson, P., Kane, T., Reynard, J., & Brennan, P. (2016). Leading Article: How Can I Optimise My Role as a Leader Within the Surgical Team? *British Journal of Oral & Maxillofacial Surgery, 54*, 847–850. https://doi.org/10.1016/j.bjoms.2016.05.035.

Grindel, C. G. (2016). Clinical Leadership: A Call to Action. *Medsurg Nursing, 25*(1), 9–16.

Gulati, R., Mikhail, O., Morgan, R. O., & Sittig, D. F. (2016). Vision Statement Quality and Organizational Performance in U.S. Hospitals. *Journal of Healthcare Management, 61*(5), 335–350. ISSN:1096-9012.

Ham, C. (2003). Improving the Performance of Health Services: The Role of Clinical Leadership. *Lancet, 361*(9373), 1978–1980.

Hamilton, P., Spurgeon, P., Clark, J., Dent, J., & Armit, K. (2008). *Engaging Doctors: Can Doctors Influence Organisational Performance?* Coventry: NHS Institute for Innovation and Improvement.

Hatler, C., & Sturgeon, P. (2013). Resilience Building: A Necessary Leadership Competence. *Nurse Leader, 11*(4), 32–34, 39. https://doi.org/10.1016/j.mnl.2013.05.007.

Hawkins, B. (2016). ASHP Statement on the Roles and Responsibilities of the Pharmacy Executive. *American Journal of Health-System Pharmacy, 73*(5), 329–332. ISSN:1079-2082.

Hlupic, V. (2014). *The Management Shift*. London: Palgrave Macmillan.

Humphreys, B., Couse, L., Sonnenmeier, R., Kurtz, A., Russell, S., & Antal, P. (2015). Transforming LEND Leadership Training Curriculum Through the Maternal and Child Health Leadership Competencies. *Maternal & Child Health Journal, 19*(2), 300–307. https://doi.org/10.1007/s10995-014-1587-8.

Johnston, C., Turpin, N., & Wynn-Jones, W. (2016). Medical Leadership in Perioperative Practice: I. *BJA Education, 16*(6), 203–208. https://doi.org/10.1093/bjaed/mkv041.

Kantanen, K., Kaunonen, M., Helminen, M., & Suominen, T. (2017). Leadership and Management Competencies of Head Nurses and Directors of Nursing in Finnish Social and Health Care. *Journal of Research in Nursing, 22*(3), 228–244. https://doi.org/10.1177/1744987117702692.

Kelly, J., Hogg, P., & Henwood, S. (2008). The Role of a Consultant Breast Radiographer: A Description and a Reflection. *Radiography, 14*(Supplement 1), e2–e10. https://doi.org/10.1016/j.radi.2008.10.003.

Khoshal, K., & Guraya, S. Y. (2016). Leaders Produce Leaders and Managers Produce Followers. *Saudi Medical Journal, 37*(10), 1061–1067.

Kilburg, R. R., & Donohue, M. D. (2011). Toward a 'Grand Unifying Theory' of Leadership: Implications for Consulting Psychology. *Consulting Psychology Journal: Practice and Research, 63*(1), 6–25. https://doi.org/10.1037/a0023053.

Kim, T. H., & Thompson, J. M. (2012). Organizational and Market Factors Associated with Leadership Development Programs in Hospitals: A National Study. *Journal of Healthcare Management, 57*(2), 113–131.

Kim, C. S., King, E., Stein, J., Robinson, E., Salameh, M., & O'Leary, K. J. (2014). Unit-Based Inter-Professional Leadership Models in Six US Hospitals. *Journal of Hospital Medicine, 9*(8), 545–550.

Kirkpatrick, I., Bullinger, B., Lega, F., & Dent, M. (2013). The Translation of Hospital Management Models in European Health Systems: A Framework for Comparison. *British Journal of Management, 24*, S48. https://doi.org/10.1111/1467-8551.12030.

Kirkpatrick, I., Hartley, K., Kuhlmann, E., & Veronesi, G. (2016). *Clinical Management and Professionalism* (pp. 325–340). Basingstoke: Palgrave Macmillan. https://doi.org/10.1007/978-1-137-38493-5_20.

Kovačič, H., & Rus, A. (2015). Leadership Competences in Slovenian Health Care / Vodstvene Kompetence V Slovenskem Zdravstvu. *Slovenian Journal of Public Health, 54*(1), 11–17. https://doi.org/10.1515/sjph-2015-0002.

Kumar, S., Kumar, N., Adhish, V. S., & Reddy, R. S. (2015). Strategic Management and Leadership for Health Professionals—Skills to Leverage Resources To Achieve Health Goals. *Indian Journal of Community Medicine, 40*(3), 158–162. ISSN:0970-0218.

Lalleman, P., Smid, G., Lagerwey, M., Shortridge-Baggett, L., & Schuurmans, M. (2016). Curbing the Urge to Care: A Bourdieusian Analysis of the Effect of the Caring Disposition on Nurse Middle Managers' Clinical Leadership in Patient Safety Practices. *International Journal of Nursing Studies, 63*, 179–188. https://doi.org/10.1016/j.ijnurstu.2016.09.006.

Langabeer, J. R., & Galeener, C. A. (2008). Measuring Board Activity in Governance of Not-For-Profit Healthcare. *Texas Public Health Journal, 60*(1), 22–25.

LeBrasseur, R., Whissell, R., & Ojha, A. (2002). Organisational Learning, Transformational Leadership and Implementation of Continuous Quality Improvement in Canadian Hospitals. *Australian Journal of Management (University of New South Wales), 27*(2), 141.

Leenstra, N. F., Jung, O. C., Johnson, A., Wendt, K. W., & Tulleken, J. E. (2016). Taxonomy of Trauma Leadership Skills: A Framework for Leadership Training and Assessment. *Academic Medicine, 91*(2), 272–281. https://doi.org/10.1097/ACM.0000000000000890.

Lehr, B., Ostermann, H., & Schubert, H. (2011). Schwerpunkt: Competence-Based Demands Made of Senior Physicians: An Empirical Study to Evaluate Leadership Competencies. *Zeitschrift Fuer Evidenz, Fortbildung Und Qualitaet Im Gesundheitswesen, 105*(Panta rhei – Alles fliesst), 723–733. https://doi.org/10.1016/j.zefq.2010.08.006.

Levey, S., Hill, J., & Greene, B. (2002). Leadership in Health Care and the Leadership Literature. *Journal of Ambulatory Care Management, 25*(2), 68–74. ISSN:0148-9917.

Love, D. B., & Ayadi, M. F. (2015). Redefining the Core Competencies of Future Healthcare Executives Under Healthcare Reform. *Administrative Issues Journal: Education, Practice & Research, 5*(2), 3–16. ISSN:2153-7615.

MacLeod, L. (2015). Toppling the 3-Legged Stool: The Nurse Leader's Role. *Nurse Leader, 13*(6), 68–71. ISSN:1541-4612.

McAlearney, A. S. (2010). Executive Leadership Development in U.S. Health Systems. *Journal of Healthcare Management, 55*(3), 206–222. American College of Healthcare. ISSN: 1096-9012.

McBride, A. B. (2017). Serving on a Hospital Board: A Case Study. *Nursing Outlook, 65*, 372–379.

Mintzberg, H. (2011). To Fix Health Care, Ask the Right Questions. *Harvard Business Review, 89*(10), 44.

Mitchell, L., & Boak, G. (2009). Developing Competence Frameworks in UK Healthcare: Lessons from Practice. *Journal of European Industrial Training, 33*(8–9), 701–717.

Moen, C., & Prescott, P. (2016). A Values-Based Approach to Medical Leadership. *British Journal of Hospital Medicine, 77*(11), 624–629.

Mountford, J., & Webb, C. (2009). When Clinicians Lead. *McKinsey Quarterly, 2*, 44–53.

NHS. (2010). *Medical Leadership Competency Framework; Enhancing Engagement in Medical Leadership* (3rd ed.). Coventry: NHS Institute for Innovation and Improvement. Retrieved from https://www.leadershipacademy.nhs.uk/wp-content/uploads/2012/11/NHSLeadership-Leadership-Framework-Medical-Leadership-Competency-Framework-3rd-ed.pdf.

Ohlson, S. M., & Anderson, M. A. (2015). Ability Emotional Intelligence of Nurse Managers in the Midwestern United States. *Asia-Pacific Journal of Oncology Nursing, 2*(2), 82–88. https://doi.org/10.4103/2347-5625.155733.

Patnaik, S. K., Gupta, S. K., Kant, S., & Pillay, R. (2017). Analysing Competencies of Indian Healthcare Leaders. *International Journal of Research Foundation of Hospital and Healthcare Administration, 5*(1), 47–53.

Pereira, C. M. M., & Gomes, J. F. S. (2012). The Strength of Human Resource Practices and Transformational Leadership: Impact on Organisational Performance. *International Journal of Human Resource Management, 23*(20), 4301–4318. ISSN:0958-5192.

Pihlainen, V., Kivinen, T., & Lammintakanen, J. (2016). Management and Leadership Competence in Hospitals: A Systematic Literature Review. *Leadership in Health Services (1751–1879), 29*(1), 95–110. https://doi.org/10.1108/LHS-11-2014-0072.

Pirozek, P., Komarkova, L., Leseticky, O., & Hajdikova, T. (2015). Corporate Governance in Czech Hospitals After the Transformation. *Health Policy, 119*(8), 1086–1095. https://doi.org/10.1016/j.healthpol.2015.05.002.

Poikkeus, T., Leino-Kilpi, H., & Katajisto, J. (2014). Supporting Ethical Competence of Nurses During Recruitment and Performance Reviews – The Role of the Nurse Leader. *Journal of Nursing Management, 22*(6), 792–802.

Popescu, G. H., & Predescu, V. (2016). The Role of Leadership in Public Health. *American Journal of Medical Research, 3*(1), 273–279.

Prybil, L. D., Dreher, M. C., & Curran, C. R. (2014). Nurses on Boards: The Time Has Come. *Nurse Leader, 12*, 48–52.

Reichenpfader, U., Carlfjord, S., & Nilsen, P. (2015). Leadership in Evidence-Based Practice: A Systematic Review. *Leadership in Health Services (1751–1879), 28*(4), 298. https://doi.org/10.1108/LHS-08-2014-0061.

Rick, C. (2014). Competence in Executive Nursing Leadership for the 21st Century: The 5 Eyes. *Nurse Leader, 12*, 64–66. https://doi.org/10.1016/j.mnl.2014.01.005.

Rosenman, E. D., Ilgen, J. S., Shandro, J. R., Harper, A. L., & Fernandez, R. (2015). A Systematic Review of Tools Used to Assess Team Leadership in Health Care Action Teams. *Academic Medicine, 90*(10), 1408–1422.

Saravo, B., Netzel, J., & Kiesewetter, J. (2017). The Need for Strong Clinical Leaders – Transformational and Transactional Leadership as a Framework for Resident Leadership Training. *PLoS One, 12*(8), 1–13. https://doi.org/10.1371/journal.pone.0183019.

Scully, N. J. (2015). Leadership in Nursing: The Importance of Recognising Inherent Values and Attributes to Secure a Positive Future for the Profession. *Collegian, 22*(4), 439–444. ISSN:1322-7696.

Shariff, N. J. (2015). A Delphi Survey of Leadership Attributes Necessary for National Nurse Leaders' Participation in Health Policy Development: An East African Perspective. *BMC Nursing, 14*(13), 1–8.

Siddiqi, S., Masud, T., Nishtar, S., Peters, D., Sabri, B., Bile, K., et al. (2009). Framework for Assessing Governance of the Health System in Developing Countries: Gateway to Good Governance. *Health Policy, 90*(1), 13–25.

Silva, V. L. d. S., Camelo, S. H. H., Soares, M. I., Resck, Z. M. R., Chaves, L. D. P., dos Santos, F. C., et al. (2017). Leadership Practices in Hospital

Nursing: A Self of Manager Nurses. *Revista da Escola de Enfermagem da USP, 51*, e03206. https://doi.org/10.1590/s1980-220x2016099503206.

Size, T. (2006). Leadership Development for Rural Health. *North Carolina Medical Journal, 67*(1), 71–76.

Squires, M., Tourangeau, A., Spence Laschinger, H. K., & Doran, D. (2010). The Link Between Leadership and Safety Outcomes in Hospitals. *Journal of Nursing Management, 18*(8), 914–925. https://doi.org/10.1111/j.1365-2834.2010.01181.x.

Stempniak, M. (2013). Value-Based Leadership: Is Your Hospital Management Team Prepared for the Future? *H&HN Hospitals & Health Networks, 87*(5), 41.

Stevenson, S. (2015). Supervising Mental Health Clinicians in the Context of Complex Organisational Dynamics. *Journal of Social Work Practice, 29*(4), 445–456. https://doi.org/10.1080/02650533.2014.956305.

Storkholm, M. H., Mazzocato, P., Savage, M., & Savage, C. (2017). Money's (Not) on My Mind: A Qualitative Study of How Staff and Managers Understand Health Care's Triple Aim. *BMC Health Services Research, 17*, 1–9. https://doi.org/10.1186/s12913-017-2052-3.

Taylor, R., & Martindale, S. (2013). Clinical Leadership in Primary Care. *Primary Health Care, 23*(5), 32–38.

The King's Fund. (2011). *The Future of Leadership and Management at NHS*. London: The King's Fund.

Thorpe, R., Gold, J., & Lawler, J. (2011). Locating Distributed leadership. *International Journal of Management Reviews, 13*, 239–250. https://doi.org/10.1111/j.1468-2370.2011.00303x.

Till, A., Dutta, N., & McKimm, J. (2016). Vertical Leadership in Highly Complex and Unpredictable Health Systems. *British Journal of Hospital Medicine (17508460), 77*(8), 471. https://doi.org/10.12968/hmed.2016.77.8.471.

Turner, S., Seel, M., Trotter, T., Giuliani, M., Benstead, K., Eriksen, J. G., et al. (2017). Defining Leaders in Radiotherapy: Defining a Leader Role Curriculum for Radiation Oncology: A Global Delphi Consensus Study. *Radiotherapy and Oncology, 123*, 331–336. https://doi.org/10.1016/j.radonc.2017.04.009.

Valori, R. M., & Johnston, D. J. (2016). Leadership and Team Building in Gastrointestinal Endoscopy. *Best Practice & Research Clinical Gastroenterology, 30*(3), 497–509. https://doi.org/10.1016/j.bpg.2016.04.007.

Veronesi, G., & Keasey, K. (2012). A (New) Model of Board of Directors: Evidence from the National Health Service. *International Journal of Public Sector Management, 25*(4), 272–286.

Veronesi, G., Kirkpatrick, I., & Vallascas, F. (2013). Clinicians on Board: What Difference Does It Make? *Social Science and Medicine, 77*, 147–155.

Veronesi, G., Kickpatrick, I., Sturdy, A., Oliver-Blanco, A., & Reguera, N. (2018). The Impact of Management Consultants on Public Service Efficiency. *Policy & Politics*. https://doi.org/10.1332/030557318X15167881150799.

Vinot, D. (2014). Transforming Hospital Management à la francaise. The New Role of Clinical Managers in French Public Hospitals. *International Journal of Public Sector Management, 27*(5), 406. https://doi.org/10.1108/IJPSM-06-2012-0067.

Wang, D., Waldman, D. A., & Zhang, Z. (2014). A Meta-Analysis of Shared Leadership and Team Effectiveness. *Journal of Applied Psychology, 99*(2), 181.

West, M., Armit, K., Loewenthal, L., Eckert, R., West, T., & Lee, A. (2015). *Leadership and Leadership Development in Healthcare: The Evidence Base*. London: Faculty of Medical Leadership and Management.

White, K. R., Pillay, R., & Huang, X. (2016). Article: Nurse Leaders and the Innovation Competence Gap. *Nursing Outlook, 64*, 255–261. https://doi.org/10.1016/j.outlook.2015.12.007.

Wolf, J. A. (2008). Health Care, Heal Thyself! An Exploration of What Drives (and Sustains) High Performance in Organizations Today. *Performance Improvement, 47*(5), 38–45.

Yielder, J. (2006). Leadership and Power in Medical Imaging. *Radiography, 12*, 305–313. https://doi.org/10.1016/j.radi.2005.07.006.

6

Leadership Capability Through Personal Insight and Leadership Identity

Leadership and Human Personal Characteristics

There are some 200 definitions of leadership with a multitude of hypotheses about what a leader is and does. Leadership can connote 'images of powerful, dynamic individuals who command victorious armies, direct corporate empires from atop gleaming skyscrapers or shape the course of nations' (Yukl 2010: 19). Or it can be interpreted as a form of social interaction that takes place at all levels, that is, it is non-hierarchical and contextual. Where leaders are the most senior members of the organisation faced with, for example, significant VUCA forces, the expectation is that they will be responsive and adaptable and have competences in strategy setting and abilities in pushing through organisational change. But faced with operational challenges, the ability to engage multi-skilled, multilayered, multi-functional teams or apply critical thinking to complex supply chain problems, for example, may be deemed to be more apt transactional or devolved leadership with an inclusive style. In some cases, leaders will be exceptional or heroic people who deal with unique circumstances or

P. Turner, *Leadership in Healthcare*, Organizational Behaviour in Health Care,
https://doi.org/10.1007/978-3-030-04387-2_6

crises; in others, leadership will be that activity undertaken by many people during business as usual, a normal part of the operation of the organisation.

The reason that it's so difficult to clarify whether there is a best practice or most appropriate leadership style is due not only to the contextual nature of leadership but also that leadership is an 'essentially contested concept' (Grint 2005: 17), with differing opinions, interpretations, and emphases. The previous narrative outlined some of these perspectives in which leadership was seen as a formal, senior-level activity determined by position in the organisational hierarchy on the one hand or a non-hierarchical phenomenon that is 'socially constructed between work-group members' at multiple levels, on the other (Marchiondo et al. 2015: 892). Between the base and the apogee of leadership theory, it was argued that the constitutive nature of leadership in fact required different actions depending on how situations are framed underscoring the importance of context—and the necessity to shape that context (Hodgson et al. 2015: 456). In this scenario there is no 'one right way' to lead and no simple binary solution that will facilitate a choice between leadership style A and leadership style B. The decision on how to lead therefore rests with an individual's understanding of her or his strengths in leadership and how these can be best developed or deployed in the organisational context within which leadership is required.

Throughout this melange of ideas and concepts, it's possible to look at the characteristics of leadership through one of a series of norms. The first is through the personification of the leader or 'who we are,' that is, who leaders are as individuals that makes them leaders, or by seeing leadership as a result, leadership as a position, or leadership as a process (Grint 2005: 19). There are merits in analysing the categories in this way, because each has a strong foundation in the overall canon of leadership. However, in the development of a model by which leaders in the health sector can frame their own response to the challenges they face, it is the objective of this chapter to focus on the 'leader as person' norm and in so doing address questions about an individual leader's style and identity. The basis of this is personal insight or reflection as the means by which a leader will understand her or his motivation to lead, 'generic' skills and expertise already present to do so, and context skills—professional credibility or understanding organisational dynamics, for example—specific to the health sector and the environment within which this leadership activity takes place.

In the health sector, the scope of the challenge of what it means to be a leader can be gauged from the 119 competences in 8 domains (systems thinking, political leadership, collaborative leadership, leadership and communication, leading change, emotional intelligence, leadership, organisational learning and development and ethics and professionalism) found in Czabanowska et al.'s (2014) excellent pan-European study. Amongst the competences were those specifically relevant to the sector such as 'understand current public health issues and engage in systemic change to address them' and 'promote the European and national public health agenda.' But there were also those which would be identified more generally, such as 'understand reflective leadership and demonstrate that all leadership begins from within,' 'translate broad strategies into practical terms for others,' and 'exercise the sensitivity needed to communicate with diverse cultures and disciplines' (Czabanowska et al. 2014: 853). Groups of these competences present in an individual leader, set in a particular context, would influence not only the success of any outcomes but also the style of leadership, that is, whether that person was a transformational or transactional leader, a hero or a servant leader, or indeed one of the many other variations on the theme. In some cases, leaders would have competences in articulating an organisational vision or mission and the values that support it. In other cases, the leader would be less concerned about creating the context (through vision and mission) than achieving operational objectives for which such competences as 'delivering results under pressure' or 'making change work' would be appropriate. In all cases, the effectiveness of leaders and their qualities will include the engagement, well-being, and satisfaction of health professionals and their teams (Bigelow and Arndt 2005; Ribeiro Chavaglia et al. 2013; Chobanuk and James 2015; Shanafelt et al. 2015). The question that remains is which style or which set of leadership competences fit the particular needs of the organisation and the individual leaders within that organisation.

Sense Making from a Contested Concept

Three questions are important in addressing this conundrum in the quest for sense making around the subject of leadership in health. First, what is leadership?; second, what does a leader do?; and third, is there a best fit leadership style? Amongst the categorisations in answering the first question and outlined in Chaps. 3 and 4 include leadership based on person or trait, behaviour, power-influence, result, process, or situation and local leadership theories including functional leadership or group and team leadership (Grint 2005; Yukl 2010; Edger 2012). The second question, what a leader does, is addressed by outlining the specific challenges faced by an organisation and, from these, distinguishing the role of the ***leader***, who sits at the head of an organisation, department, or business unit in dealing with these challenges, and that of ***leadership*** which is a social phenomenon that occurs at many organisational levels and points. In this consideration, there is also the added question of the difference between leadership and management, one which remains unresolved as the debate about the distinct characteristics of each rumbles on (Yukl 2010; Ellis and Bach 2015). There's a good deal of material available to those wishing to understand and develop leader and leadership concepts in response to the first two questions of what a leader is and what a leader does. What is left unanswered is the third question about how to identify a best fit leadership style and its associated competencies.

At organisational level, this means matching the demand for leaders and leadership, determined by the context within which the organisation finds itself and the strategy by which it intends to achieve its objectives, with the supply of those in leadership positions or being developed into such positions, who have the appropriate knowledge, attitudes, skills, and behaviours for these circumstances. At an individual level, therefore, it is important for leaders to establish their own leadership style and identity and articulate how these are relevant to the leadership needs of the organisation. Understanding both the context for leadership and the individual leader's ability to perform successfully in that context is an important consideration (Jodar et al. 2016). An organisation will seek to match its leadership capability with the demands placed on it; the individual leader will seek to ensure that her or his capability is aligned to these needs.

So, on the assumption that leadership is not prescribed because of a hierarchical organisational position, the question is how leadership and leader-follower relationships develop in organisations and the relational and social processes involved and being seen as a leader (DeRue and Ashford 2010: 629). The model for leadership in healthcare outlined in Chap. 5 highlighted three areas in which health sector leadership might address these questions—leadership capability, professional credibility, and understanding organisational dynamics. It is proposed in this chapter that leaders in the health context adopt a process of personal insight to establish their own leadership strengths and weaknesses against this model, use this insight to create a leadership identity based on real and clear leadership capabilities, and execute their leadership actions against these capabilities.

Personal Insight: 'All Leadership Begins from Within'

Personal insight occurs at the point where self-analysis meets self-knowledge resulting in a deep understanding on the part of an individual leader or aspirational leader about their own suitability in the leadership role. It involves understanding of 'how one is perceived by other people, how the professional thinks and analyses situations, and how he/she contributes to his/her own relationship and leadership' (Rothke 2014: 54). In practice this means that an individual leader will develop self-awareness from the perspective of their own personal lens (Grint 2005: 33) and answer the question 'how can I ensure that my approach to leadership is the right one for my organisation?' Personal insight is concerned with knowledge, skills, attitudes, and behaviours in response to this question against criteria or competences as to what constitutes leadership in any particular organisation. Ultimately it will contribute to a 'preferred leadership style' used to adapt and deal with a specific context, developing strengths or filling gaps in leadership requirements for a particular situation (because some face challenges that go beyond their individual capacities). And in this respect, the process of personal insight will highlight not only strengths but also an understanding of personal barriers to leadership, overcoming which will play a significant role in leadership success (Taylor 2014: 9–10; Day et al. 2014; Bish et al. 2015: 181). Such self-reflection and self-awareness are therefore integral actions in identifying and developing leadership capability and the leadership identity that arises from it. Self-knowledge will help to create leader identity in areas such as self-confidence, empathy, meaning, strength, and integration, in which meaning was the definition of leadership held by an individual, 'whereas strength refers to the extent to which an individual identifies as a leader' (Waite et al. 2014; Ezziane 2012: 262; Johnston et al. 2016; Jodar et al. 2016; Miscenko et al. 2017: 606). Since all leadership begins from within, acquiring this understanding is the foundation from which to develop a leadership style and is a significant regulator of leadership behaviour (Mastrangelo et al. 2004: 446; Hendricks et al. 2010: 253; Czabanowska et al. 2014; Fernandez et al. 2015; Zheng and Muir 2015; Purdy 2016: 12; Hunt 2017: 1223). Personal insight is a contributor to identifying a best fit leadership style for the rapidly changing environment that characterises health and will be a significant contribution to organisational effectiveness, to the achievement of the objectives of person-centred care, safe care, and effective care and the creation of an effective workplace culture (Moen and Prescott 2016; Adegoke 2017). Figure 6.1 shows the relationship between personal insight, leadership identity, and leadership action.

This approach to leadership builds on identified authentic strengths, traits, or behaviours and uses these in the context within which leadership action takes place, a principle that has been applied to health sector leaders in multiple geographies (see inter alia Robbins et al. 2001; Amestoy et al. 2009; Hendricks et al. 2010; Bimray and Jooste 2014). Such knowledge forms the core of the leader's identity. The counterparty of this reflection is that an individual will understand her or his weaknesses or areas for self-development in respect of the requirements of leadership.

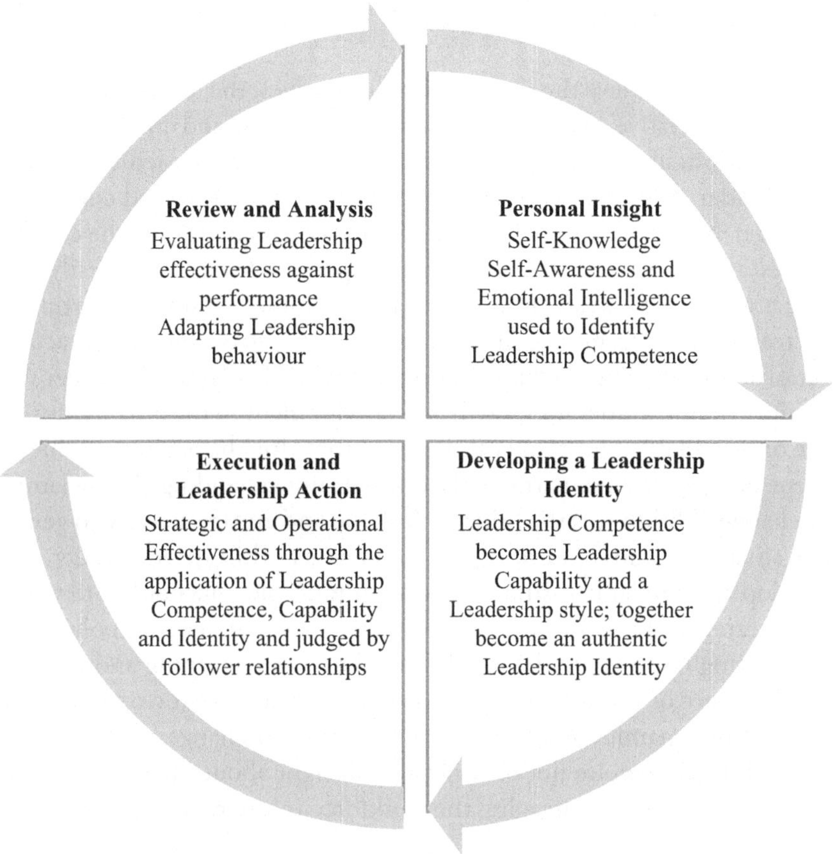

Fig. 6.1 Best fit leadership: from personal insight to leadership identity to leadership action

Personal Insight, Leadership Competence, and Leadership Capability

Personal insight provides the basis against which a leader will measure or match her or his leadership capability against that which has been identified as necessary to lead the organisation in its unique context. The model for health sector leadership in Chap. 5 outlined some of the competence areas that might be included in this calculation. It's possible to categorise these into three important groupings:

- **Creating Meaning and Purpose**

In order to achieve the organisation's objectives, the leader will create a 'strategic narrative' which articulates the meaning and purpose of the organisation, unit, department, or team, aligns this to the achievement of stakeholder objectives, and demonstrates how those involved contribute to this narrative. To do so will require self-assessment against the competences associated with this important aspect of leadership. Firstly, the leader will seek to create meaning for the organisation, unit, department, or team—its strategy and individual roles translate this into practical actions. This is ability in 'knowing-interpreting.' Secondly, the leader will identify opportunities for growth and development in the organisation—she or he will drive for results and act as a force for change in the achievement of these results, particularly through understanding the dynamics of change. Within this the leader will shape and engage actively to generate situations and opportunities for change. Thirdly, the leader will develop and implement strategies to align multiple stakeholders to vision and strategy; she or he will act as an advocate, influencing policy and negotiating resources to deliver. The need to create meaning and purpose is a key part of the role of the leader in the health sector organisation. Given the dynamics and the ensuant pressure to change, this aspect of leadership will require not only personal insight about the need to do so but also a deftness in engaging the workforce in the resulting strategy.

- **Engaging and Motivating the Workforce**

So, having outlined the purpose of the organisation, unit, department, or team and its mission, vision, and strategy and articulated how this is operationalised in the form of a strategic narrative or a statement of meaning, the second group of competences are those associated with converting this into practice and the engagement and motivation of the workforce. The competences associated with this aspect are the ability to mobilise the potential of the organisation as a whole or individual departments/teams. To do so will require that the leader engages and motivates a broad section of the health workforce. She or he will understand the importance of followership through demonstrating emotional intelligence and the impact of actions on others. Throughout, the leader will assess and act on factors that contribute to individual, team, or organisational objectives, including when and where to prioritise clinical outcomes amongst competing objectives. The leader will do so by engaging and empowering, coaching, mentoring, and developing. This may be aligned with a wider objective of developing successors to ensure either continuity or change of strategy, stewardship, and policy. In all cases the leader will act as a role model for multicultural and diversity leadership.

The two competence sets associated with setting direction and engaging the workforce to achieve the goals to which this direction leads will require the ability to adapt to change if this is needed, since strategy is rarely constant.

- **Adapting and Responding to Change**

The leadership competences associated with personal insight remain conceptual until they become operationalised by actions on the part of the leader and articulated in the form of a leadership identity. The third significant grouping therefore concerns the capability associated with transformation and change not only on the part of the organisation but also on the part of the individual leader. Personal insight will highlight areas of strength, and these can be assessed against the required competences for adaptation and change. Of particular importance is the ability to perform well in a VUCA environment—and be able to take decisions, in spite of ambiguity (Love and Ayadi 2015). Having done so, the leader will anticipate the impact of decisions and plan accordingly. An awareness of the existing perceived leadership 'style' and that determined by the context of the organisation is critical and the development of a leadership identity in which these factors are integrated equally. The leader will be able to mediate leadership identity using insight and hindsight to adapt leadership behaviour. However, this will need to be authentic, a requirement of the contemporary leader together with being reliable, truthful, and transparent as a means of earning trust and respect. To do so is facilitated by adopting a collaborative style which will enable the leader to operate effectively across networks and boundaries.

Personal insight is gained through a process of self-analysis against which an individual leader can assess her or his leadership capability against the requirements of the organisation as determined by competence to achieve a particular set of strategic or operational goals. Effective leadership will occur at the intersection of capability 'supply' and organisational—unit, team, or individual—'demand.'

Developing a Leadership Identity: Personal and Relational Insight

Hence, from personal insight and the assessment of the outcomes against leadership competences will emerge leadership identity which is the version of leadership that an individual wants to project; 'leadership influence relies on the communication of a desired leader identity to potential follower' (Croft et al. 2015: 115; Owens 2016). Its bases are both personal and relational insights which conceptualise how individuals come to be seen (by themselves and by others) as leaders (DeRue and Ashford 2010; Marchiondo et al. 2015: 893). Those who undertake leadership will have an identity which informs leadership action and reinforces the action once taken, based on capability and contributing to authenticity. Figure 6.2 outlines some of the key elements in leadership identity development. First, there is a period of identity negotiation where a leader would test the fit of her or his style (an identity proposal); second, there is identity balance, validating or otherwise this particular style; thirdly task interaction takes place in search as the leader and followers strive to achieve an objective and finally any identity conflicts would be adapted accordingly (Lührmann and Eberl 2007: 118).

Those in formal, mainly Senior Leadership positions have a leadership identity reinforced by the institutional validity of being in the role at a particular level. The challenge for those in such positions is to ensure that this identity is enacted credibly since hierarchical status alone is only one contributory factor. Claiming to be a leader is not sufficient in and of itself to fully explain the perceptions of leadership; 'other's' acceptance (or rejection) of the claims also shapes judgements of leadership in groups. This notion is consistent with a *logic of appropriateness* conceptualised as

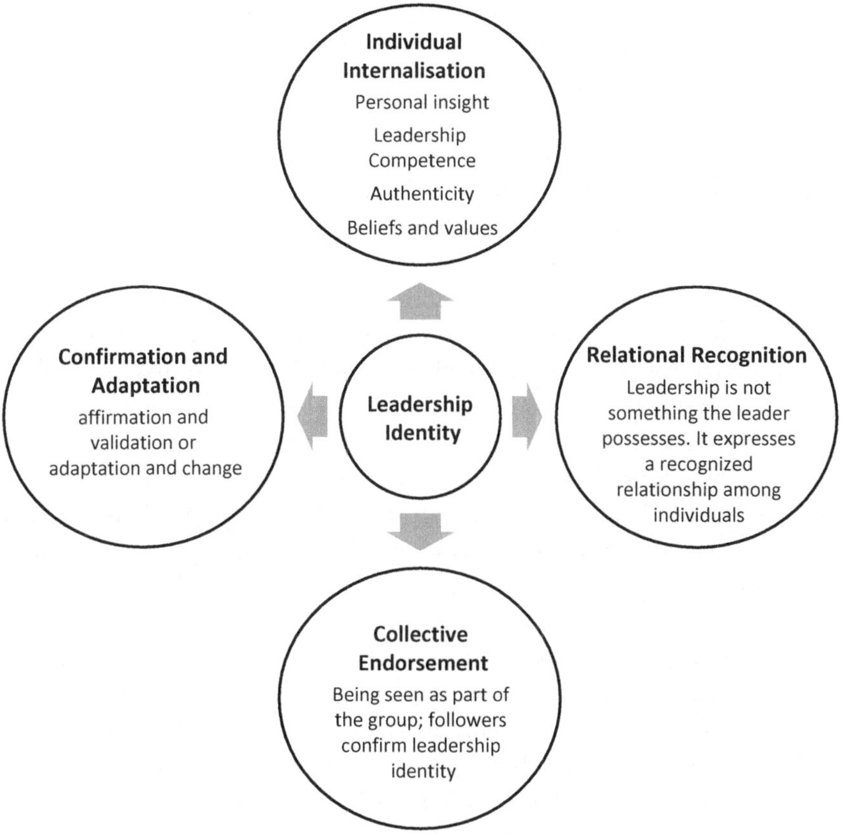

Fig. 6.2 Four elements of leadership identity

a metaphoric question: 'What does a *person* like me [or him/her] (identity) *do* (rules) in a *situation* like this (recognition) given this *culture* (group)?' (Marchiondo et al. 2015: 904). The importance for acceptance applies equally to those not in formal leadership roles but all those who take on leadership activity. In both cases leadership identity is a precursor to claiming leadership recognition with the suggestion that:

> leadership identity is coconstructed in organizations when individuals claim and grant leader and follower identities in their social interactions. Through this claiming-granting process, individuals internalize an identity

> as leader or follower, and those identities become relationally recognized through reciprocal role adoption and collectively endorsed within the organizational context. (DeRue and Ashford 2010: 627)

There are two theoretical bases to this assumption. In the first, identity theories focus on individual (dyadic) processes between leaders and followers where identity theories examine how individuals define themselves with others and how they are identified by them. 'Leadership is considered to be effective if there are corresponding individual identities of leaders and followers.' In the second, social identity theory is based on the idea that 'people who are perceived to match their group's social identity are more likely to be endorsed as leaders' (Lührmann and Eberl 2007: 121). There is evidence to support these concepts. Research in US healthcare organisations, for example, concluded that 'the competencies of those formally designated leaders in hierarchical organizations are only strengthened when those in follower roles are able to step up and demonstrate the same behaviors' (Baker et al. 2011: 357). If the identity of a leader doesn't correspond to the leadership needs of the team unit or organisation, there will be challenges. A weak level of followership will compound a lack of belief in the objectives. It is important that identity is acted out with integrity, fairness, and consistency (Robinson et al. 2013; Lorber et al. 2016; Berghout et al. 2017). The leadership characteristics that inspire action in others include a way of thinking, acting, and communicating which 'gives some leaders the ability to inspire those around them' and that 'people don't buy what you do but why you do'. Leadership identity is a means of projecting this.

Developing a Leadership Identity: Bridging the Gap Between Clinical and Managerial Objectives

The creation of a leader identity in the health sector environment faces the challenge of 'overcoming differences in clinical and managerial perspectives and in the corresponding effort required in brokering relationships between professionals' (Hodgson et al. 2015: 456). The results of research in several geographies reflect this telling point and moving into new roles requiring the construction of a leader identity in addition to a professional identity can be an emotional transition for individuals, because it challenges other social or professional identities. Such a dilemma was found in studies in the UK, amongst primary healthcare nurses in South Africa and in New Zealand (Miskelly and Duncan 2014; Daire and Gilson 2014; Croft et al. 2015: 116). It was argued that having a strong motivation to lead was critical to overcoming the challenges of transition from the professional to the leadership identity (Mascia et al. 2015). And the willingness to do so was then underpinned by the ability to lead with confirmation from within and to the leader that the role and style are appropriate. The effective leader will adapt style and/or behaviour to the context, based on feedback and within the boundaries of the individual leader's identity/authenticity and competence, combining internalisation processes and external confirmation, that is, external recognition from both individuals and the group over which leadership takes place. Finally linking leadership identity with the reinforcement of professional identity starting with the acceptance of the leadership role and the accompanying responsibilities were features of successful transition to the leadership role.

The final consideration is the growing interest in and influence of authentic leadership that is seen across the sector (inter alia Hlongwane and Olivier 2017; Fernandes Carvalho et al. 2016; Malik et al. 2016). Indeed, a leadership identity which embraces this aspect will be of value in a sector whose very ethos is steeped in authenticity. But authenticity by itself is not leadership. 'It is a person-centered cognitive construct that focuses the alignment between the self—including knowledge of one's needs, emotions, personality, and values—and one's actions' (Chang and Diddams 2009: 1). It is a psychological paradigm based on 'the knowledge, acceptance, and behavioural responses of a person, which is rooted in a person's core and ethical values, high standards, convictions, emotions, and motives,' self-awareness, and unbiased balanced information processing (Waite et al. 2014). Beliefs and values as part of leadership identity feature strongly in creating an authentic approach. So much so that where there are discrepancies between professed and actual beliefs or values, the manager or leader 'should do some soul searching about what he really values in order to learn and grow as an individual and as a manager' (Graber and Kilpatrick 2008; Jodar et al. 2016). Authenticity will normally be effective in the leadership paradigm when leaders create transparent, shared relationships with followers acknowledging or addressing weaknesses as well as strengths. Those with authenticity as part of their identity will have empathy, respect, trustworthiness, reliability, and believability, and an authentic leader will be perceived by others as naturally open, hopeful, optimistic, and resilient, will exhibit warmth and relationship-centred principles, and will be an inspiration in respected professional and personal environments (Waite et al. 2014; Weiss et al. 2017).

Personal insight forms the basis of a leadership identity which reflects an individual's leadership capability against the competences needed to deliver an organisation's objectives. However, individual success at leadership will only occur if these conceptual findings are converted into action in the context of that specific organisation.

Execution and Leadership Action: Contextual Awareness

The third aspect of best fit leadership (Fig. 6.1) concerns the ability to apply contextual awareness to leadership action. This is based on the assumption that different leadership styles will either be a response to the organisation's particular challenges or influence the way the organisation deals with them. This is contextual awareness and means understanding aspects of the situation that are relevant to direction and objective setting. 'It is important to understand the external events and trends that will impact performance and require adjustments in strategy and work processes. It is also important to understand the processes and people within the organisation' (Yukl 2010: 192). In both instances there will be greater chance of success if the leader's style or identity converges with those of followers, is compatible with (or used to determine) the culture of the organisation, and is aligned to the goals of the organisation. But even within this, there is no 'right' way to lead, and studies in health sector organisations have shown the relevance of diverse leadership styles to suit particular contexts. A pilot study of senior medical staff in emergency departments, for example, showed that, when using the Myers-Briggs Type Indicator (ENTJ), thinking and judging were strong features of senior clinicians (Boyd and Brown 2005), whilst in contrast, a study of health executives found that the most common Myers-Briggs Type was ISTJ (Lawrence 2010). The paradigm that leadership is contextual is reinforced by these findings.

After DeRue and Ashford (2010)

The 'best fit' leader will have an identity which is authentic and reflects her or his values and beliefs, but also reflects knowledge, skills, attitudes, and behaviours set against the needs or objectives of the organisation. The closer the fit between need, preference, and actuality, the closer the fit to authenticity.

Execution and Leadership Action: Mediating Leadership Identity Through Emotional Intelligence

A particular leadership style will manifest itself once execution and action take place. In some cases, the context of the organisation means that leaders who are predominantly transformational will succeed because of their recognition of the need for colleagues who are better placed to deliver process reengineering or operational excellence, whilst those who are predominantly transactional will require colleagues who are better able to engage the workforce in transformation and change. Understanding of this point will be enhanced by the leader's level of awareness both of the strategic context and the human one. For the latter, emotional intelligence is an asset. It is the ability to express and manage one's emotions in relationships with others and consists of self-awareness and an accurate self-assessment (Xavier 2005). Emotional intelligence is defined as 'the ability to assess an individual's and others' emotions through emotional awareness, discern the impact of those emotions, and then use that information to positively affect behavior' (Kozub et al. 2016: 145). It is a cooperative combination that blends intelligence and emotion to influence a person's ability to cope with environmental demands and pressures (Czabanowska et al. 2014), and for some, though not all, 'the simple process of learning how to better understand and respond to emotions (in yourself and others) is all it takes for leaders to improve a host of behaviours that are critical to their performance' (Bradberry and Antonakis 2015: 22). Emotional intelligence is distinct from personality and composed of four branches: emotion perception, emotion facilitation, emotion understanding, and emotion management, which may be useful in supporting the idea of personal insight as a prerequisite of effective leadership in health.

Whilst there has been some scepticism about emotional intelligence and perceived 'hyperbolic claims' (Antonakis et al. 2009), some such as Ezziane (2012) argue that emotional intelligence is a key facet of clinical leaders in a devolved construct. Amongst the determinants of emotional intelligence are *self-awareness*, understanding (and confidence) gained by realistic self-assessment; *social skill*, the ability to communicate and build relationships/teams; *self-regulation*, self-control and the ability to adapt to changing circumstance; and *social awareness*, empathy and awareness of the dynamics of the organisation. It is an area of interest to healthcare professionals in general (Di Fabio et al. 2014: Kim and Lee 2016; Celik 2017; Samiuddin et al. 2017) and specifically to studies of its impact on health leadership which have ranged across health sector organisations from, inter alia, Slovenia to Nigeria to the UK and USA (Larkin 2015; Lorber et al. 2016; Uzonwanne 2016; Ali and Terry 2017). A study of global organisations noted that cultural and emotional intelligences provide a framework for better understanding cross-cultural leadership and help to clarify possible adaptations that need to be implemented in leadership (Alon and Higgins 2005). The desired outcomes of such awareness are effective interpersonal skills being able to cultivate strong working relationships and effectiveness in collaborating and cooperating within and outside the profession (Shariff 2015). Furthermore, there is a significant relationship between emotional intelligence and transformational leadership amongst clinical leaders (Larkin 2015; Crowne et al. 2017). Emotional intelligence can contribute to improved patient outcomes and can enhance the practice environment such that clinical leaders 'must be able to recognise and regulate their emotions and manage those of others' (Grindel 2016: 13).

Whilst personal insight and the development of a leadership identity can be a conscious process through such developmental approaches as coaching or mentoring helped by 360 tools, MBTI, or assessment against competencies (see Chaps. 10 and 11), or part of the subconscious element of leading whereby self-reflection and assessment form part of the leader's psychological make-up, complementary to these will be assessments for emotional intelligence such as the Mayer-Salovey-Caruso Emotional Intelligence Test and the Emotional Quotient Inventory (Hall et al. 2015), both of which have been used in health sector environments. The former assesses emotional intelligence against four branches which are perceiving emotions, using emotions to facilitate thinking, understanding emotions, and managing emotions, whilst the latter uses five composite scales which are self-perception, self-expression, interpersonal, decision-making, and stress management. The power of the process has been acknowledged amongst diverse groups of health professionals (Hall et al. 2015: 1895; Ohlson and Anderson 2015: 87). The predilection or ability to gain self-knowledge may well be a feature of the leader's level of emotional intelligence. And being led by an individual with whom followers have high relational interest increases the intentional mobilisation of followers, and a leader who advances the interests of a collective is perceived as offering more authentic leadership and is more likely to inspire followership (Steffens et al. 2016; Slater et al. 2017). This relational interest will be enhanced when followers perceive that the leader is able to respond to circumstance and isn't committed to a monolithic approach. The ability to adapt is critical.

Case Study: Leadership in British Healthcare—A Dynamic and Evolving Model

Michelle Fitzgerald-Shaw, National Programme Lead: Talent Management, NHS Leadership Academy

Leaders in the health sector have a significant impact on the societies and communities that their organisations serve. Their effectiveness will not only influence the quality of care given and positive patient outcomes but will also go a long way to determining whether the workforce is engaged in the complex and difficult challenges that they face. Evidence from academics and practitioners has shown that to achieve positive outcomes will require clear team objectives, high levels of participation, and a commitment to excellence throughout the whole organisation. Leadership can provide these essential requirements. It was to this end that in 2013, the NHS Leadership Academy, together with colleagues and partners throughout the UK, developed a model that would begin to explain the features of best practice leadership that could be used in the wide variety of organisations and many different healthcare settings that existed in the UK (NHS 2013).

The most important facets of leadership were identified along nine 'dimensions' or groups of activity against which UK health leaders could develop. Each of the dimensions contained a series of desired leadership behaviours on a four-part scale which ranged from 'essential' through 'proficient' and 'strong' to 'exemplary.' The idea was that these dimensions and their accompanying descriptions would help to understand how leadership behaviour affected the organisation, its teams, and individual members of the health workforce. Leaders would be able to rate themselves on this scale and decide how best to move up the scale in their self-development.

The *nine dimensions of leadership behaviour* were as follows:

- 'Inspiring shared purpose: Valuing a service ethos; curious about how to improve services and patient care; behaving in a way that reflects the principles and values of the NHS
- Leading with Care: Having the essential personal qualities for leaders in health and social care; understanding the unique qualities and needs of a team; providing a caring, safe environment to enable everyone to do their jobs effectively
- Evaluating Information: Seeking out varied information; using information to generate new ideas and make effective plans for improvement or change; making evidence-based decisions that respect different perspectives and meet the needs of all service users
- Connecting our service: Understanding how health and social care services fit together and how different people, teams or organisations interconnect and interact

- Sharing the Vision: Communicating a compelling and credible vision of the future in a way that makes it feel achievable and exciting
- Engaging the team: Involving individuals and demonstrating that their contributions and ideas are valued and important for delivering outcomes and continuous improvements to the service
- Holding to account: agreeing clear performance goals and quality indicators; supporting individuals and teams to take responsibility for results; providing balanced feedback
- Developing Capability: Building capability to enable people to meet future challenges; using a range of experiences as a vehicle for individual and organisational learning; acting as a role model for personal development
- Influencing for results: deciding how to have a positive impact on other people; building relationships to recognise other people's passions and concerns; using interpersonal and organisational understanding to persuade and build collaboration' (NHS 2013)

These dimensions applied to all those designated as leaders in the NHS regardless of the size of unit for which they were responsible. Experience of implementation of the model for leadership led to refinements, and in 2016 NHS Improvement highlighted four critical capabilities for NHS leaders which were:

- 'systems leadership for staff who are working with partners in other local services on 'joining up' local health and care systems for their communities
- established quality improvement methods that draw on staff and service users' knowledge and experience to improve service quality and efficiency
- inclusive and compassionate leadership, so that all staff are listened to, understood and supported, and that leaders at every level of the health system truly reflect the talents and diversity of people working in the system and the communities they serve
- talent management to support NHS-funded services to fill senior current vacancies and future leadership pipelines with the right numbers of diverse, appropriately developed people' (NHS 2016)

Leadership in British healthcare is a critical factor in the delivery of effective health services across society. The type of leadership and its nature is very much contextual, and the frameworks that have evolved over the past five years reflect this point, responding to the need for different types of leadership in different scenarios—but underpinned by a belief in the values and ethics for which the National Health Service is renowned.

Review and Analysis: Adapting Leadership Behaviour

Since leadership is a socially complex and adaptive process (DeRue 2011), the ability to respond to the continuous change that is a feature of the modern health sector environment is important. Indeed, because leadership in health is formed by 'individual leaders practicing within a specific context of effective work relationships occurring throughout an organization, mediated through conversations' (Eubank et al. 2012: 242), adapting leadership style to best fit might be seen as an essential prerequisite to success. Adaptive leadership is a concept developed by Heifetz et al. (2009) and 'considers crises to be opportunities and offers a set of guiding principles that help to direct the organization's resilience while building mutual trust and creativity among administration, staff, and community' (Raney 2014: 312). A study of leadership in Brazilian hospitals concluded that 'leaders must continuously look for improvements in their own skills to exercise the leadership, anticipating the future, being creative and equipped to conduct processes of change, always promoting patients as protagonists and subjects of their care' (Ribeiro Chavaglia et al. 2013: 453); and recognition of the necessity of adaptive leadership has permeated several aspects of health sector with positive outcomes amongst paramedics in India (Mantha et al. 2016) and nurse and physician adaptive leadership behaviours in the USA (Adams et al. 2013), as well as potential to deal with the challenges facing family medicine where it was concluded that 'a whole person focus and healing relationships can be developed by learning the process skills of adaptive leadership' (Eubank et al. 2012: 249). Adaptive leadership behaviours corresponded to and complemented doctor practices with positive impacts on health outcomes and doctor-patient communication (Thygeson et al. 2010). One point of view argued that 'tough problems are often avoided by stakeholders and almost always are adaptive in nature. Thus they can only be addressed with adaptive change involving all stakeholders, which is why only adaptive leadership should be called real leadership' (Haeusler 2010: 14).

Those in leadership positions have a role to play in initiating change on the one hand but on the other must themselves adapt to change in order to remain effective, and 'while there are many leadership styles, the approach to any change must be appropriate to the demands of the situation' (Donnelly 2017: 154). There is a need for health sector leaders to 'demonstrate leadership behaviors or styles that are appropriate for the constantly changing, complex and turbulent health care delivery system' (Casida and Pinto-Zipp 2008). Adapting leadership behaviours is critical to the success in dealing with these changes (Hertig et al. 2016). To do so whilst maintaining the authenticity, beliefs, and values derived from personal insight is not straightforward. An awareness of self and others is one such way. With this point goes the ability to relate to a diverse set of people and learn to be effective 'in a broad range of situations by developing a range of behaviours' (Gray et al. 2010: 17). In critical care teams, effective leadership was characterised by both clear and unambiguous behaviour but most importantly to this section was adaptable to situational demands and, as an additional point, shared between team members (Künzle et al. 2010).

Conclusions and Implications for Practice

Whilst accepting that there is no right or wrong way to lead, it is important to bear in mind that the success of any leadership style or identity will depend on the context in which they are applied and how they are applied. Recognition of the former is a critical skill for health sector leaders, whilst leadership capability in the latter may be the difference between success and failure. In some cases, leaders will be exceptional and heroic; in others, leadership will be business as usual and a normal part of the operation of the organisation. In both cases personal insight is important to address the questions: am I a leader?; if so, what kind of a leader?; and how can I ensure that my approach to leadership is the right one for my organisation? The appropriate response will be for the leader, whether she or he is one in a formal position or one who has assumed leadership to deal with a particular scenario facing the organisation to reflect on four key areas: firstly, to acquire personal insight into leadership strengths, values, and beliefs; secondly, to craft this leadership capability into a leadership identity that is accepted by followers; thirdly, to implement leadership that is appropriate to circumstance and that builds on strengths and identity; and finally, to adapt or modify behaviour depending on the context within which leadership takes place.

Some of the key conclusions are:

- The **self-reflecting leader** evaluates performance as an ongoing process and with the benefit of insight and hindsight adapts behaviour accordingly.
- **Personal insight is important for a leader** or potential leader to realise her or his strengths and to use this information to be more effective once insight is translated into action. Such knowledge can be acquired through feedback gained by established human resource processes which include 360-degree appraisal, assessments, or coaching and mentoring.
- Personal insight is the **deep understanding of one's own leadership capabilities, values and beliefs, and preferred leadership style**. It is the basis of identifying leadership capability in any given context.
- A process for developing leadership capability therefore is to **reflect on personal strengths** and areas for development as provided by self-analysis or through third-party feedback, of which 360-degree appraisal is a common form; use the identified capability to **form a leadership identity** which is communicated by behaviour and leadership action and recognised as authentic by followers; **execute leadership actions in a way that is sensitive to the people** and operational context within which leadership takes place; and **evaluate the outcomes of leadership** with a view to adapting if necessary.
- In so doing it is assumed that leadership style is influenced by three factors: firstly, by **the skills and expertise already present in the leader**, which may be professional knowledge as in the case of clinical leadership or more generic leadership attributes such as 'creating value' or 'meeting the challenges of change'; secondly, **the ability to deliver to objectives through the direct or indirect influence of people**; and thirdly, **contextual factors that are at play in the approach to leadership challenges**—both within and outside of the organisation.

The ability of the leader to adapt his or her behaviour to the prevailing circumstances or need of the organisation is a conclusion that has been borne out by evidence from different health sector contexts.

References

Adams, J. A., Bailey, D. E., Jr., Anderson, R. A., & Thygeson, M. (2013). Finding Your Way Through EOL Challenges in the ICU Using Adaptive Leadership Behaviours: A Qualitative Descriptive Case Study. *Intensive & Critical Care Nursing, 29*(6), 329–336. https://doi.org/10.1016/j.iccn.2013.05.004.

Adegoke, K. A. A. (2017). Novice to Transformational Leader – A Personal Critical Reflection. *International Practice Development Journal, 7*(1), 1–12. https://doi.org/10.19043/ipdj.71.010.

Ali, S., & Terry, L. (2017). Exploring Senior Nurses' Understanding of Compassionate Leadership in the Community. *British Journal of Community Nursing, 22*(2), 77.

Alon, I., & Higgins, J. M. (2005). Global Leadership Success Through Emotional and Cultural Intelligences. *Business Horizons, 48*(6), 501–512. ISSN:0007-6813.

Amestoy, S., Cestari, M., Thofehrn, M., & Milbrath, V. (2009). Personal Characteristics That Influence the Development of a Nurse Leader. *Acta Paulista De Enfermagem, 22*(5), 673–678.

Antonakis, J., Ashkanasy, N. M., & Dasborough, M. T. (2009). Theoretical and Practitioner Letters: Does Leadership Need Emotional Intelligence? *The Leadership Quarterly, 20*(2), 57–262. ISSN:1048-9843.

Baker, S. D., Mathis, C. J., & Stites-Doe, S. (2011). An Exploratory Study Investigating Leader and Follower Characteristics at U.S. Healthcare Organizations. *Journal of Managerial Issues, 23*(3), 341.

Berghout, M. A., Fabbricotti, I. N., Buljac-Samardzic, M., & Hilders, C. M. (2017). Medical Leaders or Masters – A Systematic Review of Medical Leadership in Hospital Settings. *PLoS One, 12*(9), e0184522. https://doi.org/10.1371/journal.pone.0184522.

Bigelow, B., & Arndt, M. (2005). Transformational Change in Health Care: Changing the Question. *Hospital Topics, 83*(2), 19–26.

Bimray, P. B., & Jooste, K. (2014). A Conceptual Framework of the Resemblance in Self-Leadership and Professional Core Values of Nurses in the South

African Context. *African Journal for Physical, Health Education, Recreation & Dance, 1*, 197–216.

Bish, M., Kenny, A., & Nay, R. (2015). Factors That Influence the Approach to Leadership: Directors of Nursing Working in Rural Health Services. *Journal of Nursing Management, 23*(3), 380–389. https://doi.org/10.1111/jonm.12146.

Boyd, R., & Brown, T. (2005). Pilot Study of Myers Briggs Type Indicator Personality Profiling in Emergency Department Senior Medical Staff. *Emergency Medicine Australasia, 17*(3), 200–203. https://doi.org/10.1111/j.1742-6723.2005.00723.x.

Bradberry, T., & Antonakis, J. (2015). Is Emotional Intelligence a Good Measure of Leadership Ability. *HRMagazine, 60*(9), 22.

Casida, J., & Pinto-Zipp, G. (2008). Leadership-Organizational Culture Relationship in Nursing Units of Acute Care Hospitals. *Nursing Economic$, 26*(1), 7–15.

Celik, G. O. (2017). The Relationship Between Patient Satisfaction and Emotional Intelligence Skills of Nurses Working in Surgical Clinics. *Patient Preference & Adherence, 11*, 1363–1368. https://doi.org/10.2147/PPA.S136185.

Chang, G., & Diddams, M. (2009). Hubris or Humility: Cautions Surrounding the Construct and Self-Definition of Authentic Leadership. *Academy of Management Annual Meeting Proceedings, 2009*(1), 1–6. https://doi.org/10.5465/AMBPP.2009.44247841.

Chobanuk, J., & James, K. (2015). Leadership Special Interest Group: What Is Leadership? *Canadian Oncology Nursing Journal, 25*(1), 114–117.

Croft, C., Currie, G., & Lockett, A. (2015). The Impact of Emotionally Important Social Identities on the Construction of a Managerial Leader Identity: A Challenge for Nurses in the English National Health Service. *Organization Studies, 36*(1), 113.

Crowne, K. A., Young, T. M., Goldman, B., Patterson, B., Krouse, A. M., & Proenca, J. (2017). Leading Nurses: Emotional Intelligence and Leadership Development Effectiveness. *Leadership in Health Services (1751–1879), 30*(3), 217. https://doi.org/10.1108/LHS-12-2015-0055.

Czabanowska, K., Smith, T., Könings, K. D., Sumskas, L., Otok, R., Bjegovic-Mikanovic, V., et al. (2014). In Search for a Public Health Leadership Competency Framework to Support Leadership Curriculum–A Consensus Study. *European Journal of Public Health, 24*(5), 850–856. https://doi.org/10.1093/eurpub/ckt158.

Daire, J., & Gilson, L. (2014). Does Identity Shape Leadership and Management Practice? Experiences of PHC Facility Managers in Cape Town, South Africa. *Health Policy and Planning, 29 Suppl 2*, ii82–ii97. https://doi.org/10.1093/heapol/czu075.

Day, M., Shickle, D., Smith, K., Zakariasen, K., Moskol, J., & Oliver, T. (2014). Training Public Health Superheroes: Five Talents for Public Health Leadership. *Journal of Public Health, 36*(4), 552–561. ISSN:1741-3842.

DeRue, D. S. (2011). Adaptive Leadership Theory: Leading and Following as a Complex Adaptive Process. *Research in Organizational Behavior, 31*, 125–150. https://doi.org/10.1016/j.riob.2011.09.007.

DeRue, D. S., & Ashford, S. J. (2010). Who Will Lead and Who Will Follow? A Social Process of Leadership Identity Construction in Organizations. *Academy of Management Review, 35*(4), 627–647. https://doi.org/10.5465/AMR.2010.53503267.

Di Fabio, A., Bernaud, J., & Loarer, E. (2014). Emotional Intelligence or Personality in Resistance to Change? Empirical Results in an Italian Health Care Context. *Journal of Employment Counseling, 51*(4), 146–157. https://doi.org/10.1002/j.2161-1920.2014.00048.x.

Donnelly, T. (2017). Leadership: Briefing and Debriefing in the Operating Room. *Journal of Perioperative Practice, 27*(7), 154–157.

Edger, C. (2012). *Effective Multi-Unit Leadership: Local Leadership in Multi-Site Situations*. Farnham: Gower Applied Research Press.

Ellis, P., & Bach, S. (2015). *Leadership, Management and Team Working*. London: Sage Publications.

Eubank, D., Geffken, D., Orzano, J., & Ricci, R. (2012). Teaching Adaptive Leadership to Family Medicine Residents: What? Why? How? *Families, Systems, & Health, 30*(3), 241–252. https://doi.org/10.1037/a0029689.

Ezziane, Z. (2012). The Importance of Clinical Leadership in Twenty First Century Healthcare. *International Journal of Health Promotion and Education, 50*(5), 261–269.

Fernandes Carvalho, A. G., Kowal Olm Cunha, I. C., Pazetto Balsanelli, A., & Bernardes, A. (2016). Authentic Leadership and the Personal and Professional Profile of Nurses. *Acta Paulista De Enfermagem, 29*(6), 618–625. https://doi.org/10.1590/1982-0194201600087.

Fernandez, C., Noble, C., Jensen, E., & Steffen, D. (2015). Moving the Needle: A Retrospective Pre- and Post-Analysis of Improving Perceived Abilities Across 20 Leadership Skills. *Maternal & Child Health Journal, 19*(2), 343–352. https://doi.org/10.1007/s10995-014-1573-1.

Graber, D. R., & Kilpatrick, A. O. (2008). Establishing Values-Based Leadership and Value Systems in Healthcare Organizations. *Journal of Health & Human Services Administration, 31*(2), 179–197.

Gray, I., Field, R., & Brown, K. (2010). *Effective Leadership, Management and Supervision in Health and Social Care*. Exeter: Learning Matters.

Grindel, C. G. (2016). Clinical Leadership: A Call to Action. *Medsurg Nursing, 25*(1), 9–16.

Grint, K. (2005). *Leadership: Limits and Possibilities*. Basingstoke: Palgrave Macmillan.

Haeusler, J. C. (2010). Medicine Needs Adaptive Leadership. *Physician Executive, 36*(2), 12–15.

Hall, C. M., Murphy Enright, S., White, S. J., & Allen, S. J. (2015). A Quantitative Study of the Emotional Intelligence of Participants in the ASHP Foundation's Pharmacy Leadership Academy. *American Journal of Health-System Pharmacy, 72*(21), 1890–1895. https://doi.org/10.2146/ajhp140812.

Heifetz, R., Grashow, A., & Linsky, M. (2009). *The Practice of Adaptive Leadership: Tools and Tactics for Changing Your Organisation and the World*. Boston, MA: Harvard Business Press.

Hendricks, J. M., Cope, V. C., & Harris, M. (2010). A Leadership Program in an Undergraduate Nursing Course in Western Australia: Building Leaders in Our Midst. *Nurse Education Today, 30*(Leadership for Learning Special Issue), 252–257. https://doi.org/10.1016/j.nedt.2009.12.007.

Hertig, J. B., Hultgren, K. E., & Weber, R. J. (2016). Using Contemporary Leadership Skills in Medication Safety Programs. *Hospital Pharmacy, 51*(4), 338–344. https://doi.org/10.1310/hpj5104-338.

Hlongwane, V., & Olivier, B. (2017). Authentic Leadership Influences on Organisational Commitment in a South African State Hospital. *Journal of Psychology in Africa, 27*(5), 400–404.

Hodgson, D., Bresnen, M., Hyde, P., Hodgson, D., & Hassard, J. (2015). Leadership Talk: From Managerialism to Leaderism in Health Care After the Crash. *Leadership, 11*(4), 451–470.

Hunt, M., Jr. (2017). The Power of Great Expectations. *American Journal of Health-System Pharmacy, 74*(16), 1221–1228. https://doi.org/10.2146/ajhp170.

Jodar, I., Solà, G., Gené, I., Badia, J., Hito, P. D., Osaba, M. C., et al. (2016). Self-Perception of Leadership Styles and Behaviour in Primary Health Care. *BMC Health Services Research, 16*(1), 572.

Johnston, C., Turpin, N., & Wynn-Jones, W. (2016). Medical Leadership in Perioperative Practice: I. *BJA Education, 16*(6), 203–208. https://doi.org/10.1093/bjaed/mkv041.
Kim, B., & Lee, J. (2016). Research Article: Relationships Between Personal Traits, Emotional Intelligence, Internal Marketing, Service Management, and Customer Orientation in Korean Outpatient Department Nurses. *Asian Nursing Research, 10*, 18–24.
Kozub, E., Brown, L., & Ecoff, L. (2016). Strategies for Success: Cultivating Emotional Competence in the Clinical Nurse Specialist Role. *AACN Advanced Critical Care, 27*(2), 145–151. https://doi.org/10.4037/aacnacc2016771.
Künzle, B., Kolbe, M., & Grote, G. (2010). Ensuring Patient Safety Through Effective Leadership Behaviour: A Literature Review. *Safety Science, 48*, 1–17. https://doi.org/10.1016/j.ssci.2009.06.004.
Larkin, H. (2015). The New Health Care CEO: In a Rapidly Changing Field, Effective Leaders Require 'Learning Agility' and 'Emotional Intelligence' as Much–or More–Than Traditional Skills. *H&HN Hospitals & Health Networks, 22*(6).
Lawrence, E. T. (2010). Myers-Briggs and Psychological Type and Change Style for Hospital Executives. *Journal of Psychological Issues in Organizational Culture, 1*(2), 6. https://doi.org/10.1002/jpoc.20020.
Lorber, M., Treven, S., & Mumel, D. (2016). The Examination of Factors Relating to the Leadership Style of Nursing Leaders in Hospitals. *Naše Gospodarstvo, 62*(1), 27–36. https://doi.org/10.1515/ngoe-2016-0003.
Love, D., & Ayadi, M. F. (2015). Redefining the Core Competencies of Future Healthcare Executives Under Healthcare Reform. *Administrative Issues Journal: Education, Practice & Research, 5*(2), 3–16. ISSN:2153-7615.
Lührmann, T., & Eberl, P. (2007). Leadership and Identity Construction: Reframing the Leader-Follower Interaction from an Identity Theory Perspective. *Leadership, 3*(1), 115. https://doi.org/10.1177/1742715007073070.
Malik, N., Dhar, R. L., & Handa, S. C. (2016). Authentic Leadership and Its Impact on Creativity of Nursing Staff: A Cross Sectional Questionnaire Survey of Indian Nurses and Their Supervisors. *International Journal of Nursing Studies, 63*, 28–36. https://doi.org/10.1016/j.ijnurstu.2016.08.004.
Mantha, A., Coggins, N. L., Mahadevan, A., Strehlow, R. N., Strehlow, M. C., & Mahadevan, S. V. (2016). Adaptive Leadership Curriculum for Indian

Paramedic Trainees. *International Journal of Emergency Medicine, 9*, 1–7. https://doi.org/10.1186/s12245-016-0103-x.

Marchiondo, L. A., Myers, C. G., & Kopelman, S. (2015). The Relational Nature of Leadership Identity Construction: How and When It Influences Perceived Leadership and Decision-Making. *The Leadership Quarterly, 26*, 892–908. https://doi.org/10.1016/j.leaqua.2015.06.006.

Mascia, D., Russo, S. D., & Morandi, F. (2015). Exploring Professionals' Motivation to Lead: A Cross-Level Study in the Healthcare Sector. *The International Journal of Human Resource Management, 26*(12), 1622–1644. https://doi.org/10.1080/09585192.2014.958516.

Mastrangelo, A., Eddy, E. R., & Lorenzset, S. J. (2004). The Importance of Personal and Professional Leadership. *The Leadership and Organisation Development Journal, 25*(5), 435–451.

Miscenko, D., Guenter, H., & Day, D. V. (2017). Am I a Leader? Examining Leader Identity Development Over Time. *The Leadership Quarterly, 28*, 605–620. https://doi.org/10.1016/j.leaqua.2017.01.004.

Miskelly, P., & Duncan, L. (2014). 'I'm Actually Being the Grown-Up Now': Leadership, Maturity and Professional Identity Development. *Journal of Nursing Management, 22*(1), 38–48.

Moen, C., & Prescott, P. (2016). A Values-Based Approach to Medical Leadership. *British Journal of Hospital Medicine, 77*(11), 624–629.

NHS. (2013). *The Healthcare Leadership Model: Nine Dimensions of Leadership Behaviour*. Leeds: NHS Leadership Academy. Retrieved from https://www.leadershipacademy.nhs.uk/wp-content/uploads/2014/10/NHSLeadership-LeadershipModel-colour.pdf.

NHS. (2016). *Developing People – Improving Care*. London: NHS Improvement. Retrieved from https://improvement.nhs.uk/resources/developing-people-improving-care.

Ohlson, S. M., & Anderson, M. A. (2015). Ability Emotional Intelligence of Nurse Managers in the Midwestern United States. *Asia-Pacific Journal of Oncology Nursing, 2*(2), 82–88.

Owens, P. (2016). Leadership Identity. *The CEO Magazine.*

Purdy, N. (2016). Impact of a Leadership Development Institute on Professional Lives and Careers. *Nursing Leadership (1910–622X), 29*(2), 10–30.

Raney, A. F. (2014). Agility in Adversity: Integrating Mindfulness and Principles of Adaptive Leadership in the Administration of a Community Mental Health Center. *Clinical Social Work Journal, 42*(3), 312–320. https://doi.org/10.1007/s10615-014-0487-0.

Ribeiro Chavaglia, S. R., Dela Coleta, M. F., Dela Coleta, J. A., Costa Mendes, I. A., & Trevizan, M. A. (2013). Adaptation and Validation of the Charismatic Leadership Socialized Scale. *Acta Paulista De Enfermagem, 26*(5), 444–454.

Robbins, C. J., Bradley, E. H., & Spicer, M. (2001). Developing Leadership in Healthcare Administration: A Competency Assessment Tool. *Journal of Healthcare Management / American College of Healthcare Executives, 46*(3), 188–202.

Robinson, M., MacNeily, A., Afshar, K., McInnes, C., Lennox, P., Carr, N., et al. (2013). Original Reports: Leadership in Canadian Urology: What Is the Right Stuff. *Journal of Surgical Education, 70*, 606–612. https://doi.org/10.1016/j.jsurg.2013.04.013.

Rothke, S. E. (2014). Organizational Insight for Physician Leaders: A Critical Perspective. *Physician Executive, 40*(2), 54–56.

Samiuddin, K., Ishtiaq, A., & Syed Zaheer Abbas, K. (2017). The Role of Emotional Intelligence in Hospital Administration: A Case Study from Pakistan. *Cross-Cultural Management Journal, 19*(1), 39–46.

Shanafelt, T. D., Gorringe, G., Menaker, R., Storz, K. A., Reeves, D., Buskirk, S. J., et al. (2015). Original Article: Impact of Organizational Leadership on Physician Burnout and Satisfaction. *Mayo Clinic Proceedings, 90*, 432–440. https://doi.org/10.1016/j.mayocp.2015.01.012.

Shariff, N. J. (2015). A Delphi Survey of Leadership Attributes Necessary for National Nurse Leaders' Participation in Health Policy Development: An East African Perspective. *BMC Nursing, 14*(1), 13. ISSN:1472-6955.

Slater, M. J., Turner, M. J., Evans, A. L., & Jones, M. V. (2017). Capturing Hearts and Minds: The Influence of Relational Identification with the Leader on Followers' Mobilization and Cardiovascular Reactivity. *The Leadership Quarterly, 29*(3), 365–442. https://doi.org/10.1016/j.leaqua.2017.08.003.

Steffens, N. K., Mols, F., Haslam, S. A., & Okimoto, T. G. (2016). True to What We Stand for: Championing Collective Interests as a Path to Authentic Leadership. *The Leadership Quarterly, 27*, 726–744. https://doi.org/10.1016/j.leaqua.2016.04.004.

Taylor, D. L. (2014). Perioperative Leadership: Managing Change with Insights, Priorities and Tools. *AORN Journal, 100*(1), 8–26, 27–29.

Thygeson, M., Morrissey, L., & Ulstad, V. (2010). Adaptive Leadership and the Practice of Medicine: A Complexity-Based Approach to Reframing the Doctor–Patient Relationship. *Journal of Evaluation in Clinical Practice, 16*(5), 1009–1015. https://doi.org/10.1111/j.1365-2753.2010.01533.x.

Uzonwanne, F. C. (2016). Practising Male, in a "Woman's World": Gender, Age and Dimensions of Emotional Intelligence Among Nurse Leaders in Northern Nigeria. *Gender & Behaviour, 14*(3), 778.

Waite, R., McKinney, N., Smith-Glasgow, M. E., & Meloy, F. A. (2014). The Embodiment of Authentic Leadership. *Journal of Professional Nursing, 30*, 282–291. https://doi.org/10.1016/j.profnurs.2013.11.004.

Weiss, M., Razinskas, S., Backmann, J., & Hoegl, M. (2017). Authentic Leadership and Leaders' Mental Well-Being: An Experience Sampling Study. *The Leadership Quarterly, 29*(2), 253–364. https://doi.org/10.1016/j.leaqua.2017.05.007.

Xavier, S. (2005). Are You at the Top of Your Game? Checklist for Effective Leaders. *Journal of Business Strategy, 25*(3), 35–42.

Yukl, G. (2010). *Leadership in Organisations*. London: Pearson.

Zheng, W., & Muir, D. (2015). Embracing Leadership: A Multi-Faceted Model of Leader Identity Development. *Leadership & Organization Development Journal, 36*(6), 630–656. https://doi.org/10.1108/LODJ-10-2013-0138.

7

The Importance of Professional Credibility

Credible Leaders Who 'Span the Divide'

Leadership capability is a source of authority; professional credibility is a source of legitimacy. A combination of both will create respect and trust by peers and engagement with followers. The challenge is how to do so in health sector organisations with often complex people and organisational dynamics. This chapter will analyse a meaning for the term professional credibility and identify how health sector leaders incorporate it into their leadership identity—a particular issue because they operate in a world that spans managerial and clinical logics, managerial and clinical objectives, and managerial and clinical decision-making processes. In this environment, health leaders are often faced with a balancing act between the two sets of priorities: expected to build on strengths when they converge and resolve tensions when they don't (Hunn 2016). This implies that not only do they require 'the ability to envision a compelling future' (Thompson et al. 2008: 371) but also the capacity to realise that future, to develop innovative solutions, and to get others to support them. Professional credibility complements leadership capability in achieving these stretching goals. Integrated healthcare requires leadership both ***by***

P. Turner, *Leadership in Healthcare*, Organizational Behaviour in Health Care,
https://doi.org/10.1007/978-3-030-04387-2_7

and ***for*** those in clinical, managerial, technical, professional, and administrative roles (American Medical Association 2015). Leadership decisions in health are made in this unique context.

The forces driving the convergence of profession and leadership are plentiful, comprising external factors outlined in the VUCA narrative in Chap. 2 and internal ones based on the complexity, fluidity, and the highly skilled technical and professional health workforce. For these reasons, it is argued that a purely mechanical, rational, and predictable approach to health sector leadership is impracticable because the pluralistic nature of health sector organisations demands strength of organisational knowledge, 'professional' legitimacy, and an abundance of social capital (Goorapah 1997; Thompson et al. 2008; Kaiser et al. 2012; Loh et al. 2016; Pascuci et al. 2017: 4). There are common factors in the leader's ability to deliver to these requirements. For example, the model for health sector leadership included such generic competences as the ability to create meaning for the organisation and translate broad strategy into practical actions and ability in 'knowing-interpreting,' acting as a force for change, understanding the dynamics of change, and mobilising the potential and capacities across organisations and of members of the organisation as a whole or individual departments/teams. In addition, the capability to engage and motivate a broad section of the workforce by understanding the importance of followership is an important competence. However, leaders in health also need to build social capital by demonstrating professional credibility, a requirement that is necessary not only to provide context to strategy or objective setting but also in ensuring that followers have trust in the ability of the leader to lead against some of the unique demands of the sector. Evidence from Africa, Brazil, the USA, and the UK has raised the importance of the professional credibility attribute (Brooke et al. 1998; Shariff 2015; Manley and Titchen 2017; Pascuci et al. 2017).

The Meaning of Professional Credibility in the Health Sector

For the purposes of the leadership model proposed in this book, professional credibility is related to knowledge and insight into the particular area or sphere of health sector activity in which the organisation operates.

It means being knowledgeable about practice (Fisher 2005) but not necessarily expert at practice, and it requires an understanding of the unique context within which this practice takes place. So, whilst clinical leadership requires leadership capability and clinical competence, wider organisational leadership will require leadership capability and an understanding of, rather than mastery of, clinical context, issues, and outcomes. Professional credibility in the former example, clinical leadership, is earned by qualification, experience, and successful practice. In the latter it is earned from contextual knowledge, experience, and successful practice. The argument is that a leadership style, for example, transformational leadership, will be enhanced by a level of professional credibility relevant to the role and the unique milieu of health. Professional credibility is not confined to those in clinical roles but to all of those who undertake leadership activity.

Professional credibility goes hand in hand with personal credibility and is a reputation that an individual builds up over time based on factors such as knowledge, trust, integrity, and the consistent behaviours and actions that reinforce these. It is not something that individuals can bestow on themselves but is, in all cases, the result of the perceptions of others. An individual will be regarded as having credibility by team members through her or his deep, demonstrable knowledge of the environment in which they operate, success in delivering outcomes in this environment, balance and fairness in leading a workforce in the unique milieu of health, and transparency in dealings with all stakeholders. Professional credibility builds on these concepts and of the ability of 'sense making' in a climate of volatility or unpredictability but will include additional factors such as qualification in a specific field, experience of delivering strategy or operations in health's complex multi-agency environments, successful performance in the professional context, and a commitment to acquiring and maintaining knowledge in the sphere. In some cases, professional credibility will come from mastery of a particular domain (e.g. clinical, medical, technical); in others it will come from mastery of the understanding of a context, such as that in the successful general management of a hospital, specialist health unit, or health sector support function—technology in health or human resources in health. The broad spread of those covered by the concept means that professional credibility and its relationship with leadership capability have been the subject of considerable debate. For some, the logic of management discourse has been internalised into both professional role and identity, making it a valid and integrated part of the role of the health sector leader (Salvatore et al. 2012; Veronesi et al. 2015: 1031). For others, there is the ongoing potential for conflict between professional and managerial logics (Berghout et al. 2017). In its worst case 'getting involved in leadership and management is moving away from the perceived altruistic activity of clinical practice' (Loh et al. 2016: 314), and those who take on formal medical leadership roles are perceived as having gone to the 'dark side.'

Nevertheless, there is a perception that when health solutions are developed, they would be enhanced by the professional credibility on the part of those advocating such solutions. The reasons for this arise from general leadership theory in which a leader is 'granted' leadership because of her or his competence (Marchiondo 2015: 903) and a specific example because in health sector organisations 'decisions and actions result from political, interpretive and symbolic aspects more than from essentially rationalistic approaches' (Pascuci et al. 2017: 4). Tensions are neither universal nor inevitable, and whilst 'specific patterns of professionalism reinforce resistance towards managerial measures,' some aspects of professionalism have been transformed by management measures or have facilitated the incorporation of managerial tools (Salvatore et al. 2012: 629). The interdependency between regimes can mediate some of the more negative perceptions between professionalism and managerialism.

> Hitherto, scholarship shows that professionalism and management are frequently framed as contradictory. However, a number of contextual and situated analyses have concluded that interplay between professionalism and management results more often in co-existence, co-optation, mediation, negotiating, merging and (strategic) adaptation rather than in clashes, hegemony and resistance. (Salvatore et al. 2012: 637)

Numerous organisational positions and scenarios ensure that clinical and medical professionalism and management or leadership remain complex interrelated subjects. A critical challenge for health sector leaders is to reconcile these positions in an environment where clinical or medical professionalism is interpreted in a sociocultural context, where goal orientations and ethics can be different to those of management, and in which overlaps and tensions can result (Martin et al. 2013).

Becoming a Visible, Accessible, and Authoritative Presence

Professional credibility is particularly relevant to health because of the accentuation of the outcomes of leadership activity. Whereas leaders in all sectors will invariably find themselves under the spotlight about their organisation's performance and sometimes simultaneously under a sharper, more focused critique directed towards a single specific issue, the lights that shine on health sector leaders are often brighter, sharper, and in many cases more prolonged. To deal with this, both leadership capability and professional credibility are important in relation to the process of making decisions and the perceived efficacy of their outcomes (Gabris et al. 2001). So, the chances of successful transformation and change in health may be improved where the leader is an accepted and 'credible insider' (Denis et al. 2000), combining specified and formal leadership responsibilities with credibility in clinical, medical, professional, technical, or business leadership in 'a sphere of situated and wider influence' (Stoddart et al. 2014: 52). Decisions will be made, in part from inherent, developed, or experienced knowledge or insight (leadership capability) and in part from knowledge generated by having the right focus on activity in the right places (through professional credibility and understanding). Studies in the USA and UK reinforce the importance of professional credibility through the 'visible, accessible and authoritative presence' (Patrick et al. 2011: 450; Lawrence and Richardson 2014), that is, the manifestation of it. In this context, the transfer of health professional skills to broader health organisation decision-making is in multiple forms. Roles can be generic, which fill the space between specialists focusing on the organisation of care and treatment, increasingly integrating care and cure activities, or extended which develop new ways of providing health service provision by shaping 'organisation-oriented' healthcare delivery (de Bont et al. 2016; Noordegraaf 2016: 783). A professional logic, underpinning a managerial logic, may be a formula for effective change. And in reverse, where managerial logic informs professional logic—perhaps in the frame of talent management or technological innovation—a combination of leadership capability and professional credibility is a desired objective.

Examples of this intertwinement include those where a clinical professional adopts leadership roles such as Nurse or Physician Executives requiring leadership and managerial acumen in addition to clinical knowledge as well as systems-based practice and professionalism, and in order to have credibility with peers, 'it is critical for a physician to be recognized as accomplished in one's field before taking on medical leadership roles' (Simms et al. 1985; Hernandez 2010; Bhatia et al. 2015), or where leadership roles overlap those of professional ones (Kumar et al. 2015: 161). The challenge is to develop both into a viable health leadership proposition and identity. But it isn't just in clinical roles that the question of professional credibility stands out. A Canadian study of organisational leadership concluded that

> the hospital CEO is responsible for the management of complex services involving substantial financial resources and large numbers of people with diverse specialized skills which he or she usually does not share. No move can be contemplated without considering the role and reactions of professional staff whose power and autonomy may be perpetuated not only through their specialized expertise, but also through structural mechanisms. (Denis et al. 2000)

Professional credibility will contribute to a relationship of trust with followers based on a perception that the leader understands the context and therefore takes informed and insightful decisions from this base. It is important to health sector leaders because

> trust is vital for the leader, and leaders who make personal connections by establishing trust with followers tend to be more effective. If a follower trusts a leader, then trust in the organization also can increase, and trust in an organization has been shown to be positively associated with work engagement, sharing of knowledge, teamwork, and employee performance. (Penny 2017: 611)

There are benefits to combining leadership and professional credibility in the health sector. Figure 7.1 highlights some of the characteristics of these two areas as well as possible outcomes.

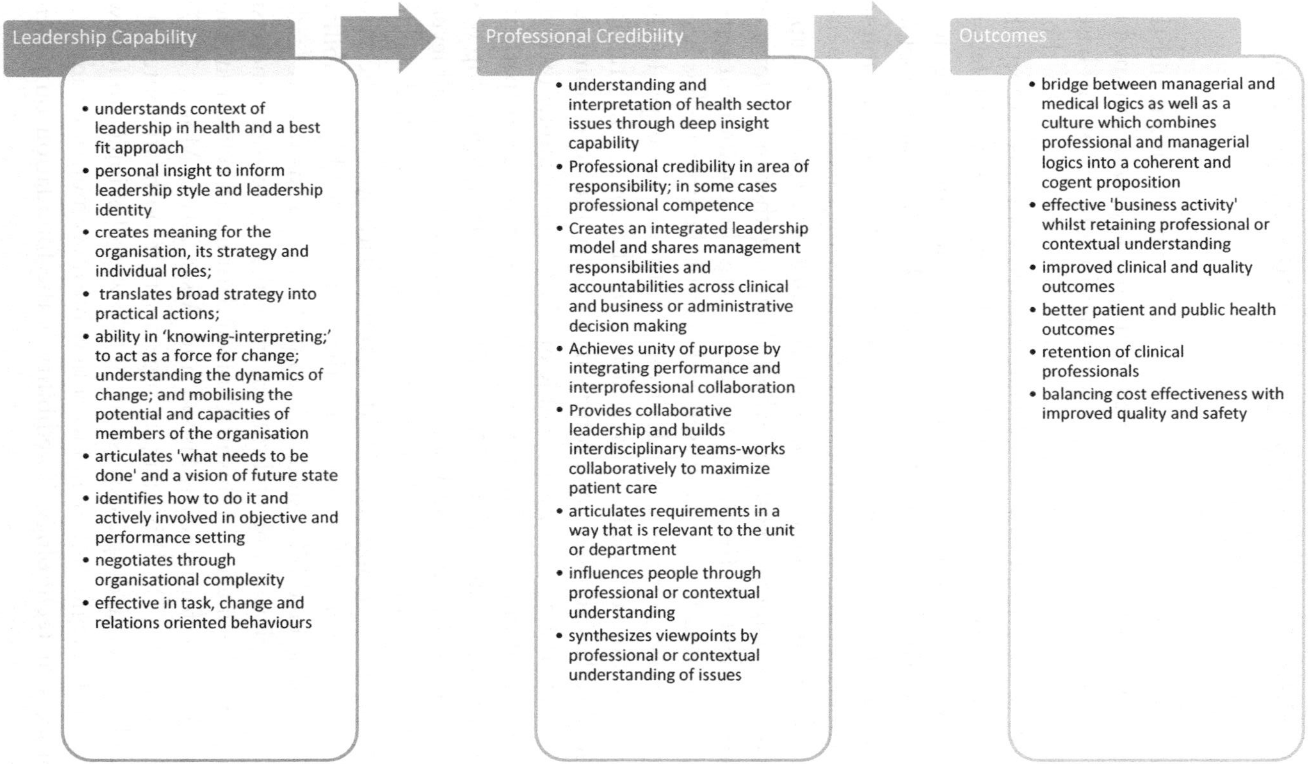

Fig. 7.1 Leadership capability, professional credibility, and improved outcomes

Professional Credibility, Leadership Capability, and Leadership Identity

A critical route for successful integration of the professional and the managerial is in the form of a viable leadership identity as outlined in Chap. 6. There are theoretical underpinnings in support of this based on the fundamental that leadership is a relationship between those who wish to lead and those who choose to follow. In this respect, the term follower isn't used in an inferior or subordinate way. It refers to health professional colleagues who accept and buy in to the decisions or recommendations made by someone in a leadership position including peers or those in Senior Leadership positions. For this equation to work, leaders require the respect and esteem of organisational members and external stakeholders, through demonstrable leadership capability and professional credibility which come together in the form of a leadership identity. The model for identifying the component parts of leadership identity was discussed earlier, and the premise has been validated across geographic divides from California to Kenya. In the former, professional credibility was earned by the consistent practice of Senior Leaders across several functions (clinical, financial, administrative) and being visible and accessible in a health environment which had a significant impact on redirecting time and energy to the patient, with positive outcomes (Manss 2017: 68). In the latter, leadership was inclusive and deliberative and perceived by the workforce at all levels to be fair because of the credibility of the leader who 'reached out to different actors and negotiated with them to participate in the processes' (Barasa et al. 2017: 109). Furthermore, leadership capability and professional credibility and their contribution to an effective leadership identity played a pivotal role in, inter alia, innovation amongst nursing staff, the success of hospital consolidation and transition, and surgical team performance (Masood and Afsar 2017; Morris 2017; Barling et al. 2017). This analysis suggests that both attributes are invaluable in persuading a diverse set of fellow professionals to follow a particular strategic path, embrace a new business model, or adopt a new process or technology. 'Credibility is the foundation on which leaders and constituents will build grand dreams of the future … especially in uncertain times, leadership credibility is essential in generating confidence among constituents' (Kouzes and Posner 2011: 2). In the health sector it is an advantage, if not a requirement, that professionals who assume leadership roles have substance knowledge—to grasp the relationship of decisions to the larger health organisation or community served—as well as leadership and management competencies (Politis 2005; Size 2006; Kantanen et al. 2017). The fusion of leadership capability and professional credibility is one that applies at many levels where leadership activity takes place.

Professional Credibility and Leadership Competence

There is a strong case then for combining leadership capability with professional credibility as a contribution to an organisation's success in the health sector. The challenge facing leaders is to understand the competences associated with this objective. Having undertaken a process of gaining personal insight from self-reflection, from which emanated a deeper understanding of relevant knowledge, skills, attitudes, and behaviours, an individual will have begun to develop a leadership identity. The question of professional credibility can be viewed in the same light in determining the extent that those in leadership roles have it at sufficient levels to ensure followership from a professional health workforce spanning clinical, medical, technical, and administrative roles and how this might be developed. The model for health sector leadership included in Chap. 5 outlined a series of competences associated with professional credibility which can help to develop this part of the health leader's identity. These can be grouped under two headings as outlined below.

- **Unity of Purpose by Strategic and Operational Balance**

The question is how to create value by combining clinical, managerial, and managerial logics. And so, the first group of competences concerns the necessity of integration and collaboration in trying to achieve a unity of purpose and a balance between strategy and operations. Professional credibility means that the leader recognises the necessity of a multi-professional response to often complex and ambiguous challenges and adopts a collaborative approach to these. This will require the leader to create a model that ensures that management responsibilities and accountabilities are shared across clinical and business or administrative decision-making functions. This will contribute to a desired unity of purpose because it facilitates performance and interprofessional collaboration. A contribution to this is to build alliances and partnerships with clinical, medical, and managerial colleagues to ensure effective outcomes as well as establishing professional contacts and networks with experts outside of the organisation. To do so will require an understanding of patient and consumer healthcare expectations and requirements and the context within which these take place. To help, professional intuition and evidence-based outcomes in decision-making are necessary, and this requires the application of both professional and managerial competences to organisational challenges. In summary, these competences are particularly focused on ensuring that the links between professional (e.g. clinical) and managerial outcomes are forged, that synergies are sought as a result, and that tensions are dealt with by transparency of decision-making, building collaboration, and effective multifunctional teams.

- **Alignment of Professional Domain with Organisational Objectives**

The second categorisation of the competences associated with leadership and professional credibility seeks to ensure the alignment between a professional area and the overall organisational objectives—thereby mitigating any source of tension. To do so will require an understanding of the importance of clinical integration and coordination of care and hence insight into the fundamentals of the care delivery process. In this respect, having professional credibility will add value to decisions about innovations, new methods, technologies, or opportunities for the delivery of healthcare and contribute to gaining followership in their acceptance and implementation. This will be undertaken in a context of professional accountability and responsibility in which the leader will act as a role model and demonstrate the core elements of professionalism—including a high level of ethical behaviour and commitment to the professional values of the organisation. During this process the leader will actively seek and be able to acquire new knowledge in either a specific professional discipline or a broader contextual understanding of the implications of decisions on health outcomes.

These two groups of competences are intended to be indicative. Each organisation will adapt its competence sets to its specific needs and environment, and it is likely that the professional credibility element of the model will vary. Whichever competences are chosen will, when combined with leadership capability, be articulated in the form of a health leadership identity.

Professional Credibility: Task, Change, and Relations

The application of the above will depend on the context within which leadership takes place which might be the delivery of new systems and processes designed to improve operational performance; or they might be strategic changes to a business model as a way of addressing health needs; they might be the need to integrate multiple agencies to ensure the best allocation of resource or they might be about improving workforce engagement. Understanding how the two foundations for health sector leadership are manifested can take place by looking at leadership through one of the three lenses as outlined in Chaps. 3 and 4. At its most general, leadership is composed of **task-oriented behaviours** which are intended to improve business or operational processes, **change-oriented behaviours** which are a response to external forces such as the examples in the VUCA analysis in Chap. 2, and **relations-oriented behaviours** which deal with the engagement and direction of people (Yukl 2010: 392). On the one hand, there is an argument that the leadership skills necessary to influence in these three ways are generic and portable, so that a leader in one sector or role could transfer to another and apply successfully the same skills or approaches. On the other hand, there is the argument that the unique context of the health sector requires leaders who have a knowledgeable, insightful, and specific understanding of the health environment for them to be successful. Hence, not only was the leaders' awareness of how they themselves were situated important; (Saxena et al. 2017) but the unique context within which identity was articulated. Indeed, when the performance determinants of leaders are analysed in more detail, there is a strong case for arguing that achievement in any of the three 'metacategories' outlined above (task, change, relations) would be enhanced by the professional credibility of the leader in question. Professional knowledge and insight would add value to such activities as structural reform, knowledge acquisition, organisational learning, and goal setting, which are seen as some of the activities needed to influence performance (Yukl 2010: 393).

Capability to perform strongly in both areas will allow health sector leaders to 'span the divide' between profession and organisation and contribute to the achievement of organisational goals. This premise can also apply to leadership in its broadest sense—that is, where it is non-hierarchical and contextual (Lv and Zhang 2017). It is in this domain where professional credibility overlaps with **task-oriented behaviour**, which is how a leader performs the management functions of planning, organising, controlling, and seeking subordinates' commitment (Ceri-Booms et al. 2017). In a US study of the implementation of evidence-based practice (EBP), it was found that leadership capability in the integration and 'institutionalisation' of EBP reflected a complex set of actions in which 'leaders engaged in strategic behaviors related to one theme, Planning-Organizing-Aligning, which demonstrated underlying vision-focused and systems-oriented thinking' (Stetler et al. 2014: 221). Not only did these leaders create a vision but made plans to sustain it—task-oriented leadership behaviour based on professional understanding of how change would be implemented. These findings were also present in an earlier review which found that 'two of the most prominent factors impacting the implementation of EBP were strong leadership and mastery of practice-related skills' (Sandström et al. 2011: 213). Professional credibility affects how followers regard such decisions. Not only does it give team members a clear sense of direction and purpose, but they do so in a perception that the person giving the direction is doing so based on contextual knowledge and insight.

In addition to the task-orientated leadership behaviour outlined above, **change-oriented behaviour** also benefits from professional credibility and its contribution to leadership identity. Hence, building and sustaining a culture, which involves change to health sector practices or organisational transformation, requires those responsible to demonstrate more than leadership capability. This is a specific challenge for health sector leaders in senior roles because they are required to demonstrate that they have insight in clinical, medical, operational, or technical matters whilst at the same time demonstrating insight in leadership or business management knowledge, skills, attitudes, and behaviours. Practice evidence suggests that it was important for health leaders in both the USA and China to support change management and wider business administration through their understanding of context (Godfrey et al. 2014; Bai et al. 2017) and to create a supportive culture to institutionalise change by the creation of 'norms, artifacts, and expectations reflective of such a culture therefore needed to be identified or created and inculcated into behaviors.' In these examples leaders acted as role models in the implementation of new behaviours. Professional credibility facilitated this and 'leaders deliberatively influenced, through many differently themed leadership behaviors, the way things were to be done in the organization' (Stetler et al. 2014: 223).

The third area in which professional credibility can enhance leadership identity is in **relations-oriented behaviour**. A leader who has 'executive presence' is someone who exerts influence over and above that conferred by formal authority. Amongst the factors that contribute to this presence are status and reputation, confidence, communication ability, engagement skills, interpersonal integrity, values in action, intellect and expertise, and outcome delivery ability (Dagley and Gaskin 2014). In the health sector, the equivalent construct to executive presence is professional credibility because this demonstrates that the health leader understands the context and has knowledge and insights that can inform leadership decisions. Leaders who are able to inspire, induce, activate, engage, motivate, encourage, and engage others will be critical to the success of a specific project (such as the implementation of evidence-based practice) or to the achievement of wider organisational objectives (Sandström et al. 2011: 215; Stetler et al. 2014). A combination of leadership support and professional credibility was described as addressing individual concerns and encouraging staff.

In addition to the types of context within which leadership in health takes place—task, change, or relations—as outlined above, there are organisational dependencies which will also influence and be influenced by professional credibility. These are the roles covered by Executive, clinical, and devolved leadership.

Professional Credibility and Executive Leadership

Executive Leadership responsibilities involve a balancing act in resource allocation between clinical priorities and broader organisational objectives. Hence there is a necessity on the part of the leader to draw together the logics of management and medicine in pursuit of the provision of better care and improved population health in a cost-efficient way. The role of the leader in the quest for these objectives is to articulate a vision and make sure that there is alignment of operational resources and practices behind it to ensure high quality of care, equitably and efficiently delivered, through the engagement of multidisciplinary teams of clinicians, nurses, allied health professionals, and support services such as finance, HR, and IT. Professional credibility enhances the prospects of this ideal outcome and in Executive roles might be seen as a prerequisite to successful organisational change or innovation. In this respect the senior health leader who is perceived as having professional knowledge, understanding, or insight is in a better position to persuade the workforce to accept or follow a particular narrative. This can take on several forms and is not only clinical or medical competence. Instead it can be insight and deep knowledge about how health organisations are run from a 'business' or operational point of view in which the knowledge would be about the impact of decisions on clinical outcomes.

In some instances, professional credibility is enshrined in formal authority since a health sector organisation will take account of professional credentials when selecting those for certain formal leadership positions and 'formal authority contributes to the legitimacy of the leader and to trust in the leader, and hence to the establishment of an effective leadership relationship' (Boas and Galit 2017: 582). It provides a framework within which followers can do their jobs and helps to move towards a common goal. Studies in the UK and Canada concluded that leadership traits alone were not deemed to be sufficient to push through project implementation and additional professional attributes were needed (Nwabueze 2011: 342; Lavoie-Tremblay et al. 2012; Dearing et al. 2017: 9). Executive Leaders who were able to demonstrate their professional knowledge and insights could use these in effecting organisational transformation. Specifically, through their leadership roles, health executives 'have the opportunity to lead by example when implementing research-based practices in health care. As an integral part of their function, they have the possibility to communicate with key administrators and other health professionals, encourage others to use research evidence, transfer knowledge between colleagues, and their own use of RBE' (Lavoie-Tremblay et al. 2012: 191). Such an observation applies to those in formal leadership roles with direct influence over a health organisational unit but also informally by demonstrating the combination of leadership and professional credibility across the organisation.

Professional Credibility and Clinical Leadership

The diversification and reconfiguration of the health workforce over the past decade has been driven by a variety of factors generating new business or operating models. Such workforce reconfiguration is part of 'a growing international trend in healthcare policy to redistribute resources on the basis of professional accomplishment rather than historical workforce hierarchies and roles.' Clinical professionals are becoming more active in leadership and management. They are increasingly involved in leading on service transformation, beyond their own area of clinical expertise, creating direction and aligning others around it, and influencing others across a broad range of stakeholders, managing services, teams, or organisations (Wilson 2013).

Formally through the membership of governing Boards or taking up Executive and Management roles and informally by being involved in day-to-day decisions outside of the clinical arena, there are benefits to the organisation across a number of fields where this happens. Examples in the USA and Europe have shown that 'greater clinical participation in hospital board-level discussions can have an impact on clinical quality outcomes' (Veronesi et al. 2015: 1031); in Australia the involvement of doctors in the development of the health system was linked to improvements in the retention of clinical professions, culture change, better patient and public health outcomes, and balancing cost-effectiveness with improved quality and safety. This comes about because effective clinical leadership can facilitate the take-up of new systems and processes such as IT developments (Ingebrigtsen et al. 2014; Sebastian et al. 2014). The trend means that some health professionals taking on leadership roles (such as those in extended roles outlined earlier) are considered to be 'hybrids' because they straddle two domains, bridging the gap but influenced by different interests and priorities. Resolving the best fit model for such roles, though, remains unclear. For the hybrid role to work, such leaders or managers (seeking authority and legitimacy) 'must be able to relate to the existing cultural 'codes' and thus to acknowledge the discourse of management, on the one hand, and understand and heed clinical needs, on the other' (Salvatore et al. 2012: 630).

It is for these reasons that clinical leadership is a vital part of the delivery of high-quality care and is important to uni-professional and multi-professional teams in a range of professional groups to ensure effective solutions and seamless care-stretching across professional and organisational boundaries (Edmonstone 2011). Appointing people into leadership roles who can span the divide, to act as linking pins between the worlds of what may be referred to as 'business' management and that of professional (e.g. clinical or medical) management, can be a significant success factor for all health sector organisations. And so, the second group of leaders to whom professional credibility applies concerns those in clinical or medical leadership roles where, since health sector leaders do not achieve success in isolation but through collaboration with others, leadership capability is a critical element to complement professional best practice (Manley and Titchen 2017). And yet combining professional capability with leadership capability in the case of clinicians is one of the most complex leadership challenges facing the sector. In the first place, the definition of clinical leadership remains an area of debate varying from being 'conceptualized in literature either as physicians with formal managerial roles or physicians who act as informal 'leaders' in daily practices' (Berghout et al. 2017). It has been argued that the role of a health sector leader (particularly clinical leadership) could be seen as a first among equals with the role of problem-solving through inclusive processes. In this respect clinical leadership is a broad term and refers to clinicians who demonstrate leadership as they complete their technical responsibilities without a formal leadership designation or title. Professional credibility could be obtained in several ways including medical excellence and training in a speciality or commitment to clinical work (Berghout et al. 2017; Gauld 2017: 5). Nevertheless, whilst there are many examples requiring medical leaders to undertake general management and leadership activities in addition to their professional, clinical, or medical role, the transition from pure clinical practice to a combined clinical leadership role can be problematic. The challenge was articulated in a recent US study where, despite transitioning into leadership roles, clinical professionals retained a strong primary identity as a clinician (Quinn and Perelli 2016), leading to a dilemma about which area to prioritise in terms of leadership practice.

There is evidence about how success might be achieved. Firstly,

> medical leaders must carry out general management and leadership activities and acts to balance between management and medicine, because these physicians must accomplish both organizational and medical staff objectives. To perform effectively, credibility among medical peers appeared to be the most important factor, followed by a scattered list of fields of knowledge, skills and attitudes. (Berghout et al. 2017: 1)

In a recent study, the logic of this was based on the idea that clinical professionals were more influenced by their peers than by managers, due to the socialised nature of the medical profession. It was argued that to perform effectively, credibility among professional peers was an important factor (Shariff 2015; Berghout et al. 2017). Other global studies reinforced the point where professional credibility was necessary to influence both health policy and operational leadership (Shariff 2015;

Loh et al. 2016). The NHS Leadership Academy (2011) published its Clinical Leadership Competency Framework outlining the importance of five domains which were demonstrating personal qualities, working with others (by developing networks and building relationships), managing services, improving services, and setting direction. The objective was to embed leadership and management learning outcomes into the work of clinicians (McKimm and Swanwick 2011).

Secondly, there is the dilemma of full- or part-time leadership. In the case of those in a part-time leadership capacity, the challenge was greater than those who had moved to full time, that is, former physicians who had transitioned from clinician to full-time leadership roles and who 'view themselves and are viewed by others unambiguously as both physicians and organizational leaders, demonstrating the two roles are, indeed, compatible' (Quinn and Perelli 2016: 719) and that those who are active in this way 'can influence others and improve the health care system' (Vaterlaus Patten and Sauer 2017). In one study, three of the five most frequently practised leadership behaviours related to developing and sharing clinical acumen and that passion and credibility in clinical work were important for clinical leaders. This is an essential legislative leadership role and is one of ensuring continued professionalism by building consensus amongst other professionals, resolving disputes, and improving morale and cohesion in health teams. The clinical leader also has a role in shaping decisions either at a strategic or operational level that may go beyond those embraced by the specific role. This can be achieved by one in the leadership position who has the trust of multiple stakeholders. Professional credibility enhances this perception (Ivany and Hurt 2007).

Professional Credibility and Devolved Leadership

It was noted earlier that organisational knowledge and professional legitimacy were important for those in leadership positions because they added to credibility and to the engagement of frontline staff. The move towards a more devolved form of leadership in health sector organisations increases the importance of this point since leadership is seen to occur at multiple levels. When followers perceive that 'the unique characteristics of their manager fit their own pre-existing schemata for leader prototypes (e.g., being competent and sociable), the manager will more likely be seen as a leader than a non-leader' (Chiu et al. 2017: 334). But how does a leader without a formally confirmed leadership role establish legitimacy? Since health sector decisions are increasingly collective efforts, the ability to facilitate the diverse and valuable voices who can contribute is in itself a valuable leadership attribute. In such situations, professional credibility can provide a bridge or pathway. The phenomenon of leadership is to a large extent a social phenomenon, and research has shown that one of the most important influencing tactics on having a significant and positive relationship with both task- and relations-oriented outcomes was rational persuasion (Boas and Galit 2017; Lee et al. 2017); then engaging social groupings is an aspect of leadership where it has been devolved through the organisation.

Developing a proposition for the health unit, department, or team will increasingly fall to more people as leadership becomes devolved throughout the organisation. For this process to be successful, and to achieve followership, then professional credibility will be essential. This is a case in point in Brazil with the move away from a purely welfare-based system. 'Professionalisation has been translated predominantly as enhancing financial performance, from the adoption of management methodologies from companies operating in the market … focusing mainly on efficiency and profitability, classically where managerial and medical logics cross paths'. However, the complexity of health organisations means that professional credibility is important in transforming 'intentions into actions and meaningful outcomes with effectiveness and legitimacy while remaining committed to the organization's core values and beliefs' (Pascuci et al. 2017: 3). A rationalistic-managerialist lens would be enhanced significantly if it was underpinned by professional credibility at multiple levels. In some health systems this shift towards distributed models of leadership has given a greater role to clinical leaders, and whereas clinical leadership was once considered as 'leadership *for* clinicians, *by* clinicians' (Divall 2015), there has been a growing recognition that professional leadership can add inherent value to broader organisational decision-making in relation to patient experience, clinical outcomes, workforce engagement, and organisational performance. However, a number of challenges have been highlighted including clinical leaders struggling with a lack of role definition by comparison with their clinical role and that of maintaining a hybrid clinical-managerial role (Divall 2015). The challenge is for clinical leaders to maintain a professional identification and a leadership or management identity. When they do so, it benefits the quality and output of team decision-making in contexts of informational complexity (Meyer et al. 2016).

Professional credibility requires a deep understanding of the context within which health decisions are taken. When this is added to the leadership skills based on contemporary management principles, including 'followership, team-building, tracking and assessing progress, storytelling and communication, and cultivating innovation' (Hertig et al. 2016: 338), then there is a good chance of promoting and achieving all of which that promote transformational change.

Leadership in Healthcare Organisations

Ryan Changcoco and Gaby Ammatuna, Association for Talent Development, Washington, USA

There are challenges when clinicians (perhaps a nurse, physician, or health professional) are promoted, because of stellar performance, into leadership roles which require a completely different type of skill set. These are compounded firstly by the complexity of healthcare systems, which in today's world are often bigger, more complicated, and considerably more challenging to administrate than organisations in other industries, and secondly by various external factors driving change in healthcare today. The effects of not having those with the right leadership skills in post can be significant, and according to the Center for Creative Leadership,[1] nearly 40% of CEOs fail within their first 18 months on the job, and turnover within the C-suite is nearly 20%. The trickle-down consequences of the mismatch between skills demand and supply can be felt at just about every single part of the organisation: the quality of care drops,[2] burnout and job

[1] https://www.ccl.org/wp-content/uploads/2015/04/addressingLeadershipGapHealthcare.pdf.

[2] https://www.ncbi.nlm.nih.gov/pmc/articles/PMC1765760/.

dissatisfaction increases amongst staff,[3] and the financial effects can be disastrous.[4]

Before we can better understand the solution for the issues presented above, it is important to figure out why organisations don't recognise often enough the need to find the right type of leader. Historically, clinical and technical skills, as well as academic qualifications, were the main factors on determining the selection of leaders within healthcare organisations. And while it's effective to have a clinical mindset within a clinical setting,[5] the failures of healthcare CEOs often have nothing to do with their skill as a clinician. According to a report by Becker's Hospital Review, physician integration, consolidation, reimbursement, population health, and understanding patients as consumers are some of the many complex challenges leaders are confronting today. However, a leader who has not developed the skills of being able to influence at a high level, driving consensus, and building coalition will find achieving successful management of these challenges extremely difficult, if not impossible.[6]

The Solution (From Clinical Expert to Strategic Leader)

The jump from being an individual contributor and clinical expert into a leadership role is not an impossible one, but it is not easy. According to ATD Author Alan Patterson, moving from a technical expert into a strategic leadership position is anything but linear. If left to their instincts, many technical experts can find themselves guided by the gravitational pull for more knowledge and experience as the gateway into leadership. To compound the issue, organisations often are willing co-conspirators in this endeavour by promoting their best individual contributors with the most expertise into management positions. The problem: technical expertise alone does not define leadership success.

The evolution into strategic leadership positions occurs across three dimensions:

- technical expertise—the content-specific knowledge and experience an individual needs to execute the job effectively
- relationship management—the ability to engage and influence others for both immediate and long-term job success

---

[3] https://www.psychologytoday.com/us/blog/pressure-proof/201506/the-impact-poor-leadership-burnout-job-satisfaction.

[4] http://www.nchl.org/Documents/Ctrl_Hyperlink/doccopy3309_uid6102014456192.pdf.

[5] https://www.dovepress.com/the-importance-of-clinical-leadership-in-the-hospital-setting-peer-reviewed-fulltext-article-JHL.

[6] https://www.beckershospitalreview.com/hospital-management-administration/10-reasons-healthcare-leaders-fail-and-how-to-prevent-them.html.

- organisational savvy—understanding the business and working as a partner and strategist to achieve customer outcomes

In a recent interview, Patterson states that strategic leaders see beyond the flurry of everyday activity. They see the bigger picture. They need to understand how the work of their team connects to the rest of the organisation. They look beyond functional silos to create a line of sight from where they sit to the ultimate customer, the one that pays the bills. They realise the value they bring is by working as partners and strategists to the organisation.

Because they see the bigger picture, strategic leaders are more willing to take the risks associated with their economic viability. They look to the future and create a strategic vision and a plan for how to get from here to there. The business needs this type of leader, the ones who push and prod—who ask 'Why?' and 'What if?' and challenge the status quo. These leaders realise that, without continuous change and reinvention, the healthcare institution could disappear.

Many organisations have begun to tackle this very issue by installing leadership programmes for individual contributors who self-select as future leaders. Take, for example, Baltimore-based Johns Hopkins Medicine's Leadership Development Program (LDP), which is a sponsored leadership development initiative designed to foster diversity and inclusion among their future leaders. Their mission is to develop an understanding of effectiveness in the organisational culture, prepare for the challenges of healthcare reform, strengthen bonds and communication among and between faculty and administrators, and advance leaders within the organisation. Among their programme goals are to:

- Strengthen JHM's long-term organisational viability by developing leaders for the twenty-first century to foster innovative and sustaining solutions to complex problems
- Develop JHM leaders who can contribute to solving current challenges and contributing to future initiatives throughout the system and support the three missions of JHM
- Improve the JHM operating environment by building trusting relationships that break down barriers, facilitate communication, and foster (the practice of better medicine and better service) research, education, and clinical care
- Retain emerging leaders by providing a prestigious and challenging learning experience, which can lead to new opportunities and promotion
- Develop JHM leaders who value and enthusiastically appreciate diversity inclusion

- Develop JHM leaders who value teamwork and foster collegial working relationships[7]

There is evidence-based scientific literature on organisational development that suggests leading a complex system such as a healthcare institution has less chance of continued success. An option is to apply these competencies throughout the continuum of care in the organisation and then consistently put them into practice and vigilance. While full changes or improvements might not be visible immediately, healthcare leaders who adopt this perspective can get all staff moving in the same direction and working with a common purpose in the short and middle term.

Many would characterise these competencies as soft skills, which by their name are typically not considered as important as those things that we consider hard skills. Our perspective as talent development experts is that we would prefer to think of the competencies mentioned as 'critical skills,' which must be part of the toolkit of every healthcare leader who wants to contribute to a healthy team and service organisation, therefore better outcomes for the patients.

Lastly, a consistent execution of these competencies will make a profound difference in the performance of each professional individually now and into the future.

Conclusions and Implications for Practice

Professional credibility is regarded as an important course of legitimacy, influence, and recognition (Berghout et al. 2017). So, in addition to the generic competencies or prerequisites for effective leadership, such as decision-making, role clarity, and organisational alignment, there is an added dimension in the health sector where professional credibility is seen as adding value to the leadership role. In a UK study, clinical credibility was the platform on which leadership credibility could be built, involving clinical system leadership, the facilitation of culture change, and the prioritisation of person-centred, safe, and effective care across patient pathways (Manley and Titchen 2017), whilst in the USA, physician understanding and support in the delivery of care have been

[7] https://www.hopkinsmedicine.org/fac_development/career_path/leadership/leadership_dev_prgm.html.

identified as critical success factors (Baldwin et al. 2011). And it was found that medical leadership was necessary to overcome any divisions between 'medical and managerial logics' in hospitals.

Studies have suggested that successful leadership in the health sector depends on the performance against the 'how' of impacting on the organisation and the 'what' as in what needs to be done. The 'how' depends on interpersonal competence since it depends on achieving followership and hence the ability to influence social behaviour. The 'what' is focused on the activities necessary to achieve an objective. But in the health sector these are accentuated by professional credibility of the person answering the how and what needs to be done. Leaders in this sector are often under significant pressure at both organisational level, for example, performance against KPIs, and in response to specific issues such as local patient care or outcomes. It is important, therefore, for the health sector leader to demonstrate not only those leadership skills that would be expected of the leader of any organisation in any sector but also the knowledge and insights that are necessary to navigate the complexities of the health environment. This assumption forms the basis of arguing that professional credibility will be a foundation on which successful leadership is built in the sector. The following are the conclusions in this respect:

- **Leadership capability gives authority, whilst professional credibility gives legitimacy**. A combination of both will contribute to respect, trust, and engagement with peers and followers. The challenge facing those who lead in health sector organisations is how to achieve both given complex organisational, people, and process dynamics.
- **Professional credibility is related to knowledge and insight into the particular area or sphere of health sector activity in which the organisation operates**. Professional credibility is being knowledgeable about practice and the unique context within which this practice takes place or needs to take place.
- **Professional credibility will lead to a relationship of trust with followers based on a perception that the leader understands the context** and therefore takes informed, knowledgeable, and insightful decisions based on this.

- **Professional credibility goes hand in hand with leadership capability to create a health sector leadership identity** that combines the two effectively.

In all respects, professional credibility is a critical success factor to organisational strategy setting, change, and innovation in the health sector.

References

American Medical Association. (2015). *Integrated Leadership for Hospitals and Health Systems: Principles for Success*. Retrieved from https://www.ama-assn.org/sites/default/files/media-browser/public/about-ama/ama-aha-integrated-leadership-principles_0.pdf.

Bai, Y., Gu, C., Chen, Q., Xiao, J., Liu, D., & Tang, S. (2017). The Challenges That Head Nurses Confront on Financial Management Today: A Qualitative Study. *International Journal of Nursing Sciences, 4*, 122–127. https://doi.org/10.1016/j.ijnss.2017.03.007.

Baldwin, K. S., Dimunation, N., & Alexander, J. (2011, July–August). Health Care leadership and the Dyad model. *Physician Executive Journal, 37*(4), 66–70.

Barasa, E. W., Molyneux, S., English, M., & Cleary, S. (2017). Hospitals as Complex Adaptive Systems: A Case Study of Factors Influencing Priority Setting Practices at the Hospital Level in Kenya. *Social Science & Medicine, 174*, 104–112. https://doi.org/10.1016/j.socscimed.2016.12.026.

Barling, J., Akers, A., & Beiko, D. (2017). The Impact of Positive and Negative Intraoperative Surgeons' Leadership Behaviors on Surgical Team Performance. *The American Journal of Surgery, 215*(1), 14–18. https://doi.org/10.1016/j.amjsurg.2017.07.006.

Berghout, M. A., Fabbricotti, I. N., Buljac-Samardzic, M., & Hilders, C. M. (2017). Medical Leaders or Masters? A Systematic Review of Medical Leadership in Hospital Settings. *PLoS One, 12*(9), e0184522. https://doi.org/10.1371/journal.pone.0184.

Bhatia, K., Morris, C. A., Wright, S. C., Takayesu, J. K., Sharma, R., & Katz, J. T. (2015). Leadership Training for Residents: A Novel Approach. *Physician Leadership Journal, 2*(2), 76–80.

Boas, S., & Galit, E. S. (2017). Reflections on Leadership, Authority, and Lessons Learned. *The Leadership Quarterly, 28*(4), 578–583. https://doi.org/10.1016/j.leaqua.2017.06.004.

de Bont, A., van Exel, J., Coretti, S., Ökem, Z. G., Janssen, M., Hope, K. L., et al. (2016). Reconfiguring Health Workforce: A Case-Based Comparative Study Explaining the Increasingly Diverse Professional Roles in Europe. *BMC Health Services Research, 16*, 1–14. https://doi.org/10.1186/s12913-016-1898-0.

Brooke, P. J., Hudak, R. P., Finstuen, K., & Trounson, J. (1998). Management Competencies Required in Ambulatory Care Settings. *Physician Executive, 24*(5), 32–38.

Ceri-Booms, M., Curşeu, P. L., & Oerlemans, L. A. (2017). Task and Person-Focused Leadership Behaviors and Team Performance: A Meta-Analysis. *Human Resource Management Review, 27*(1), 178–192. https://doi.org/10.1016/j.hrmr.2016.09.010.

Chiu, C.-Y. C., Balkundi, P., & Weinberg, F. J. (2017). When Managers Become Leaders: The Role of Manager Network Centralities, Social Power, and Followers' Perception of Leadership. *The Leadership Quarterly, 28*(2), 334–348. https://doi.org/10.1016/j.leaqua.2016.05.004.

Dagley, R., & Gaskin, C. J. (2014). Understanding Executive Presence: Perspectives of Business Professionals. *Consulting Psychology Journal: Practice and Research, 66*(3), 197–211. ISSN:1065-9293.

Dearing, J. W., Beacom, A. M., Chamberlain, S. A., Meng, J., Berta, W. B., Keefe, J. M., et al. (2017). Pathways for Best Practice Diffusion: The Structure of Informal Relationships in Canada's Long-Term Care Sector. *Implementation Science, 12*, 1–13. https://doi.org/10.1186/s13012-017-0542-7.

Denis, J.-L., Langley, A., & Pineault, M. (2000). Becoming a Leader in a Complex Organization. *Journal of Management Studies, 37*, 1063–1100. https://doi.org/10.1111/1467-6486.00217.

Divall, B. (2015). Negotiating Competing Discourses in Narratives of Midwifery Leadership in the English NHS. *Midwifery, 31*(11), 1060–1066. ISSN:0266-6138.

Edmonstone, J. (2011). The Development of Strategic Clinical Leaders in the National Health Service in Scotland. *Leadership in Health Services, 24*(4), 337–353. https://doi.org/10.1108/17511871111172376.

Fisher, M. T. (2005). Exploring How Nurse Lecturers Maintain Clinical Credibility. *Nurse Education in Practice, 5*, 21–29. https://doi.org/10.1016/j.nepr.2004.02.003.

Gabris, G. T., Golembiewski, R. T., & Ihrke, D. M. (2001). Leadership Credibility, Board Relations, and Administrative Innovation at the Local Government Level. *Journal of Public Administration Research and Theory: J-PART, 11*(1), 89–108.

Gauld, R. (2017). Clinical Leadership: What Is It and How Do We Facilitate It? *Journal of Primary Health Care, 9*(1), 5–8.

Godfrey, M. M., Andersson-Gare, B., Nelson, E. C., Nilsson, M., & Ahlstrom, G. (2014). Coaching Interprofessional Health Care Improvement Teams: The Coachee, the Coach and the Leader Perspectives. *Journal of Nursing Management, 22*(4), 452–464. https://doi.org/10.1111/jonm.12068.

Goorapah, D. (1997). Clinical Competence/Clinical Credibility. *Nurse Education Today, 17*(4), 297–302.

Hernandez, J. S. (2010). The Spectrum of Medical Leadership Roles. *Physician Executive, 36*(5), 56–59.

Hertig, J. B., Hultgren, K. E., & Weber, R. J. (2016). Using Contemporary Leadership Skills in Medication Safety Programs. *Hospital Pharmacy, 51*(4), 338–344. https://doi.org/10.1310/hpj5104-338.

Hunn, L. (2016). Preparing for Ward Management: A Neonatal Network Perspective. *Infant, 12*(2), 44–48.

Ingebrigtsen, T., Georgiou, A., Clay-Williams, R., Magrabi, F., Hordern, A., Prgomet, M., et al. (2014). Review: The Impact of Clinical Leadership on Health Information Technology Adoption: Systematic Review. *International Journal of Medical Informatics, 83*, 393–405. https://doi.org/10.1016/j.ijmedinf.2014.02.005.

Ivany, C., & Hurt, P. H. (2007). Enhancing the Effectiveness of the Psychiatric Chief Resident. *Academic Psychiatry, 31*(4), 277–280.

Kaiser, R. B., McGinnis, J. L., & Overfield, D. V. (2012). The How and the What of Leadership. *Consulting Psychology Journal: Practice and Research, 64*(2), 119–135. https://doi.org/10.1037/a0029331.

Kantanen, K., Kaunonen, M., Helminen, M., & Suominen, T. (2017). Leadership and Management Competencies of Head Nurses and Directors of Nursing in Finnish Social and Health Care. *Journal of Research in Nursing, 22*(3), 228–244. https://doi.org/10.1177/1744987117702692.

Kouzes, J. M., & Posner, B. Z. (2011). Leadership Is a Relationship. In *Credibility*. Hoboken, NJ: John Wiley & Sons, Inc. https://doi.org/10.1002/9781118983867.ch1.

Kumar, S., Kumar, N., Adhish, V. S., & Reddy, R. S. (2015). Strategic Management and Leadership for Health Professionals – Skills to Leverage

Resources to Achieve Health Goals. *Indian Journal of Community Medicine, 40*(3), 158–162. ISSN:0970-0218.

Lavoie-Tremblay, M., Anderson, M., Bonneville-Roussy, A., Drevniok, U., & Lavigne, G. L. (2012). Nurse Executives' Perceptions of the Executive Training for Research Application (EXTRA) Program. *Worldviews on Evidence-Based Nursing, 9*(3), 186–192. https://doi.org/10.1111/j.1741-6787.2011.00218.x.

Lawrence, N., & Richardson, J. (2014). To Explore and Understand the Leadership Experiences of Modern Matrons, Within an Acute NHS Trust. *Journal of Nursing Management, 22*, 70–79. https://doi.org/10.1111/j.1365-2834.2012.01432.x.

Lee, S., Han, S., Cheong, M., Kim, S. L., & Yun, S. (2017). How Do I Get My Way? A Meta-Analytic Review of Research on Influence Tactics. *The Leadership Quarterly, 28*(1), 210–228. https://doi.org/10.1016/j.leaqua.2016.11.001.

Loh, E., Morris, J., Thomas, L., Bismark, M. M., Phelps, G., & Dickinson, H. (2016). Shining the Light on the Dark Side of Medical Leadership – A Qualitative Study in Australia. *Leadership in Health Services, 29*(3), 313–330. https://doi.org/10.1108/LHS-12-2015-0044.

Lv, C.-M., & Zhang, L. (2017). How Can Collective Leadership Influence the Implementation of Change in Health Care? *Chinese Nursing Research, 4*(4), 182–185. ISSN:2095-7718.

Manley, K., & Titchen, A. (2017). Facilitation Skills: The Catalyst for Increased Effectiveness in Consultant Practice and Clinical Systems Leadership. *Educational Action Research, 25*(2), 256–279.

Manss, G. (2017). Implementation of Daily Senior Leader Rounds Using a Transformational Leadership Approach. *Nurse Leader, 15*, 65–69. https://doi.org/10.1016/j.mnl.2016.08.012.

Marchiondo, L. (2015). The Relational Nature of Leadership Identity Construction: How and When It Influences Perceived Leadership and Decision-Making. *The Leadership Quarterly, 26*(5), 892–908. ISSN:1048-9843 Online ISSN:1873-3409.

Martin, G. P., Leslie, M., Minion, J., Willars, J., & Dixon-Woods, M. (2013). Between Surveillance and Subjectification: Professionals and the Governance of Quality and Patient Safety in English Hospitals. *Social Science & Medicine, 99*, 80–88. https://doi.org/10.1016/j.socscimed.

Masood, M., & Afsar, B. (2017). Transformational Leadership and Innovative Work Behavior Among Nursing Staff. *Nursing Inquiry, 24*(4), n/a. https://doi.org/10.1111/nin.12188.

McKimm, J., & Swanwick, T. (2011). Leadership Development for Clinicians: What Are We Trying to Achieve? *Clinical Teacher, 8*(3), 181–185. https://doi.org/10.1111/j.1743-498X.2011.00473.x.

Meyer, B., Burtsher, M. J., Jonas, K., Feese, S., & Arnrich, B. (2016). What Good Leaders Actually Do: Micro-Level Leadership Behaviour, Leader Evaluations, and Team Decision Quality. *European Journal of Work and Organizational Psychology, 25*(6), 773–789.

Morris, B. (2017). Frontline Leadership During Hospital Consolidation. *Radiation Therapist, 26*(2), 200–202.

NHS. (2011). *Clinical Leadership Competency Framework.* NHS Leadership Academy, NHS Institute for Innovation and Improvement, Coventry House, University of Warwick Campus, Coventry, CV4 7AL. ISBN:978-1-907045-88. Retrieved from https://www.leadershipacademy.nhs.uk/wp-content/uploads/2012/11/NHSLeadership-Leadership-Framework-Clinical-Leadership-Competency-Framework-CLCF.pdf.

Noordegraaf, M. (2016). Reconfiguring Professional Work: Changing Forms of Professionalism in Public Services. *Administration & Society, 48*(7), 783.

Nwabueze, U. (2011). Implementing TQM in Healthcare: The Critical Leadership Traits. *Total Quality Management & Business Excellence, 22*(3), 331–343. https://doi.org/10.1080/14783363.2010.532338.

Pascuci, L. M., Meyer Junior, V., & Crubellate, J. M. (2017). Strategic Management in Hospitals: Tensions Between the Managerial and Institutional Lens. *BAR – Brazilian Administration Review, 14*(2), 1.

Patrick, A., Laschinger, H. K. S., Wong, C., & Finegan, J. (2011). Developing and Testing a New Measure of Staff Nurse Clinical Leadership: The Clinical Leadership Survey. *Journal of Nursing Management, 19*, 449–460. https://doi.org/10.1111/j.1365-2834.2011.01238.x.

Penny, S. M. (2017). Serving, Following, and Leading in Health Care. *Radiologic Technology, 88*(6), 603–620.

Politis, J. D. (2005). Dispersed Leadership Predictor of the Work Environment for Creativity and Productivity. *European Journal of Innovation Management, 8*(2), 182. https://doi.org/10.1108/14601060510594693.

Quinn, J. F., & Perelli, S. (2016). First and Foremost, Physicians: The Clinical Versus Leadership Identities of Physician Leaders. *Journal of Health Organization and Management, 30*(4), 711–728. https://doi.org/10.1108/JHOM-05-2015-0079.

Salvatore, D., Numerato, D., & Fattore, G. (2012). The Impact of Management on Medical Professionalism: A Review. *Sociology of Health & Illness, 34*(4), 626–644.

Sandström, B., Borglin, G., Nilsson, R., & Willman, A. (2011). Promoting the Implementation of Evidence-Based Practice: A Literature Review Focusing on the Role of Nursing Leadership. *Worldviews on Evidence-Based Nursing, 8*(4), 212–223. https://doi.org/10.1111/j.1741-6787.2011.00216.x.

Saxena, A., Desanghere, L., Stobart, K., & Walker, K. (2017). Goleman's Leadership Styles at Different Hierarchical Levels in Medical Education. *BMC Medical Education, 17*(1), 169.

Sebastian, A., Fulop, L., Dadich, A., Fitzgerald, A., Kippist, L., & Smyth, A. (2014). Health LEADS Australia and Implications for Medical Leadership. *Leadership in Health Services (1751–1879), 27*(4), 355. https://doi.org/10.1108/LHS-03-2014-0028.

Shariff, N. J. (2015). A Delphi Survey of Leadership Attributes Necessary for National Nurse Leaders' Participation in Health Policy Development: An East African Perspective. *BMC Nursing, 14*(1), 1–8. https://doi.org/10.1186/s12912-015-0063-0.

Simms, L. M., Price, S. A., & Pfoutz, S. K. (1985). Nurse Executives: Functions and Priorities. *Nursing Economic$, 3*(4). ISSN:0746-1739.

Size, T. (2006). Leadership Development for Rural Health. *North Carolina Medical Journal, 67*(1), 71–76.

Stetler, C. B., Ritchie, J. A., Rycroft-Malone, J., & Charns, M. P. (2014). Leadership for Evidence-Based Practice: Strategic and Functional Behaviors for Institutionalizing EBP. *Worldviews on Evidence-Based Nursing, 11*(4), 219–226. https://doi.org/10.1111/wvn.12044.

Stoddart, K., Bugge, C., Shepherd, A., & Farquharson, B. (2014). The New Clinical Leadership Role of Senior Charge Nurses: A Mixed Methods Study of Their Views and Experience. *Journal of Nursing Management, 22*, 49–59.

Thompson, A. D., Grahek, M., Phillips, R. E., & Fay, C. L. (2008). The Search for Worthy Leadership. *Consulting Psychology Journal: Practice and Research, 60*(4), 366–382. https://doi.org/10.1037/1065-9293.60.4.366.

Vaterlaus Patten, E., & Sauer, K. (2017). Practice Applications: The Framework and Future Opportunities for Leadership in Clinical Dietetics. *Journal of the Academy of Nutrition and Dietetics*. ISSN:2212-2672. https://doi.org/10.1016/J.Jand.2017.06.363.

Veronesi, G., Kirkpatrick, I., & Altanlar, A. (2015). Clinical Leadership and the Changing Governance of Public Hospitals: Implications for Patient Experience. *Public Administration, 93*(4), 1031–1048. https://doi.org/10.1111/padm.12183.

Wilson, K. (2013). How to Be an Effective Clinical Leader. *Health Services Journal*.

Yukl, G. (2010). *Leadership in Organisations*. London: Pearson.

8

Understanding Organisational Dynamics

Organisational Dynamics: Where Twenty-First Century Transformation Meets Twentieth-Century Structure

Volatility, uncertainty, complexity, and ambiguity in the health environment, combined with the emergence of groundbreaking healthcare technologies and new business models, mean that health sector leaders are faced with significant strategic challenges and choices in their quest to deliver quality of care in a way that is cost-effective or market competitive. For some health sector organisations, twenty-first century transformation has met or collided with twentieth-century organisational structure. And whilst many have responded with new types of organisational design, an increased amount of health process reengineering, and a fresh look at strategy and leadership, others have struggled to navigate the perfect storm of forces. In all cases, individual success, which in turn will create the conditions of organisational success, will be grounded in leadership capability, professional credibility, and knowledge of the context within which strategy is formulated—effective leaders engage in both professional leadership behaviours and personal leadership behaviours

P. Turner, *Leadership in Healthcare*, Organizational Behaviour in Health Care,
https://doi.org/10.1007/978-3-030-04387-2_8

(Mastrangelo et al. 2004). However, an additional factor in the leadership equation is that of understanding organisational dynamics, that is, those forces which influence how an organisation is structured, operates, and responds to opportunity or threat and which are determined by strategy, history, culture, language, politics, and process. Leadership in this context requires the ability to deal with the 'rich interconnectivity' of organisational behaviour, where 'adding the word rich to interconnectivity means that when things interact, they change one another in unexpected and irreversible ways' (Uhl-Bien and Arena 2017: 9). For contemporary health sector leaders, levels of complexity and the richness of interconnectivity are unprecedented.

Organisational dynamics may be shaped by national or regional health policy and involve large-scale health sector units. In these circumstances the ability to navigate between multiple agencies and systems using strategic and tactical nous will be critical—between public or private ways of delivering healthcare, for example, and their different dimensions of organisational commitment (Top et al. 2015: 1259). A further level of dynamic, in line with the particular focus of this chapter, will be that which occurs at health sector organisation, unit, department, or team level. Here, different modus operandi will require awareness on the part of the leader about the opportunities for transformation and change, what organisational factors will enhance them, and what obstacles might hinder them. The capability to deal with such forces is encapsulated in the term 'understanding organisational dynamics' and is the third element of the model for leadership in health. The questions that arise here are: where do organisational dynamics fit into the overall canon of leadership theory and how are they manifested in practice style?

Complexity and Rich Interconnectivity

To begin with, setting objectives and crafting a strategy to achieve them are important facets of the roles of Senior Leaders. Using personal insight as the basis of leadership capability, a leadership identity to reflect an appropriate approach, and having professional credibility to ensure the engagement of colleagues in all disciplines and at all levels will provide a foundation on which strategy can be built. However, if the resulting objectives are to be translated into practical success, then an understanding of the dynamics of the organisation will also be a factor for consideration. This means leaders who are able to combine effectiveness in both tangible elements of strategy and the intangibility of organisational culture and its associated complexities. But, there are many definitions of leadership and a vast number of leadership styles and theories as organisations and individuals search for an ideal or best practice approach. Understanding how these both influence and depend on organisational dynamics is therefore important.

Leadership is increasingly interpreted as a contextual phenomenon, flexing and adapting to a rapidly changing environment. It involves multiple conceptual levels because it can occur, for instance, between an individual leader and individual followers, groups of followers, and/or entire organisations (Basistic et al. 2017). In the health sector, the subjects of leader and leadership have produced 'waves' of theory and practice over time ranging from situational leadership to transformational and more recently 'authentic' and devolved leadership—as outlined in Chap. 4. The key influencers were internal organisational culture, external health context, individual propensity, and style history. It is this multiplicity of factors that has led some to conclude that the health sector is distinctive from leadership in other business settings (Chapman et al. 2014: 283; Kim et al. 2016: 375). Whilst trait theory argued that effective leaders were those who demonstrated combinations of qualities through cognition or personality, style or behaviour theories of leadership considered 'how leaders actually behave and what they choose to do can make a radical difference in how others perceive them as leaders and the nature of the outcomes their organisations produce' (Kilburg and Donohue 2011: 8). However, it is in the area of the contingency theory of leadership where understanding of the dynamics of the organisation is particularly appropriate. Contingency theory means that there is no single, best practice, but that internal and external forces combine to influence the way a leader adapts his or her leadership style. As organisational structures evolve, they require greater collaboration between units, departments, and teams with leaders simultaneously coordinating both vertical (traditional leadership) and horizontal (contemporary leadership) relationships and processes. A single best practice approach is unlikely in these circumstances, and different organisational and environmental situations and contexts will require different leadership perspectives (Kilburg and Donohue 2011: 8; Reichenpfader et al. 2015: 310). Such a narrative is particularly relevant to health because of the complexity of national, regional, and local organisational structures and the constant change which is an accompanying feature. It is unlikely that any single approach to leadership would have universal applicability. The 'leader as person' norm outlined in Chap. 6 reflects this point of view.

In this melange of structure and scope, understanding organisational dynamics is a key aspect of leadership insight, and negotiating pathways through multiple organisational constructs is an essential leadership capability. This applies at a macro level, where the search for efficient or more economical ways of producing healthcare which might consist of public sector health provision, private health provision, or mixed markets of public, private, and third sector providers (Waring and Bishop 2013). Organisational types and structures will proliferate. And at the micro level, health organisations follow traditional academic specialities—such as radiology, anaesthesiology, or surgery (Porter and Teisberg 2006)—or, as is increasingly the case, integrating diverse health and social service organisations to enhance delivery, sustainability, and affordability. Added to this complexity, patient outcomes are no longer dependent solely upon excellent clinical management at the clinician-patient level but also on tiers of supporting processes, microsystems, and organisations that can determine the provision of good quality care. Negotiating a way through these many layers in the delivery of positive health outcomes is core to the health sector leader's role.

Organisational Complexity, Transformation, and Change

The identification of relevant competences is one step in the process of understanding organisational dynamics. It is the application of these competences that will decide whether a particular approach to leadership will succeed in the context of the various factors which constitute organisational dynamics and their importance to transformation and change, hence the conclusion that health sector leaders will need to be 'politically perceptive, adaptive to rapid change and chaos, and highly adept in decision making, team building, and collaboration' (Opollo et al. 2014). A combination of competence and competency will be critical. This applies to where models of intervention in any of these constructs are affected by such things as changes in demand or technology developments (e.g. within a hospital care system integrating specialist and emergency care or a primary care system functioning as a source of treatment and 'a gatekeeper to specialist care' (Pencheon 2015: 1335)). It is the role of the leader to re-engage and adapt. In these circumstances, the ability to craft a way through a variety of structures and different groups of professionals will be essential as will the ability to work across multiple professions and agencies to provide comprehensive and coordinated services (Valentijn et al. 2015: 2). At the most senior levels, the Executive's focus will be to position the organisation strategically for future success and operationally through a coherent implementation plan. How to effect this transformation will depend on the leader's understanding of methods and processes that suit the specific dynamics in the organisation, where they can place effort for change and the likely cultural or process inhibitors to change. Influence, capital, and contextual understanding are three 'organising themes' required by leaders in these circumstances (Graber and Kilpatrick 2008; Bish et al. 2015: 383). Studies from China, France, and the USA have shown that the ability to negotiate organisational barriers was important to achieve collaboration and culture change, and leadership and management performance relied on good organisational understanding through networks and the legitimacy acquired from them. The observation is particularly important as care delivery becomes more integrated and a more complex interdisciplinary, nonlinear, and dynamic process (Vinot 2014: 406; Larkin 2015; Valentijn et al. 2015: 10). In all cases and at all levels, leaders in the health sector will need knowledge of the organisation, the ebbs and flows of power, the cultural context within which people work, and the methods and processes for achieving change. Leadership capability and professional credibility are important, but knowing how the organisation works; the levers to pull or the buttons to press are equally so.

Knowledge, Insight, and Systems Thinking

The model for health sector leadership outlined in Chap. 5 put forward the view that a combination of competences would be an appropriate response to the leadership challenges that characterised the health sector. A group of these competences were aligned with the requirement to understand organisational dynamics. Further analysis means that it is possible to characterise leadership capabilities into three key areas, these being organisational knowledge and insight, systems thinking, and professional workforce engagement. Once again, the competences highlighted below are not meant to be definitive, more an indication of the type of approach that would be envisaged. It is likely that health sector organisations will have their own unique perspectives on this.

- **Organisational Knowledge and Insight**

The first grouping or category of competence for understanding organisational dynamics can be referred to as knowledge and insight and arises because of the heterogeneity and complexity of health sector organisations. A key consideration here is the type and structure of the organisation within which leadership takes place. Leading in a bureaucratic hierarchy, for example, may have different implications to those of leading in, say, a matrix or network. This isn't to favour one structure over the other, but to draw attention to the ability to adapt leadership style if it is necessary to do so. Organisational knowledge and insight are two factors that will be important in how the leader responds. In this respect and at a Senior Leadership level, understanding the implications of working with Boards and how these may differ between different types of governance structure is a critical competence. Getting the Board on Board will be necessary when aligning strategy to organisation and organisation to strategy and identifying processes for initiating, sustaining, and organising change that are relevant to the structure and culture of specific organisations, units, departments, or teams. This will require not only the power that resides with positional leadership but also the influence which will impact on change—including organisational politics. Within these dynamics, the leader will be sensitive to and understand the implications of diverse cultures and disciplines and will adapt leadership style in an appropriate way. Throughout, the leader will need to ensure that, where possible, plans and actions remain flexible. Organisational knowledge will also include an understanding of the impact of decision-making within one unit, department, or team on units outside of the immediate sphere of operations, and hence the second factor, the ability to lead or interface with others across different health systems, units, departments, or teams.

- **Systems Thinking**

Systems thinking arises because of the complexity of processes that can be a feature of health sector organisations. Here, leaders are increasingly faced with the challenge of joining up the outcomes of any decisions they make in one unit, department, or team and the effect these may have not only on the immediate recipients of the decision but on those after—along a supply chain, for example—and beyond. The ability to finesse, to have a perspective that goes beyond the immediate physical or temporal nature of decisions, is known as systems thinking. The characteristics of this include working effectively across organisations and agencies in the achievement of the organisation's objectives and an understanding of the need for connection, as well as sharing of information. Collaborating with others outside of the immediate area of responsibility to drive system change and being resilient in its delivery are critical and an understanding that collective action is important. Providing leadership to multiple groupings, or interdisciplinary teams simultaneously—the organisation as a whole, its teams, and individuals—will be necessary.

A third set of competences associated with understanding organisational dynamics is that concerned with engaging a diverse workforce drawn from across several professional or operational disciplines. These two groupings are focused on the implications of structure and process and require knowledge and ability on the part of the leader to deliver strategies across boundaries. Within both areas there is the dependency on engaging professionals from different skill areas in the 'solutions' that are proposed.

- **Professional Workforce Engagement**

The ability to engage a workforce made up of diverse skills and professions is a key area of competence. The health sector leader will require knowledge of the shape and structure of the organisation for which they have responsibility, an understanding of the people who make up this structure, and the specific cultural context within which they operate. Understanding organisational dynamics therefore means understanding people dynamics and the ability to mobilise these to the achievement of the unit, department, or team's objectives. Understanding and being able to inspire a vision that has the 'buy in' and is operationalised at every level through having a coherent narrative and setting clear, aligned objectives for all units, departments teams, and individuals are specific to employee engagement. This is complemented by promoting a sense of common ownership of the organisation and its reputation and relating this to the specifics of the unit, department, or team for which the leader has responsibility. Both of these will help to create a working environment that supports innovation, risk taking, and ownership of professional practice and set a positive team climate which integrates diverse viewpoints for the good of the organisation as a whole.

These competences are both strategic and relate to the dynamics of the whole organisation and tactical or operational relating to the dynamics of the unit, department, or team and their relationships. They will require the leader to be aware of macro-level demands (such as of the Board, its policies, and the operating principles by which the organisation makes its decisions) and micro-level ones concerned with resource allocation to individual areas. It will require an understanding of the culture of the organisation and how the leader engages individuals and teams. The success of the leader will be dependent on her or his capability in crafting an approach or an identity based on deep understanding (insight) into how the organisation works, where its fast streams are and where its blockages or silos are, and what needs to be done to break these down.

Formalised Rules or Adaptive Environments: The Scope of Organisational Dynamics

The application of competence and competency will be dependent upon the nature of strategy and policy setting, decision-making, and decision operationalisation, often in a sequence of challenge and response. On the one hand, there may be 'formalised rules and written formal procedures to ensure the management and governance of the health care providers act in accord with espoused values. These may relate to internal business processes, patient quality services, safety and satisfaction, organisational learning and growth, and finance' (Shukri and Ramli 2015). However, formality may not always be present and as healthcare becomes more complex, different, more adhocratic processes may emerge requiring that 'contemporary healthcare management and communication networks need to become adaptive and support innovation to be effective' (Hunt et al. 2016: 51). Successful outcomes will require those in leadership positions to recognise such diversity in structure and processes, adapt their leadership style based on this knowledge, and manage with and through the dynamics. In some cases, the leader will adopt the rules and processes and in others will use her or his knowledge of organisational dynamics to change them. Within the unit, the dynamics will arise out of the setting and implementing of strategy, policy, and stewardship and their impact on structure and process, whilst outside of the health unit, there will be the dynamics of inter-organisation or inter-agency collaboration. Throughout the organisations there will be a culture—the informal rules that determine how people act or behave—against which policy and strategy are set.

Where there is convergence, a situation whereby strategy and policy are in line with what professionals in the workforce understand and accept and with which they are engaged, there will be more harmony in change or transformation. It is the role of the leader to offer a strategic narrative and operational solutions to facilitate this. To do so leadership actions will be based on the competences outlined above in the categories of organisational knowledge and insight, systems thinking, and professional workforce engagement and will be achieved by brokering, participating, mediating, and relationship building (Thorpe et al. 2011). Where these are applied successfully, the challenges to transformation outlined in Kotter's classic work (1996)—failing to create a sufficiently powerful guiding coalition, permitting obstacles to block the new vision, and neglecting to anchor changes firmly in the corporate culture—can be dealt with.

The concepts of negotiating and navigating as leadership approaches have been viewed in the context of organisational theory (McKimm and Phillips 2009). The explanation being that in the first incarnation, the organisation was a complex machine in which trait and great man theories of leadership were apposite. Second, where the organisation was a complex organic structure, transformational and transactional leadership styles were predominant. In the third example, where the organisation was a loose agglomeration of complex organisms, contingency theories, distributed leadership, and complex adaptive leadership were necessary. There is a possibility that the health sector leader will face all three scenarios and organisational awareness therefore is an important attribute. This occurs at strategic level through the Board, at operational level through the unit or department, and at team level and across boundaries with multiple agencies (McKimm and Phillips 2009: 15; Ezziane 2012). The scope of these dynamics is shown in Fig. 8.1.

The navigation will involve balancing the abstract of organisational design on the one hand and the specificity of individual needs on the other. The various stakeholders are 'placed at the heart of the management process and not be considered as static players or as interfering external claims makers' and understanding organisational dynamics recognises 'the heterogeneity of stakeholders … different groups come into salience, depending on the context. As the context shifts, so do the relevant stakeholders' (Beaulieu and Pasquero 2002: 55). It is possible to identify four groups of such stakeholders who have a key role to play in organisational dynamics, namely, the Board, the unit and its managers, teams of health professionals, and finally organisational dynamics across health service providers—multiple or single agency.

Internal-Single Unit- Getting the Board on Board	**Internal-Single Unit-** Negotiating through unit or team dynamics	**External-single agency-** collaboration and cooperation	**External-multiple agencies-** Building relational capital with partners
• Understanding the implications of working with boards and within governance structures. • creating a narrative for the organisation's future that reflects stakeholder objectives • negotiating this narrative through Board member needs and issues • aligning strategy to suit present and future needs • recognising the importance of political impact of strategy • demonstrating capability in contextual, educational, interpersonal, analytical, political and strategic dimensions • Promoting a sense of common ownership of the organisation and its reputation- brokers and mediates in areas of contention	• understanding the organisation's unique culture and processes • Managing the processes of influence that can impact on the change including organisational politics • Being sensitive to and understands the leadership of diverse cultures and disciplines • engaging stakeholdersin creating and implementing strategy • planning organising, setting objectives in a way that is aligned to organisational culture and systems understood by teams • understanding of the dynamics of embedding change in the organisation's processes. • building influence, capital and contextual understanding • acknowledging the importance of team dynamics	• collaborating and cooperating with colleagues outside of the immediate unit as a partnership • Providing leadership to multiple groupings simultaneously-organisation as a whole, teams and individuals • Providing leadership across interdisciplinary teams • building relational capital with partners • recognising differences in culture and systems and adapting behaviour accordingly	• collaborating and cooperating with colleagues outside of immediate unit • building relational capital with partners • understanding political impact and negotiates with partner organisations accordingly • Providing leadership across interdisciplinary teams • building relationships across boundaries • providing information relevant to partner organisations

Fig. 8.1 The scope of organisational dynamics and required leadership actions

'Getting the Board on Board'

The first such group is the Board of the organisation. As the senior policy-making structure in health sector organisations, providing strategic leadership, setting direction and objectives, and establishing the governance by which this is delivered, the Board will consist of a Chair and a diverse range of Executive and non-Executive Directors. Their purpose is to provide effective governance and to build service user, public, and stakeholder confidence that local, regional, or national healthcare is being effectively managed for quality and safety and that investment is allocated to the best health outcomes. The Boards are proactive in strengthening governance processes for quality and efficiency and seek the engagement of members in strategic initiatives. Good corporate governance can make a significant difference to health outcomes (Emslie et al. 2006; Jumaa 2008; Millar et al. 2013; Tsai et al. 2015). On the one hand, the Board can provide strategic direction, a mechanism for performance improvement by sharing knowledge and values, 'a shared process of top-level organizational leadership, policy making and decision making. Although the governing board has the ultimate accountability, the CEO, senior management and clinical leaders are involved in top-level functions' (Abor et al. 2008: 48; Tuan 2012). On the other it can relate to business processes such as finance or operational efficiency. The work of the Board is to establish policies, to make decisions that affect the working of the organisation, and to be accountable for the actions that follow those policies and decisions (Chelliah et al. 2016: 4). Three considerations are important, these being Board dynamics, the dimensions of Board effectiveness, and the type of Board structure that is in place.

A range of theories and approaches to Board dynamics have been highlighted. *Agency theory*, for example, explains the Board as a way of holding members of the workforce at all levels to account for their performance (Millar et al. 2013); *stewardship theory* seeks to maximise the contribution of the workforce to wider organisational goals by nurturing a culture of shared values and goals; *stakeholder theory* 'elaborates the notion that health care organisations comprise a range of overlapping interests, both competing and cooperative,' and the emphasis is on how different stakeholder interests can be addressed, integrated, and balanced (Martins et al. 2014). In all of these cases, the role of the Board is to interpret and represent the views of those with a stake in ensuring the delivery of good quality care and to make trade-offs between different stakeholders including employees, regulators, patients, and the public, which when effective can increase the likelihood of knowledge translation into policy and practice (Makan et al. 2015; Mannion et al. 2017: 279). Finally with *resource dependence theory*, the Board gives specialised expertise or knowledge as well as external networks or resources (Mannion et al. 2017). The contextual nature of organisations means that best practice governance will not always follow broadly defined standards but will be influenced by contextual factors which contribute to fitting governance responses. 'Such a process would translate contingency theory into a useful practice' (Chelliah et al. 2016: 20). The choice of governance approach is variable, but the desired outcomes are consistent. Hence, understanding the unique dimensions of Board-level operation in any one organisation remains important. Completing the picture of Board-level dynamics are the six dimensions of Board effectiveness including those related to context, education (ensuring that all Board members are well-informed about the organisation and the professions working there as well as the Board's own roles, responsibilities, and performance), an interpersonal relationship, an analytical dimension, one related to politics (positive relationships between stakeholders), and finally a strategic dimension in which the Board helps to shape organisational direction and helps ensure a strategic approach to the organisation's future (Mannion et al. 2017: 280). Against each of these dimensions, there is an emphasis on ensuring that those who gain access to Board-level membership should be equipped with the relevant capabilities to the context of which understanding organisational dynamics is a key component.

The relevant theory and the assessment of dimensions of effectiveness will vary from situation to situation. In some cases, a Board will be supportive and engaged in, for example, clinical issues. In others, the focus will be on responding to external forces. The taxonomy of governance reflects multiple dynamics at Board level within which successful health sector leadership would have to plot a course (Jones et al. 2016; Shah et al. 2017). The influence held by health sector leaders will depend on the recognition of the importance of understanding organisational dynamics at Board level and the ability to negotiate a path through them.

To do so requires excellent organisational skills (Pidgeon 2017). Amongst these will be knowledge of the operating process of the Board and how it affects not only the mission and strategy but also the culture, as well as understanding the interests or approaches of Board members. The objective is to engage Board members—*Getting Boards on Board*—to secure commitment to the strategic direction of the organisation (Walton and Mullinix 2016; McBride 2017). The second aspect is to ensure shared responsibility between the Board and the Executive Leadership of the organisation, for outcomes including quality and patient safety and meeting the needs of the community and stakeholders. This is a mutually advantageous approach which will require a clear appreciation of roles and responsibilities and respect for differences. Hence health professionals in leadership positions will need to extend their outlooks and 'move beyond competence to being able to work effectively in unpredictable and changing healthcare contexts' on the one hand and being able to develop effective partnerships at multiple levels on the other (Jumaa 2008: 926; Goeschel et al. 2010; Wilson Pecci 2014; McBride 2017). This extension to the recognised boundaries of leadership competence will require professionals who understand the dynamics of Board-level operations including core governance functions such as the development of policy, resource allocation, and legal authority and oversight and understand how to influence their direction or maximise the benefits of their outcomes.

Negotiating Through Unit, Department, or Team Dynamics: Culture, Values, Symbols, and Language

The second level of organisational dynamics occurs at unit, department, or team level. In this context, unit strategy acts as the enabler and 'is the craft of figuring out which purposes are both worth pursuing and capable of being accomplished' (Rumelt 2011: 66). The dynamics which influence strategy are the power of culture, values, symbols, and language; of policies, processes, and routines; of historical experience or memory of change and transformation; and of the views of professional specialists and generalists. Leadership success will be associated with making the mission clear to all of these vested interests as a means of holding the organisation together and enabling it to perform effectively (Drucker 2006 quote from 1992) and ensuring that the organisation (its design and processes) is adapted to the strategy (Kaplan and Norton 2006) or in a contemporary description that the alignment of the organisation's objectives and strategy is facilitated by an alignment with culture, systems, and processes. There is the need to ensure that the organisation's policies and procedures provide the basis of justice and fairness for stakeholders (Bowie 2000: 190).

At this level, leaders adapt their behaviour to accomplish the mission of the organisation helped by an understanding of organisational culture and dynamics with recognition that the unique circumstances or situation will have an effect such that 'each leader must provide leadership to the individuals within the organisation' and be systematic in the way she or he contributes to the maintenance of an effective organisation (Mastrangelo et al. 2004: 439). Healthcare organisations are groups of individuals who act interconnectedly in 'pluralistic organisations where divergent objectives, including the care of individual patients and specific patient populations, are positioned within a cost control environment and where interplay occurs among a multitude of actors, including healthcare professionals, managers and community groups, linked together in ambiguous power relationships' (Aubry et al. 2014: 1334). In such an environment, difficulties may arise between different parts of the organisation because actions may create overlaps and misconceptions (Lewis 2012). In some cases there is a cohabitation between hierarchy and new forms of organisation and hence multidimensional structures and hybrid forms. Such an environment requires leaders to become active forces of innovation and change by identifying inhibitors and enhancers, and working from the 'living present' ensures that strategy constructs an organisation's future. In this context, organisational dynamics is concerned with 'properties of stability and instability, regularity and irregularity, predictability and unpredictability' (Stacey 2011: 28; Tran and Voyer 2015). The leaders who understand these dynamics will be in a better position to influence the course of strategy to achieve the organisation's goals and objectives.

There are lessons from research and practice in respect of understanding organisational dynamics at unit level. In the first place, bringing together diverse talents to achieve the collaboration necessary to effect change and transformation will require an intelligent mix of short-term action and longer-term nurturing, and it will require setting the right balance between the needs of individuals and the organisation as a whole and between private interest and public knowledge (Senge et al. 2007). Studies in Canada, Switzerland, and the UK found that successful approaches recognised the relationships between strategy, structure, and culture accordingly; communicated information about the meaning and purpose of changed strategy had a preparedness to adapt where necessary and recognition on the part of leaders that embedding change in the organisational culture was critical if the benefits of the change were to be sustained (LeBrasseur et al. 2002; Mitleton-Kelly 2011; Alimpic 2013). This requires insightful action on the part of the leader in holding together the diversity of talents necessary for organisational success (Mastrangelo et al. 2004: 437; Grint 2005: 37). Understanding the depth of talent, where such talent is located in teams, and how to mobilise the talent to achieve goals are of primary importance.

Finally understanding team dynamics—intra- or cross organisation—can have significant, positive effect on the level of organisational commitment, and the need for effective teams in the modern healthcare environment therefore has emerged as a factor in the response to volatile and unpredictable external forces, 'with the need for expanded and improved teamwork to integrate and apply knowledge and technology, comes the need for improved leadership to make teamwork more efficient and effective' (LeBrasseur et al. 2002; Gokce et al. 2014; Donnelly 2017; Pidgeon 2017; Smits et al. 2014: 300). Evidence suggests that a variety of outcomes are influenced by the leader's ability to work with the dynamics of teams. But to do so will require excellence in execution (Bowers et al. 2011; Lingard et al. 2012; Kumar et al. 2014: 208; Bowen 2015). In Australia, India, the UK, and Sweden, the importance of leaders taking into account the effects of policy and structural changes on interprofessional teamwork was emphasised, recommending that leaders should recognise and minimise any negative effects of changes on the functioning of interprofessional teams, whilst in India, experiences in integrated service delivery of community health were seen to be improved where teamwork and building trust were components of practice, even where this meant 'ceding territory and seeing beyond one's own interests' were highlighted (Valsecchi et al. 2012; Klarare et al. 2013: 1067; Mishra 2014; Bentley et al. 2018). In Ireland and the USA, studies showed that team leadership was an important organisation development issue (Taplin et al. 2013; Kennedy et al. 2015).

The evidence for the principles of effective team working and the leadership implications highlights certain key features in ensuring there is a common purpose and goals, effective communication and the facilitation of an environment where there is a good team spirit. Furthermore, mutual respect among team members gives rise to a willingness to share knowledge and learning and to raise concerns (Williams 2016: 140). Collaboration, cooperation, and understanding the organisational dynamics in which these flourish are fundamental to the achievement of goals in the modern, complex health service organisation.

Building Relational Capital Through Partnership: Multiple or Single Agency

Increasingly, leadership in the health sector is concerned with crossing the boundaries of specific units to achieve organisational outcomes or change to build relational capital with leaders in other agencies, units, departments, or teams. Hence, the third and fourth aspects of understanding organisational dynamics relate to multi-unit or inter-agency working. It is possible to explain this in terms of social interaction, recognising the power of networks in developing and influencing the spread of management knowledge and practice. Indeed, the translation of key health initiatives into practice requires the internal capacity of healthcare organisations to engage in knowledge mobilisation by professional associations, collaboration, and implementation networks. Health leaders create organisational culture and processes that facilitate collaboration and are able to harness or direct it to the achievement of healthcare goals. This means dealing with differences in leadership or management styles and cultures across agencies and reconciling between them (Baxter et al. 2008; Stacey 2011: 32; Harvey et al. 2014; Bresnen 2017). The role of the leader will be to ensure that she or he has knowledge of the dynamics of the organisation which can be used positively to enhance the opportunity for successful interface (business as usual, processes or transformation, and change) within or between partners.

Where leadership takes place across organisational boundaries or in multidisciplinary teams, the understanding and management of these dynamics can be critical because 'if either contractual or managerial governance systems are too strong and perceived as excessively controlling, they can lead to … demoralisation' or different professional goals and boundaries may inhibit progress (Baxter et al. 2008: 125; Williams 2016: 140). In such cases the leadership across boundaries means proactive involvement in decision-making and the ability to negotiate change accordingly through compromise. The contemporary health sector leader has a broad perspective of the organisations across which she or he operates and avoids seeing the scope of leadership as a 'narrowed, disjointed perception' in which the 'world is an assemblage of separate things that have somehow come together' (Cacioppe 1997: 340). In practice, the leader's insight will be about how her or his organisation, unit, or team functions with both written and unwritten rules. Where this happens, collective leadership can establish a vision, create trust, and contribute to workforce engagement, as well as a culture of learning and creating continuous improvement. Regardless of the style of leadership, there is recognition of the need for an environment of adaptation and change, which in turn would require an understanding of that environment, its dynamics, and the ways in which change could take place. Findings in healthcare organisations in India, China, and France confirm that empowerment and commitment on the part of health leaders had an impact on multiple organisational outcomes, not least of which were employee engagement, job satisfaction, and quality of work life (Yang et al. 2014; Malik et al. 2016; Lv and Zhang 2017). There are benefits to the organisation and to individual members of the health workforce from leadership that is able to work through the dynamics to produce a positive workplace. The success in so doing will influence the way they engage in social interactions with colleagues, staff, and patients and thus participate in the co-creation of some aspects of context (Tsai 2011; Meier 2015: 1116).

Where health professionals span organisational boundaries, trust and engagement are priorities; and inter-organisational learning can be enhanced by socialisation, shared experience, the conversion of tacit knowledge into explicit knowledge, shared ambition, interests and mutual gains, relationship dynamics, organisational dynamics, and process management (Kok et al. 2015; Valentijn et al. 2015; Heskestad et al. 2016: 2). It is the role of the leader to facilitate these because to do so will improve cost management, quality of care, and patient outcomes. Forming partnerships is used to promote integrated service delivery across health and social service systems. Relationship dynamics have a significant effect on the success of any partnership and highlight the importance of building relational capital during the developmental phase. Trust-based governance mechanisms are critical to integration.

Case Study: Leadership in Healthcare in China—The Challenges and the Responses

Feirong Wang and Xiaoxian Zhu

The healthcare system of China is comprised of both public and private medical institutions and often funded through insurance programmes. The primary point-of-care access is often through public hospitals, which are considered to be the most important health facilities as a result, providing both outpatient and inpatient care. The hospitals are generally located within cities and built-up urban areas. In addition to care provision, these hospitals also burden the responsibility for the majority of teaching, training, and research. However, as a result of changing socio-economic environment and demands, several challenges have arisen in regard to accessible and affordable hospital healthcare.

Amongst these challenges are firstly growing consumerism and patient engagement in costs for which China has undertaken significant healthcare reforms including the launch of the New Rural Co-operative Medical Care System in an overhaul of the healthcare system, with the intention of providing affordable heath provisions for the rural poor; secondly, the increasing complexity to operate physician practices; and thirdly, growing tensions between doctors and patients due to scarce resources.

To cope with the challenges and changes in China, leaders in healthcare have adopted a positive attitude and started to make responses in the following ways:

- **Effective Leaders Driving Organisational Change**

With the increasing demands for healthcare access, there have been changes to organisational management structure across the healthcare industry. Leaders are essential for improving organisational efficiency and performance and for enhancing patient safety and creating healthy work environments. The leadership potential of managers has gradually become the focus of attention at home and abroad.

- **Through Transformational Leadership**

Various forms of transformational leadership styles can be incorporated into organisational leadership structure, in order to inspire and promote employee outputs, but it is essential that different styles that are appropriate to healthcare environments be available, to maximise relationships between different types of followers and their needs. In practice, authentic leadership is needed to maintain passion for the vision 'always be what is best for our patients' in healthcare in China.

Tension in doctor-patient relationship can impact upon doctor and nurse interactions in China. The importance of maintaining these dynamics cannot be understated due to the significant importance of trust between multidisciplinary workers. The leaders in healthcare in China have proactively explored the solutions to avoid the barriers to communication and improve cultural and healthcare environments. It is also brought to leaders' attentions to take care of the well-being of medical staff within themselves.

During and after period of conflict, authentic leadership is a relational leadership style purported to promote a healthy work environment that influences staff performance and organisational outcome. Authentic leaders are able to enhance the engagement, motivation, commitment, satisfaction, and involvement required from staff to constantly improve their work and performance outcomes through the development of personal identification with the leader and social identification with the work unit/organisation. Further leadership styles that could be incorporated into a medical framework in China include servant leadership (Northouse 2016) that well fits in its national culture.

- **Collaboration Between R&D with Outside Research Institutes**

This can be used to develop new technology and medicine to improve treatment provisions for difficult, newly emerging, and miscellaneous diseases.

Difficult miscellaneous diseases are a common issue that impacts upon the healthcare industry. In order to secure contracts, it may prove prevalent to encourage engagements with well-known prestigious hospitals, leaders acting in a flagship role that functions in terms of directional leadership and example for others as 'Champion Hospitals.' Through such 'Champion Hospitals,' a union between other hospitals, research institutes, and medical colleges and companies can collaboratively work together to develop new technologies and medicines holistically to improve treatment of disease more efficiently, with a potential to increase treatment access at the same time.

- **To Form a Healthcare Ecosystem**

In order to further enhance and drive forth healthcare provision, a healthcare ecosystem needs to be established, including healthcare organisational side (the operation of multidisciplinary care teams, academic departments, hospitals), insurance companies, and government. Through the formation of a symbiotic relationship, leaders in healthcare in China acted as a supporter, a strategist, and a facilitator in this process, to drive a supportive ecosystem—provision and resource capabilities can be shared more efficiently, to reduce 'doubling-up' on equipment, training focus, and wasteful practices when more efficient systems could be integrated and shared between centres regionally to improve the care provision of more services whilst removing stresses and burdens from health practitioners and treatment centres.

Effective leadership as an essential part of the transformation of the healthcare system in China has been recognised at all levels.

Conclusion and Implications for Practice

Leadership success in health sector organisations will be grounded in leadership capability and professional credibility but will also require knowledge about how to navigate and negotiate through the complexity of the diverse and complex organisation structures that are a feature of the sector. In this respect understanding organisational dynamics is a core leadership capability. Organisational dynamics are internal and external forces determined by the organisation's strategy, structure, history, culture, politics, and process.

The key components of this capability are:

- **At Board level, understanding organisational dynamics means recognition of the need to co-create a vision for the organisation's future that reflects stakeholder objectives**, the ability to negotiate the vision through Board member needs and issues whilst influencing strategy stewardship and policy to suit present and future needs, recognising the importance of any political impact.

- **At organisational, unit, or departmental level, the leader will have an understanding of the organisation's unique culture and processes**, is able to engage stakeholders in creating and implementing strategy, and then plans, organises, and sets objectives in a way that is aligned to organisational culture and systems understood by teams. Finally, the leader will have an understanding of the dynamics of embedding change in the organisation's processes, through building influence, capital, and contextual understanding.
- **At team level the leader will acknowledge the importance of team dynamics** and actively works to ensure effective team working.
- In the quest for integration across agencies, **the leader will have the ability to collaborate with colleagues outside of immediate unit**, is able to build relational capital with partners, understands the potential political impact of inter-agency working and negotiates with partner organisations accordingly, and provides information relevant to partner organisations.

Leadership in the health sector will require individuals who have critically appraised their own strengths in respect of the demands of a particular context or situation, adapted their leadership style accordingly, ensured that their leadership identity is an authentic account of their strengths and role, and applied this in such a way that they are able to navigate the idiosyncratic cultural characteristics of their organisation. The three elements of personal insight, professional credibility, and understanding organisational dynamics form the basis of a model for leadership that will apply to whichever leadership style are present.

References

Abor, P. A., Abekah-Nkrumah, G., & Joshua Abor, J. (2008). An Examination of Hospital Governance in Ghana. *Leadership in Health Services, 21*(1), 47–60. https://doi.org/10.1108/17511870810845905.

Alimpic, Z. (2013). New Growth Platform Framework for Swiss Acute Hospitals – An Empirical Study for the Development of Dynamic Capabilities. *Serbian Journal of Management, 8*(2), 185–199.

Aubry, M., Richer, M., & Lavoie-Tremblay, M. (2014). Governance Performance in Complex Environment: The Case of a Major Transformation in a University Hospital. *International Journal of Project Management, 32*(8), 1333–1345.

Basistic, S., Cerne, M., & Vogel, B. (2017). Just How Multi-Level Is Leadership Research? A Document Co-Citation Analysis 1980–2013 on Leadership Constructs and Outcomes. *The Leadership Quarterly, 28*(1), 86–103.

Baxter, K., Weiss, M., & Grand, J. L. (2008). The Dynamics of Commissioning Across Organisational and Clinical Boundaries. *Journal of Health Organization and Management, 22*(2), 111–128.

Beaulieu, S. A., & Pasquero, J. A. (2002). Reintroducing Stakeholder Dynamics in Stakeholder Thinking. *The Journal of Corporate Citizenship, 2002*(6), 53. https://doi.org/10.9774/Gleaf.4700.2002.Su.00007.

Bentley, M., Freeman, T., Baum, F., & Javanparast, S. (2018). Interprofessional Teamwork in Comprehensive Primary Healthcare Services: Findings from a Mixed Methods Study. *Journal of Interprofessional Care, 32*(3), 274–283. https://doi.org/10.1080/13561820.2017.1401986.

Bish, M., Kenny, A., & Nay, R. (2015). Factors That Influence the Approach to Leadership: Directors of Nursing Working in Rural Health Services. *Journal of Nursing Management, 23*(3), 380–389. https://doi.org/10.1111/jonm.12146.

Bowen, D. J. (2015). Becoming a Nimble Leader: Leading Teams Through Change Requires Agility and Masterful Execution. *Healthcare Executive, 30*(6), 8.

Bowers, L., Nijman, H., Simpson, A., & Jones, J. (2011). The Relationship Between Leadership, Teamworking, Structure, Burnout and Attitude to Patients on Acute Psychiatric Wards. *Social Psychiatry and Psychiatric Epidemiology, 46*(2), 143–148. https://doi.org/10.1007/s00127-010-0180-8.

Bowie, N. (2000). A Kantian Theory of Leadership. *The Leadership and Organisation Journal, 21*(4), 185–193.

Bresnen, M. (2017). *Managing Modern Healthcare: Knowledge, Networks and Practice*. New York: Routledge.

Cacioppe, R. (1997). Leadership Moment by Moment. *Leadership and Organisation Development Journal, 18*(7), 335–345.

Chapman, A. N., Johnson, D., & Kilner, K. (2014). Leadership Styles Used by Senior Medical Leaders. *Leadership in Health Services (1751–1879), 27*(4), 283. https://doi.org/10.1108/LHS-03-2014-0022.

Chelliah, J., Boersma, M., & Klettner, A. (2016). Governance Challenges for Not-for-Profit Organisations: Empirical Evidence in Support of a Contingency Approach. *Contemporary Management Research, 12*(1), 3–23. https://doi.org/10.7903/Cmr.14538.

Donnelly, T. (2017). Leadership: Briefing and Debriefing in the Operating Room. *Journal of Perioperative Practice, 27*(7), 154–157.

Drucker, P. (2006). What Executives Should Remember. *Harvard Business Review, 84*(2), 144–152.

Emslie, S., Oliver, C., & Bruce, J. (2006). Getting Governance Right at Board Level: The Policy Governance Approach to Building Better National Health Service Boards. *Clinician in Management, 14*(2), 69–77.

Ezziane, Z. (2012). The Importance of Clinical Leadership in Twenty First Century Health Care. *International Journal of Health Promotion and Education, 50*(5), 261–269.

Goeschel, C. A., Wachter, R. M., & Pronovost, P. J. (2010). Medical Ethics: Responsibility for Quality Improvement and Patient Safety. Hospital Board and Medical Staff Leadership Challenges. *Chest, 138*, 171–178. https://doi.org/10.1378/chest.09-2051.

Gokce, B., Guney, S., & Katrinli, A. (2014). Does Doctors' Perception of Hospital Leadership Style and Organizational Culture Influence Their Organizational Commitment? *Social Behavior & Personality: An International Journal, 42*(9), 1549–1561.

Graber, D. R., & Kilpatrick, A. O. (2008). Establishing Values-Based Leadership and Value Systems in Healthcare Organizations. *Journal of Health & Human Services Administration, 31*(2), 179–197.

Grint, K. (2005). *Leadership: Limits and Possibilities*. Basingstoke: Palgrave Macmillan.

Harvey, G., Boaden, R., Kislov, R., Kislov, R., Harvey, G., Boaden, R., et al. (2014). Rethinking Capacity Building for Knowledge Mobilisation: Developing Multilevel Capabilities in Healthcare Organisations. *Implementation Science, 9*, 166.

Heskestad, R. N., Aase, K., & Storm, M. (2016). Inter-Organisational Learning Among Health Care Professionals: A Learning Arena to Address Transitional Care of the Elderly. *International Journal of Integrated Care (IJIC), 16*(6), 1–3. https://doi.org/10.5334/ijic.2778.

Hunt, C. S., Landry, R. T., & Kerr, B. J. (2016). Formal Leaders' Perceptions of Informal Leaders. *Radiology Management, 38*(4), 51–57.

Jones, A., Lankshear, A., & Kelly, D. (2016). Giving Voice to Quality and Safety Matters at Board Level: A Qualitative Study of the Experiences of Executive

Nurses Working in England and Wales. *International Journal of Nursing Studies, 59*, 169–176. https://doi.org/10.1016/j.ijnurstu.2016.04.007.

Jumaa, M. (2008). The 'F.E.E.L.' Good Factors in Nursing Leadership at Board Level Through Work-Based Learning. *Journal of Nursing Management, 16*(8), 992–999. https://doi.org/10.1111/J.1365-2834.2008.00953.X.

Kaplan, R. S., & Norton, D. P. (2006). How to Implement a New Strategy Without Disrupting Your Organisation. *Harvard Business Review, 84*(3), 100–109.

Kennedy, N., Armstrong, C., Woodward, O., & Cullen, W. (2015). Primary Care Team Working in Ireland: A Qualitative Exploration of Team Members' Experiences in a New Primary Care Service. *Health & Social Care in the Community, 23*(4), 362–370. https://doi.org/10.1111/Hsc.12150.

Kilburg, R. R., & Donohue, M. D. (2011). Toward a 'Grand Unifying Theory' of Leadership: Implications for Consulting Psychology. *Consulting Psychology Journal: Practice and Research, 63*(1), 6–25. https://doi.org/10.1037/A0023053.

Kim, R. H., Gaukler, G. M., & Lee, C. W. (2016). Improving Healthcare Quality: A Technological and Managerial Innovation Perspective. *Technological Forecasting and Social Change, 113*(Part B), 373–378. https://doi.org/10.1016/j.techfore.2016.09.012.

Klarare, A., Lundh, H. C., Fürst, C. J., & Fossum, B. (2013). Team Interactions in Specialized Palliative Care Teams: A Qualitative Study. *Journal of Palliative Medicine, 16*(9), 1062. https://doi.org/10.1089/jpm.2012.0622.

Kok, M. C., Dieleman, M., Broerse, J. W., Kea, A. Z., Datiko, D. G., Taegtmeyer, M., et al. (2015). A Qualitative Assessment of Health Extension Workers' Relationships with the Community and Health Sector in Ethiopia: Opportunities for Enhancing Maternal Health Performance. *Human Resources for Health, 13*, 80.

Kotter, J. P. (1996). *Leading Change*. Boston, MA: Harvard Business Review Press.

Kumar, S., Deshmukh, V., & Adhish, V. S. (2014). Building and Leading Teams. *Indian Journal of Community Medicine, 39*(4), 208–213. https://doi.org/10.4103/0970-0218.143020.

Larkin, H. (2015). The New Health Care CEO: In a Rapidly Changing Field, Effective Leaders Require 'Learning Agility' and 'Emotional Intelligence' as Much–or More–Than Traditional Skills. *H&HN Hospitals & Health Networks, 22*(6).

LeBrasseur, R., Whissell, R., & Ojha, A. (2002). Organisational Learning, Transformational Leadership and Implementation of Continuous Quality

Improvement in Canadian Hospitals. *Australian Journal of Management (University of New South Wales), 27*(2), 141.

Lewis, A. (2012). Organisations Adjusting to Change: A Discussion of the Impact of an Improving Access to Psychological Therapies (IAPT) Service on the Organisational Dynamics of an Existing Psychological Therapies Department. *Counselling Psychology Review, 27*(1), 22–29.

Lingard, L., Vanstone, M., Fleming-Carroll, B., Lowe, M., Sinclair, L., Rashotte, J., et al. (2012). Conflicting Messages: Examining the Dynamics of Leadership on Interprofessional Teams. *Academic Medicine, 87*(12), 1762–1767.

Lv, C., & Zhang, L. (2017). Original Article: How Can Collective Leadership Influence the Implementation of Change in Health Care? *Chinese Nursing Research, 4*, 182–185. https://doi.org/10.1016/j.cnre.2017.10.005.

Makan, A., Fekadu, A., Murhar, V., Luitel, N., Kathree, T., Ssebunya, J., et al. (2015). Stakeholder Analysis of the Programme for Improving Mental Health Care (PRIME): Baseline Findings. *International Journal of Mental Health Systems, 9*(1), 1–12. https://doi.org/10.1186/s13033-015-0020-z.

Malik, N., Dhar, R. L., & Handa, S. C. (2016). Authentic Leadership and Its Impact on Creativity of Nursing Staff: A Cross Sectional Questionnaire Survey of Indian Nurses and Their Supervisors. *International Journal of Nursing Studies, 63*, 28–36.

Mannion, R., Davies, H., Jacobs, R., Kasteridis, P., Millar, R., & Freeman, T. (2017). Do Hospital Boards Matter for Better, Safer, Patient Care? *Social Science & Medicine, 177*, 278–287. https://doi.org/10.1016/j.socscimed.2017.01.045.

Martins, F. A., Ferreira-da-Silva, A., & Machado-Santos, C. (2014). Gestão dos Stakeholders na Captação de Recursos nos Hospitais Filantrópicos e Religiosos. *RAC – Revista De Administração Contemporânea, 18*, 65–85. https://doi.org/10.1590/1982-7849rac20141527.

Mastrangelo, A., Eddy, E. R., & Lorenzst, S. J. (2004). The Importance of Personal and Professional Leadership. *The Leadership and Organisational Development Journal, 25*(5), 435–451.

McBride, A. B. (2017). Serving on a Hospital Board: A Case Study. *Nursing Outlook, 65*, 372–379. https://doi.org/10.1016/j.outlook.2016.12.006.

McKimm, J., & Phillips, K. (2009). *Leadership and Management in Integrated Services*. Exeter: Learning Matters.

Meier, N. (2015). Configurations of Leadership Practices in Hospital Units. *Journal of Health Organization and Management, 29*(7), 1115–1130. https://doi.org/10.1108/JHOM-01-2014-0009.

Millar, R., Mannion, R., Freeman, T., & Davies, H. T. (2013). Hospital Board Oversight of Quality and Patient Safety: A Narrative Review and Synthesis of Recent Empirical Research. *Milbank Quarterly, 91*(4), 738–770. https://doi.org/10.1111/1468-0009.1203.

Mishra, A. (2014). 'Trust and Teamwork Matter': Community Health Workers' Experiences in Integrated Service Delivery in India. *Global Public Health, 9*(8), 960–974. https://doi.org/10.1080/17441692.2014.934877.

Mitleton-Kelly, E. (2011). A Complexity Theory Approach to Sustainability: A Longitudinal Study in Two London NHS Hospitals. *Learning Organization, 18*(1), 45–53.

Northouse, P. G. (2016). *Leadership, Theory and Practice* (7th ed.). Thousand Oaks, CA: Sage Publications Inc.

Opollo, J. G., Lloyd-Busby, A., Foreman, K., & Richardson, D. (2014). Nursing Administrative Officer: Transforming Nursing Leadership in Acute-Care Hospitals. *Nurse Leader, 12*, 84–90. https://doi.org/10.1016/j.mnl.2014.04.005.

Pencheon, D. (2015). Mini-Symposium: Making Health Care More Sustainable: The Case of the English NHS. *Public Health, 129*, 1335–1343. https://doi.org/10.1016/j.puhe.2015.08.010.

Pidgeon, K. (2017). The Keys for Success: Leadership Core Competencies. *Journal of Trauma Nursing, 24*(6), 338–341. https://doi.org/10.1097/JTN.0000000000000322.

Porter, M. E., & Teisberg, E. (2006). *Redefining Health Care*. Boston, MA: Harvard Business School Press.

Reichenpfader, U., Carlfjord, S., & Nilsen, P. (2015). Leadership in Evidence-Based Practice: A Systematic Review. *Leadership in Health Services, 28*(4), 298–316.

Rumelt, R. (2011). *Good Strategy, Bad Strategy*. London: Profile Books.

Senge, P. M., Lichtenstein, B. B., Kaeufer, K., Bradbury, H., & Carroll, J. S. (2007). Collaborating for Systemic Change. *MIT Sloan Management Review, 48*(2), 44–53.

Shah, G. H., Sotnikov, S., Leep, C. J., Jiali, Y., & Van Wave, T. W. (2017). Creating a Taxonomy of Local Boards of Health Based on Local Health Departments' Perspectives. *American Journal of Public Health, 107*(1), 72–80.

Shukri, N. M., & Ramli, A. (2015). Organizational Structure and Performances of Responsible Malaysian Healthcare Providers: A Balanced Scorecard Perspective. *Procedia Economics and Finance, 28*, 202–212. https://doi.org/10.1016/S2212-5671(15)01101-6.

Smits, S. J., Bowden, D., Falconer, J. A., & Strasser, D. C. (2014). Improving Medical Leadership and Teamwork: An Iterative Process. *Leadership in Health Services (1751–1879), 27*(4), 299–315. https://doi.org/10.1108/LHS-02-2014-0010.

Stacey, R. D. (2011). *Strategic Management and Organisational Dynamics: The Challenge of Complexity to Ways of Thinking About Organisations*. Harlow: Financial Times Prentice Hall.

Taplin, S. H., Foster, M. K., & Shortell, S. M. (2013). Organizational Leadership for Building Effective Health Care Teams. *Annals of Family Medicine, 11*(3), 279–281. https://doi.org/10.1370/afm.1506.

Thorpe, R., Gold, J., & Lawler, J. (2011). Locating Distributed Leadership. *International Journal of Management Reviews, 13*, 239–250. https://doi.org/10.1111/j.1468-2370.2011.00303x.

Top, M., Akdere, M., & Tarcan, M. (2015). Examining Transformational Leadership, Job Satisfaction, Organizational Commitment and Organizational Trust in Turkish Hospitals: Public Servants Versus Private Sector Employees. *International Journal of Human Resource Management, 26*(9), 1259–1282. https://doi.org/10.1080/09585192.2014.939987.

Tran, V., & Voyer, B. (2015). Fostering Innovation: An Organisational Perspective. *British Journal of Healthcare Management, 21*(3), 141.

Tsai, Y. (2011). Relationship Between Organizational Culture, Leadership Behavior and Job Satisfaction. *BMC Health Services Research, 11*, 98.

Tsai, T. C., Jha, A. K., Gawande, A. A., Huckman, R. S., Bloom, N., & Sadun, R. (2015). Hospital Board and Management Practices Are Strongly Related to Hospital Performance on Clinical Quality Metrics. *Health Affairs, 34*(8), 1304–1311.

Tuan, L. T. (2012). Clinical Governance: A Lever for Change in Nhan Dan Gia Dinh Hospital in Vietnam. *Clinical Governance: An International Journal, 17*(3), 223–247. https://doi.org/10.1108/14777271211251345.

Uhl-Bien, M., & Arena, M. (2017). Complexity Leadership: Enabling People and Organizations for Adaptability. *Organizational Dynamics, 46*, 9–20.

Valentijn, P. P., Ruwaard, D., Vrijhoef, H. M., de Bont, A., Arends, R. Y., & Bruijnzeels, M. A. (2015). Collaboration Processes and Perceived Effectiveness of Integrated Care Projects in Primary Care: A Longitudinal Mixed-Methods Study. *BMC Health Services Research, 15*(1), 1–12. https://doi.org/10.1186/s12913-015-1125-4.

Valsecchi, R., Wise, S., Mueller, F., & Smith, C. (2012). The Practice of Teamwork in Health Industry Call Centres. *Employee Relations, 34*(3), 288–305.

Vinot, D. (2014). Transforming Hospital Management à la Francaise: The New Role of Clinical Managers in French Public Hospitals. *International Journal of Public Sector Management, 27*(5), 406–416. https://doi.org/10.1108/IJPSM-06-2012-0067.

Walton, A. L., & Mullinix, C. (2016). Increasing the Number of Oncology Nurses Serving on Boards. *Clinical Journal of Oncology Nursing, 20*(4), 440–442. https://doi.org/10.1188/16.CJON.440-442.

Waring, J., & Bishop, S. (2013). McDonaldization or Commercial Re-stratification: Corporatization and the Multimodal Organisation of English Doctors. *Social Science & Medicine, 82*, 147–155. https://doi.org/10.1016/j.socscimed.2012.12.023.

Williams, J. (2016). Effective Team Working to Improve Diabetes Care in Older People. *Journal of Diabetes Nursing, 20*, 137–141.

Wilson Pecci, A. (2014). No Nurses on Your Hospital Board? Why Not? *Healthcare Leadership Review, 33*(11), 8–9.

Yang, J., Liu, Y., Chen, Y., & Pan, X. (2014). Original Article: The Effect of Structural Empowerment and Organizational Commitment on Chinese Nurses' Job Satisfaction. *Applied Nursing Research, 27*, 186–191. https://doi.org/10.1016/j.apnr.2013.12.001.

9

Linking Leadership and Succession Planning

Succession Planning in the Health Sector Provides Continuity

A leadership model for health comprising of leadership capability established through personal insight, the creation of a leadership identity, professional credibility, and an understanding of organisational dynamics provides a framework against which an organisation can identify the leadership attributes which are best fit to its own specific circumstances and against which individuals can assess their own ability to lead in those circumstances. The desired outcome of this organisational and self-evaluation will be people in leadership roles who can craft and implement strategy using their strengths to navigate through the complexity of their environment. However, leadership is not a finite proposition. The well-governed health organisation will include its ongoing leadership requirements as part of its strategic review process and to keep 'CEO succession as a standing board agenda item because it ensures a multilayered, multi-generational process' (Walker et al. 2018: 24). The extent of this 'future fit' leadership assessment will, at different ends of the strategy spectrum, be based on ensuring either continuity (of strategy, policy, stewardship,

P. Turner, *Leadership in Healthcare*, Organizational Behaviour in Health Care,
https://doi.org/10.1007/978-3-030-04387-2_9

and culture) or transformation (to new care or business models) in response to changing circumstances. The identification of Senior Leaders who are able to deliver against these scenarios is referred to as succession planning. Its advantages are many including information and insight based on procedural rationality which in turn can lead to a greater quantity and quality of succession candidates (Schepker et al. 2018); the consequences of not having a succession plan equally so, including paying executive search firms to find suitable executive replacements or paying external professionals to cover executive activity; and the less visible costs of employee uncertainty, are delayed strategic decision-making and loss of talent. Succession planning and management should therefore support strategic planning, strategic thinking, and operational efficiency (Rothwell 2010; Berns and Klarner 2017: 84).

Succession planning can be located inside a broader group of resourcing and development processes which includes leadership and management resourcing, strategic and operational workforce planning, competence analysis, and human resource development. Figure 9.1 shows the relationship between these processes. The objective of succession planning is the identification of key or business-critical positions and the development of talented people who are able to fill them. It is a process that is recognised by international organisations such as the United Nations or World Health Organization, where systematic succession planning over a five-year horizon is considered of critical importance to human resources for health, identifying key needs for intellectual talent and leadership and preparing people for present and future work responsibilities (Sukayri 2016). In addition, national organisations such as the NHS (2015) and, relevant to this section, groups of or individual health organisations have also recognised its importance. Succession planning gives the opportunity to reduce organisational turbulence associated with leadership change, to develop successors over time; it provides increased motivation for those involved as well as potential for increased productivity and retention; and it helps to increase workforce engagement as a whole if 'a transparent and inclusive culture is developed to demonstrate that succession is open to all' (NHS 2015).

In the first of the above examples, succession planning ensures continuity by filling identified, critical, leadership or management roles with

Fig. 9.1 The relationship between workforce planning and succession planning and management

people who are committed to delivering a strategy that has been agreed by the board, nurturing a culture that is already in place, and adopting stewardship and policy that is consistent with both. In the second, succession planning can be used to deliver the opposite, by bringing in or developing people to leadership or management roles who are committed to transformation and change, to question what has gone before, and to deliver a new culture, 'appointing a new CEO, could be used as a mechanism to adapt to environmental contingencies' (Berns and Klarner 2017: 87). In either case succession planning is a process to deliver competent leaders to meet organisational needs critical to role fulfilment (Carriere et al. 2009; Dilworth et al. 2011: 68), particularly in the most senior positions. The choices made to the positions of successor and their source have important implications for long-term performance (Schepker et al. 2017: 701).

This interpretation of succession planning as it relates to Senior Leadership or Executive positions is one that has become established over time. However, in addition to identifying and developing leaders or Executives, succession planning is increasingly seen as a way of ensuring a supply of talent into other health sector roles. In this case, succession planning becomes succession management, closely resembling workforce planning and embracing a broader range of positions and people. Overall, it might be assumed that succession planning has the objectives of ensuring that people are identified who can fill senior executive positions in specific units within a region, in the short term for risk management and in the medium to long term to ensure strategic continuity, that the organisation has identified Executives and Managers who are able to fulfil succession roles, and that there are processes in place for the development of talented people to fill them (NHS 2015). Its scope, remit, and projected outcomes vary, depending on the context within which it takes place.

Succession Planning in the Health Sector Satisfies Multiple Objectives at Multiple Levels

The profile of succession planning has been raised across several geographies because of, inter alia, rising CEO turnover, accelerating retirements, a shortage of management-ready talent, and the implications of transformation, change, and integration (Trepanier and Crenshaw 2013; Silver et al. 2016; Smith 2018). Succession planning is an important aspect of human resource development to deal with these issues (Sharma and Goyal 2010; Purohit and Verma 2013) and is a key responsibility for health sector Boards of Directors (Di and Santos-António 2008). Examples from the USA, the UK, China, and India portray succession planning across a broad range of scenarios from Senior Leadership and managerial roles to those relating to technical or specialist ones. It provides the basis for establishing the optimum mix of internal and external recruitment and the associated levels of leadership or management development.

In its most common form, succession planning is used for internal continuity of leadership (Tae Hyun 2012: 15; Scholes and Trapani 2017: 193). The need to supply capable people in this group means that succession planning is essential to sustaining the organisation's strategy such that many embed it into both their operational and strategic plans (Martin and Holskey 2013: 36; Ellinger et al. 2014: 369; Waxman and Delucas 2014; Scholes and Trapani 2017). Firstly, external stakeholders will want to ensure that they achieve the maximum return on their investment by the delivery of strategy from leaders of a like mind to those who agreed to the strategy; secondly, those at Board level will want to ensure that strategy is delivered in a seamless way by people who understand external (social, political and market forces) and internal dynamics (organisational structures and culture) and have the credibility to negotiate its implementation; thirdly, senior executives will require an understanding that their efforts remain valid by continuity in the strategy to which they have signed up; fourthly, employees will want confidence in the organisation's leadership by having in place people who have knowledge of the organisation and professional credibility to work within it; and most importantly, service users will want to feel confidence in the services they are receiving by having trust and faith in a well-managed entity based on continuous improvement. Succession planning for continuity then responds to the observation that 'it's absolutely vital that healthcare organizations think about who will manage a facility not just in the day-to-day but over the long term as well' (HLSC 2017: 4). It is at the heart of leadership development and an essential business strategy because it enhances the ability to achieve orderly transitions and maintain productivity levels (Tae Hyun 2012: 14). There are benefits to be had from ensuring that those who carry through the strategy have the same insight, understanding, and commitment as those who initiated it. However, an alternative perspective views succession planning as a facilitator of change in strategic or operational direction. To achieve either, it is 'a strategic process involving identification, development and evaluation of intellectual capital, ensuring leadership continuity within an organisation' (Titzer et al. 2013: 972), or 'a deliberate and proactive process of identifying key, generally senior-level positions' which if became vacant would be detrimental to the organisation's performance (Kurec 2012: 23).

A third perspective on succession planning has also emerged in more recent times. So, whilst it is primarily regarded as a way of providing a sufficient quantity of leaders, with the right knowledge, skills, attitudes, behaviours, identity, professional credibility, and organisational understanding (Carriere et al. 2009; Baron et al. 2010; Griffith 2012: 901; Titzer et al. 2013; Turner 2017), either for continuity or transformation, other factors have begun to have an influence. In this respect, succession planning can be a process to deal with areas of talent scarcity amongst health professionals at all levels. For example, in nursing, global shortages have made the adoption of succession planning a priority ('the urgency for nurse succession planning has been described as a universal need' (Sherman et al. 2014: 186)), with a proactive and deliberate strategy necessary to ensure a sufficient number of replacements for leavers in all roles and an adequate leadership pipeline—of which succession planning is a key component (Griffith 2012; Titzer et al. 2013; Acree-Hamann 2016: 161). The need is so strong in some areas that it is recommended that succession planning and succession management should be added to the strategic planning of all healthcare facilities and given a high priority designation. Where succession planning is referred to as a response to talent shortages in professional areas, it is closely aligned to the approach adopted under strategic or operational workforce planning. Nevertheless, the terminology of succession planning and management now has a wide sweep.

As a final consideration, succession planning is also associated with financial and operational criteria. Performance, sustainability—in, for example, acute care hospitals—(Trepanier and Crenshaw 2013), and strategic organisational governance are three such areas. It is argued that having successors ready to fill critical posts when required helps improve operational conditions and the bottom line giving a competitive edge and may determine which organisations thrive. Positive outcomes include an enhancement of skills in a clinical setting and a contribution to uninterrupted service delivery (Tae Hyun 2012: 20; Kittscha 2017). Overall, succession planning might be referred to as a process with which to support the organisation as it tries to 'manage the current workforce changes effectively as well as forecast and plan according to future human capital needs, such as when the organisation grows, and build a talent agile culture to lead the way' (Martin 2015).

The strategic needs of the organisation, whether these be continuity or transformation, will inform the loci or priorities to which the main activity of succession planning is targeted. In most cases, 'succession planning helps organisations refresh their leaders to continue meeting the challenges of a dynamic operating environment by identifying how positions will be filled as both planned and unplanned departures occur. Succession planning is considered a part of strategic planning … succession planning means building bench strength and developing a pipeline of strong and capable leaders including at executive level and board directors' (Varhegyi and Jepsen 2017: 111). But there are other variations on the theme. In this respect, succession planning takes place at multiple levels and in multiple forms focusing on different loci depending on the circumstances facing the organisation. It is possible to identify four types of succession planning or management in the health sector. The first two types are concerned with succession planning for Board, Senior Leadership, Executive, and Management roles. This is the more traditional definition of succession planning, identifying critical roles, individuals with potential to fill these roles, and development plans to ensure that they have the requisite abilities once appointed. There are however two other types of succession planning which have been prompted by talent shortages in professional, clinical, or medical roles on the one hand and administrative or technical ones on the other. In these cases, succession planning is an ongoing and flexible process and might be referred to as succession management.

A characteristic of both types is the

> growing focus on identifying and developing groups of jobs to enable potential successors to be identified for a variety of roles. So, jobs might be clustered by role, function and/or level so that the generic skills required for particular roles can be developed. The aim is to develop pools of tal-

> ented people, each of whom is adaptable and capable of filling a number of roles. Because succession planning is concerned with developing longer-term successors as well as short-term replacements, each pool will be considerably larger than the range of posts it covers. (CIPD 2017)

From its traditional focus of concentrating on Board or most Senior Leaders in the organisation, succession planning has been used to support both continuity and transformation at multiple levels. And in recent times its scope has extended to provide a methodology for anticipating and dealing with talent shortages in key areas. In addition, the succession process as an annual event has changed to become a more dynamic, multiphase activity. The key attributes of each are discussed in more detail below.

Succession Planning for Board, Senior, Executive, and Management Roles

Executive Leadership changes are critical turning points for many organisations, and recognition of this has led to a high level of interest from both practitioners and management scholars into the 'predictors, consequences and contingencies' (Berns and Klarner 2017: 83) of succession into leadership roles. The classical definition of succession planning concerns the short- and long-term replacement of Board members, Chief Executive Officers, or Presidents/Vice Presidents. On the assumption that transitions in leadership positions can undermine sustainable positive changes, it is argued that few decisions are more important for a healthcare organisation than the choice of who will lead it today and for the future and the development activities that are planned for identified successors (Capuano 2013: 136; Patidar et al. 2016). The criticality of an effective approach is captured by the observation 'when senior executives leave an organisation through retirement, choice or more controversial reasons, how well that organisation manages the transition will reverberate for years to come' (Sammer 2015: 40), such that 'succession planning for the CEO and other top officers in a hospital or health system is a mission-critical board responsibility' (Walker et al. 2018: 23). Identifying the roles to which these observations apply and the people able to fill these roles in the present day or into the future may be seen as being of strategic as well as operational importance.

The second aspect of succession planning is related to those in Executive or Management roles below the hierarchical level of Board or CEO. Wholesale shortages of Executives which occurred in many commercial sectors during a period referred to as 'the Talent Wars' were also a feature of health (Turner 2017). Indeed, in the USA, the National Centre for Healthcare Leadership, whilst noting that the quality of leadership had a clear and direct relationship to the quality of care provided by healthcare organisations, also recognised that there were a number of barriers challenging the recruitment, development, and retention of healthcare leaders. The organisation advocated well-developed succession plans as one of the features of high-achieving organisations. As a result, the concept of succession planning was extended to include a broader range of Executives than those only at Board level. In this interpretation, succession planning was a process of identifying staff members who have the potential and motivation to move up into leadership positions at Executive or Senior Management Team level and then providing a series of developmental tools to ensure their preparation for the roles including coaching, mentoring, training, and hands-on experience (Santamour 2016: 6). This approach was justified, because most leaders were promoted from within the organisation (Westphal 2009). Leadership positions at multiple levels were therefore included within the succession planning process, and those considered were assessed against the leadership competences for that specific organisation, although universal scoping methodologies, such as Collins' five levels or Lombardo and Eichinger's competencies framework (Capuano 2013: 137), were often used.

In both of these examples, succession planning is largely a formalised process of identification, assessment, and development of people who are able to move into leadership positions and is a crucial factor in ensuring the 'supply' of those with leadership capability, professional credibility, and an understanding of organisational dynamics (both for continuity and change). In its broadest form, 'the concept is multileveled, covering executive, middle management, and clinical leadership. It is also contextual in that it can encompass nursing administration, research, or education' (McCallin et al. 2009: 41). For the most senior positions, identifying desired leadership competences was considered to be the foundation of succession from which to inform subsequent elements of talent management such as leadership development (Titzer et al. 2013); in other contexts the ability to function as a leader, to influence and direct, is important through to the point of care. However, 'Executive succession planning is not simply about replacing the Chief Executive. Important front-end work involves defining desired executive qualifications while aligning succession with strategic objectives, often giving rise to significant Executive and Board introspection around critical environmental trends and resulting organizational imperatives, resource requirements, and adaptive goals. Ongoing internal management development increasingly surrounds the process, contributing to employee retention, leadership capacity and greater continuity for successful executive transition' (McKee and Froelich 2016: 588).

Executive-level succession planning 'incorporates those actions, activities and interventions intended to ensure that capable, motivated and talented individuals are ready to assume the leadership roles for which they have been selected' (Griffith 2012: 901–902). Research has shown the positive effects of succession planning in health though these were stronger in competitive health markets than in monopolistic markets (Patidar et al. 2016). A working definition of succession planning in these two areas might therefore be:

> *Succession planning for senior and executive leadership in the health sector is a formalised and systematic process for identifying individuals with leadership capability who are able to fill identified senior roles in the short term; and individuals with leadership potential to fill identified senior roles in the medium to long term. It is a process that is aligned to the strategy of the organisation and includes the identification and assessment of ability and potential; the development of that ability and potential and the deployment of individuals to identified key roles to fulfil that potential.*

This covers those in the most senior roles in the organisation. However, succession planning is a term that has broadened in its scope in recent times, and two further derivatives are discussed in more detail below.

Succession Management to Maximise Talent Potential and Minimise Key Talent Shortages in Professional, Clinical, Medical, Business, Administrative, and Technical Roles

There is a growing recognition of the need for healthcare organisations to develop clinical leadership to achieve their strategic objectives and increase workforce continuity and capacity (Currie and Grundy 2011). Hence, more recently, the concept of succession planning has become that of succession management bearing a close resemblance to strategic workforce planning. For example, it was noted that 'as experienced nurses continue to leave the workforce and patient acuity levels rise, acute care hospitals are challenged to meet the demand for competent nursing care' (Jones 2017: 64). Key professional roles, such as nurse managers, have seen talent shortages brought about by a number of factors, not least of which is demographic change as 'baby boomers' retire from the workforce (Kosterlitz and Lewis 2017: 397), although there is still work to do at this level since a proactive succession management approach is not always in place (a recent study found that around a third of high performers involving acting or potential ward managers were involved in succession activity (Kellner et al. 2016: 518)). Developing individuals with the right knowledge, skills, experience, and ability in clinical practice is critical for both workforce capacity and hence continuity. But since expertise for clinical roles as advanced nursing practice takes considerable time to develop, succession planning for such key roles is crucial (Currie and Grundy 2011: 934). Furthermore, the necessity to achieve operational or financial excellence in health sector organisations has created a demand for those who are effective in such areas. There are talent shortages as a result and so the emphasis on succession management into these roles. Once again, the process is closely aligned to the broader subject of workforce planning. In this respect the assumption is based on identifying 'which team members may leave in the next year and where there may be opportunities and gaps within the team. Try to anticipate who may retire, transfer, leave for personal or family issues, or choose to pursue other opportunities outside' (Maxwell 2004: 285). In these demographic and social shifts, succession planning has been identified as 'an essential task' that is more important than ever. However, in addition to being an important part of the day-to-day management process, this has prompted the need for a more systematic role to workforce planning under the title of succession planning, the main goal of which is to provide continuity in the provision of health services (Stichler 2008; Rafferty 2013). In this respect, it can extend to many professional roles where 'succession planning is more than putting a team member on a management course. It is about having a long-term vision of the team and the potential it has to grow and develop' (Fowler 2016: 674).

So, as well as satisfying the need to recognise people who will be able to fulfil leadership roles, succession management is increasingly used as a process for addressing talent shortages in other situations (Griffith 2012; Titzer et al. 2013; Sherman et al. 2014: 193). In this respect there is an overlap between succession planning and talent management and the two are often used interchangeably or in partnership. 'Talent management and succession planning constitute a systematic process for preparing people to meet an organisation's needs for leadership and talent over time. Failure to prioritise talent management and succession management often leads to a steady attrition of high potential individuals or to the retention of people with outdated skills' (Satiani et al. 2014: 544).

A working definition of succession management as it applies to a wide range of professional roles might be as follows:

> *Succession management in the health sector is a dynamic, transparent and inclusive process of ensuring the right people with the right skills in the right place at the right time to fulfil management or key professional roles. It is closely aligned to the Strategic Workforce Plan and includes the identification of areas of key talent opportunity; assessment of individuals who have the potential to take advantage of that opportunity; of processes to facilitate the movement of individuals into key identified roles and the creation of development programmes to ensure inclusivity and diversity in the succession process.*

Whether succession is achieved through effective planning or fluid and flexible management will require a well thought through process if it is to be successful. It is important to have planned and systematic processes in place which will be developed to ensure that the methodology of succession fits the culture of the organisation. The way in which this might be achieved is discussed below.

The Processes of Succession Planning and Management

There are a variety of interpretations about the way succession planning and management can be undertaken. Rothwell (2010), for example, has highlighted the top-down approach, the market-driven approach, the career planning approach, the futuring approach, and the rifle approach. In whatever definition is adopted, however, an effective process will underpin the ability to achieve the objectives set. In its most straightforward form, succession planning is about identifying leadership and 'business-critical positions' and developing identified people with the skills or potential to assume these positions. It is concerned with planning current and future leadership needs and ensuring development opportunities are put in place for those with the potential to fill them, noting that potential successors are not only technically skilled and competent but also have leadership qualities and behaviours aligned to the organisation's vision and values (NHS 2017). The extent and definitions of leadership or critical posts of course vary from organisation to organisation in the ways outlined above. Developing a succession planning process that fits the requirements of the organisation is the challenge.

A criticism of succession planning is that it has been traditionally seen as an event, a one-off annual analysis of the organisation's strategic workforce plan. Or, in some organisations, succession planning is a form of replacement planning, in which names of candidates to high-level roles are matched to individuals who are ready to take on the role immediately or have potential to do so in a relatively short period. In this process succession planning was a snapshot of the organisation, its leaders, and potential leaders. But the occurrence of VUCA factors outlined in Chap. 2 means that at a time of fast-moving change, the snapshot quickly fades or becomes out of date. The volatility of the health sector environment creates multiple and sometimes conflicting objectives, whilst the increasing complexity requires people to lead who have the capability to evaluate multiple scenarios and confidence to cope with each. It is because of this that, increasingly, succession planning is becoming more than the process of 'finding another body to hire into the practice when someone waves the "white flag" of retirement' (Falci 2016: 10) or 'a document to dust off when someone retires' (HLSC 2017: 5). There is recognition of the value of succession planning as an ongoing process, one that is proactive to change. A more holistic approach not only involves integration between the organisation's strategic direction and the supply of people to deliver this but also the satisfaction of operational demands through a more systematic, planned approach. This depends on having in place a process that is suited to the needs of the organisation, has the 'buy in' of the Board and Senior Leaders, is delivered in a way that is transparent and inclusive, and has at its heart a respect for diversity in those identified to succession positions. It includes assessment of organisational need at strategic level, the identification of individuals who are able to or have the potential to fulfil that need, the development of individuals to build on leadership strengths, and the creation of opportunities for individuals to gain experience in areas to which they have little exposure in preparation for future leadership roles. A process for succession planning and management is included at Fig. 9.2.

There are six possible component parts to the process and these are discussed in more detail below.

- **The creation of a strategic workforce plan aligned to the strategic plan to provide insights into key succession challenges over an agreed period—one, three, or five years, identifying short- and long-term succession priorities**

Information on the status of the health workforce is a critical issue at a macro or national level and at a professional level from nursing to radiography and in a health network (McCallin et al. 2009; Capuano 2013; Waters et al. 2013; Knapp et al. 2017). At organisational level, the Board will use this information to undertake an evaluation of how the direction of the organisation from strategic long-range goals, as well as operating

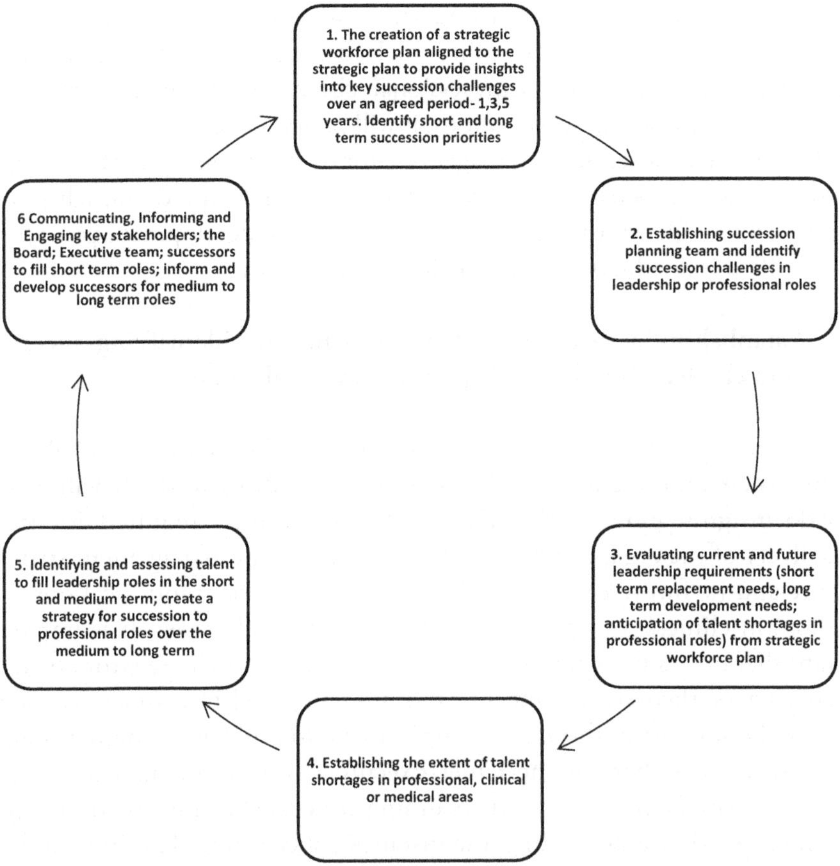

Fig. 9.2 A process of succession planning in the health sector (Sources: Ellinger et al. 2014; Evans 2016; Nissan and Eder 2017)

and financial opportunities and challenges, will impact on the workforce as a whole. This will lead to the creation of a strategic workforce plan giving insight into the likely or possible leadership requirements over a period of one to three or one to five years depending on the timescale of the strategic planning cycle. The strategic workforce plan will be closely aligned to the organisation's strategic business or operational plan (Wolf 2015: 1), with the objective of the right people, in the right place, at the right time with the right level of skills. This is seen as a 'core process of human resource management' (Baron et al. 2010: 4).

The insights provided by the strategic workforce plan will form the basis of both succession planning for leadership or executive roles and succession management for professional, clinical, medical, and technical roles. In health sector organisations, it will be 'patient centred and involve an assessment of service needs against supply' (Baron et al. 2010: 37). In some cases, leadership succession planning is prompted, initially, by replacement identification. In others it will lead to development plans for identified individuals over the medium to long term.

- **Establishing a succession planning team and identifying succession challenges in leadership or professional roles**

After the first stage outlined above, there will be some clarity about how the workforce is aligned to current and future needs. It will provide insights about leadership and Executive roles required for the delivery of the organisation's objectives, the current management structure and its future direction, and finally the numbers and locations of those in clinical, medical, or professional roles. However, it is important that once succession planning and management change from being abstract or theoretical concepts and are converted into practice, they have the support of those in Senior Leadership positions, whether these are Board members or the Chief Executive and her or his team. The second part of the succession planning process therefore is to engage senior decision-makers. In some instances, succession planning will be informal or quasi-formal in which 'programs may be documented and use generally accepted forms or templates in which managers identify required competencies, candidate readiness, and development plans' (Nissan and Eder 2017: 79). However, for many, a formal process of succession planning will be more in line with the organisation culture and values. It will consist of a succession planning committee with a firm understanding of the mission and vision of the organisation (Kurec 2012), including Board members and the CEO, or have a more operational flavour where the succession 'group' consisted of the CEO, Chief Operating Officer, Chief Medical Officer, and the Senior VP of HR (Capuano 2013: 137). The process of succession planning 'starts with the creation of a team of leaders who can review the organizational chart and workforce in the context of the strategic plan' and an objective approach to identifying candidates for leadership roles (Ellinger et al. 2014: 371; Evans 2016).

- **Evaluating current and future leadership requirements (short-term replacement needs, long-term development needs, anticipation of talent shortages in professional roles) from the strategic workforce plan**

The strategic workforce plan facilitates analysis and debate about the existing position from both a quantitative and qualitative perspective and 'provides the base case for succession planning' (NHS 2015: 8). The outputs of the analysis will be the number of leadership and managerial roles, the number of people in these roles, and the extent of identified successors to them. And given the broader definition of succession in the contemporary organisation, the analysis will extend to professional, specialist, or technical roles. The analysis will cover the number of roles and people and an analysis of the knowledge and skills required and available in these roles. The analysis will determine the type of leaders in place, the skills that are present, and the alignment of quantity and quality to competitive or organisational strength. In this case the succession plan will focus on either developing leaders, managers, or clinical professionals with these skills or bringing in new people from outside of the organisation who have such experiences elsewhere (NHS 2015). Succession planning provides the opportunity to establish what is core to any key role and what skills and competencies are required to fulfil it (Scholes and Trapani 2017: 193). Formal succession planning will be a broadly communicated process that defines positions for succession planning and assesses the potential talent pool from which development activity can take place (Nissan and Eder 2017). The outputs of the strategic workforce plan and the deliberations of the succession team will inform this decision and provide information about short- and long-term leadership 'replacement' needs. This is a critical process since part of getting the right talent is evaluating the current leadership environment (OR Manager 2015).

- **Establishing the extent of talent shortages in professional, clinical, or medical areas**

Global talent shortages in the health sector will have an impact on attracting and retaining talented people to succession roles. The shortages are not attributable to a single cause nor confined to a single country or region. But they will require sophisticated national and organisational talent strategies to deal with complex scenarios (Turner 2017). In some geographies, healthcare is amongst the fastest-growing sectors of the economy with demand for different and new types of health worker and associated leadership leading to significant talent shortages. In this case active intervention was advocated in both succession and associated talent management activities. In the USA, UK talent availability is a critical success factor for the National Health Service, whilst in Asia shortages of talent referred to as the 'talent crunch' means that the recruitment of many professional sectors (Simon et al. 2013; Satiani et al. 2014; Lorenzetti 2016), as well as those in leadership and possible succession roles, is a priority for many organisations. In India, where healthcare is a major driver in the economy and growth through a mixed approach of public investment, privatisation, and the development of new business approaches to healthcare delivery, and it was noted that the scarcity of skilled health professionals was both severe and ubiquitous (Srinivasan and Chandwani 2014). The implications for succession planning and management are significant. An understanding of the extent of talent shortages as they apply to succession roles in the particular organisation is therefore an important part of the succession process.

- **Identifying and assessing talented individuals to fill leadership roles in the short and medium term and creating a strategy for succession to professional roles over the medium to long term**

Once key roles have been established, it is important to identify those people in the organisation who are able to fill them. This will include those with leadership potential as part of the definition of succession planning, but also those with potential in professional areas or those where talent shortages occur. Both approaches emphasise the importance of strategic workforce planning, the identification of critical roles, and people with potential to supply these roles from internal or external labour markets. In the former, a key part of the process is assessing a 'pool' of candidates who are able to move into leadership roles (Dilworth et al. 2011: 68). This will take place against the context of the attributes associated with leadership capability, professional credibility, and understanding of the organisational dynamics outlined in the model for leadership in health, that is, which individuals already demonstrate these attributes and are ready to move into succession positions or those with the potential, with development, to move into such positions at a future date (say one to three years). In so doing, it is recommended to chart the depth and breadth of the talent pool and provide critical experience, know-how, and new competencies to assume key roles. 'Key individuals' capabilities should be assessed to ensure which individuals among the organisation's top talent are the best fit for critical roles.' This assessment should be conducted against valid benchmarks for both current positions and for new roles likely to exist in the future. The basis of assessment will be a combination of internal leadership competences identified and externally assessed competences for such roles. Having identified individuals who fulfil these criteria, they can then be matched to different opportunities leading to personal development personal strategies and plans (Swan and Moye 2009; Walker et al. 2018: 25). This process is the point at which supply and demand converge and:

> It is clear that a strategic match between support for the development of individuals and identified service need will be required in the future. It is the prediction of organizational need and the targeting of appropriate individuals to meet that need which is the hallmark of effective succession planning. (Currie and Grundy 2011: 939)

The key to effective succession planning is to put in place a programme that is aligned to the organisation's strategy (OR Manager 2015); and so an intrinsic part of succession planning is development to assist identified individuals to achieve their potential. 'Although management positions have been traditional places to develop aspiring leaders, flatter organisational hierarchies and the consolidation of managerial roles mean that high-potential … leaders may struggle to access situations in which they can acquire organizational knowledge' (McCallin et al. 2009).

- **Communicating, informing, and engaging key stakeholders, the Board, Executive team, and successors to fill short-term roles and informing and developing successors for medium- to long-term roles**

An important factor in succession planning and management is the communication of intent (why is the organisation undertaking the process), desired outcomes (what will be the benefits of developing a succession programme to the organisation), and the impact on individuals. The achievement of these will be facilitated by effective communications at Board level in order to anchor key decisions (such as elimination of a candidate, making an offer to a candidate) with the full board (Wolf 2015: 2). But it is also important that there is 'transparency around what is to be expected of the person who undergoes a succession programme and what he or she can expect from the people who facilitate them is essential' and that 'communicating upward and laterally concerning the management of the organization' is part of the succession planning process (Fibuch and Van Way 2012: 45; Scholes and Trapani 2017: 193). The role of the line manager is a critical success factor in ensuring adequate support is provided (Currie and Grundy 2011: 940).

These steps are by no means definitive, and as both academic research and practitioner experience in health have shown, the process adopted will very much depend on the context within which succession planning takes place.

The Post-Succession Phase: Succession Management Is Business Management

Whilst traditionally much of the empirical research into succession planning has reflected 'an event-based perspective,' the practical evidence on succession is more reflected as a continuous process, and this would seem to be an appropriate position for health sector organisations to take. At the highest level, succession planning is a key strategic process by which organisational responsibility is passed from the current to future leadership (Fibuch and Van Way 2012; Berns and Klarner 2017: 83). However, as discussed above, the contemporary definition of succession planning includes a broader range of leadership and management positions than covered previously, and the concept has been extended to roles in which talent is scarce on a worldwide basis. The interpretations of succession therefore mean that it has both strategic and operational resonance. But in any case, it is important that succession planning and succession management are not regarded as one-off isolated events. There is evidence that once succession decisions have been made, there are benefits from an ongoing review. At CEO level, for example, it is argued that 'the board needs to continuously evaluate the new CEO on the basis of her post-succession strategic decision making and resultant performance, to control and optimize the CEO succession process' (Berns and Klarner 2017: 93). In addition, the Board will have accumulated succession experience which allows them to reflect on and improve future succession processes. This is an indicator to revisit succession plans periodically. At one level, there is the case to integrate succession plan reviews into the Board's CEO evaluation (Gamble and Ingersoll 2017: 21) and, at another, to ensure that succession management becomes business management.

The need for post-succession management as an ongoing process applies to roles other than those at Senior Leadership level. On the one hand, all executive and management roles would benefit from a dynamic process (rather than a static one-off activity), whilst on the other, the fluid and global nature of talent mobility means that specialist and professional roles would also come within the remit of succession as a management process rather than a strategic 'event.' In this respect there is support for the concept of succession management as business management.

Case Study: Leadership Development and Succession Planning in North American Healthcare Organisations

Leadership Succession Planning Is an Essential Part of Organisational Governance

Succession planning in North American healthcare organisations is seen as a strategic imperative because it contributes to continuity of leadership and strategy, gives reassurance to external stakeholders that the organisation is well governed and managed, and creates confidence in service users that outcomes will remain positive and belief from the professional workforce that leadership is in place to ensure that their best interests are dealt with. It is a bastion against external shortages of health sector talent, provides cultural continuity, and is a comfort to those looking for solidity in the way the organisation is led (Titzer and Shirey 2013; Turner 2017). There is evidence that succession management practices are associated with positive health organisation performance metrics, including patient satisfaction (Groves 2017). It has been applied to those in general management positions, clinical roles, and health professional roles, and organisations such as the Ronald Reagan UCLA Medical Center Northwestern Memorial, Cleveland Clinic, and New York City Hospital systems have adopted succession planning for key roles (Turner 2017). For it to be successful, the common attributes include a commitment and buy in to the concept on the part of the organisation and the allocation of resource to its implementation. There are lessons to be learned from research and practice evidence in this area.

Firstly, it is deemed important to have an approach which integrates strategic planning, current and future leadership analysis, and the alignment of succession planning with the leadership needs identified in the organisational strategy. This will highlight the number and location of roles for which succession is seen as a critical activity.

This will be supported by, secondly, a qualitative perspective which outlines the nature of future leadership roles, giving the required competence, competency, knowledge, skills, attitudes, and behaviours for these roles.

And finally, the analysis of demand for successors and the potential supply of people suitable roles will be complemented by the identification of people who can fill positions immediately or have the potential to do so in the future, based on a 'best fit' assessment process around performance and potential.

Succession planning therefore combines a variety of techniques for identifying mission-critical roles and those who have the potential to fill such roles, increasingly using new tools and techniques (including algorithms of performance) under the heading of 'the science of measurement' (Buzachero 2017). The homogeneity of succession planning in North America centres on recognition of its importance; the heterogeneity on the diversity of development practices to deliver it.

Leadership Development Blends Formal Education and Experiential Activities

Once acceptance has been gained, then succession planning can inform a range of human resource activities including recruitment, retention, mentoring, and administration and can also provide insights for future development of healthcare succession planning frameworks (Cadmus 2006; Carriere et al. 2009; Titzer and Shirey 2013). The outcome of the process will be insight into the roles which are critical for future performance and a pipeline of individuals who are either succession ready or for whom leadership development is necessary to enable individuals to take on succession roles. It is at this point where leadership development for successors becomes a priority. In most contemporary cases, there is no single development activity. Instead leadership development associated with succession is a mix or blend of varied but complementary activities, including formal leadership programmes and informal initiatives.

Leadership development will mostly begin with the assessment or evaluation of individuals through leadership review sessions. From these, a structured leadership development programme will be designed, the content of which will be aligned with leadership competences (Ramseur et al. 2018). There will be common elements to this programme (such as leadership competence and the development of a leadership identity) and elements geared to the unique needs of individuals in the leadership pipeline. The heterogeneity of leadership development in succession planning is reflected in a wide range of studies including in Pennsylvania where highly focused development plans prioritised experiential learning, coaching, and mentoring (Capuano 2013); in Virginia where leadership development included project-related assignments, mentoring, coaching, and job shadowing (Martin and Holskey 2013); in California where development included expanded responsibilities to give an opportunity to gain experience (Kirincic and Bass 2018); in Kentucky where the emphasis was on-the-job training, intensive coaching, mentoring, and education (Walker et al. 2018); and in Ontario where formal leadership development was combined with job rotation, special projects, and coaching (Dilworth et al. 2011). Throughout, it was recognised that those in the succession process accepted responsibility for promoting their own career development (Beyers 2006; Miodinski and Hines 2013).

Conclusion

A number of forces are creating uncertainty in the health sector, explained by one or all of those included in the acronym VUCA, which means volatility, uncertainty, complexity, and ambiguity. To deal with these, it is argued that new approaches to succession planning are required which take account of new delivery models and strategies. The traditional 'next up' approach to succession may not be sufficient to tap into the well of leadership talent. Instead 'bench strength development' (Buzachero 2017) covers a broad range of those with the potential to succeed in mission-critical leadership positions. Many organisations in the North American health sector have risen to this challenge and have put in place innovative, multidimensional leadership development programmes for those who have been identified as or aspire to leadership positions.

Conclusions and Implications for Practice

Succession planning in the health sector is used in one of two ways. Firstly, it is **a process for identifying individuals with leadership capability who are able to fill critical senior roles in both the short and longer term**. It is a process that is aligned to the strategy of the organisation. Amongst the activities associated with it are identification, assessment, development, and deployment. It has been used to address continuity in leadership on the one hand or by bringing in or developing people to leadership or management roles who can deliver transformation and change. The second aspect can be referred to as succession management. In this incarnation, succession processes are used to ensure a supply of talent into those roles where talent shortages are a feature.

Many organisations adopt a systematic process to succession planning or management which begins with the preparation of a strategic workforce plan, closely aligned to the business or strategic plan and used to highlight areas where succession will be needed over a defined period which can be from one to five years. This forms the demand part of the succession equation and will include not only those in the most senior roles but Executives and Managers at all levels and areas where talent shortages are likely to occur because worldwide demand for health workers exceeds the supply of those professionals. Succession planning and management are designed to ensure a supply of appropriately qualified people, with the right knowledge, skills, attitudes, and behaviours to fill critical roles. The ways in which this is achieved can be through internal assessment and development or a strategic recruitment plan.

The governance of the whole process can be facilitated by a succession team of Senior Leaders and HR professionals (Turner and Kalman 2014).

- **Succession planning is a contextual phenomenon** that is used to address a diverse series of challenges faced by health sector organisation.
- It will be most effective when it **demonstrates clarity about how it will support the delivery of goals and objectives.**
- **Succession planning has an organisation-wide focus** in the contemporary health sector organisation that covers succession planning for Senior Leaders and Executives on the one hand, but also addresses talent shortage issues in professional areas on the other.
- **It is more effective when there is defined ownership of the succession process** (a succession committee, senior executives, and line managers) and an understanding of the key roles for which succession is needed.
- A critical success factor will be **the support of the CEO, and a defined succession process converges with business or operational processes**—such as strategic or business planning.

In conclusion, succession planning and management are essential health sector practice that enable an organisation to 'future fit' its leadership and professional workforce against the requirements of its forward strategy.

References

Acree-Hamann, C. (2016). A Call to Action: Succession Planning Needed. *Newborn and Infant Nursing Reviews, 16*, 161–163. https://doi.org/10.1053/j.nainr.2016.07.001.

Baron, A., Clake, R., Pass, S., & Turner, P. (2010). *Workforce Planning*. London: CIPD Publications.

Berns, K. D., & Klarner, P. (2017). A Review of the CEO Succession Literature and a Future Research Program. *Academy of Management Perspectives, 31*(2), 83–108. https://doi.org/10.5465/Amp.2015.0183.

Beyers, M. (2006). Nurse Executives' Perspectives on Succession Planning. *Journal of Nursing Administration, 36*(6), 304–312.

Buzachero, V. (2017). High-Performance Succession Planning: Changing Times Require Fresh Thinking When Hospitals Choose New Leaders. *Trustee, 70*(8), 5–7.

Cadmus, E. (2006). Succession Planning: Multilevel Organizational Strategies for the New Workforce. *Journal of Nursing Administration, 36*(6), 298–303.

Capuano, T. A. (2013). Achieving Succession Planning and Implementation: One Healthcare Network's Story. *Healthcare Management Forum, 26*, 136–144. https://doi.org/10.1016/j.hcmf.2013.06.003.

Carriere, B. K., Muise, M., Cummings, G., & Newburn Cook, C. (2009). Healthcare Succession Planning: An Integrative Review. *Journal of Nursing Administration*. Retrieved from www.ncbi.nlm.nih.gov/pubmed/19955970.

CIPD. (2017). *Succession Planning*. Retrieved from https://www.cipd.co.uk/knowledge/strategy/resourcing/succession-planning-factsheet#7314.

Currie, K., & Grundy, M. (2011). Building Foundations for the Future: The NHS Scotland Advanced Practice Succession Planning Development Pathway. *Journal of Nursing Management, 19*(7), 933–942. https://doi.org/10.1111/j.1365-2834.2011.01299.x.

Di, Z., & Santos-António, N. (2008). The Frozen River Model and Chinese State-Owned Hospital Reform. *Chinese Economy, 41*(3), 90–101. https://doi.org/10.2753/CES1097-1475410306.

Dilworth, K., Lankshear, S., Cava, M., Aldred, J., Hawkes, N., Lefebre, N., et al. (2011). The Top 30 Rising Stars Program: An Inter-Organizational Approach to Leadership Succession Planning. *Healthcare Management Forum, 24*, 68–71. https://doi.org/10.1016/j.hcmf.2011.01.006.

Ellinger, L. K., Trapskin, P. J., Black, R., Kotis, D., & Alexander, E. (2014). Leadership and Effective Succession Planning in Health-System Pharmacy Departments. *Hospital Pharmacy, 49*(4), 369–375. ISSN:0018-5787.

Evans, J. L. T. (2016). Three First Steps for Effective Succession Planning. *American Nurse Today, 11*(9), 36–40.

Falci, C. (2016). Managing to Succeed. Radiology Succession Planning. *Radiology Today, 17*(7), 10–11.

Fibuch, E., & Van Way, C. W., III. (2012). Succession Planning in Health Care Organizations. *Physician Executive, 38*(5), 44–47.

Fowler, J. (2016). Succession Planning. *Dental Nursing, 12*(12), 674–675.

Gamble, D., & Ingersoll, C. (2017). Avoiding the Sacrificial Lamb: Steps to a Stronger Succession Plan: What Are the Barriers to Creating a Succession Plan? How Can You Overcome Them? *Nonprofit World, 35*(7), 20–21.

Griffith, M. B. (2012). Effective Succession Planning in Nursing: A Review of the Literature. *Journal of Nursing Management, 20*(7), 900–911. ISSN:0966-0429.

Groves, K. S. (2017). Examining the Impact of Succession Management Practices on Organizational Performance: A National Study of U.S. Hospitals. *Health Care Management Review*. https://doi.org/10.1097/HMR.0000000000000176.

HLSC. (2017). Succession Planning: A Long-Term Safety Essential for Facility Managers. *Healthcare Life Safety Compliance, 20*(11), 4–6.

Jones, S. (2017). Succession Planning: Creating a Case for Hiring New Graduates. *Nursing Economics, 35*(2), 64–87.

Kellner, A., Townsend, K., Wilkinson, A., Lawrence, S. A., & Greenfield, D. (2016). Learning to Manage: Development Experiences of Hospital Frontline Managers. *Human Resource Management Journal, 26*(4), 505–522. https://doi.org/10.1111/1748-8583.12119.

Kirincic, P., & Bass, K. (2018). CEO Succession: A Strategic Imperative: Hospitals Can Use a 3-Phase Process to Ace a Leadership Transition. *Trustee, 71*(4), 5–7.

Kittscha, J. (2017). Succession Planning in Stomal Therapy: A Six-Step Model. *Journal of Stomal Therapy Australia, 37*(1), 14–16.

Knapp, K., Wright, C., Clarke, H., McAnulla, S., & Nightingale, J. (2017). The Academic Radiography Workforce: Age Profile, Succession Planning and Academic Development. *Radiography, 23*(Suppl. 1), 48–52. https://doi.org/10.1016/j.radi.2017.05.012.

Kosterlitz, M., & Lewis, J. (2017). From Baby Boomer to Millennial: Succession Planning for the Future. *Nurse Leader, 15*, 396–398.

Kurec, A. S. (2012). Succession Planning: A Forgotten Strategy. *Clinical Leadership and Management Review, 26*(4), 22. ISSN:1527-3954.

Lorenzetti, L. (2016). The Health Care Hiring Boom. *Fortune, 173*(4), 192–193. ISSN:0015-8259.

Martin, A. (2015). Leadership: Talent Management: Preparing a 'Ready' Agile Workforce. *International Journal of Pediatrics and Adolescent Medicine, 2*(3–4), 112–116. ISSN:2352-6467.

Martin, J. A., & Holskey, M. P. (2013). Succession Planning for Magnet® Program Director. *American Nurse Today, 8*(9), 36–39.

Maxwell, M. (2004). Human Resource Solutions. Putting Success into Succession Planning. *Nursing Economic$, 22*(5), 285–286.

McCallin, A., Bamford-Wade, A., & Frankson, C. (2009). Leadership Succession Planning: A Key Issue for the Nursing Profession. *Nurse Leader, 7*40–744. https://doi.org/10.1016/j.mnl.2009.07.008.

Mckee, G., & Froelich, K. (2016). Executive Succession Planning: Barriers and Substitutes in Nonprofit Organizations. *Annals of Public & Cooperative Economics, 87*(4), 587–601. https://doi.org/10.1111/Apce.12129.

Miodinski, K., & Hines, P. (2013, January–February). Leadership Development and Succession Planning in Case Management. *Professional Case Management, 18*(1), 5–12. https://doi.org/10.1097/NCM.0b013e31826b12a7.

NHS. (2015). From Succession Planning to Succession Management. *Talent and Talent Management Insights*, NHS Leadership Academy.

NHS. (2017). *Portsmouth Hospitals NHS Trust; Succession Planning.* Retrieved from http://www.porthosp.nhs.uk/Learning/succession-planning.htm.

Nissan, J., & Eder, P. (2017). Four Dimensions of Designing Succession Plans. *OD Practitioner, 49*(3), 79–81.

OR Manager. (2015). Strategic Succession Planning Essential to OR Economic Success. *OR Manager, 31*(1), 1.

Patidar, N., Gupta, S., Azbik, G., & Weech-Maldonado, R. (2016). Succession Planning and Financial Performance: Does Competition Matter? *Journal of Healthcare Management, 61*(3), 215–227. ISSN:1096-9012.

Purohit, V., & Verma, R. K. (2013). A Study of Human Resource Development Climate in Government Health Centres in India. *Journal of Health Management, 15*(3), 431–443. https://doi.org/10.1177/0972063413491878.

Rafferty, C. (2013). Nurse Practitioner Succession Planning: Forward Thinking or Just an After-Thought? *Australian Health Review.* Retrieved from www.ncbi.nlm.nih.gov/pubmed/23838033.

Ramseur, P., Fuchs, M. A., Edwards, P., & Humphreys, J. (2018). The Implementation of a Structured Nursing Leadership Development Program for Succession Planning in a Health System. *Journal of Nursing Administration, 48*(1), 25–30. https://doi.org/10.1097/NNA.0000000000000566.

Rothwell, W. J. (2010). *Effective Succession Planning.* New York: AMACOM.

Sammer, J. (2015). Teams Must Follow Best Practices in Succession Planning: Executive Departures Are Inevitable, but Your Organization Doesn't Have to Flounder During the Transition. *Behavioral Healthcare, 35*(2), 40–41.

Santamour, B. (2016). Is Everybody Ready? *H&HN: Hospitals & Health Networks, 90*(11), 6.

Satiani, B., Sena, J., Ruberg, R., & Ellison, E. C. (2014). Practice Management: Talent Management and Physician Leadership Training Is Essential for

Preparing Tomorrow's Physician Leaders. *Journal of Vascular Surgery, 59*, 542–546. https://doi.org/10.1016/j.jvs.2013.10.074.

Schepker, D. J., Youngsang, K., Patel, P. C., Thatcher, S. M. B., & Campion, M. C. (2017). CEO Succession, Strategic Change, and Post-Succession Performance: A Meta-Analysis. *The Leadership Quarterly, 28*(6), 701–720.

Schepker, D. J., Nyberg, A. J., Ulrich, M. D., & Wright, P. M. (2018). Planning for Future Leadership: Procedural Rationality, Formalized Succession Processes, and CEO Influence in CEO Succession Planning. *Academy of Management Journal, 61*(2), 523. https://doi.org/10.5465/amj.2016.0071.

Scholes, J., & Trapani, J. (2017). Succession Planning: A Case for Revisiting the Process in Critical Care. *Nursing in Critical Care, 22*(4), 193–194. https://doi.org/10.1111/nicc.12308.

Sharma, D. K., & Goyal, R. C. (2010). *Hospital Administration and Human Resource Management* (5th ed.). New Delhi: PHI Learning.

Sherman, R. O., Patterson, P., Avitable, T., & Dahle, J. (2014). Perioperative Nurse Leader Perspectives on Succession Planning: A Call to Action. *Nursing Economic$, 32*(4), 186–203.

Silver, M. P., Hamilton, A. D., Biswas, A., & Warrick, N. I. (2016). A Systematic Review of Physician Retirement Planning. *Human Resources for Health, 14*, 1–16. https://doi.org/10.1186/s12960-016-0166-z.

Simon, M. A., Gunia, B., Martin, E., Foucar, C. E., Kundu, T., Ragas, D. M., et al. (2013). Path Toward Economic Resilience for Family Caregivers: Mitigating Household Deprivation and the Health Care Talent Shortage at the Same Time. *Gerontologist, 53*(5), 861–873. ISSN:0016-9013.

Smith, B. E. (2018). *Top 12 Healthcare Trends for 2018*. San Diego, CA: AMN Healthcare.

Srinivasan, V., & Chandwani, R. (2014). HRM Innovations in Rapid Growth Contexts: The Healthcare Sector in India. *International Journal of Human Resource Management, 25*(10), 1505–1525. ISSN:0958-5192.

Stichler, J. F. (2008). Succession Planning: Why Grooming Their Replacements Is Critical for Nurse Leaders. *Nursing for Women's Health, 12*, 525–528. https://doi.org/10.1111/j.1751-486X.2008.00387.x.

Sukayri, R. M. (2016). *Succession Planning in the United Nations System Organizations*. Geneva: United Nations Joint Inspection Unit.

Swan, B., & Moye, J. (2009). Perspectives in Ambulatory Care. Growing Ambulatory Care Nurse Leaders: Building Talent from the Primed Pipeline. *Nursing Economic$, 27*(4), 251–254.

Tae Hyun, K. (2012). Succession Planning in Hospitals and the Association with Organizational Performance. *Nursing Economic$, 30*(1), 14–20.

Titzer, J. L., & Shirey, M. R. (2013). Nurse Manager Succession Planning: A Concept Analysis. *Nursing Forum, 48*(3), 155–164. https://doi.org/10.1111/nuf.12024.

Titzer, J., Phillips, T., Tooley, S., Hall, N., & Shirey, M. (2013). Nurse Manager Succession Planning: Synthesis of the Evidence. *Journal of Nursing Management, 21*(7), 971–979. ISSN:0966-0429.

Trepanier, S., & Crenshaw, J. T. (2013). Succession Planning: A Call to Action for Nurse Executives. *Journal of Nursing Management, 21*(7), 980–985. ISSN:0966-0429.

Turner, P. A. (2017). *Talent Management in Healthcare*. Basingstoke: Palgrave Macmillan.

Turner, P. A., & Kalman, D. (2014). *Make Your People Before You Make Your Products*. London: Wiley.

Varhegyi, M. M., & Jepsen, D. M. (2017). Director Succession Planning in Not-for-Profit Boards. *Asia Pacific Journal of Human Resources, 55*(1), 106–126. https://doi.org/10.1111/1744-7941.12101.

Walker, L., Fineran, C., & Giella, T. (2018). Succession Planning: An Investment in Leadership Continuity and Success. *Trustee, 71*(1), 23–25.

Waters, K. P., Zuber, A., Willy, R. M., Kiriinya, R. N., Waudo, A. N., Oluoch, T., et al. (2013). Kenya's Health Workforce Information System: A Model of Impact on Strategic Human Resources Policy, Planning and Management. *International Journal of Medical Informatics, 82*, 895–902. https://doi.org/10.1016/j.ijmedinf.2013.06.004.

Waxman, K., & Delucas, C. (2014). Succession Planning: Using Simulation to Develop Nurse Leaders for the Future. *Nurse Leader, 12*, 24–28. https://doi.org/10.1016/j.mnl.2014.07.009.

Westphal, J. (2009). The Effect of Workforce Shortages on Nurse Leader Turnover and Succession in U.S. Hospitals. *Western Journal of Nursing Research, 31*(8), 1084–1085. https://doi.org/10.1177/0193945909342528.

Wolf, S. E. (2015). How to Best Conduct CEO Succession Planning (Cover Story). *Corporate Governance Advisor, 23*(5), 1–4.

10

Assessing Health Professionals for Succession and Leadership Roles

Health Sector Leaders Set Direction, Craft Strategy, and Engage Their Teams

Effective leadership is seen as an important factor in navigating through the volatility, uncertainty, complexity, ambiguity, and the 'myriad of wicked problems' (Czabanowska et al. 2014b: 1046; Trastek et al. 2014: 377; Reuben Olugbenga et al. 2016) that characterise the health sector. And so, having the right leaders in the right place at the right time with the right skill sets is a strategic imperative. Putting in place organisational structures populated with a leadership cadre of individuals with appropriate competences will therefore be a significant contribution to the ability of the organisation to deal with transformation and change. The challenges facing organisations in this environment are to identify those competences and match them against the availability of current leaders (or those with leadership potential). Leadership assessment is one way of achieving this ideal. It is a process that combines information on an individual's achievement against measurable objectives (performance analytics), with information based on interpretations of competence, capability, and potential (behavioural analytics), to identify

P. Turner, *Leadership in Healthcare*, Organizational Behaviour in Health Care,
https://doi.org/10.1007/978-3-030-04387-2_10

people who are ready for defined leadership roles or who have the potential to be so at some point in the future. The observation that 'it is essential to determine now if your board and executive team have the skill sets needed to shepherd the organization' (Stempniak 2013: 41) resonates across geographies. The basis for this assessment is the model for health sector leadership outlined in Chap. 5, which put forward competence 'clusters' in three elements, these being leadership capability, professional credibility, and an understanding of organisational dynamics. However, its contextual nature means that there is unlikely to be a single best practice model of leadership, and so leadership assessment will be based on a best fit approach that suits the specific environment in which an organisation operates.

As organisations evolve, so will their leadership requirements (Greiner 1998) and this will affect the competence mix. For example, new organisations in the sector may focus on developing a service and identifying a 'market' to which the service can be supplied. Health leadership in this case will be adaptive, responsive, and entrepreneurial to deal with the opportunity and its associated ambiguity. But in another example, more mature health organisations will require leaders who can build a period of sustained growth, installing structure and implementing processes accordingly, that is, an initial period of transformation, followed by effective 'transaction' as processes are put in place to deal with growth or change. And in the final stage of an organisation's evolution, strong interpersonal collaboration will be required of leaders to overcome the constraints of bureaucratic systems and processes. In each of these examples, the organisation will seek to put in place leaders who are able to deliver immediate requirements and a leadership cadre that can ensure continuity of success in the longer term. A priority facing all health sector organisations is to identify people with potential to fill leadership roles in these and other scenarios, assess them against external benchmarks or specific internal organisational criteria, and develop them to maximise the delivery of potential outcomes. Competence and competency aligned to the organisation's strategy are the established criteria used in this process.

Competence is an internal characteristic of a person or the possession of a required skill, knowledge, qualification, or capacity; and competency is an observable action of a person (Fraser et al. 2016) or 'the underlying characteristic of a person that leads to or causes effective and outstanding performance' (Kovačič and Rus 2015: 13). In the past competence and competency were separate and distinctive terms (CIPD 2017); but, more recently, the two are used interchangeably and in the health sector in a variety of different contexts (see inter alia, Calhoun et al. 2008; Lurie 2012; Brownie et al. 2014; Kanjananat et al. 2015; Pihlainen et al. 2016; Phan Van and Nguyen Duc 2017; American College of Healthcare Executives 2018). Assessment can be aligned to the competences for a specific post or role or to provide specific individuals to fill those posts, or a pipeline of those with the potential to fill a range of future leadership positions. A possible assessment model applicable to health sector organisations and incorporating competences is shown in Fig. 10.1 and forms the basis for this chapter. The objective is to establish the quantitative and qualitative demand for leadership roles and ensure that this demand is fulfilled by a supply of leaders who have been assessed against clusters of competences relevant to immediate and longer-term need.

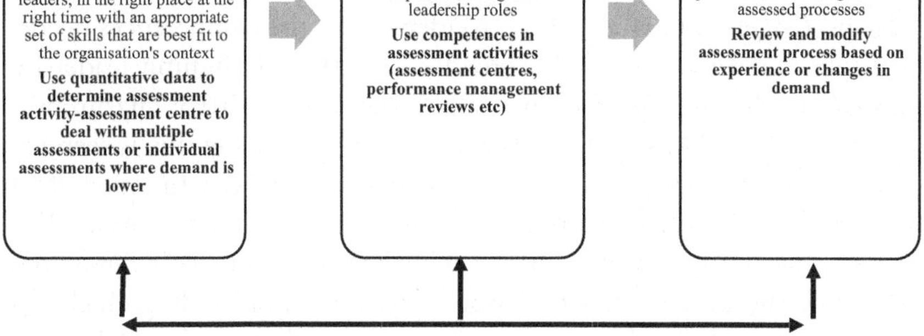

Fig. 10.1 An assessment process for leadership in health sector organisations

Identifying the Demand for Leadership Roles: Quantitative Analysis

An important precondition to any assessment activity therefore is a clear understanding of the number of leadership positions to be filled; in which unit, department, or team; in which professional, technical, or business area; and an estimate of the potential change in these numbers caused by known strategy or proposed practice (continuous linear change) or anticipated by more disruptive change such as reorganisation or merger. The number of roles will include Board-level posts, Executives, and the organisation's senior managers. The information on the impact of organisational strategy on structure and leadership is the quantitative demand side of strategic workforce planning, which is a core process of human resource management with the objective of the right number of people with the right skills, in the right place, at the right time to deliver short- and long-term organisation objectives. The strategic workforce plan is an output providing a view on which leadership assessment and development can be based (Crethar et al. 2009; Fibuch and Van Way 2012; Ellinger et al. 2014). Its role is to anticipate change and to provide a sufficient number of leaders to 'shape' the organisation to deal with both expected and unexpected events and provide continuity. It provides valuable information to support the organisation in its quest to be flexible and agile through effective leadership (Turner 2010).

In the health sector, workforce planning has been applied in a variety of scenarios from operational planning, such as the RAFAELA system in Finland (Fagerström et al. 2014), to identifying the competences needed in professional sectors, to the broader objective of aligning leadership capability to future need (see inter alia Gillespie et al. 2013; Fitzsimmons and Rose 2015; Martin 2015; Turner 2017). Nationally this is seen as a vital area to prepare people 'to embrace change and can functionally as well as behaviourally take on key roles within the organizations as effective strategic leader' (Martin 2015), whilst organisationally it can help to overcome the complexities of supply, retention, and funding challenges (Townsend et al. 2011). The quantitative analysis provides visibility of the scale of the leadership challenge that is to be addressed. However, demand is not only determined quantitatively (the required numbers of those in leadership positions) but qualitatively with the required competences for such roles.

Identifying the Demand for Leadership Roles: Qualitative Analysis

The second part of the process, therefore, is to highlight the type of competence required in the leadership roles anticipated by the above analysis. Such competence will contain elements of strategic capability as well as that of the operationalisation of strategy once agreed. In this respect implementation capability is associated with the skills, resources, and, most importantly, leadership for each proposed strategy and its component tasks (Berman et al. 2011: 9; Trustee 2015: 3). And whilst acknowledging that behaviour does not always fit a 'rational actor model,' it is still possible to adopt a systematic process with (to some extent) predictable results (CIPD 2015). Individual leadership competences will include personal elements such as emotional intelligence or authenticity (Fernandes Carvalho et al. 2016; Storberg-Walker and Gardiner 2017: 351; Hanold 2017) and organisational elements such as the ability to inspire a vision that is operationalised at every level (West et al. 2015: 5), able to work across organisations and agencies in the achievement of own organisation's objectives or an understanding of the implications of working with Boards and within governance structures. Competences will be focused on the ability to turn concept into practice and through this to create meaning for the organisation, its strategy, and individual roles. Core leadership skills therefore include both strategic awareness and operational competence such as network development (the ability of leaders to build relationships) and expertise in leading across various agencies across demographics (Stempniak 2013; Reichenpfader et al. 2015; Kalaitzi and Czabanowska 2016). The qualitative, competence-based analysis will be used to inform the type of assessment methods deployed. For the purposes of leadership assessment, clusters of competences will be grouped together, thereby reflecting a holistic view of the leader's role.

Applications of leadership competence identification and analysis in the health sector range from competence-based core areas in leadership and for the professional development of physicians to the competences of leaders in mobilising and engaging the workforce in US 'Magnet' hospitals. It was related to work role performance and organisational commitment and patient satisfaction, with typical findings of key leadership characteristics of knowledge about healthcare delivery and performance and knowledge about business and finance (Lehr et al. 2011; Ulrich et al. 2014; CCL 2016; Calzone et al. 2017; Sundean 2017: 5). In Europe there had been a focus on leadership competences within the healthcare sector in Slovenia (Kovačič and Rus 2015) and in the UK with the development of the Clinical Leadership Competency Framework, 'to build leadership awareness and capability across the health service' (Long et al. 2011: 111). Further examples of the use of competences in leadership assessment and development are found in India (Usha Marath 2015), where the application of leadership competences could have a possible impact on healthcare reform and health policy and implementation, in the development of Directors of Nursing with a particular emphasis on the importance of role competences (Spicer et al. 2010), and in nurse leadership development in Brazil (Fernandes Carvalho et al. 2016). In Korea research amongst 216 nurse managers in 7 cities found 42 competences together with 181 behavioural indicators (Kim and Kim 2016), whilst in Japan competences were identified for effectiveness in the field of community medicine (Kainuma et al. 2018). A synthesis of some of these competence analyses used in the sector was the basis for the model for healthcare leadership outlined in Chap. 5.

The research supports the idea that 'numerous competency frameworks, competency libraries and assessments are available off-the-shelf and organisations have been using them for many years to map the leadership competencies required for the success of their organisations … Leadership competencies can be seen as the result of a leader's experience, wisdom and ability to perform effectively on leadership tasks that are presented to them in an organisational context, and which have cognitive, behavioural, emotional, and meta-level components'(West et al. 2015: 19). The application of competence assessment in the health environment is ubiquitous, and, in spite of the observation that no two lists of competences 'ever seem to be the same and no consensus exists as to which traits or characteristics or competences are essential or optional' (Grint 2005: 34), the model has been adopted as an assessment framework by health organisations. For many it is an essential prerequisite to identifying leaders who will provide best fit to the organisation in its quest to achieve positive organisational outcomes for the many and diverse stakeholders.

The model for health sector leadership included a list of competences against each of the three identified components although it is recognised that the junction of managerial and medical logics requires this to be used in a nuanced way (Schultz and Pal 2004) since there is debate about which are most relevant and how these should be applied in the unique context of health. It is possible to adapt the framework to systems, methods, and processes for assessment. In practice, this has resulted in a broad range of applications including those through the performance management process and those used in formal and dedicated assessment 'events' such as competence-based interviews or assessment centres, to a range of diagnostic tools involving 360-degree appraisal, psychological or behavioural profile tests, and emotional intelligence assessments. In some cases, organisationally administered assessment is preferred, in others self-assessment and one-to-one coaching or mentoring feedback. In the case of professional credibility, peer review and feedback or the role in expert or professional organisations is used towards assessing the appropriateness of an individual for leadership roles. Finally, employee attitude surveys provide a rich source of assessment data on the performance of an individual leader or potential leader.

The quantitative and qualitative analyses resulting from the strategic workforce plan and competence identification provide the basis for leadership assessment in numbers of leaders and their required attributes. However, there are few consistent best practice guidelines for leadership assessment against these criteria, and so the next stage will be to put in place assessment processes that are best fit to the culture of the organisation.

Leadership Assessment Processes in Health Sector Organisations

As health systems evolve to meet changing operational and delivery system demands, 'so too must the organisation's leadership. The shift toward value-based care and population health management places new demands on the organisation, requiring new competences and skill sets … with a change in strategic direction often comes the need to assess and develop new competencies' (Trustee 2015: 2). Hence leadership assessment processes in the health sector are as heterogenous as leadership definitions, reflecting the richness of experience brought about by the contextual nature of strategy and operations. Research carried out in the USA, for example, found over 80 studies relating to leadership assessment including 61 team leadership assessment tools. These assessed against behaviours, skills, or characteristics to define leadership as well as leadership style (Rosenman et al. 2015). There is additional evidence of the use of a range of sophisticated assessment tools for leaders and managers in the UK, Finland, India, and across Asia (Stefl 2008; Hui-Gek Ang et al. 2016; Garman and Scribner 2011; Kantanen et al. 2015; Algarni et al. 2017). The continued popularity of leadership assessment is based on a long-standing assertion that leaders benefit from detailed and actionable information about the existence of any gap between their current skills and future potential. The overall objective of the process is to address these by ensuring a good competence and cultural fit between role and individual, in a way that is objective and consistent (Watson 2008; Sinar and Wellins 2016; Fisher and Wilmoth 2017).

Notwithstanding the diversity of approaches, assessment may be divided into formal processes which are organisationally led or those that are more informal and involve self-assessment or self-management by individuals. In traditional models, health sector leaders have been assessed against a wide range of qualities including their clinical skills, academic accomplishments, and administrative or interpersonal skills. However, more recently additional factors such as contemporary fiscal management and regulatory requirements are included in the process (Lanier and Rose 2008: 974). Table 10.1 is a snapshot of where and how these have been applied in each of the areas of the leadership model outlined in Chap. 5.

Table 10.1 Leadership assessment using a leadership competence framework for Senior Leaders, Executives, and Managers

Leadership criteria	Leadership competence and primary assessment method
Leadership capability	**Performance management and review, assessment centre, 360-degree, self-assessment processes, one-to-one coaching or mentoring feedback**
	Creates meaning for the organisation, its strategy, and individual roles
	Translates broad strategy into practical actions; has ability in 'knowing-interpreting'
	Identifies opportunities for growth and development of the organisation—drives for results
	Acts as a force for change and understands the dynamics of change
	Shapes and engages actively to generate situations and opportunities for change
	Mobilises the potential and capacities of members of the organisation as a whole or individual departments/ teams
	Engages and motivates a broad section of the health workforce—understands the importance of followership
	Assesses and acts on factors that 'contribute to or impede individual, team, or organizational success'
	Develops and implements 'strategies to align stakeholders to organizational mission and vision'
	Acts as advocate, influences policy, and negotiates resources to deliver strategy
	Performs well in a VUCA environment—able to take decisions, in spite of ambiguity
	Psychological or behavioural profile tests, emotional intelligence assessment, competence-based interview performance management and review, assessment centre, one-to-one coaching or mentoring feedback
	Anticipates impact of decisions and plans accordingly
	Demonstrates emotional intelligence and impact of actions on others
	Prioritises clinical outcomes amongst competing objectives
	Empowers others, develops, and mentors to 'create a strong team with diverse skills and perspectives'
	Develops successors to ensure either continuity or change of strategy, stewardship, and policy
	Shares critical information and seeks input from employees
	Acts as a role model for multicultural and diversity leadership
	Awareness of existing perceived leadership 'style' and the perceived required leadership style determined by the context of the organisation
	Able to mediate leadership identity, uses insight and hindsight to adapt leadership behaviour
	Acts with integrity, is authentic, reliable, truthful, and transparent as a means of earning trust and respect
	Adopts a collaborative style
	Operates effectively across networks and boundaries

(*continued*)

Table 10.1 (continued)

Leadership criteria	Leadership competence and primary assessment method
4.1.1.1.1.1. Professional credibility	**Peer review and feedback, performance management and review, role in expert or professional organisations, leadership assessment centre, 360-degree, one-to-one coaching or mentoring feedback**
	Creates an integrated leadership model and shares management responsibilities and accountabilities across clinical and business or administrative decision-making
	Establishes professional contacts and networks with experts outside the organisation
	Provides an authoritative source of advice to professional colleagues
	Encourages a high level of ethical behaviour and commitment to the professional values of the organisation
	Balances the ethics of care to the individual with care to the community
	Acts as role model for professional leadership in clinical and medical disciplines
	Understands the core elements of medical professionalism
	Performance management and review, leadership assessment centre, 360-degree, one-to-one coaching or mentoring feedback
	Understands the fundamentals of the care delivery process including how physicians make clinical decisions
	Practises and promotes professional accountability and responsibility
	Demonstrates commitment to professional welfare in the form of 'mentoring-nurturing' colleagues
	Identifies innovations, new methods, technologies, or opportunities for the delivery of healthcare
	Actively seeks and is able to acquire new knowledge
	Creates value by combining clinical, medical, and managerial logics
	Achieves unity of purpose by integrating performance and interprofessional collaboration
	Provides collaborative leadership and builds interdisciplinary teams—works collaboratively to maximise patient care
	Builds alliances and partnerships with clinical, medical, and managerial colleagues to ensure effective outcomes
	Understands patient and consumer healthcare expectations and requirements
	Understands the importance of clinical integration and coordination of care
	Uses both professional intuition and evidence-based outcomes in decision-making
	Applies both professional or managerial competence to organisational challenges

(*continued*)

Table 10.1 (continued)

Leadership criteria	Leadership competence and primary assessment method
4.1.1.1.1.2. Understanding organisational dynamics	**Performance management and review, leadership assessment centre, 360-degree, one-to-one coaching or mentoring feedback, employee attitude surveys**
	Understands and is able to inspire a vision that is operationalised at every level
	Works across organisations and agencies in the achievement of own organisation's objectives
	Understands implications of working with Boards and within governance structures
	Aligns strategy to organisation and organisation to strategy
	Sets clear, aligned objectives for all teams, departments, and individual staff
	Promotes a sense of common ownership of the organisation and its reputation
	Identifies strategies for initiating, sustaining, and organising change—fosters positive change
	Manages the processes of influence that can impact on the change including organisational politics
	Creates a work environment that supports innovation, risk taking, and ownership of professional practice
	Collaborates to drive system change and is resilient in its delivery
	Employee attitude surveys, performance management and review
	Sets a positive team climate
	Engages in dialogue to solve disputes and to solve critical problems
	Integrates divergent viewpoints for the good of the organisation as a whole
	Understands that collective action is a critical success factor
	Understands the need for connection, as well as sharing of information in an uncertain (VUCA) environment
	Provides leadership to multiple groupings simultaneously—organisation as a whole, teams, and individuals
	Provides leadership across interdisciplinary teams
	Is sensitive to and understands leadership of diverse cultures and disciplines—acts as cultural role model
	Ensures that plans and actions remain flexible to take account of the needs and work commitments of others
	Understands and explains financial, accounting, and other performance or business measures

Sources: CMDA (2006), Wolf (2008), Mitchell and Boak (2009), NHS (2010), Garman and Scribner (2011), Lehr et al. (2011), Hatler and Sturgeon (2013), Stempniak (2013), Czabanowska et al. (2014a), Day et al. (2014a), Hlupic (2014), Poikkeus et al. (2014), Rick (2014), Dauvrin and Lorant (2015), American Medical Association (2015), Fernandez et al. (2015), Humphreys et al. (2015), Kantanen et al. (2015), Kovačič and Rus (2015), Love and Ayadi (2015), Rosenman et al. (2015), West et al. (2015), Hui-Gek Ang et al. (2016), Leenstra et al. (2016), White et al. (2016), Patnaik et al. (2017)

There is practical value in matching assessment processes to competence frameworks which explains their continuing popularity. But there is inevitably a rider in that organisations are not driven by any single form of leader-dominated rationality, and 'too often the criteria for the selection of leaders is based on leadership theory rather than leadership practice. In fact, leadership is a complex, multi-faceted process and the translation of theory to practice is 'never simply a unilinear act of transmission' (Grint 2007: 232–233). And as leadership moves from a traditional to an emergent style, new competences will emerge because of the distribution of formal power and decision-making, the creation of interactive informal networks, and a learning mindset (Hlupic 2014). So, leaders will eschew a top-down ethos and move towards a direction that is derived from network activity, who use inspiration and intuition instead of toughness and control and who are comfortable with adaptation through decentralised systems. However, these considerations complement competence-based frameworks which can be adapted to accommodate inspirational characteristics.

For many organisations, the need for a transparent process in selecting those to move into leadership positions and to comply with corporate governance guidelines on appointments that are likely to be present requires a formal approach to assessment. Such a process will identify which are critical to the role and then establish a battery of tests against which to assess individual, leadership style, and cultural fit, as well as team leadership (Trustee 2015; Rosenman et al. 2015). The foundation for assessing leadership potential in this way is based on the assumption that 'personality variables and other stable personal attributes to leaders' effectiveness … provide a substantial empirical foundation for the argument that traits do matter in the prediction of individuals' effectiveness as leaders. Many theorists have gone beyond traits, emphasizing extensive lists of abilities, competencies, and skills that are essential for leadership effectiveness' (Gowing et al. 2008: 436).

However, not all assessment is through the scientific or psychometric means. Informal assessments that rely on observation rather than measurement also have a part to play. For example, it is suggested that 'at a very high level, board readiness can be summarized in the 3T trifecta: time, talent, and treasure. One must have the time to devote to board work, the talents (knowledge, skills, and expertise) needed for the specific board role and organization, and the treasure or philanthropic capacity to contribute to the organization' (Sundean 2017: 5). In this argument, talent can be measured through some of the processes outlined above but requirements such as 'treasure' or philanthropy less so.

Formal Organisation-Led Assessment Processes

Three formal organisation-led assessment processes are common in the health sector environment. These are performance management and reviews, competence-based interviews, and leadership assessment centres.

Performance assessment, associated with leadership and management practice, is a powerful tool because when it is directed to specific goals and objectives, there are positive correlations with clinical and economic performance (Lega et al. 2013). Whilst recognising evidence of the structuralist argument of the potential inequalities and power imbalance (Hewko and Cummings 2016) contained within performance management, contemporary processes should, in theory, ensure the application of transparency and fairness. Performance assessment will be relevant to demonstrate whether those in leadership roles have delivered to objectives by their effective leadership approach or adapted to new working environments and mechanisms (Chunharas and Davies 2016) and whether they are able to learn from their interactions at an operational level (identified as leadership ability through personal insight in the model for leadership). Any potential subjectivity can be mediated by complementing this process with assessment centres, self-assessment, 360-degree feedback, or peer review (Picker-Rotem et al. 2008). Data can be used independently or supplemented with that from a second common assessment process, the competence-based interview. Appointments to many, if not all, leadership roles will involve an interview seeking to answer the question 'is this the right person for the right job at the right time' which underscores the case for evidence-based recruitment and appointment practices (Cohen 2011: 103), as a way of improving suitability and performance (Hadley et al. 2015). Competence-based interviews can take place at the most senior level to 'ensure board members reflect the constellation of qualifications necessary to lead healthcare organizations within a complex and changing healthcare system' (Sundean 2017: 6) and as a tool at all levels of the leadership and management hierarchy or network.

A third part of the formal assessment process is that related to leadership assessment centres, which are designed to measure across the range of competences and their component parts. They are used for selection purposes as well as promotion and professional development and require candidates to complete a number of different tasks, combining behavioural ratings and cognitive and personality assessments obtained from multiple sources (CIPD 2016, 2018). Assessment centres provide valid information for recruitment, promotion, and development decisions for leadership positions. Their application has become widespread in and their appeal is attributed to recognised high predictive validity and perceived fairness. Meta-analytic studies have shown that they are effective in predicting performance ratings and person-organisation fit. They have solid content and criterion-related validity and are an established way of identifying people with leadership potential through a standardised set of procedures. Such centres measure competences, including job-specific behaviours and skills as well as personality and attitudinal dimensions, and are ideally suited for leadership roles. Establishing well-developed, methodologically sound leadership assessment tools will enhance the ability of organisations to have an impact on team performance and patient outcomes (Gowing et al. 2008; Petrides et al. 2010: 227; Rosenman et al. 2015: 1419; Herd et al. 2016: 31). Assessment centres are effective for organisations to observe and evaluate individual skills, behaviours, and abilities and how they match up with competences required for positions, organisational levels, or career moves. The major advantage of an assessment centre is that it uses a broad range of subject areas to provide the opportunity to 'observe and evaluate a participant on a number of separate occasions in a range of different situations' (NHS Leadership Academy 2012; Sackett et al. 2017). The design of such centres includes role plays, in-tray exercises, analysis exercises, and psychometric assessments. The centres include interviews, situational tests, and psychometric tests related to personality or aptitude. Often leadership assessment centres are physical locations, with multiple candidates and assessors present. The alternative to 'bricks and mortar' involves the greater use of technology to increase flexibility in creating virtual centres (Gowing et al. 2008; Yukl 2010: 49).

Self-Assessment Methods in an Organisational Context

Formal methods of assessment outlined above can be complemented or supplemented (rarely replaced) by self-assessment for leadership roles fitting within the concept of self-determination theory, 'a theory of motivation arguing that people are inherently proactive in mastering their inner drives and emotions to achieve their potential' (Giri et al. 2017: 398). Self-assessment is prompted by self-motivation and driven by the opportunity for individuals to move into or develop leadership roles. Such processes have been used in different contexts and for different purposes in health sector organisations, from Board self-assessment as a way of assessing Board performance through a combination of quantitative and qualitative measurements of Board, committee, and individual performance, which allowed individuals and Boards to identify any 'leadership gaps,' or potential for improvement (Walker Company 2018), to self-assessment based on a 'map of the non-technical skills necessary for effective clinical leadership … applied as a self-assessment and improvement tool' (Jalil et al. 2018). In the UK self-assessment provided a guide to an individual's competence in particular leadership domains including demonstrating personal qualities, working with others, managing services, improving services, and setting direction. In addition, assessment tools such as the Clinical Leadership Competency Framework, Medical Leadership Competency Framework, and the Managerial Practices Questionnaire have also been used (NHS 2012; Agnew and Flin 2014). Other applications of self-assessment for leadership competence in Brazil, Kenya, and the USA were in the context of nurse leadership and coaching, of assessing leadership skills in primary care and hospitals, as a way of improving leadership decision-making, and of assessing readiness for Healthcare Boards (Mogere and Muga

2014; Pereira Cardoso et al. 2014; Jodar I Solà et al. 2016; Sundean 2017; Lean Keng and AlQudah 2017). Self-assessments against competences were put in place for leaders at the 'bedside, unit level, and department level' so that leaders 'can support the new strategic plan by increasing attention to competencies related to healthcare finance, economics, and delivery models. Additional competencies to develop included evidence-based practice, risk taking, innovation, and use of reflective practice. Mentoring and active learning strategies are recommended for programme delivery' (Beckman and Warshawsky 2017: 18), and in a further example (Day et al. 2014b), a leadership competence model was used in the creation of a self-assessment tool to identify areas of strengths.

Within this framework, the use of the 360-degree process is common—also referred to as multi-sourced feedback—because it requires input from subordinates, peers, and superiors and compares self-ratings from individual health leaders with those provided by their peers and other groups (Spurgeon 2008; West et al. 2015; Sikes et al. 2015: 64). This has been used in the sector as the basis for a broad range of development interventions including insight into strengths and weaknesses, enhancing culture change, enhancing team effectiveness, and identifying development needs (Wood et al. 2006: 185). It has also been proposed as a means of Senior Leaders demonstrating evidence of distilling organisational and embedding them into practice (CIPD 2014). It involves the individual and several others with whom they work completing a questionnaire assessing behaviours and effectiveness. The use of this methodology has been demonstrated in the sector as an effective tool in the development of both interpersonal skills and leadership acumen and has been widely applied using tools such as the Leadership Practices Inventory (LPI) developed by Kouzes and Posner (2007) and the Physicians Universal Leadership-Teamwork Skills Education (PULSE) 360 to assess perceptions of a leadership, teamwork, and clinical practice style (Hageman et al. 2015). In a study by the American College of Surgeons, 360-degree evaluation was found to provide the basis of a practical, systematic, and subjectively accurate assessment of performance (Nurudeen et al. 2014). Indeed, 'research on 360-degree feedback of managers has consistently shown that ratings of managers predict team performance and employee satisfaction. Furthermore, leaders who receive such feedback have shown significant improvement in their follow-up.

Additionally, leadership effectiveness may increase by as much as 60% in development programs that use it' (Gregory et al. 2017: 3566). The 360-degree method in assessing leadership potential and behaviours such as the 'big five factors' of personality *extraversion*, *openness to experience*, *conscientiousness*, *agreeableness*, and *emotional stability* or other identified leadership assessment criteria can be useful where rigour and practical relevance are applied and with some caveats (Wood et al. 2006; Langford et al. 2017).

It is likely that organisations will choose an assessment process that has cultural fit. For some, the competence interview is sufficient; for others rigorous assessment centres will be the norm. There are strengths in each of the methods, with the common objective of ensuring that the process is fair and transparent. The assessment of leaders 'can and should be based on robust theory with strong empirical support and evidence of what works in health care' (West et al. 2015: 23). It is a good practice to ensure that assessment processes are reviewed continuously to ensure their continued effectiveness and to ensure that any learning points, such as from assessment centres, for example, are collected and used in improving future practice (British Psychological Society 2015; CIPD 2015).

Case Study: Bright and Dark Sides of Leadership in Polish Healthcare Organisations

Professor Tomasz Ingram, the University of Economics in Katowice, Faculty of Economics, Department of Entrepreneurship and Innovation Management

Healthcare units located in transition economies such as Poland face radical change and are continuously encountering unpredictable shifts in the modes of financing, system-imposed demands, and ownership structure (Rurik and Kalabay 2009). The Polish healthcare system is therefore composed of large, publicly owned hospitals with a long history and tradition on the one hand and relatively young, privately owned healthcare units rivalling their public competitors for public and private funds (Orlewska 2011) on the other. The challenge facing Polish healthcare units is to match their leadership styles to those of new market and organisational conditions and requirements.

In this respect, organisational researchers and practitioner emphasise the role of leadership in all organisations, regardless of their size, branch, or age (Bolman and Deal 2017). Unsurprisingly, there are numerous studies that focus attention on diverse aspects of leadership, also in the healthcare organisations. Previous research results reveal that irrespective of the economic and political systems healthcare units operate in, leadership plays important role in driving organisational results (Cummings et al. 2010). Although the issues, facets, and aspects of leadership in well-developed countries seem to be well explained, it seems even more challenging and interesting to study leadership in transition economies. It is a fruitful avenue for empirical studies considering fast, unpredictable, and frequently system-driven changes (Murauskiene et al. 2013) that tend to affect social systems to a large degree.

For the purposes of a study into the Polish healthcare sector in 2017, two types of leadership were investigated. The first, transformation leadership, is broadening and elevating followers' goals and providing them with confidence to perform beyond the expectations specified in the implicit or explicit exchange agreement (Dvir et al. 2002: 735). The second, destructive leadership, refers to systematically and repeatedly performed behaviour that disrupts the fundamental interests of the organisation by undermining and obscuring realisation of organisational goals and job tasks, wasting resources, and hindering effectiveness, motivation, well-being, or job satisfaction of employees (Einarsen et al. 2007). The basic research question reflected how these two types of leadership coexist and to what extent they allow for an explanation of two facets of organisational performance (job satisfaction and organisational commitment).

In the first instance, we have carried out exploratory factor analyses to discover and better understand the internal structure of our research constructs. These analyses revealed that transformational leadership, organisational commitment, job satisfaction, and task uncertainty are composed of one factor each, and destructive leadership is explainable using three main components: ineffective leadership, ego-oriented leadership, and offensive leadership.

The research results lead to several important conclusions as follows:

- In Polish private and public healthcare units, both transformational leadership and destructive leadership behaviours occur simultaneously.
- The level of destructive leadership behaviours in studied Polish healthcare institutions is very low, but ineffective leadership behaviours appear to be demonstrated more than in private sector ones.
- Transformational leadership in Polish healthcare (public and private) organisations influences positively both organisational commitment and job satisfaction, and that effect can be clearly observable.
- The higher the level of ineffective leadership behaviours, the lower the organisational commitment of subordinates. From our control variables (age, experience, supervisor's age, and supervisor's experience), only supervisor's experience explained employee commitment. In particular, the higher the supervisors' experience, the lower the employees' commitment.

- Healthcare organisations do not differ in terms of the transformational leadership style of their managers (according to surveyed employees).

Our study brings also implications for managerial practice. In particular, it seems rational to focus rather on developing transformational leadership skills among managers in the healthcare organisations while they tend to drive organisational commitment and job satisfaction among employees. Thus, promoting transformational leadership skills seems to pay back to organisations and teams at the healthcare organisations, and fostering and developing these skills among managers might bring highly appreciated results such as increased job satisfaction and organisational commitment. On the other hand, managers should also focus attention on the ineffective leadership behaviours, paying attention to individuals who, by their sheer lack of managerial skills, undermine the realisation of organisational goals and hinder motivation and effectiveness of their employees. The research results briefly described above suggest that the role leadership plays in healthcare organisations in transition economies is critical to successful outcomes.

Conclusion and Implications for Practice

The identification of leaders for health sector organisations is not something that can be left to chance because in order to deal with the dynamic VUCA forces that are prevalent in the sector, effective leadership at all levels will be required. Such leadership provides objectives and direction to the organisation and is also able to engage the workforce in the pursuit of both. The challenge of identifying those who are able to assume such responsibilities is complex as was highlighted by a systematic review of literature on the subject which found 30 different activities, and specific reference to medical leadership, the issues of innovation, and multidisciplinary collaboration involving skills in influence, empowerment, and communication were identified (Berghout et al. 2017). Nevertheless, and in spite of the complexity, assessing those with best fit leadership competence and competency is vital to the success of the organisation.

The creation of a competence framework provides the foundation on which this assessment can be built and which will contribute to having the right leaders in the right place at the right time. The objective will be to create effective leaders and with new or enhanced skills. In so doing, the key conclusions from this chapter are as follows:

- **Identifying the organisation's existing leadership bench strength and assessing those who are able to move into leadership positions in the future are key considerations** and structured assessment processes help to achieve these goals.
- Competences are the basis of this assessment where ***competence* is an internal characteristic of a person or the possession of a required skill, knowledge, qualification, or capacity** and *competency* is an observable action of a person.
- **A competence framework combines the required areas of strength and performance into definable and measurable clusters.** These attributes were described as a model for health sector leadership, of which the key areas were personal insight as a way of identifying leadership capability at both organisational and individual levels, professional credibility as a way of bridging managerial and clinical or medical logics, and an understanding of the dynamics of the organisation within which leadership was to take place.
- Assessments of leadership should be clearly linked to conceptual frameworks for leadership as applied in the specific organisation, recognising that **such frameworks are 'flexible and complex and vary according to the demands of a particular business strategy of an organisation.'** A combination of competence and competency factors within each of these three areas was proposed as a means of assessing best fit leadership for any organisation.
- An array of tools and methods of assessment are used by health sector organisations including **performance management, competence-based interviews, assessment centres, 360-degree or multi-sourced feedback, and self-assessment.** There is no 'best way' to assess but the choice is dependent on the organisation's culture and its capability.

The range of competencies required by leaders in health sector organisations is broad and ranges from the ability to 'scan and search for new information, "connect the dots" between incidents that appear to be unrelated with limited cues and recognize patterns or ideas that suggest potential opportunities in the myriad cues or signals that they receive' (White et al. 2016: 258) through to the ability to develop a vision, convert this into a meaningful strategy, and deliver this in a way that engages the workforce, all of which are geared to improved health or societal outcomes.

References

Agnew, C., & Flin, R. (2014). Senior Charge Nurses' Leadership Behaviours in Relation to Hospital Ward Safety: A Mixed Method Study. *International Journal of Nursing Studies, 51*(5), 768–780. https://doi.org/10.1016/j.ijnurstu.2013.10.001.

Algarni, N., Mclaughlin, P., & Al-Ashaab, A. (2017). Developing a Framework to Improve Leadership Performance in Healthcare Organisations: The Case of the Kingdom of Saudi Arabia. *BMJ Leader, 1*, A2–A3.

American College of Healthcare Executives. (2018). *Healthcare Leadership Competencies.* Retrieved from https://www.ache.org/newclub/resource/competencies.cfm.

American Medical Association. (2015). *Integrated Leadership for Hospitals and Health Systems: Principles for Success.* Retrieved from https://www.ama-assn.org/sites/default/files/media-browser/public/about-ama/ama-aha-integrated-leadership-principles_0.pdf.

Beckman, D., & Warshawsky, N. (2017). Assessing Competencies Needed to Lead in an ACA World. *Kentucky Nurse, 65*(2), 18.

Berghout, M. A., Fabbricotti, I. N., Buljac-Samardzic, M., & Hilders, C. M. (2017). Medical Leaders or Masters?—A Systematic Review of Medical Leadership in Hospital Settings. *PLoS One, 12*(9), e0184522. https://doi.org/10.1371/journal.pone.0184522.

Berman, P., Pallas, S., Smith, A. L., Curry, L., & Bradley, E. H. (2011). *Improving the Delivery of Health Services: A Guide to Choosing Strategies.* The World Bank: Open Knowledge Repository (OKR).

Bolman, L. G., & Deal, T. E. (2017). *Reframing Organizations: Artistry, Choice, and Leadership* (6th ed.). Cambridge: John Wiley & Sons.

British Psychological Society. (2015). *The Design and Delivery of Assessment Centres.* Leicester, UK: British Psychological Society. Retrieved from https://www1.bps.org.uk/system/files/user-files/DivisionofOccupationalPsychology/public/inf234_assess_centres_final.pdf.

Brownie, S., Thomas, J., McAllister, L., & Groves, M. (2014). Australian Health Reforms: Enhancing Interprofessional Practice and Competency Within the

Health Workforce. *Journal of Interprofessional Care, 28*(3), 252–253. https://doi.org/10.3109/13561820.2014.881790.

Calhoun, J., Dollett, L., Sinioris, M. E., Wainio, J. A., Butler, P. W., Griffith, J. R., et al. (2008). Development of an Interprofessional Competency Model for Healthcare Leadership. *Journal of Healthcare Management, 53*(6), 375–389.

Calzone, K. A., Jenkins, J., Culp, S., & Badzek, L. (2017). Hospital Nursing Leadership Led Interventions Increased Genomic Awareness and Educational Intent in Magnet® Settings. *Nursing Outlook*. https://doi.org/10.1016/j.outlook.2017.10.010.

Centre for Creative Leadership. (2016) *Addressing the Leadership Gap in Healthcare*. White Paper: Centre for Creative Leadership.

Chinese Medical Doctors Association. (2006). Retrieved from www.cmda.net/cmdaenglish/about.php.htm.

Chunharas, S., & Davies, D. S. C. (2016). Leadership in Health Systems: A New Agenda for Interactive Leadership. *Health Systems & Reform, 2*(3), 176–178. https://doi.org/10.1080/23288604.2016.1222794.

CIPD. (2014). *Cultivating Trustworthy Leaders*. London, UK: Chartered Institute of Personnel and Development (with the University of Bath).

CIPD. (2015). *A Head for Hiring: The Behavioural Science of Recruitment and Selection*. London, UK: Research Report, Chartered Institute of Personnel and Development.

CIPD. (2016). *Assessment Centres*. London, UK: Chartered Institute of Personnel and Development. Retrieved from https://www.cipd.co.uk/knowledge/fundamentals/people/recruitment/selection-factsheet#7267.

CIPD. (2017). *Competency and Competence Frameworks*. London, UK: Chartered Institute of Personnel and Development. Retrieved from https://www.cipd.co.uk/knowledge/fundamentals/people/performance/competency-factsheet.

CIPD. (2018). *Selection Methods*. London, UK: Chartered Institute of Personnel and Development. Retrieved from https://www.cipd.co.uk/knowledge/fundamentals/people/recruitment/selection-factsheet#7267.

Cohen, K. R. (2011). The Case for Evidence-Based Human Capital Management: There Are Financial Benefits to Evidence-Based Recruitment, Selection, Development, and Retention—Underscoring the Need for Finance Executives to Become Actively Involved in Initiatives to Manage Their Organizations' Talent. *Healthcare Financial Management, 65*(8), 102–107.

Crethar, M. P., Phillips, J. N., Stafford, P. J., & Duckett, S. J. (2009). Leadership Transformation in Queensland Health. *Australian Health Review, 3*, 357–364.

Cummings, G. G., MacGregor, T., Davey, M., Lee, H., Wong, C. A., Lo, E., et al. (2010). Leadership Styles and Outcome Patterns for the Nursing Workforce and Work Environment: A Systematic Review. *International Journal of Nursing Studies, 47*(3), 363–385.

Czabanowska, K., Smith, T., Könings, K. D., Sumskas, L., Otok, R., Bjegovic-Mikanovic, V., et al. (2014a). In Search for a Public Health Leadership Competency Framework to Support Leadership Curriculum—A Consensus Study. *European Journal of Public Health, 5*, 850.

Czabanowska, K., Rethmeier, K. A., Lueddeke, G., Smith, T., Malho, A., Otok, R., et al. (2014b). Public Health in the 21st Century: Working Differently Means Leading and Learning Differently. *European Journal of Public Health, 6*, 1047.

Dauvrin, M., & Lorant, V. (2015). Leadership and Cultural Competence of Healthcare Professionals: A Social Network Analysis. *Nursing Research, 64*(3), 200–2010. https://doi.org/10.1097/NNR.0000000000000092.

Day, D. D., Hand, M. W., Jones, A. R., Kay Harrington, N., Best, R., & LeFebvre, K. B. (2014a). The Oncology Nursing Society Leadership Competency Project: Developing a Road Map to Professional Excellence. *Clinical Journal of Oncology Nursing, 18*(4), 432–436. https://doi.org/10.1188/14.CJON.432-436.

Day, M., Shickle, D., Smith, K., Zakariasen, K., Moskol, J., & Oliver, T. (2014b). Training Public Health Superheroes: Five Talents for Public Health Leadership. *Journal of Public Health, 36*(4), 552–561. https://doi.org/10.1093/pubmed/fdu004.

Dvir, T., Eden, D., Avolio, B. J., & Shamir, B. (2002). Impact of Transformational Leadership on Follower Development and Performance: A Field Experiment. *Academy of Management Journal, 45*(4), 735–744.

Einarsen, S., Aasland, M. S., & Skogstad, A. (2007). Destructive Leadership Behaviour: A Definition and Conceptual Model. *The Leadership Quarterly, 18*(3), 207–216.

Ellinger, L. K., Trapskin, P. J., Black, R., Kotis, D., & Alexander, E. (2014). Leadership and Effective Succession Planning in Health-System Pharmacy Departments. *Hospital Pharmacist, 9*(4), 369–375. https://doi.org/10.1310/hpj4904-369.

Fagerström, L., Lønning, K., & Andersen, M. H. (2014). The RAFAELA System: A Workforce Planning Tool for Nurse Staffing and Human Resource Management. *Nursing Management—UK, 21*(2), 30–36. https://doi.org/10.7748/nm2014.04.21.2.30.e1199.

Fernandes Carvalho, A. G., Kowal Olm Cunha, I. C., Pazetto Balsanelli, A., & Bernardes, A. (2016). Authentic Leadership and the Personal and Professional Profile of Nurses. *Acta Paulista De Enfermagem, 29*(6), 618–625. https://doi.org/10.1590/1982-0194201600087.

Fernandez, C. P., Noble, C. C., Jensen, E., & Steffen, D. (2015). Moving the Needle: A Retrospective Pre- and Post-Analysis of Improving Perceived Abilities Across 20 Leadership Skills. *Maternal and Child Health Journal, 19*(2), 343–352. https://doi.org/10.1007/s10995-014-1573-1.

Fibuch, E., & Van Way, C. W., III. (2012). Succession Planning in Health Care Organizations. *Physician Executive, 38*(5), 44–47.

Fisher, E. M., & Wilmoth, M. C. (2017). Do I Take the Job? Assessing Fit with the Organization. *Journal of Professional Nursing, 34*(2), 82–86. https://doi.org/10.1016/j.profnurs.2017.08.003.

Fitzsimmons, M. J., & Rose, R. (2015). Designing Structure to Meet Demands, and Recruiting Talent to Achieve Results. *Nurse Leader, 13*(1), 1–84. ISSN:1541-4612.

Fraser, A. B., Stodel, E. J., & Chaput, A. J. (2016). Curriculum Reform for Residency Training: Competence, Change, and Opportunities for Leadership. *Canadian Journal of Anaesthesia, 63*(7), 875–884.

Garman, A., & Scribner, L. (2011). Leading for Quality in Healthcare: Development and Validation of a Competency Model. *Journal of Healthcare Management, 56*(6), 373–382. ISSN:1096-9012.

Gillespie, B. M., Hamlin, L., Polit, D. F., & Chaboyer, W. (2013). The Influence of Personal Characteristics on Perioperative Nurses' Perceived Competence: Implications for Workforce Planning. *Australian Journal of Advanced Nursing, 30*(3), 14–25. ISSN:0813-0531.

Giri, P., Aylott, J., & Kilner, K. (2017). Self-Determining Medical Leadership Needs of Occupational Health Physicians. *Leadership in Health Services (1751–1879), 30*(4), 394–410. https://doi.org/10.1108/LHS-06-2016-0029.

Gowing, M., Morris, D., Adler, S., & Gold, M. (2008). The Next Generation of Leadership Assessments: Some Case Studies. *Public Personnel Management, 37*(4), 435–455.

Gregory, P. J., Harmon, L., Robbins, B., & Schwaitzberg, S. D. (2017). Leadership Development in a Professional Medical Society Using 360-Degree Survey Feedback to Assess Emotional Intelligence. *Surgical Endoscopy and Other Interventional Techniques, 31*(9), 3565–3573.

Greiner, L. E. (1998). Evolution and Revolution as Organizations Grow. *Harvard Business Review, 76*(3), 55–68.

Grint, K. (2005). *Leadership: Limits and Possibilities*. Basingstoke, Hampshire, UK: Palgrave Macmillan.

Grint, K. (2007). *Learning to Lead: Can Aristotle Help Us to Find the Road to Wisdom*. Retrieved from https://lea.sagepub.com/content/3/2/231.

Hadley, L., Black, D., Welch, J., & Penlington, C. (2015). Encouraging Formative Assessments of Leadership for Foundation Doctors. *The Clinical Teacher, 12*(4), 231–235. https://doi.org/10.1111/tct.12289.

Hageman, M. G. J. S., Ring, D. C., Gregory, P. J., Rubash, H. E., & Harmon, L. (2015). Do 360-Degree Feedback Survey Results Relate to Patient Satisfaction Measures? *Clinical Orthopaedics and Related Research, 473*(5), 1590–1597. https://doi.org/10.1007/s11999-014-3981-3.

Hanold, M. (2017). Toward a New Approach to Authentic Leadership: The Practice of Embodied Dialogical "Thinking" and the Promise of Shared Power. *Advances in Developing Human Resources, 19*(4), 454. https://doi.org/10.1177/1523422317728940.

Hatler, C., & Sturgeon, P. (2013). Resilience Building: A Necessary Leadership Competence. *Nurse Leader, 11*(4), 32–34. https://doi.org/10.1016/j.mnl.2013.05.007.

Herd, A. M., Alagaraja, M., & Cumberland, D. M. (2016). Assessing Global Leadership Competencies: The Critical Role of Assessment Centre Methodology. *Human Resource Development International, 19*(1), 27–43.

Hewko, S. J., & Cummings, G. G. (2016). Performance Management in Healthcare: A Critical Analysis. *Leadership in Health Services, 29*(1), 52–68. https://doi.org/10.1108/LHS-12-2014-0081.

Hlupic, V. (2014). *The Management Shift*. London: Palgrave Macmillan.

Hui-Gek Ang, Meng-Yeow Koh, Jeremy, Jeffrey Lee, & Yong-Hao Pua. (2016). Development and Preliminary Validation of a Leadership Competency Instrument for Existing and Emerging Allied Health Professional Leaders. *BMC Health Services Research, 16*, 64. ISSN:1472-6963.

Humphreys, B., Couse, L., Sonnenmeier, R., Kurtz, A., Russell, S., & Antal, P. (2015). Transforming LEND Leadership Training Curriculum through the Maternal and Child Health Leadership Competencies. *Maternal & Child Health Journal, 19*(2), 300–307. https://doi.org/10.1007/s10995-014-1587-8.

Jalil, R., Soukup, T., Akhter, W., Sevdalis, N., & Green, J. A. (2018). Quality of Leadership in Multidisciplinary Cancer Tumor Boards: Development and Evaluation of a Leadership Assessment Instrument (ATLAS). *World Journal of Urology, 36*(7), 1031–1038.

Jodar I Solà, G., Gené I Badia, J., Hito, P. D., Osaba, M. C., & Del Val García, J. L. (2016). Self-Perception of Leadership Styles and Behaviour in Primary Health Care. *BMC Health Services Research, 16*(1), 572.

Kainuma, M., Kikukawa, M., Nagata, M., & Yoshida, M. (2018). Competencies Necessary for Becoming a Leader in the Field of Community Medicine: A Japanese Qualitative Interview Study. *BMJ Open, 8*, e020082. https://doi.org/10.1136/bmjopen-2017-020082.

Kalaitzi, V., & Czabanowska, K. (2016). Women's Leadership in Healthcare—The Three Faceted Quest. *European Journal of Public Health, 26*(1), 1. https://doi.org/10.1093/eurpub/ckw166.018.

Kanjananat, T., Wipada, K., Raymoul, N., & Thitinut, A. (2015). Development of a Competency Assessment Scale for Head Nurses in Community Hospitals. *Pacific Rim International Journal of Nursing Research, 19*(2), 122–134.

Kantanen, K., Kaunonen, M., Helminen, M., & Suominen, T. (2015). The Development and Pilot of an Instrument for Measuring Nurse Managers' Leadership and Management Competencies. *Journal of Research in Nursing, 20*(8), 667–677. ISSN:1744-9871.

Kim, S. Y., & Kim, J. K. (2016). A Study on the Classification of Nursing Management Competencies and Development of Related Behavioral Indicators in Hospitals. *Journal of Korean Academy of Nursing, 46*(3), 375–389. https://doi.org/10.4040/jkan.2016.46.3.375.

Kouzes, J. M., & Posner, B. Z. (2007). *The Leadership Challenge*. San Francisco: Jossey Bass.

Kovačič, H., & Rus, A. (2015). Leadership Competences in Slovenian Health Care / Vodstvene Kompetence V Slovenskem Zdravstvu. *Slovenian Journal of Public Health, 54*(1), 11–17. https://doi.org/10.1515/sjph-2015-0002.

Langford, P. H., Dougall, C. B., & Parkes, L. P. (2017). Measuring Leader Behaviour: Evidence for a 'Big Five' Model of Leadership. *Leadership & Organization Development Journal, 38*(1), 126–144.

Lanier, W. L., & Rose, S. H. (2008). The Contemporary Medical Community: Leadership, Mentorship, and Career Choices. *Mayo Clinic Proceedings, 83*(9), 974–977.

Lean Keng, S., & AlQudah, H. I. (2017). Assessment of Cognitive Bias in Decision-Making and Leadership Styles Among Critical Care Nurses: A Mixed Methods Study. *Journal of Advanced Nursing, 73*(2), 465–481. https://doi.org/10.1111/jan.13142.

Leenstra, N. F., Jung, O. C., Johnson, A., Wendt, K. W., & Tulleken, J. E. (2016). Taxonomy of Trauma Leadership Skills: A Framework for Leadership

Training and Assessment. *Academic Medicine, 91*(2), 272–281. https://doi.org/10.1097/ACM.0000000000000089.

Lega, F., Prenestini, A., & Spurgeon, P. (2013). Is Management Essential to Improving the Performance and Sustainability of Health Care Systems and Organizations? A Systematic Review and a Roadmap for Future Studies. *Value in Health, 16*(1), S46–S51.

Lehr, B., Ostermann, H., & Schubert, H. (2011). Schwerpunkt: Competence-Based Demands Made of Senior Physicians: An Empirical Study to Evaluate Leadership Competencies. *Zeitschrift Fuer Evidenz, Fortbildung Und Qualitaet Im Gesundheitswesen, 105* (Panta rhei—Alles fliesst), 723–733. https://doi.org/10.1016/j.zefq.2010.08.006.

Long, P. W., Lobley, K., Spurgeon, P. C., Clark, J. C., Balderson, S., & Lonetto, T. M. (2011). The CLCF: Developing Leadership Capacity and Capability in the Clinical Professions. *International Journal of Clinical Leadership, 17*(2), 111–118.

Love, D. B., & Ayadi, M. F. (2015). Redefining the Core Competencies of Future Healthcare Executives under Healthcare Reform. *Administrative Issues Journal: Education, Practice, and Research, 5*(2), 3–16.

Lurie, S. J. (2012). History and Practice of Competency-Based Assessment. *Medical Education, 46*(1), 49–57. https://doi.org/10.1111/j.1365-2923.2011.04142.x.

Martin, A. (2015). Leadership: Talent Management: Preparing a 'Ready' Agile Workforce. *International Journal of Pediatrics and Adolescent Medicine, 2*(3–4), 112–116. ISSN:2352-6467.

Mitchell, L., & Boak, G. (2009). Developing Competence Frameworks in UK Healthcare: Lessons from Practice. *Journal of European Industrial Training, 33*(8–9), 701–717.

Mogere, D. M., & Muga, R. (2014). Assessment of Management and Leadership Skills, Competencies and Ability Among Health Care Managers Working in Level 3, 4 and 5 Hospitals, Nyanza Province—Kenya. *Value in Health, 3*, A148.

Murauskiene, L., Janoniene, R., Veniute, M., & Karanikolos, M. (2013). Lithuania: Health System Review. *Health Systems in Transition, 15*(2), 1–150.

NHS. (2010). *Medical Leadership Competency Framework; Enhancing Engagement in Medical Leadership*. 3rd ed. Retrieved from https://www.leadershipacademy.nhs.uk/wp-content/uploads/2012/11/NHSLeadership-Leadership-Framework-Medical-Leadership-Competency-Framework-3rd-ed.pdf.

NHS. (2012). *The Leadership Framework—Self Assessment Tool*. London, UK: NHS Leadership Academy.

Nurudeen, S. M., Kwakye, G., Berry, W. R., Chaikof, E. L., Lillemoe, K. D., Millham, F., et al. (2014). Can 360-Degree Reviews Help Surgeons? Evaluation of Multisource Feedback for Surgeons in a Multi-Institutional Quality Improvement Project. *Journal of the American College of Surgeons, 221*(4), 837–844.

Orlewska, E. (2011). Challenges and Changes in the Polish Healthcare System. *Society and Economy, 33*(3), 575–594.

Patnaik, S. K., Gupta, S. K., Kant, S., & Pillay, R. (2017). Analysing Competencies of Indian Healthcare Leaders. *International Journal of Research Foundation of Hospital and Healthcare Administration, 5*(1), 47–53.

Pereira Cardoso, M. A., Ramos, L. H., & D'Innocenzo, M. (2014). Coaching Leadership: Leaders' and Followers' Perception Assessment Questionnaires in Nursing. *Einstein (16794508), 12*(1), 66–74.

Petrides, K. V., Weinstein, Y., Chou, J., Furnham, A., & Swami, V. (2010). An Investigation into Assessment Centre Validity, Fairness, and Selection Drivers. *Australian Journal of Psychology, 62*(4), 227–235. https://doi.org/10.1080/00049531003667380.

Phan Van, T., & Nguyen Duc, T. (2017). A Leadership and Managerial Competency Framework for Public Hospital Managers in Vietnam. *AIMS Public Health, 4*(4), 418–429. https://doi.org/10.3934/publichealth.2017.4.418.

Picker-Rotem, O., Schneider, A., Wasserzug, S., & Zelker, R. (2008). Nursing Leaders of Tomorrow: A Peer Selection Process. *Journal of Nursing Management, 16*(8), 915–920. https://doi.org/10.1111/j.1365-2834.2008.00878.x.

Pihlainen, V., Kivinen, T., & Lammintakanen, J. (2016). Management and Leadership Competence in Hospitals: A Systematic Literature Review. *Leadership in Health Services (1751–1879), 29*(1), 95–110. https://doi.org/10.1108/LHS-11-2014-0072.

Poikkeus, T., Leino-Kilpi, H., & Katajisto, J. (2014). Supporting Ethical Competence of Nurses During Recruitment and Performance Reviews—The Role of the Nurse Leader. *Journal of Nursing Management, 22*(6), 792–802.

Reichenpfader, U., Carlfjord, S., & Nilsen, P. (2015). Leadership in Evidence-Based Practice: A Systematic Review. *Leadership in Health Services (1751–1879), 28*(4), 298. https://doi.org/10.1108/LHS-08-2014-0061.

Reuben Olugbenga, A., Nicola, N., Katharine Ann, W., Zhanming, L., & Annette, D. (2016). Outcomes and Impact of Training and Development in Health Management and Leadership in Relation to Competence in Role: A

Mixed-Methods Systematic Review Protocol. *International Journal of Health Policy and Management, 5*(12), 715–720. https://doi.org/10.15171/ijhpm.2016.138.

Rick, C. (2014). Competence in Executive Nursing Leadership for the 21st Century: The 5 Eyes. *Nurse Leader, 12*, 64–66. https://doi.org/10.1016/j.mnl.2014.01.005.

Rosenman, E. D., Ilgen, J. S., Shandro, J. R., Harper, A. L., & Fernandez, R. (2015). A Systematic Review of Tools Used to Assess Team Leadership in Health Care Action Teams. *Academic Medicine, 90*(10), 1408–1422.

Rurik, I., & Kalabay, L. (2009). Primary Healthcare in the Developing Part of Europe: Changes and Development in the Former Eastern Bloc Countries That Joined the European Union Following 2004. *Medical Science Monitor, 15*(7), PH78–PH84.

Sackett, P. R., Shewach, O. R., & Keiser, H. N. (2017). Assessment Centres Versus Cognitive Ability Tests: Challenging the Conventional Wisdom on Criterion-Related Validity. *Journal of Applied Psychology, 102*(10), 1435–1447. https://doi.org/10.1037/apl0000236.

Schultz, F. C., & Pal, S. (2004). Who Should Lead a Healthcare Organization: MDs or MBAs? *Journal of Healthcare Management, 49*(2), 103–116.

Sikes, D., Jestes, E., LeClair-Smith, C., & Yates, R. R. (2015). Using a 360° Feedback Evaluation to Enhance Interprofessional Collaboration. *Nurse Leader, 13*, 64–69. https://doi.org/10.1016/j.mnl.2014.10.002.

Sinar, E., & Wellins, R. S. (2016). Cracking the Code to Leader Growth. *TD: Talent Development, 70*(3), 36–41.

Spicer, J. G., Guo, Y., Liu, H., Hirsch, J., Zhao, H., Ma, W., et al. (2010). Collaborative Nursing Leadership Project in the People's Republic of China. *International Nursing Review, 57*(2), 180–187. https://doi.org/10.1111/j.1466-7657.2009.00769.x.

Spurgeon, T. (2008). Multi-Source Feedback: The Importance of Enhanced Self-Reflection in the Context of Leadership Competences. *International Journal of Clinical Leadership, 16*(3), 143–148.

Stefl, M. E. (2008). Common Competencies for All Healthcare Managers: The Healthcare Leadership Alliance Model. *Journal of Healthcare Management, 53*(6), 360–373. ISSN:1096-9012.

Stempniak, M. (2013). Value-Based Leadership: Is Your Hospital Management Team Prepared for the Future? *H&HN Hospitals & Health Networks, 87*(5), 41.

Storberg-Walker, J., & Gardiner, R. A. (2017). Authentic Leadership in HRD—Identity Matters! Critical Explorations on Leading Authentically. *Advances in Developing Human Resources, 19*(4), 350–361. https://doi.org/10.1177/1523422317728731.

Sundean, L. J. (2017). Healthcare Board Competency Survey for Nurses: Assessing Board Readiness. *Nursing Economic$, 35*(6), 295–303.

Townsend, E. A., Polatajko, H. J., Craik, J. M., & von Zweck, C. M. (2011). Introducing the Leadership in Enabling Occupation (LEO) Model. *Canadian Journal of Occupational Therapy, 78*(4), 255–259. https://doi.org/10.2182/cjot.2011.78.4.7.

Trastek, V. F., Hamilton, N. W., & Niles, E. E. (2014). Leadership Models in Health Care—A Case for Servant Leadership. *Mayo Clinic Proceedings, 89*(3), 374–381.

Trustee. (2015). Leadership Assessment and Competencies. *Trustee, 68*(6), 12.

Turner, P. A. (2010). *Reflections on Workforce Planning*. London, UK: Chartered Institute of Personnel and Development.

Turner, P. A. (2017). *Talent Management in Healthcare*. Basingstoke, UK: Palgrave Macmillan.

Ulrich, B., Lavandero, R., & Early, S. (2014). Leadership Competence: Perceptions of Direct Care Nurses. *Nurse Leader, 12*, 47–50. https://doi.org/10.1016/j.mnl.2014.03.012.

Usha Marath, R. (2015). Impact of Leadership Development Package on Leadership Competencies of Undergraduate Nursing Students. *Asian Journal of Nursing Education & Research, 5*(2), 221–228. https://doi.org/10.5958/2349-2996.2015.00044.0.

Walker Company. (2018). *Using your Board of Trustees Self-Assessment to Improve Leadership Effectiveness.* Retrieved from https://www.mnhospitals.org/Portals/0/Documents/Trustees/briefs-resources/governance-self-assessment.pdf.

Watson, C. (2008). Assessing Leadership in Nurse Practitioner Candidates. *The Australian Journal of Advanced Nursing, 26*(1), 67–76.

West, M., Armit, K., Loewenthal, L., Eckert, R., West, T., & Lee, A. (2015). *Leadership and Leadership Development in Healthcare: The Evidence Base.* London: Faculty of Medical Leadership and Management.

White, K. R., Pillay, R., & Huang, X. (2016). Article: Nurse Leaders and the Innovation Competence Gap. *Nursing Outlook, 64*, 255–261. https://doi.org/10.1016/j.outlook.2015.12.007.

Wolf, J. A. (2008). Health Care, Heal Thyself! An Exploration of What Drives (and Sustains) High Performance in Organizations Today. *Performance Improvement, 47*(5), 38–45.

Wood, L., Hassell, A., Whitehouse, A., Bullock, A., & Wall, D. (2006). A Literature Review of Multi-Source Feedback Systems Within and Without Health Services, Leading to 10 Tips for Their Successful Design. *Medical Teacher, 28*(7), 185–191. https://doi.org/10.1080/01421590600834286.

Yukl, G. (2010). *Leadership in Organisations*. London: Pearson.

11

Leadership Development Practices

High-Quality Leadership: High-Quality Healthcare

Effective leadership in health sector organisations is associated with high-quality care, improved societal outcomes, and organisational performance across a range of measures (Reichenpfader et al. 2015; Kyratsis et al. 2016; McSherry and Pearce 2016; Gauld 2017; Mutale et al. 2017). These include positive results for 'patients, caregivers and their work environments, organisations and the healthcare system' (Purdy 2016: 30). However, with the recognition of the importance of leadership comes the recognition of challenge and complexity in its definition and execution. A range of 'VUCA' factors have disrupted the delivery of healthcare, and even though there is a significant amount of investment flowing into the sector, the demand for health service continues to outstrip its supply. To mitigate this, additional factors and initiatives including new organisational designs or the impact of technology continue to offer opportunities that are exciting for the prospect of health, but with few guidelines as to how to ensure their effective delivery. The challenge of health sector leaders, therefore, is to make sense of these multiple developments and

P. Turner, *Leadership in Healthcare*, Organizational Behaviour in Health Care,
https://doi.org/10.1007/978-3-030-04387-2_11

craft a course through which their organisations can thrive and improve both clinical outcomes and satisfaction for patients, providers, and other stakeholders (Blumenthal et al. 2012). To do so means that health sector leaders will need to be 'politically perceptive, adaptive to rapid change and chaos, and highly adept in decision making, team building, and collaboration' (Opollo et al. 2014: 85). Having insight and understanding about the context and the organisation as well as professional credibility and well-honed leadership skills will be essential. It is here where leadership development assumes importance because it is able to address these issues. However, in the same way that leadership cannot be viewed in a binary way—there is no simple choice between a right way to lead and a wrong way—and no simple choice in the way to develop people into leadership roles. The health sector has a wide range of leadership development activities that are a response to complex environmental factors and diverse organisational structures.

To help in navigating the complexities of the health environment, a 'model for health care leadership' was proposed in Chap. 5 within which leadership and its many variables could be accommodated. The model consisted of three core elements—leadership capability, professional credibility, and an understanding of organisational dynamics. A series of competences and competencies were aligned to each to make the model useful to those looking to assess people for leadership positions at Senior Leadership, Executive, and Management levels. It is also possible to use such a framework to identify leadership development needs and their possible solutions. This chapter will analyse how organisations in the sector have chosen to develop people for the wide variety of health leadership roles. In this context, leader training represents initiatives 'aimed at individual-level concepts, whereas leadership development takes a more integrated approach that involves the interplay between leaders and followers and socially based concepts (Lacerenza et al. 2017: 1687). In addition to the improvements in performance that would be expected of leadership development in other sectors, its incidence in health has additional dimensions since 'the quality of leadership can mean the difference between life and death' (Vlasich 2017: 327). Leadership development with this observation as a qualifier takes the concept to a new level.

There Is a Difference Between Learning About Leadership and Leadership Development

Because of 'the rapid pace of change, competing priorities, resource scarcity and all manner of other challenges we face on a constant basis' (Vlasich 2017: 327), the need for excellent leadership within the sector is significant. It is regarded as a solution but also a major human capital challenge; and in order to achieve a maximum return on the investment in its design and delivery, those responsible for leadership development will need to be astute in setting it against clearly defined objectives. Leadership development is an intervention to improve the abilities of people to lead, often based on structured frameworks (McAlearney 2010). But leadership is more than understanding the precepts on which leadership and management theory are built against a list of competences, however well thought through they may be. There is a difference between learning about leadership and leadership development. The former concerns an understanding of the concepts; the latter is about concepts and how they can be applied in practice. In this respect, it is possible to group the objectives and associated activities for leadership development in the health sector into four key areas of expected output (after Hamlin and Stewart 2011):

- Firstly, **improving individual or group effectiveness and performance** contributing to 'innovative solutions to clinical and managerial problems, facilitation of service change with the multidisciplinary team, and problem-solving skills developed through extensive clinical knowledge and experience' (McGowan and Stokes 2017: 62). In the USA an educational curriculum geared to training residents incorporated creating and managing high-performance teams through alignment, communication, and integrity through a collaborative leadership style (Awad et al. 2004). Leadership capability, professional credibility, and understanding organisational dynamics will be required to achieve this outcome.

- Secondly, **improving organisational effectiveness and performance by the achievement of organisational goals through quality outputs and resource efficiency**, exemplified by linking health leadership development programmes to organisational strategy and culture (Cocowitch et al. 2013: 10). The importance of the critical engagement of those in health sector leadership with the complex environment within which leadership takes place 'may be facilitated by effective leadership development if such activities are 'inclusive, eclectic, integrated and contextually aware' (Ford 2015: 263). Understanding the dynamics of the organisation and the competences needed to navigate through them will be an essential feature.
- Thirdly, **developing knowledge, skills, and competencies to prepare leaders in health organisations who are able to craft their way through uncertainty** and develop strategies for their organisations in spite of VUCA. Leaders 'at all levels of the health-care system need to cultivate leadership skills to guide decision making and to ensure the success and viability of private practices, hospitals, and government health-care programs' (Chaudry et al. 2008: 213). This is closely related to competences in the area of leadership ability through personal insight.
- Fourthly, **enhancing human potential and personal growth and developing individuals through growth and engagement**. This particular objective or outcome complements organisational outcomes and is concerned with the effect of leadership development on the leader's personal development and outlook (Broscio 2014; Garman and Scribner 2011).

Recognition that leadership development is a process to increase organisational leadership competence and improve organisational performance underpins the argument. Leadership development therefore will take account of external context and internal factors related to ownership or governance, size, and the place of the organisation in wider health systems (Kim and Thompson 2012: 116). Its priorities will be to prepare leaders to improve organisational and workforce performance. It will do so by 'improving the skills of existing leaders to think in a more strategic and future-focused way' (MacCarrick 2014; CIPD 2015: 18, 19; Moodie 2016; SHRM 2017). At organisational level, leadership development will take place against the backdrop of the unique and specific contextual factors in the sector.

Richness and Diversity in Leadership Development

There is a richness and diversity in leadership development practices in health organisations across the world. Table 11.1 shows the wide range of development activity that has been identified from numerous sources and in several geographies. It is argued that health sector organisations have embraced the proposition that the need for leaders is too great to leave their emergence to chance and are actively engaged in developing leaders (Czabanowska et al. 2014). A point of view enhanced by increasing professional accountability, which has put pressure on healthcare professionals to develop competences in leadership and team working, incorporated into development programmes based on sound adult learning principles (Spurgeon 2008; Garman and Scribner 2011: 380). Health organisations in the USA are prominent in this area, developing evidence-based and behaviourally focused health leadership competency frameworks for use in leadership development, and subsequently, competence models have been put in place within medicine, nursing, pharmacy, and public health (Calhoun et al. 2008). Furthermore, competence was used to inform Executive Leadership Development programmes which grew in number from 2003, in parallel with leadership development, coaching, and mentoring amongst physicians, nurse leaders, and professional healthcare administrators (McAlearney 2010; Hauser 2014; Jackowski and Burroughs 2015; Henson 2016a). The successful Mayo approach recognised the importance of leadership education and development to implement effective change and for some time had tailored leadership and management education to organisational culture and need and the building of a collegial climate (Tangalos et al. 1998; Trastek 2014). Professional programmes in the region offer an array of opportunities to develop leadership abilities (Feller et al. 2016). But it isn't just in North America where leadership development is a focus for health sector organisations, and in China, programmes included relational competences such as communication and social capital as learning (Shek et al. 2017). The International College of Nursing sponsors leadership programmes for nurse leaders including Leadership in Negotiation, Global Leadership, and Leadership for Change (Opollo et al. 2014). In countries as diverse as Portugal and Zambia, there were perceived improvements in both the workplace environment and performance as a result of leadership development (Mutale et al. 2017; Silva et al. 2017: 6). And the British NHS has a long history of leadership development excellence through its Leadership Academy and associated organisational partners.

The diversity of objectives is matched by the diversity of practices. These can either be informal such as where Senior Leaders act as mentors, coaches, or career counsellors to managers and supervisors or formal to include training and structured leadership development programmes (Kim and Thompson 2012). But the broad range of leadership development activity can be grouped into four key areas. Firstly, there is the leader development associated with succession planning and management. As outlined earlier, succession planning has grown to embrace a range of activities including preparation and planning for key professional roles as well as those in leadership positions. However, for the purposes of this analysis, succession planning pertains to those in Senior Leadership positions who are being prepared for Board-level roles. Secondly, leadership development is associated with formal leadership development programmes. Thirdly, leadership development is associated with the use of coaching and mentoring. And finally, networking, assignments, and projects are seen as valuable developmental tools. The following sections outline some of the key principles behind these approaches.

Matching Leadership Development to the Model for Healthcare Leadership

It is argued that leaders in the sector 'need to develop key competencies before embracing new responsibilities related to patient-centred change. Effective leaders known for their optimism, transparency, high ethical standards and their ability to inspire and motivate their followers can have a strong impact on the quality of care provided by the health-care organizations, and training leaders to lead is an important step in creating effective leaders' (Jeyaraman et al. 2018: 78). There is evidence that many have responded to the challenge of leadership development from a wide range of imaginative programmes of activity. Table 11.1 outlines some of these.

Amongst this rich and diverse set of leadership development activities, formal programmes in line with organisational objectives and their associated competences remain the most popular method of delivery.

Leadership Development and Succession Planning

Leadership development is often an adjunct to succession planning with the objective of improving the organisation's overall leadership bench strength or with the purpose of filling specific leadership roles for which change is anticipated. The growing association has been brought about by demographic trends such as the number of those in leadership positions approaching retirement (Bonczek and Woodard 2006; Titzer and Shirey 2013); but equally prominent have been organisational dynamics such as CEO turnover, a shortage of management-ready talent, clinical leadership integration, and concerns because of worldwide shortages of those to fill Senior Leadership and managerial roles as well as for critical clinical, technical, or specialist roles (Di and Santos-António 2008; Sharma and Goyal 2010; Purohit and Verma 2013; Trepanier and Crenshaw 2013; Silver et al. 2016; Smith 2018). The strong message that permeates all is that a close alignment between leadership development and succession planning will produce benefits by increasing the leadership capacity to achieve current succession needs as well as building capability to achieve future ones. The differentiating factor for leadership development for succession planning in health sector organisations is the inclusion, not only of leadership capability development but also how to enhance professional credibility and increase understanding of organisational dynamics.

In its implementation, organisations are aware of the need to integrate leadership development and succession planning systems in ways that use resources most effectively, 'identifying and codifying high potential

Table 11.1 Leadership competencies and development activities in the health sector

Leadership criteria	Leadership development activity identified
Leadership capability	1. Linking leadership development to health unit succession plans (a) Succession planning to ensure continuity of hospital business or operational leadership (b) Succession planning for nurse executives (c) Succession management directly linking development plans to overall talent management (d) Succession leadership development based on structured activities—experiences and projects—that target leader roles in succession planning (e) Formal mentoring programmes for successors 2. Strategic alignment of leadership development to organisational goals and the competences needed to achieve them 3. Leadership development based on personal qualities such as self-belief and self-awareness, setting the direction through political astuteness and a drive for results, and delivering the service by leading change through people (a) Using leadership competences as the foundation for leadership training and assessment centres (b) Comprehensive leadership development programmes supported by talent assessments and development plans (c) Leadership development based on competence-based learning in various formats, media, and locations 4. Problem-based learning to reinforce how leadership development works best from an experiential perspective (a) Didactic modules that allowed the application of acquired knowledge (b) Use of assignments, projects, expanded responsibilities, or practices where specific leadership competencies can be developed through delineated experiences 5. Executive development through both formal workshops and self-study modules 6. Leadership development targeted towards the needs of specific groups (a) Development of executives to work in multi-unit hospital systems (b) Development of frontline clinical leader-physician leadership development (c) Formal leadership training for specialist groups (e.g. radiologists) (d) Formal leadership training for health administrators 13. Leadership development through action research and integrated work-based learning 14. Leadership development programmes that encourage and incorporate empowering behaviours 15. Offering flexibility in leadership development that balances the demands of a professional and personal life and making sure that there are no 'cultural penalties' for such flexibility 16. Including emotional intelligence education with leadership development programmes 17. Executive coaching as part of leadership development programme 18. Mentoring for nurse leaders

(*continued*)

Table 11.1 (continued)

Leadership criteria	Leadership development activity identified
	19. Coaching and mentoring for high-potential employees 20. Mentoring programmes combined with stretch assignments and job rotations 21. 360-degree assessment processes for clinical leaders converted into development opportunities and actions 22. Mentoring for wide range of employees in a hospital environment 23. Developing a healthcare leadership coaching model using action research and systems 24. Career planning advice for healthcare executives 25. Continuous education and learning—including self-learning programmes 26. Reflection sessions—regular time to review their work and identify areas that need improvement and ways to improve the service 27. Professional networking projects and Secondments 28. Sponsoring membership of professional organisations 29. Networking outside of the health sector to broaden perspectives 30. Job rotation 31. Cross departmental projects 32. Organisation-wide projects (IT systems, etc.) 33. Stretch assignments
Professional credibility	34. Succession planning and management in professional or specialist areas 35. Leadership and management development programmes which combine clinical and leadership development or leadership development with health context understanding and knowledge (a) Accepting that strong clinical leadership requires all health professionals to acknowledge that they have two jobs and 'receive appropriate training to support this' (b) Assessment against professional competences as basis for leadership programmes (c) Specific development of medical professionals in leadership skills and behaviours 36. Medical leadership aligned to cultural values 37. Executive coaching, performance coaching, and mentoring for professionals or specialists in dual leadership/clinical roles 38. Professional networking projects and Secondments 39. Professional membership organisations as a way of enhancing career development through peer learning and networking 40. Longitudinal mentoring programmes, mentoring through one-on-one, project-based mentoring, and developmental networks 41. Membership of special interest groups provides leadership development for health policy influence 42. Peer-to-peer shadowing to develop clinical leadership practices 43. Setting up peer exchange networks to obtain ongoing information and support from others on leadership development programmes

(*continued*)

Table 11.1 (continued)

Leadership criteria	Leadership development activity identified
Understanding organisational dynamics	44. Succession planning and management that take account of organisational understanding 45. Leadership and management development programmes integrating contextual, organisational knowledge 46. Diagnosis of organisational issues and adapting leadership development to their solutions 47. Development in processes for creating change, such as shaping culture, solving problems, building alliances, and/or securing resources with the proper development and support 48. Involvement of all tiers of leadership in programmes design and delivery—'going beyond the hero in leadership development' 49. High-level sponsorship and involvement—stakeholders involved in programme design and expected outcomes 50. Learning cycles/groups 51. Healthcare organisations play an active role in the commissioning and development of leadership programmes, combining academic and organisational inputs 52. Monthly group sessions facilitated by an organisational or leadership development coach or leadership coach to explore leadership concepts and to analyse 'real-life situations from the practice setting for processing, discussion, analysis, and practice within the group sessions' 53. Use of feedback which 'significantly improves the onset of transfer following a leadership training program' 54. Cross-cultural adaptation to make the leadership development relevant to the context or geography within which it takes place 55. Integrate separate cultures into a single coherent organisational approach or system through development 56. Leadership development programmes incorporate a defined service impact element to support the delivery of identifiable positive service outcomes within an organisation 57. Leadership development takes place in the context of clear, progressive pathways within the organisation over an extended period 58. Executive coaching, performance coaching, and mentoring on organisational issues 59. Professional networking projects and Secondments 60. Reunions of those on leadership programmes allowing members to reflect on progress and share experiences 61. Network development to 'accelerate the elimination of geographic or organisational "silos"' 62. Attachments, shadowing, and observation

Sources: Williamson (2005), Lacey-Haun and Whitehead (2009), Swearingen (2009), Taylor (2009), McAlearney (2010), Paterson et al. (2010), Curtis et al. (2011), Kim and Thompson (2012), Blumenthal et al. (2014), Hauser (2014), MacPhee et al. (2014), Blood et al. (2015), Fealy et al. (2015), Ford (2015), Taylor-Ford and Abell (2015), Chappell and Dervay (2016), Henson (2016b), Vatan (2016), Crowne et al. (2017), Hartzell et al. (2017), Lacerenza et al. (2017), Lalleman et al. (2017), Bárbara Souza et al. (2017), Truant and Chan (2017), SHRM (2009), Ruston and Tavabie (2010), Zoheir (2012), Cocowitch et al. (2013), Law and Aquilina (2013), Kvas et al. (2014), Waite et al. (2014), Becker and Welch (2015), Humphreys et al. (2015), Lafranconi et al. (2015), Jefferies et al. (2016), Valori and Johnston (2016), Gauld (2017), Saravo et al. (2017), Silva et al. (2017), Turner (2017)

employees, developing high potentials via project-based learning experiences and manager-facilitated workshops, establishing a flexible and fluid succession planning process, creating organization-wide forums for exposing high potential employees to multiple stakeholders, and establishing a supportive organizational culture' (Groves 2007). In addition, the alignment can contribute to a professional culture that helps to promote career development and career advancement (Hampel et al. 2010). To be effective therefore, leadership development in support of succession planning should be aligned to the strategy of the organisation, set against the competences identified to achieve this, identifying people who would be highlighted as having immediate capability or potential to fulfil such roles and then creating a sustainable plan to ensure that individuals match the expectations required. In this scenario, succession planning is central to both professional and organisational workforce planning, and it requires a strategic approach for the long term (McCallin et al. 2009). Leadership development for those who aspire to or are earmarked for Executive or Senior Leadership succession roles therefore will require development in those competences that are consistent with the longer-term direction of the organisation as well as issues such as governance, stewardship, and policy.

Applications have taken place in a diverse set of contexts including continuity of hospital business or operational leadership as well as succession development for specific professional groups, career planning and development, and mentoring with targeted development and tracking of successors (Hampel et al. 2010; Procter et al. 2010). In Canada leadership succession programmes were designed to enable leadership capacity building and included formal learning, stretch opportunities, and mentorship (Dilworth et al. 2011). In the USA such development included formal programmes, informal subgroups, mentoring, peer coaching, and individual self-development and reflection (Pintar et al. 2007). The intended components of this programme included formal learning activities, informal subgroups, mentoring, peer coaching, and individual self-development and reflection. Whilst in Brazil, leadership development against succession needs was achieved through mentoring/coaching against a set of leadership competencies that helped to create a culture of career progression (Munari et al. 2017). These examples demonstrate a richness in approach but also reflect the diversity of need depending on the specific context of the organisation.

Case Study: Developing Emerging Leaders in the British Healthcare Sector

Fiona Rodden, Consultant for Leadership and Organisational Development, Thames Valley and Wessex Leadership Academy, National Health Service, United Kingdom

The British health sector faces unprecedented workforce challenges through which health leadership, at all levels, is required to navigate. Instrumental to organisational success is the attraction, development, and retention of emerging or new leaders, the subject of which is increasingly a Board-level issue. The term 'emerging leaders' is often used to describe those new to a leadership role, who are considered high-performing and have high potential. The way in which the health sector engages and develops emerging leaders has some common ground with those in established leadership positions. However, there are possible variances which may be the result of power dynamics or generational differences. The following are conclusions about the development of emerging leaders, in the context of the health sector, based on evidence from practice-based experience:

- **Harness Impatience and Enthusiasm**

Firstly, it is important to encourage the innate enthusiasm which is a characteristic of emerging leaders. This can be achieved by identifying projects where they can have relative autonomy and freedom to innovate and with role models from whom they can learn. Projects might include defined service improvement projects, audits leading to recommendations for change, or informal patient consultations or focus groups. A critical aspect of this will be the role of managers in helping to broaden horizons, see further into the future, and identify potential consequences.

- **Develop for Resilience**

Organisational challenges require great resilience on the part of those in emerging leadership positions which can be developed by more openness of dialogue. The role of line managers will be important in recognising changing social and cultural attitudes and accepting both connectedness and a different cultural context. In such a situation, emotions and needs are verbalised regularly. Great managers support emerging leaders to develop self- and social awareness through reflection and tools (such as psychometrics or 360-degree self-assessment)—but the tool is less important than the approach—inclusive, appreciative, and strengths based; promote and role model and actively maintaining health and well-being.

- **Build on Loyalty and Values**

In the UK there is a strong cultural value for publicly provided health and care, and as a consequence the emerging leaders employed espouse those values to a high degree. Managers who, through their actions, demonstrate rather than simply verbalise that their emerging leaders are recognised and valued will earn this loyalty. Equally as a healthcare system, enabling career development across traditional organisational and sector boundaries should be actively encouraged. Talent management activity often focuses on retaining people indefinitely while experience across other agencies should be prized. In this way the organisation will develop into a system that naturally fosters greater connectivity and integration. Loyalty is a function of recognition of the value of the contribution made by emerging leaders.

- **Diversity as Strength**

Studies have suggested that the most common style of leadership in healthcare in the UK is a 'pacesetting' style which entails setting high standards and demonstrating how one should achieve them. This is being complemented by more diverse and facilitative leadership styles, and emerging leaders will both offer and benefit from this great deal. Emerging leaders most often work best for those who are honest, genuine, and present their whole self at work. A coaching and collaborative approach to elicit learning and decisions from emerging leaders helps grow confidence, abilities, and ultimately their performance. Mentoring is also a key component to developing diverse leadership styles as this individualised approach helps inexperienced leaders recognise the short- and long-term impacts of their choices and behaviours.

- **Flexible Leaders**

Emerging leaders generally expect a flexible work environment which transcends traditional job descriptions and organograms; and when handled well, this can benefit the organisation. The ways in which managers might do this include allowing flexible hours and work locations where appropriate, jointly agreeing tailored work objectives rather than focusing on standard formal job description, encouraging informal team communication, and enabling informal shadowing and other development opportunities outside of traditional boundaries and hierarchies. By increasing flexibility, managers receive greater commitment, connectivity, and adaptability in return

- **Give Regular Feedback to Emerging Leaders**

Emerging leaders generally desire more regular feedback and communication. Where managers respond to this and can give regular strength-based feedback, it will lead to greater motivation, higher productivity, and innovation. Equally this also means holding to account, not avoiding more critical feedback, and proactively managing performance through clear objectives that are reviewed regularly with feedback on behaviour and conduct as well as effort and achievement. Where expectations around levels and methods of communication are explicitly clarified, this can lead to increased satisfaction for all.

Conclusion

A new cohort of leaders is generally far more empowered than emerging leaders even a decade ago. They will follow those who meet their needs, and health organisations which want to secure high-potential and high-performing people to continue to drive forward change will need to recognise this. While generational differences will play out, many characteristics of emerging leaders apply irrespective of age. Where there are differences within a team, we know that they can either be harnessed for the benefit of the team and service, or they can lead to conflict and dysfunction. Where managers value these differences and see the benefits they bring and how to work better with them, they will see the most success for their team and individuals within. In the health service, that means saving more lives and a better patient experience.

Formal Leadership Development Programmes: 'Inclusive, Eclectic, Integrated, and Contextually Aware'

Formal leadership programmes can be transnational such as those offered by the Institute for Global Healthcare Leadership which seeks to prepare leaders to 'globally, successfully lead, collaborate and participate in global healthcare ventures, assume and effectively meet the global demands of critical healthcare leadership positions within their countries, and provide national and global consultation to effectively meet dynamic contemporary global healthcare needs' (Vlasich 2017: 328) or national such as the comprehensive programmes provided by the British NHS including the Nye Bevan programme leading to an NHS Leadership Academy Award in Executive Healthcare Leadership with the objectives to 'accelerate participants into an executive role and perform better at board level' or the structured Chief Executive and Director programmes (NHS 2018). The American Association of Colleges of Nursing (AACN) offers the Clinical Nurse Leader (CNL) initiative to prepare nurse leaders with advanced competencies in clinical leadership, care environment management, and clinical outcomes management (Kaack et al. 2018). And the Dorothy Wylie Health Leaders Institute launched leadership development initiatives in 2001 to broaden and strengthen nursing leadership in Canada to enable leaders or those with leadership potential to gain 'an insider's perspective on how others use leadership competencies to create positive results; acquiring a powerful set of practical tools that can be immediately implemented; successfully leading a change initiative in the participants' home organization; and developing meaningful networks with other healthcare leaders across the country' (Purdy 2016: 11). For most, leadership development programmes are focused on leadership knowledge, skills, and practices and to support stability and succession planning (Kim and Thompson 2012: 115).

Leadership competences often form the base case of leadership development, with assessment centres or reviews to identify individuals who would benefit from such development. Development programmes can then be designed using competence-based or problem-based learning which reinforces development, putting it in an experiential perspective. A common feature of formal development programmes is the inclusion of action learning to tackle real issues by exploring and reflecting on actual actions and practice in addition to the more traditional approach (Surinder and Marks-Maran 2014: 612). Assignments, projects, and expanded responsibilities are additional features targeted towards specific challenges (such as change or transformation) or the needs of specific groups such as Executives in multi-unit hospital systems, frontline clinical leaders, specialist groups, health administrators, and high-performing managers—'a curriculum designed specifically for surgeons may enable future programs to equip surgeons better for important leadership roles in a complex health care environment' (Taylor 2009; Blumenthal et al. 2014; MacPhee et al. 2014; Fealy et al. 2015; Taylor-Ford and Abell 2015; Pradarelli et al. 2016: 255; Purdy 2016; Hartzell et al. 2017;

Lacerenza et al. 2017; Lalleman et al. 2017; Bárbara Souza et al. 2017). The basis of differentiating between groups is to add meaningful context to development.

To avoid the criticism that 'leadership programmes in health often lack a theoretical base and a sense of how they fit in with individual or organisational goals' (McDonald 2014: 228), the alignment of the leadership development process to wider organisational strategy is emphasised. In their evidence-based analysis, Anderson and Garman (2014) concluded that this was essential for the success of any subsequent leadership development activities and characterised by Senior Leadership involvement in the process to act as mentors and learning facilitators. Clarification of the objectives of leadership development is an important criterion, and where research has taken place on this subject in the health sector, these include the achievement of organisational goals but also employee development and workforce improvement, contributing to becoming the employer of choice and to show a commitment to education, learning, training, and development (McAlearney 2010). However, the more traditional concept of leadership development as a stand-alone activity based on fixed and formal programmes is being overtaken by a more holistic view of development which involves additional practice-based modules or nodes. In addition, there is a growing recognition of the value of coaching and mentoring as part of the process integrated into the programme's overall direction. For some organisations this is part of the development process anyway, whether or not it is attached to something more formal.

Executive Coaching, Performance Coaching, and Mentoring

Whilst leadership development is often conducted through formal programmes, organisations are also recommended 'to commit to other follow-up strategies to ensure leadership behaviour flourishes … i.e., mentoring, coaching and career counselling specific to the professional's leadership career path.' The ability to test out and demonstrate leadership learning is required for leadership competencies to be embedded (Purdy 2016: 27). Coaching has been described as helping others to realise their own potential, and when applied to health professional development, it supported greater understanding of situational leadership allowing the coachee to evolve as a leader in the context of learning as a lifelong process with a positive impact on organisational objectives (Alfa-Wali 2013: 680; Law and Aquilina 2013). Executive coaching can enhance organisational efficiency and productivity, accelerating growth and performance by engaging leaders in ways that are tailored to their individuality (Schidlow and Siders 2014: 61). It offers an opportunity for exploration, conversation, and practice in a confidential setting, and it can be focused to suit the needs of individual leaders. It facilitates the process of feedback which can be invaluable in the development of new leaders and more Senior Leaders alike and can support the move from a particular level or even plateau to a higher level of performance (Robinson-Walker 2005; Sagin 2016). If implemented in a collaborative way—with a commitment to share knowledge and learn from experiences—the delivery of effective coaching can ensure that the development activity is aligned with the mission, vision, and values of the organisation (Woods 2016; Kempster and Iszatt-White 2013). In the Scottish health sector, 'co-active coaching supported deep analysis by individuals. Focus on self, rather than behaviours provoked reflection on perspectives, mindsets, beliefs and approaches which can lead to more sustainable behaviour and support service change' (Cable and Graham 2018). The process is often used in collaboration with mentoring which is a relationship whereby a more experienced colleague shares knowledge to support the development of someone with leadership potential, although it uses similar skills—questioning, listening, and clarifying—that are also associated with coaching (CIPD 2018). The use of mentoring programmes for leaders in health sector organisations is one that is growing in popularity (Blood et al. 2015; Vatan 2016).

Mentoring is valued by those with potential for leadership roles because of the contribution to personal development and the belief that such offerings 'will help them to both perform better in their current roles and prepare them for potential future positions' (McCartney 2010). Coaching and mentoring in a health sector context have been found to increase satisfaction, retention, enhanced self-awareness, feelings of support, ability to take decisions and keep to time frames, and achievement of organisational and personal goals, on the part of those mentored but also added to optimal patient outcomes. Mentoring programmes have been implemented for nurse leaders and high-potential employees, but also in a broader developmental context. Programmes were found to have a positive organisational effect in developing leadership skills and 'created positive change in leadership behaviours for both mentors and protégés and contributed toward relational job learning' (Vatan 2016: 242). It can occur through a variety of methods from peer-to-peer interactions and through working with assigned coaches or mentors (LaPaglia et al. 2017).

Professional Networking, Projects, and Assignments

A fourth area of leadership development in the health context is that of professional networking, projects, and assignments. As outlined in Chap. 2, significant change, as well as policy and procedural developments, has intensified the need for those in leadership roles, not only to remain current in their field or specialism but also to improve the quality and efficiency of healthcare in health systems, through more innovative approaches. Leadership development programmes can contribute to this, especially if they are combined with leadership knowledge and skills outside of formal programmes, a point that reinforces the idea that leaders learn from their own experiences (Boyd and Williams 2010; Cocowitch et al. 2013; Cheryl et al. 2016: 391; Feller et al. 2016); and active, self-directed learning to promote independent, lifelong learning and critical thinking forms part of this philosophy (Kirkpatrick and Brown 2006). The use of projects and assignments in leadership development is a natural extension of the development process.

Their importance increases because leadership development involves 'recognising the individual needs of each learner, current and desired skill levels, experience, personality, and the change in behaviours necessary for success … as such, a one-size-fits-all program is insufficient to develop effective leaders who can successfully navigate the constantly changing global economy' (Holt et al. 2018). The use of projects and assignments, as a complementary activity to more formalised programmes, allows leadership development to be tailored to the needs of individuals. The diverse nature of leadership is reflected in the diverse nature of projects and assignments ranging from professional networking, Secondments, peer learning, and networking and membership of special interest groups. These are features of the development of leaders in specialist care and public health leadership institutes—aimed at solving real, complex issues—physician leadership development, and nurse leadership development (Kirkpatrick and Brown 2006; Donna and Steve 2013; Surinder and Marks-Maran 2014; Cheryl et al. 2016). Peer-to-peer shadowing has also been highlighted as a way of developing clinical leadership practices (Lalleman et al. 2017). Findings showed that learning projects were associated with development of collaborations (whereas assessment tools and coaching were most often associated with increased self-awareness (Delesha et al. 2007)).

New research (Pesut and Thompson 2018) suggests that leadership development should encompass advanced levels of learning, complementing horizontal development (focusing on the acquisition and use of information, skills, and competencies) to more vertical leadership development involving more complex and sophisticated ways of thinking. The use of networking in particular and encountering and engaging with different points of view, as well as projects that take the learner outside of any 'comfort zone,' are useful techniques in the development process. This elevated sense making can be facilitated with coaching or mentoring or peer support. There are numerous (often low cost) ways in which learning from formal leadership development programmes can be supplemented by the knowledge and experience that can be gained from leadership practice as encountered on projects or assignments.

Conclusions and Implications for Practice

The 'model for healthcare leadership' with its three foundations of leadership capability, professional credibility, and an understanding of organisational dynamics and its associated competences can be used as the basis for leadership development at all levels but with particular reference in this chapter to those at Executive or Senior Leadership roles. There is a distinction between leader development, that is, training initiatives aimed at individual-level concepts, and leadership development which is a more integrated approach.

Leader and leadership development whilst being a major human capital challenge offers benefits to health sector organisations, especially when it is closely aligned to the organisation's overall objectives. Some of the findings are:

- **Leader development represents training initiatives aimed at individual-level concepts, whereas leadership development takes a more integrated approach that involves the interplay between leaders and followers and socially based concepts.**
- Its objectives can be found in one of four clusters. Firstly, **improving individual or group effectiveness and performance**; secondly, **improving organisational effectiveness and performance** by the achievement of organisational goals through quality outputs and resource efficiency; thirdly, **developing knowledge, skills, and competencies** to prepare leaders in health organisations who are able to craft their way through uncertainty; and finally, **enhancing human potential and personal growth**, developing individuals through growth and engagement.
- **There is a richness and diversity in leadership development practices** in the healthcare sector with evidence that health sector organisations have responded with a wide range of imaginative programmes of activity including formal leadership development programmes through to the use of coaches and mentors through to the use of projects and assignments as part of action-based approach.

Leadership development in the health sector is of strategic importance. It has benefits for individuals in that it allows them to reach their full potential; but it can be a critical success factor for organisations especially when the goals of leadership development are aligned to those of the organisation.

References

Alfa-Wali, M. (2013). Surgical Leadership Through Coaching. *Journal of Surgical Education, 70*(5), 680–682. https://doi.org/10.1016/j.jsurg.2013.02.003. Retrieved from http://www.sciencedirect.com/science/article/pii/S1931720413000457.

Anderson, M. M., & Garman, A. N. (2014). *Leadership Development in Healthcare Systems: Toward an Evidence-Based Approach*. Chicago, IL: National Center for Healthcare Leadership.

Awad, S. S., Hayley, B., Fagan, S. P., Berger, D. H., & Brunicardi, F. C. (2004). Core Competency: The Impact of a Novel Resident Leadership Training Curriculum. *The American Journal of Surgery, 188*, 481–484. https://doi.org/10.1016/j.amjsurg.2004.07.024.

Bárbara Souza, R., Denize Bouttelet, M., Luana Cássia Miranda, R., & Lara Gomes, R. (2017). Evidence in Nursing Leadership Development Through Action Research: An Integrative Review. *Revista Eletrônica De Enfermagem, 19*. https://doi.org/10.5216/ree.v19.4682.

Becker, E., & Welch, T. A. (2015, September). Establishing a Common Vision among Healthcare Providers. *Talent Development*, Association for Talent Development.

Blood, E., Trent, M., Gordon, C., Goncalves, A., Resnick, M., Fortenberry, J., et al. (2015). Leadership in Adolescent Health: Developing the Next Generation of Maternal Child Health Leaders Through Mentorship. *Maternal & Child Health Journal, 19*(2), 308–313. https://doi.org/10.1007/s10995-014-1619-4.

Blumenthal, D. M., Bernard, K., Bohnen, J., & Bohmer, R. (2012). Addressing the Leadership Gap in Medicine: Residents' Need for Systematic Leadership Development Training. *Academic Medicine, 87*(4), 513–522. https://doi.org/10.1097/ACM.0b013e31824a0c47.

Blumenthal, D. M., Bernard, K., Fraser, T. N., Bohnen, J., Zeidman, J., & Stone, V. E. (2014). Implementing a Pilot Leadership Course for Internal Medicine Residents; Design Considerations, Participant Impressions and Lessons Learned. *BMC Medical Education, 14*, 257.

Bonczek, M., & Woodard, E. (2006). Who'll Replace You When You're Gone? *Nursing Management, 37*(8), 30–35.

Boyd, B., & Williams, J. (2010). Developing Life-Long Learners Through Personal Growth Projects. *Journal of Leadership Education, 9*(2), 144–150.

Broscio, M. A. (2014). Career Management in Today's Healthcare Environment. *Journal of Healthcare Management, 59*(6), 395. ISSN:1096-9012.

Cable, S., & Graham, E. (2018). 'Leading Better Care': An Evaluation of an Accelerated Coaching Intervention for Clinical Nursing Leadership Development. *Journal of Nursing Management, 26*(5), 605–612. https://doi.org/10.1111/jonm.12590.

Calhoun, J., Dollett, L., Sinioris, M., Wainio, J., Butler, P., Griffith, J., et al. (2008). Development of an Interprofessional Competency Model for Healthcare Leadership … Including Commentary by Rice T. *Journal of Healthcare Management, 53*(6), 375–391.

Chappell, A., & Dervay, K. (2016). Leadership Book Club: An Innovative Strategy to Incorporate Leadership Development into Pharmacy Residency Programs. *Hospital Pharmacy, 51*(8), 635–638. https://doi.org/10.1310/hpj5108-63.

Chaudry, J., Jain, A., McKenzie, S., Richard, W., & Schwartz, R. W. (2008). Physician Leadership: The Competencies of Change. *Journal of Surgical Education, 65*(3), 213–220. https://doi.org/10.1016/j.jsurg.2007.11.014.

Cheryl, T., Trey, M., Tom, M., & Marijo, S. (2016). Evaluating a Physician Leadership Development Program – A Mixed Methods Approach. *Journal of Health Organization and Management,* (3), 390. https://doi.org/10.1108/JHOM-11-2014-0187.

CIPD. (2015). *Learning and Development.* Annual Survey Report, Chartered Institute of Personnel and Development, London.

CIPD. (2018). *Coaching and Mentoring.* Chartered Institute of Personnel and Development, London. Retrieved from https://www.cipd.co.uk/knowledge/fundamentals/people/development/coaching-mentoring-factsheet.

Cocowitch, V., Orton, S., Daniels, J., & Kiser, D. (2013). Reframing Leadership Development in Healthcare. *OD Practitioner, 45*(3), 10–18.

Crowne, K. A., Young, T. M., Goldman, B., Patterson, B., Krouse, A. M., & Proenca, J. (2017). Leading Nurses: Emotional Intelligence and Leadership Development Effectiveness. *Leadership in Health Services (1751–1879), 30*(3), 217–232. https://doi.org/10.1108/LHS-12-2015-0055.

Curtis, E. A., Sheerin, F. K., & de Vries, J. (2011). Developing Leadership in Nursing: The Impact of Education and Training. *British Journal of Nursing, 20*(6), 344–352.

Czabanowska, K., Malho, A., Schröder-Bäck, P., Popa, D., & Burazeri, G. (2014). Do We Develop Public Health Leaders? – Association between Public Health Competencies and Emotional Intelligence: A Cross-Sectional Study. *BMC Medical Education, 14*(1), 1. https://doi.org/10.1186/1472-6920-14-83.

Delesha, L. M., Karl, E. U., Steve, L. F., & Donna, R. D. (2007). Linking Learning Methods to Outcomes in Public Health Leadership Development. *Leadership in Health Services, 20*(2), 97–123. https://doi.org/10.1108/17511870710745439.

Di, Z., & Santos-António, N. (2008). The Frozen River Model and Chinese State-Owned Hospital Reform. *Chinese Economy, 41*(3), 90–101. https://doi.org/10.2753/CES1097-1475410306.

Dilworth, K., Lankshear, S., Cava, M., Aldred, J., Hawkes, N., Lefebre, N., et al. (2011). Original Article: The Top 30 Rising Stars Program: An Inter-Organizational Approach to Leadership Succession Planning. *Healthcare Management Forum, 24*, 68–71. https://doi.org/10.1016/j.hcmf.2011.01.006.

Donna, R. D., & Steve, L. F. (2013). Action-Learning Projects Used in Public Health Leadership Institutes. *Leadership in Health Services, 1*, 7. https://doi.org/10.1108/17511871311291697.

Fealy, G. M., McNamara, M. S., Casey, M., O'Connor, T., Patton, D., Doyle, L., et al. (2015). Service Impact of a National Clinical Leadership Development Programme: Findings from a Qualitative Study. *Journal of Nursing Management, 23*, 324–332.

Feller, T. T., Doucette, W. R., & Witry, M. J. (2016). Assessing Opportunities for Student Pharmacist Leadership Development at Schools of Pharmacy in the United States. *American Journal of Pharmaceutical Education, 80*(5), 1–10.

Ford, J. (2015). Going Beyond the Hero in Leadership Development; The Place of Healthcare Context, Complexity and Relationships. *International Journal of Health Policy Management, 4*(4), 261–263.

Garman, A., & Scribner, L. (2011). Leading for Quality in Healthcare: Development and Validation of a Competency Model. *Journal of Healthcare Management, 56*(6), 373–338.

Gauld, R. (2017). Clinical Leadership: What Is It and How Do We Facilitate It? *Journal of Primary Health Care, 9*(1), 5–8.

Groves, K. S. (2007). Integrating Leadership Development and Succession Planning Best Practices. *Journal of Management Development, 26*(3), 239–260.

Hamlin, B., & Stewart, J. (2011). What Is HRD? A Definitional Review and Synthesis of the HRD Domain. *Journal of European Industrial Training, 35*(3), 199–220.

Hampel, S., Procter, N., & Deuter, K. (2010). A Model of Succession Planning for Mental Health Nurse Practitioners. *International Journal of Mental Health Nursing, 19*(4), 278–286. https://doi.org/10.1111/j.1447-0349.2010.00668.x.

Hartzell, J. D., Yu, C. E., Cohee, B. M., Nelson, M. R., & Wilson, R. L. (2017). Moving Beyond Accidental Leadership: A Graduate Medical Education Leadership Curriculum Needs Assessment. *Military Medicine, 182*(7), e1815–e1822. https://doi.org/10.7205/MILMED-D-16-00365.

Hauser, M. C. (2014). Leveraging Women's Leadership Talent in Healthcare. *Journal of Healthcare Management, 59*(5), 318–322. ISSN:1096-9012.

Henson, J. W. (2016a). Developing Physician Leaders Through Professional Associations. *Journal of Healthcare Management, 61*(1), 7–10.

Henson, J. W. (2016b). Five Ideas for the Development of Successful Physician Leaders. *Journal of Healthcare Management, 61*(3), 171–175. ISSN:1096-9012.

Holt, S., Hall, A., & Gilley, A. (2018). Essential Components of Leadership Development Programs. *Journal of Managerial Issues, 30*(2), 214–229.

Humphreys, B., Couse, L., Sonnenmeier, R., Kurtz, A., Russell, S., & Antal, P. (2015). Transforming LEND Leadership Training Curriculum Through the Maternal and Child Health Leadership Competences. *Maternal and Child Health Journal, 19*(2), 300–308.

Jackowski, M. B., & Burroughs, B. (2015). The Relationships Between Self-Reported Leadership Practices, Job Satisfaction, and Demographics of Radiology Administrators. *Radiologic Technology, 87*(1), 10–20. ISSN:0033-8397.

Jefferies, R., Sheriff, I. N., Matthews, J. H., Jagger, O., Curtis, S., Lees, P., et al. (2016). Leadership and Management in UK Medical School Curricula. *Journal of Health Organization and Management, 30*(7), 1081. https://doi.org/10.1108/JHOM-03-2016-0042.

Jeyaraman, M. M., Qadar, S. Z., Wierzbowski, A., Farshidfar, F., Lys, J., Dickson, G., et al. (2018). Return on Investment in Healthcare Leadership Development Programs. *Leadership in Health Services (1751–1879), 31*(1), 77–97. https://doi.org/10.1108/LHS-02-2017-0005.

Kaack, L., Bender, M., Finch, M., Borns, L., Grasham, K., Avolio, A., et al. (2018). A Clinical Nurse Leader (CNL) Practice Development Model to Support Integration of the CNL Role into Microsystem Care Delivery. *Journal of Professional Nursing, 34*(1), 65–71.

Kempster, K., & Iszatt-White, M. (2013). Towards Co-constructed Coaching: Exploring the Integration of Coaching and Co-constructed Autoethnography in Leadership Development. *Management Learning, 44*(4), 319–336.

Kim, T. H., & Thompson, J. M. (2012). Organizational and Market Factors Associated with Leadership Development Programs in Hospitals: A National Study. *Journal of Healthcare Management, 57*(2), 113–131.

Kirkpatrick, M., & Brown, S. (2006). Leadership Development in Geriatric Care Through the Intergeneration Make a Difference Project. *Nursing Education Perspectives (National League for Nursing), 27*(2), 89–92.

Kvas, A., Seljak, J., & Stare, J. (2014). Training Needs Assessment for Leaders in Nursing Based on Comparison of Competency Models. *Organizacija, 47*(1), 66. https://doi.org/10.2478/orga-2014-0006Abstract.

Kyratsis, Y., Armit, K., Zyada, A., & Lees, P. (2016). Medical Leadership and Management in the United Kingdom. *Australasian Psychiatry, 24*(3), 240–242. https://doi.org/10.1177/1039856216635909.

Lacerenza, C. N., Reyes, D. L., Marlow, S. L., Joseph, D. L., & Salas, E. (2017). Leadership Training Design, Delivery, and Implementation: A Meta-Analysis. *Journal of Applied Psychology, 102*(12), 1686–1718. https://doi.org/10.1037/apl0000.

Lacey-Haun, L. C., & Whitehead, T. D. (2009). Leading Change Through an International Faculty Development Programme. *Journal of Nursing Management, 17*, 917–930. https://doi.org/10.1111/j.1365-2834.2008.00955.x.

Lafranconi, A., Gomes, B., Stankunas, M., Babich, S. M., Rethmeier, K. A., & Czabanowska, K. (2015). Medical Leadership – From Inspiration to Education. *The Lancet, 386*(10003), 1531–1532. https://doi.org/10.1016/S0140-6736(15)00483-3.

Lalleman, P., Bouma, J., Smid, G., Rasiah, J., & Schuurmans, M. (2017). Peer-to-Peer Shadowing as a Technique for the Development of Nurse Middle Managers Clinical Leadership: An Explorative Study. *Leadership in Health Services (1751–1879), 30*(4), 475. https://doi.org/10.1108/LHS-12-2016-006.

LaPaglia, D., Thompson, B., Hafler, J., & Chauvin, S. (2017). Training for Leadership Roles in Academic Medicine: Opportunities for Psychologists in the AAMC LEAD Program. *Journal of Clinical Psychology in Medical Settings, 24*(2), 118–123. https://doi.org/10.1007/s10880-017-9498-7.

Law, H., & Aquilina, R. (2013). Developing a Healthcare Leadership Coaching Model Using Action Research and Systems Approaches – A Case Study: Implementing an Executive Coaching Programme to Support Nurse Managers in Achieving Organisational Objectives in Malta. *International Coaching Psychology Review, 8*(1), 54–71.

MacCarrick, G. R. (2014). Professional medical leadership: A relational training model. *Leadership in Health Services (1751–1879), 27*(4), 343–354. https://doi.org/10.1108/LHS-03-2014-0024.

MacPhee, M., Dahinten, V. S., Hejazi, S., Laschinger, H., Kazanjian, A., McCutcheon, A., et al. (2014). Testing the Effects of an Empowerment-Based Leadership Development Programme: Part 1 – Leader Outcomes. *Journal of Nursing Management, 22*, 4–15.

McAlearney, A. S. (2010). Executive Leadership Development in U.S. Health Systems. *Journal of Healthcare Management, 55* (3), American College of Healthcare. ISSN:1096-9012.

McCallin, A., Bamford-Wade, A., & Frankson, C. (2009). Leadership Succession Planning: A Key Issue for the Nursing Profession. *Nurse Leader, 7*, 40–44. https://doi.org/10.1016/j.mnl.2009.07.008.

McCartney, C. (2010). 'The Talent Perspective: What Does It Feel Like to Be Talent – Managed?' Chartered Institute of Personnel and Development, London.

McDonald, R. (2014). Leadership and Leadership Development in Healthcare Settings – A Simplistic Solution to Complex Problems. *International Journal of Health Policy and Management, 3*(5), 227–229.

McGowan, E., & Stokes, E. (2017). Leadership and Leadership Development within the Profession of Physiotherapy in Ireland. *Physiotherapy Theory and Practice, 33*(1), 62–71.

McSherry, R., & Pearce, P. (2016). What Are the Effective Ways to Translate Clinical Leadership into Health Care Quality Improvement? *Journal of Healthcare Leadership, 8*(1), 11–17.

Moodie, R. (2016). Learning about Self: Leadership Skills for Public Health. *Journal of Public Health Research, 5*(1). ISSN:2279-9028.

Munari, D., Bezerra, A. L. Q., Nogueira, A. L., Rocha, B. S., Sousa, E. T., & Ribeiro, L. C. M. (2017). Leadership Succession in Nursing: Thinking and Acting Today to Ensure a Better Tomorrow; Sucessão de lideranças em enfermagem: pensar e agir hoje para garantir o amanhã. *Revista Eletrônica de Enfermagem, 19*, 1–5.

Mutale, W., Vardoy-Mutale, A., Kachemba, A., Mukendi, R., Clarke, K., & Mulenga, D. (2017). Leadership and Management Training as a Catalyst to Health System Strengthening in Low-Income Settings: Evidence from Implementation of the Zambia Management and Leadership Course for District Health Managers in Zambia. *PLoS One, 12*(7), 1–24. https://doi.org/10.1371/journal.pone.0174536.

NHS. (2018). *Programmes for Every Level of Leadership Responsibility*. NHS Leadership Academy. Retrieved from https://www.leadershipacademy.nhs.uk/programmes/.

Opollo, J. G., Lloyd-Busby, A., Foreman, K., & Richardson, D. (2014). Nursing Administrative Officer: Transforming Nursing Leadership in Acute-Care Hospitals. *Nurse Leader, 12*, 84–90. https://doi.org/10.1016/j.mnl.2014.04.005.

Paterson, K., Henderson, A., & Trivella, A. (2010). Educating for Leadership: A Programme Designed to Build a Responsive Health Care Culture. *Journal of Nursing Management, 18*, 78–83. https://doi.org/10.1111/j.1365-2834.2009.01065.x.

Pesut, D. J., & Thompson, A. (2018). Nursing Leadership in Academic Nursing: The Wisdom of Development and the Development of Wisdom. *Journal of Professional Nursing, 34*(2), 122–127. https://doi.org/10.1016/j.profnurs.2017.11.004.

Pintar, K. A., Capuano, T. A., & Rosser, G. D. (2007). Developing Clinical Leadership Capability. *Journal of Continuing Education in Nursing, 38*(3), 115–121.

Pradarelli, J. C., Jaffe, G. A., Lemak, C. H., Mulholland, M. W., & Dimick, J. B. (2016). Health Care: A Leadership Development Program for Surgeons: First-Year Participant Evaluation. *Surgery, 160*, 255–263. https://doi.org/10.1016/j.surg.2016.03.011.

Procter, N., Deuter, K., Hampel, S., Procter, N., & Deuter, K. (2010). A Model of Succession Planning for Mental Health Nurse Practitioners. *International Journal of Mental Health Nursing, 19*(4), 278–286.

Purdy, N. (2016). Impact of a Leadership Development Institute on Professional Lives and Careers. *Nursing Leadership, 29*(2), 10–30.

Purohit, V., & Verma, R. K. (2013). A Study of Human Resource Development Climate in Government Health Centres in India. *Journal of Health Management, 15*(3), 431–443. https://doi.org/10.1177/0972063413491878.

Reichenpfader, U., Carlfjord, S., & Nilsen, P. (2015). Leadership in Evidence-Based Practice: A Systematic Review. *Leadership in Health Services, 28*(4), 298–316.

Robinson-Walker, C. (2005). Reflections on Executive Coaching. *Nurse Leader*, 324–327. https://doi.org/10.1016/j.mnl.2004.11.007.

Ruston, A., & Tavabie, A. (2010). Fostering Clinical Engagement and Medical Leadership and Aligning Cultural Values: An Evaluation of a General Practice Specialty Trainee Integrated Training Placement in a Primary Care Trust. *Quality in Primary Care, 18*(4), 263–268.

Sagin, T. (2016). The Case for Executive Coaching. *Healthcare Executive, 31*(4), 60–61.

Saravo, B., Netzel, J., & Kiesewetter, J. (2017). The Need for Strong Clinical Leaders – Transformational and Transactional Leadership as a Framework for Resident Leadership Training. *PLoS One, 12*(8), 1–13. https://doi.org/10.1371/journal.pone.0183019.

Schidlow, D. V., & Siders, C. T. (2014). Executive Coaching in Academic Medicine – The Net Under the Tightrope. *Physician Leadership Journal, 1*(2), 60–64.

Sharma, D. K., & Goyal, R. C. (2010). *Hospital Administration and Human Resource Management* (5th ed.). New Delhi: PHI Learning.

Shek, D. L., Li, L., Hildie, L., & Xiaoqin, Z. (2017). The Impact of an Intensive Service Leadership Course in Mainland China: Objective Outcome Evaluation. *International Journal of Child & Adolescent Health, 10*(1), 63–71.

SHRM. (2009). *India: Building Sustainable Leadership Competency*, SHRM, Mumbai, India. Retrieved from https://www.shrm.org/hr-today/news/hr-magazine/documents/090366_india_article_sstnbl_ldrshp_fnl.pdf.

SHRM. (2017). *SHRM Research Overview: Leadership Development.* Society for Human Resource Management, USA. Retrieved from https://www.shrm.org/hr-today/trends-and-forecasting/special-reports-and-expert-views/Documents/17-0396ResearchOverviewLeadershipDevelopmentFNL.pdf.

Silva, Vânea Lúcia dos Santos, Camelo, Silvia Helena Henriques, Soares, Mirelle Inácio, Resck, Zélia Marilda Rodrigues, Chaves, Lucieli Dias Pedreschi, Santos, Fabiana Cristina dos, and Leal, Laura Andrian. (2017). Leadership Practices in Hospital Nursing: A Self of Manager Nurses. *Revista da Escola de Enfermagem da USP*, 51, e03206. Epub April 03, 2017. https://doi.org/10.1590/s1980-220x2016099503206.

Silver, M. P., Hamilton, A. D., Biswas, A., & Warrick, N. I. (2016). A Systematic Review of Physician Retirement Planning. *Human Resources for Health, 14*, 1–16. https://doi.org/10.1186/s12960-016-0166-z.

Smith, B. E. (2018). *Top 12 Healthcare Trends for 2018*. San Diego, CA: AMN Healthcare.

Spurgeon, T. (2008). Multi-Source Feedback: The Importance of Enhanced Self-Reflection in the Context of Leadership Competences. *International Journal of Clinical Leadership, 16*(3), 143–148.

Surinder, W., & Marks-Maran, D. (2014). Leadership Development Through Action Learning Sets; An Evaluation Study. *Nurse Education in Practice, 14*, 612–619.

Swearingen, S. (2009). A Journey to Leadership: Designing Nursing a Leadership Development Program. *Journal of Continuing Education in Nursing, 40*(3), 107–112. https://doi.org/10.3928/00220124-20090301-0.

Tangalos, E. G., Blomberg, R. A., Hicks, S. S., & Bender, C. E. (1998). Mayo Leadership Programs for Physicians. *Mayo Clinic Proceedings, 73*(3), 279–284.

Taylor, R. (2009). Leadership Theories and the Development of Nurses in Primary Health Care. *Primary Health Care, 19*(9), 40–46.

Taylor-Ford, R. L., & Abell, D. (2015). The Leadership Practice Circle Program: An Evidence-Based Approach to Leadership Development in Healthcare. *Nurse Leader, 13*(2), 63–68. https://doi.org/10.1016/j.mnl.2014.07.014.

Titzer, J. L., & Shirey, M. R. (2013). Nurse Manager Succession Planning: A Concept Analysis. *Nursing Forum, 48*(3), 155–164. https://doi.org/10.1111/nuf.1202.

Trastek, V. F. (2014). Leadership Models in Health Care – A Case for Servant Leadership. *Mayo Clinic Proceedings, 89*(3), 374–381.

Trepanier, S., & Crenshaw, J. T. (2013). Succession Planning: A Call to Action for Nurse Executives. *Journal of Nursing Management, 21*(7), 980–985, 0966042.

Truant, T., & Chan, R. J. (2017). Future Ready: Strengthening Oncology Nursing Leadership in the Context of Professional Oncology Nursing Organizations. *Canadian Oncology Nursing Journal, 27*(1), 2–8.

Turner, P. A. (2017). *Talent Management in Healthcare*. London: Palgrave Macmillan.

Valori, R. M., & Johnston, D. J. (2016). 12: Leadership and Team Building in Gastrointestinal Endoscopy. *Best Practice & Research Clinical Gastroenterology, 30* (Training in Gastrointestinal Endoscopy), 497–509. https://doi.org/10.1016/j.bpg.2016.04.007.

Vatan, F. (2016). A Leadership Development Program Through Mentorship for Clinical Nurses in Turkey. *Nursing Economic$, 34*(5), 242–250.

Vlasich, C. (2017). The Quest for Excellent Leadership. *Journal of Nursing Management, 25*(5), 327–328. https://doi.org/10.1111/jonm.12497.

Waite, R., McKinney, N., Smith-Glasgow, M. E., & Meloy, F. A. (2014). Or The Embodiment of Authentic Leadership. *Journal of Professional Nursing, 30*, 282–291. https://doi.org/10.1016/j.profnurs.2013.11.004.

Williamson, T. (2005). Work-Based Learning: A Leadership Development Example from an Action Research Study of Shared Governance Implementation. *Journal of Nursing Management, 13*(6), 490–499. https://doi.org/10.1111/j.1365-2934.2005.00576.x.

Woods, M. (2016). Changing the Culture of a Nursing Organization: A Case for Executive Coaching. *Nurse Leader, 14*, 267–270. https://doi.org/10.1016/j.mnl.2016.05.009.

Zoheir, E. (2012). The Importance of Clinical Leadership in Twenty-First Century Health Care. *International Journal of Health Promotion & Education, 50*(5). https://doi.org/10.1080/14635240.2012.723377.

12

Twenty Important Conclusions About Leadership in the Health Sector

Strategy, Stewardship, Policy, and Followership Depend on Effective Leadership

The health sector is in a state of flux because of powerful forces that have created an environment of complexity and fast-moving change demanding a response that is often innovative and transformative. But social and political expectations in both the definition of health and how and when it is delivered are dramatically different to previous times which means that a single transformation is not necessarily enough to deal with the issues. Instead, transformation and change are ongoing characteristics of the sector in general with health organisations in particular operating in a cycle of challenge and response. For some, twenty-first-century transformation has met twentieth-century organisation. Many have responded with new types of organisational structure, health process reengineering, new strategies, and a refreshed leadership capability. But others have struggled to navigate a course through a perfect storm of forces.

P. Turner, *Leadership in Healthcare*, Organizational Behaviour in Health Care,
https://doi.org/10.1007/978-3-030-04387-2_12

Effective leadership is critical to the success of the health sector in this context. It can lead to positive outcomes in patient-oriented, staff-oriented, or organisational measures including patient care quality and patient satisfaction; employee satisfaction and organisational commitment; productivity and team working; and interprofessional collaboration. Not only can it have an impact on the delivery of high-quality, safe, compassionate healthcare and not only can it make a difference as to how organisations in the sector are run and how they deliver services, but also how health sector organisations set themselves up for longer-term prosperity. Health sector leaders have an influence on an organisation's vision, mission, and strategy which will ultimately filter through to performance and on the type of culture that prevails and the level of innovation therein.

The delivery of effective health services requires the right leadership in the right place at the right time with the right level of capability, credibility, and knowledge of organisational dynamics. At the highest levels of the organisation, leaders will not only require knowledge of how to develop long-term strategy but also the ability to deliver it. However, the growing awareness that leadership is a non-hierarchical activity—often separate from the formal role of leader—means that interest in the subject now extends to creating a culture in which leadership can thrive at all levels of the organisation. Without effective leadership there will not be an engaged followership and this will have an impact on the quality of care and societal or business outcomes. In whatever way it is defined, leadership in the health sector carries significant responsibility. The effect of a health leader's actions impacts countless lives and the right leadership fit is therefore crucial. The nature and shape of best 'fit' is an ongoing challenge facing all organisations in the sector.

In this respect, there are many options as to the nature and definition of leadership including the leader as a person, leadership as result, leadership as position, and leadership as process. But in all cases, leadership success may be seen as a precursor to organisational success and will be grounded in leadership capability, professional credibility, and knowledge of the context within which strategy is formulated. But identifying the most appropriate definition and its application is a challenge facing all health sector organisations.

Twenty Important Conclusions About Leadership in the Health Sector

In spite of or perhaps because of the sheer number of opinions and interpretations, there is a richness about the leadership debate in health. Both academics and practitioners have engaged in a dialogue about how 'best practice' in one organisation can be transported to another. The output of this dialogue is a comprehensive range of theories and opinions which provide an essential underpinning of any model for healthcare leadership. The following represents a synthesis of some of the key points in the debate in the form of 20 important conclusions.

- **Health sector leadership has an impact on organisational strategy, stewardship, policy, governance, and structure.** Leadership in the health sector is an essential practice with the potential for a significant impact on both strategic direction and operational performance. Success in health depends on having the right leaders in the right place at the right time with the right skills. In this respect, leadership embraces a wide range of activity and influence. However, for the impact to take place, an organisation will require a leadership style and capability best fit to its specific circumstances, because leadership requirements vary by context, situation, and position.
- **Health leadership is distinctive from leadership in other business settings** which presents a significant challenge since there are few benchmarks against which 'best practice' can be assessed. Instead it is framed by unique circumstances against which an organisation has to decide on its strategic direction or operational priorities, to develop a sustainable path for creating value. In these circumstances best fit is a feasible option.
- **Health sector leadership has different emphases to leadership in other sectors.** Whilst there is an ongoing dialogue in the sector about the nature of leadership and its expected outcomes, there is a growing consensus on the role of high-performing leaders in the transformation of healthcare organisations. Health sector leaders establish direction, align people, motivate, and inspire towards a common goal in the

same way as leaders would in organisations in any industry or commercial sector. However, there are differences in some areas of health leadership from that advocated in business or management literature and practice. Health sector leaders operate in a world that spans managerial and health professional logics. And so, to have the ability to envision a compelling future and the capacity to realise that future, to develop innovative solutions, and to get others to rally round to implement these requires not only generic leadership attributes but also ones specific to the health context. In particular there is the necessity to have an understanding of both the clinical world and the organisational world. Secondly, the emphasis on the leaders and leadership's role in achieving care, compassion, courage, commitment, communication, and competency that is enshrined in healthcare organisations adds an additional dimension; and the significant human responsibility and the effect of a health leader's actions on countless lives create an extra level of scrutiny for those who lead in health.

- **Health sector leadership means a transformational style at the top of organisations.** There are some 200 definitions of leadership, each of which has interpretations about style, traits, or behaviour. At one end of a spectrum, the term leadership is concerned with powerful, dynamic individuals at the pinnacle of organisations; at the other it is a more inclusive term relating to the devolution or distribution of leadership at multiple levels. However, amongst the many definitions and applications of leadership, the transformational model has persisted at the most senior level in the health sector. In this view, health leaders identify the gap between a more traditional model of healthcare and a future emerging model and, having done so, manage through VUCA forces to develop new strategies for the future and engage and enthuse the workforce in their delivery.
- **Health sector leadership has increasingly embraced the concept of devolution from Board to Ward—from Ward to Community.** However, there is a growing recognition that leadership in health can be effective when it is inclusive and collaborative. Hence in recent times, there has been a reset of leadership emphasis shifting from Board to Ward, from Ward to Community—distributed, devolved, and inclusive leadership. This takes the point of view that leadership

processes cannot be understood apart from the social system in which they are embedded, and the behaviours of any one individual are less important than the combined behaviours of the collective whole.

- **Health sector leadership is complex—transformation, transaction, and inclusion converge towards value-based leadership.** But this is not to say that there is a binary choice between transformational and transactional, devolved, or inclusive leadership. The diverse nature of health sector organisations prevents such singularity. Hence leadership in the health sector as a whole is a melange of leadership styles and preferences.
- **Health sector leadership embraces a multiplicity of professional and managerial fields. There is a growing emphasis on leadership in clinical, professional, and technical leadership as in roles that are mainly focused on business and management issues.** Leadership in health sector organisations can either span managerial and medical or clinical logics or be rooted within one of these logics. There is a need to take account of both when analysing the subject of leadership in the sector, and whilst there are commonalities in generic leadership capabilities, there are specific requirements that differentiate some aspects of leadership from others, particularly in the question of clinical leadership. Leadership capability gives authority, whilst professional credibility gives legitimacy. There is a need for both facets in most if not all parts of health sector organisations.
- **Health sector leadership overlaps with health sector management and vice versa.** There is an ongoing debate about whether leadership is different from management with references to leadership and management as distinct concepts, but often present in the same role in the health sector. The terms leader and manager can be used interchangeably particularly when the leadership scenario in question is task or relationship oriented.
- **There are common elements in health sector leadership—an intricate fusion of characteristics, conducts, and skills.** A synthesis of the many and varied competence analyses that have taken place for leadership in the health sector highlight some of these characteristics and indicate that three areas in particular are critical. The first is ***leadership capability through personal insight and the creation of a leadership***

identity. This begins with an understanding, on the part of the leader, of the requirements of leadership, her or his abilities to meet these, and areas in which further professional leadership development will be required. Amongst the important aspects of this will be emotional intelligence and awareness, empathy, and the ability to engage and communicate. The capability is ultimately reflected in a leadership identity. The second is ***professional credibility*** which will need to be demonstrated in whichever leadership role is undertaken (medical, clinical, professional, or managerial) if followership is to be secured. The level of professional credibility, whilst applying in other commercial or business sectors, is a particular aspect of health sector leadership that requires emphasis. The third is ***understanding organisational dynamics***, a leadership skill that applies across all leadership activity if successful transformation is to be achieved.

- **Leadership capability through personal insight—'all leadership begins from within.'** Since all leadership begins from within, acquiring personal insight into leadership strengths, behaviours, and 'preferences' and using this to develop a leadership style or identity that is best fit to the organisation is an important foundation. Such personal insight will provide knowledge, which in turn will facilitate the setting of clear goals and expectations about leadership and will help to focus attention on the most important issues. It will form the basis of a leadership identity that will in turn form the modus operandi of an individual leader and how she or he goes about the task of leadership in their unique context.
- **Professional credibility is essential for health sector leaders.** A premise of leadership is that it is a relationship between those who wish to lead and those who choose to follow. For this equation to work, leaders require the respect and esteem of organisational members and external stakeholders, through demonstrable leadership capability and the creation of a leadership identity. But the approach to leadership is not homogenous. Instead, the type of behaviour will be determined by the leadership style adopted, whilst the scope will be by the environment within which leadership takes place. In most cases the leader will provide a strategic narrative to give context and situation to direction and activity of the organisation, unit, department, or

team and leadership decision-making. At the most senior levels, the leader's credibility will be important for strategic change or transformation. But at all organisational levels, where leadership occurs, the credibility of the person who assumes the leadership role will be necessary to ensure followership against a particular task or objective. Hence, it is an advantage, if not a requirement, that senior professionals who assume leadership roles have substance knowledge as well as leadership and management competencies. In creating the narrative, leaders will require not only knowledge and insight into the programme or organisation they are heading but also the ability to grasp its relationship to the larger health organisation or community served.

- **Understanding organisational dynamics is a core leadership capability.** Setting objectives and crafting a strategy to achieve them are important facets of the roles of Senior Leaders in the health sector organisation. Using personal insight to reflect on the most appropriate approach and professional credibility to ensure the engagement of colleagues at all levels will provide a foundation on which strategy can be built. However, if strategic concepts are to be translated into practical success, then understanding of the dynamics of the organisation will also be necessary. These will be framed not only in structure, process, or policy but also in history, culture, and language. Being able to combine effectiveness in both tangible, strategic elements and the intangibility of culture and its associated complexities is therefore important.
- **Leaders and leadership at Board level are responsible for governance, strategy, stewardship, and policy.** Complexity in the health sector environment, increasing scrutiny on improving performance in quality and patient outcomes, and market and regulatory forces precipitating higher levels of accountability have reinforced the need for effective governance in health sector organisations. Hence, a health sector organisation will be overseen by a leadership team usually consisting of a Board of Directors, who provide the external link to stakeholder interests whilst at the same time approving direction and strategy. The Board's members will be complemented in their role by Executive Leaders who are responsible for setting and implementing strategy and delivering performance through day-to-day operations.

- **Executive Leaders set strategy and prioritise and allocate resource.** A key challenge for the health sector leader is to bring together the 'logics of management and medicine.' To this end, if the leader can articulate a vision for the organisation, clarity about role and purpose to achieve it, and an alignment of the leadership practices of health managers behind it, this will have an impact on a range of performance indicators. Executive Leaders face the challenge of allocating their limited resources in a way that ensures high quality of care is given equitably and efficiently, which means that the management of healthcare facilities is multidisciplinary, requiring the involvement of clinicians, nurses, allied health professionals, and those responsible for providing managerial services such as from finance to HR and IT, all focused on performance excellence. Hence amongst the key challenges of health sector Executives are clarifying objectives, agreeing strategies to meet them, engaging the workforce in their delivery by encouraging individual accountability, and finally allocating sufficient resources for the achievement of the strategy.
- **Clinical leadership with the patient at the centre.** A specific challenge in the health sector is to balance clinical and managerial (business, cost management, administrative, or technical process) needs, and it is this aspect of leadership that separates the sector from others. To do so it is essential that leaders in healthcare bring an understanding of both the clinical world and organisational world and hence the importance of professional credibility to the health sector leader. One aspect of this is clinical leadership and in this respect all clinicians take on leadership responsibilities when delivering care and will be expected to act as stewards of the healthcare system, and clinical leadership at the point of service is now recognised as a central professional competency to ensure quality patient care and patient safety. Clinical leadership is putting physicians at the heart of shaping and running clinical services so as to deliver excellent outcomes for patients and populations, not as a one-off task or project, but as a core part of a clinician's professional identity. It may be interpreted in its broadest form to include all professionals: doctors, nurses, and allied care providers. There is a defined need for clinical leaders to demonstrate the versatility to work with diverse disciplines and respond to changing environments. The challenge here is to define and clarify the role of the clinical leader.

- **Devolved leadership—distribution of leadership responsibility.** There is increasing acceptance that leadership is not based on the actions of a few people at the top of organisations. Instead, leadership may be viewed as a non-hierarchical activity. Indeed, contemporary leadership models in healthcare organisations have shifted from hierarchical command and control models to those based on influential relationships that require different interactions between the leader and members of the team. Such an assumption provides the foundation for the incidence of devolved or distributed leadership. In this situation, the changing nature of organisational structures such as the replacement of hierarchy with matrices or networks means that leadership activity will exist at several levels or at different nodes on the network. Formally acknowledging this fact by extending the nomination of leaders beyond the Board or Executive team creates a new type of leadership situation. Devolved leadership can take place in a formal context by extending the scope of those covered by the leadership nomenclature or policy; or it can take place informally by dint of the fact that leadership is a response to a circumstance or situation regardless of job role or title.
- **There is a growing recognition that leadership takes place at all levels,** whereby particular circumstances or situations will require leadership action from someone who is not formally designated in a leadership role. Hence in place of the formality, there will be tacit leadership at all levels. The implication here is that individuals who find themselves in situations requiring leadership action have both willingness and a skill set that allows them to make leadership decisions and a confidence that the organisation will back them once made. Priorities for the organisation in these circumstances will be to facilitate a culture whereby members of the workforce who are forced to assume leadership positions by dint of circumstance feel empowered to do so.
- **Succession planning in the health sector provides continuity for the organisation's strategy.** A leadership model for health comprising of leadership capability established through personal insight, professional credibility, and an understanding of organisational dynamics provides a framework against which an organisation can identify the leadership

attributes which are best fit to its own specific circumstances and against which individuals can assess their own ability to lead in those circumstances. The desired outcome of this organisational and self-evaluation will be people in leadership roles who can craft and implement strategy using their strengths to navigate through the complexity of their environment. However, leadership is not a finite proposition, and so the well-governed Board will include leadership as part of its strategic review process and keep CEO succession as a standing Board agenda item because it ensures a multilayered, multigenerational process. The extent of this 'future fit' leadership assessment will be based on ensuring either continuity (of strategy, policy, stewardship, and culture) or transformation (to new care or business models) in response to changing circumstances. The identification of individuals who are able to deliver against these scenarios is referred to as succession planning, and the consequences of not doing so can be significant since Board's lack of succession planning has major implications. Succession planning can be located inside a broader group of resourcing and development processes which might include leadership and management resourcing, strategic and operational workforce planning, competence analysis, and human resource development. Its objective is the identification and development of key or business-critical positions and talented people who are able to fill them. Succession planning for leadership in the health sector is a formalised and systematic process for identifying individuals with leadership capability who are able to fill identified senior roles in the short term and individuals with leadership potential to fill identified senior roles in the medium to long term. It is a process that is aligned to the strategy of the organisation and includes identification, assessment of ability and potential, the development of that ability and potential, and deployment of individuals to identified key roles to fulfil that potential.

- **Leadership competences and competency can be identified against which leaders can be assessed.** *Competence* is an internal characteristic of a person or the possession of a required skill, knowledge, qualification, or capacity; and *competency* is an observable action of a person. Competences cover a broad range of requirements including those that are **relationship oriented,** focused on being able to connect

with key people and networks and having the ability to establish proper communication channels with colleagues and clients; **task oriented**, focused on goal achievement, persistence in removing obstacles, and the ability to deliver ideas and creativity; and **ethically oriented** including professional knowledge to create work at the highest ethical standards. Competences are presented as lists of idealised attitudes or behaviours, as a taxonomy which groups competences together where there are commonalities, or in the form of a framework against which potential leaders or managers can be assessed. Effective health sector leadership will therefore require a combination of personal attributes or inputs of an individual and the behaviours that individuals must have, or must acquire, to perform effectively in their roles. In the past competence and competency were separate and distinctive terms, but more recently, the two are used interchangeably.
- **There is richness and diversity in leadership development in healthcare.** It is argued that the need for leaders is too great to leave their emergence to chance, and so health organisations should actively engage in developing leaders. In this respect, there is a difference between learning about leadership and leadership development. Given the importance attached to leader and leadership development, it should be of no surprise that there is a richness and diversity in leadership development practices in the healthcare sector worldwide with a broad range of development activity. There is a difference between learning about leadership and leadership development.

These conclusions reflect the richness of the knowledge, skills, attitudes, behaviours, and performance of leaders and leadership in the world's health sector. Not only do health sector leaders mirror their counterparts in other sectors, but they add dimensions to the role which create a uniqueness of application. Those fulfilling such roles operate in extremely complex environments and in order to be successful require not only leadership capability but deep insight about the professional health context and an understanding of how to navigate their way through a myriad of organisational structures, cultures, and dynamics.

Index

P. Turner, *Leadership in Healthcare*, Organizational Behaviour in Health Care,
https://doi.org/10.1007/978-3-030-04387-2

N

O

P

The manufacturer's authorised representative in the EU is Springer Nature Customer Service Centre GmbH, Europaplatz 3, 69115 Heidelberg, Germany. If you have any concerns regarding our products, please contact ProductSafety@springernature.com

Printed and bound by CPI Group (UK) Ltd, Croydon, CR0 4YY

30/09/2026

02225442-0015